D1332995

THE COMPLETE VISUAL DICTIONARY

Native blaster emits bolts of kinetic force

Mustafarian gas mask with flare-guard goggles

Life-support pack

Insulated fabric

Armor made from discarded lava flea shells

Weapon controls

Dense skirt protects legs

Heat-resistant boots

MUSTAFARIAN

STAR WARS®

THE COMPLETE VISUAL DICTIONARY

Written by DAVID WEST REYNOLDS (Episodes I, II and IV–VI) and
JAMES LUCENO (Episode III)
Updates and new material by RYDER WINDHAM

Special fabrications by ROBERT E. BARNES, DON BIES,
JOHN GOODSON, NELSON HALL, & MIKE VERTA

New photography by ALEX IVANOV

MACE WINDU'S
LIGHTSABER

OBI-WAN'S
LIGHTSABER

DOOKU'S
LIGHTSABER

Foreword

I vividly remember seeing the first *Star Wars* film. Along with all the other thirteen year olds, I sat open mouthed as the Blockade Runner disappeared into the background pursued by the never-ending Star Destroyer. My life was changed forever and I was on a new course.

The summer of 1977 was spent reading the novelization of the film and dreaming of the worlds that George Lucas had created. I was already a kid who spent hours drawing underground cities with secret rooms, trap doors and amazing hidden vehicles. I was interested in what was happening below the surface and behind the scenes.

Star Wars helped to springboard my imagination and I remember thinking about what was happening just outside of Lucas' camera's view on Tatooine, Dagobah and Hoth. How did the citizens of those worlds live? If I could go there, what would I see?

I was one of the first in line to see *The Empire Strikes Back* in 1980 and I remember the impact that Yoda had on me. I was fascinated by the oldest and wisest of the Jedi. Like everyone else, at the time, I had my own version of Frank Oz's backward Yoda speak (something that I was too embarrassed to share with Frank when we were working together on the digital version of Yoda).

The 1983 release of *Return of the Jedi* was bittersweet for me. I remember wondering after the film ended whether we would ever see another *Star Wars* film. We knew that Lucas had written a fabled nine episodes, but there was only speculation back then as to whether he would ever return to this series.

It is now funny to think back to my nineteen-year-old self, the innocence of not knowing that Industrial Light & Magic would hire me and that I would spend the better part of eight years working closely with Lucas on the *Star Wars* prequels.

As the Animation Director on *The Phantom Menace, Attack of the Clones,* and *Revenge of the Sith,* I was responsible for the digital characters and creatures that inhabited Lucas' wonderful worlds. We started in 1997 with Watto, our cranky junkyard dealer and we ended in 2005 with the villainous General Grievous. For that entire time I was focused on our digital creatures and how they interacted with the human characters.

To me it is vitally important that the animators understand that they are actors working behind the scenes. For our animated characters to blend seamlessly with the live-action photography the animators must breathe a little of their own humanity into the digital characters. We collaborated with George Lucas and the terrific voice actors, like Andy Secombe as Watto and Frank Oz as Yoda, to produce the animated performances.

Visual effects and digital animation is a team event and we had enormous crews of talented artists and technicians working at Industrial Light & Magic with us to create the amazing scenes you saw up on the movie screen.

I love the images in this book. They take me back to a time when I was a young boy drawing pictures of secret buildings and magical worlds, a time when my imagination swept me away. It has been really fun for me to leaf through these pages and remember all of the astonishing places, creatures and vehicles that have sprung from George Lucas' mind. It is my hope that the images here will inspire you, too, and take you back to a galaxy, far, far away.

Rob Coleman

Rob Coleman, Animation Director,
Lucasfilm Animation, Skywalker Ranch, October 2006

Contents

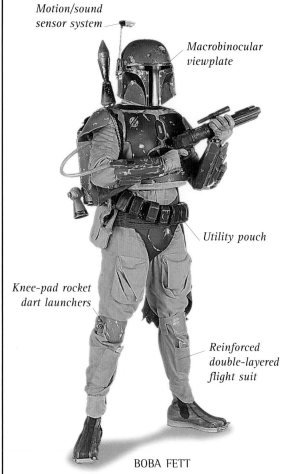

Motion/sound sensor system

Macrobinocular viewplate

Utility pouch

Knee-pad rocket dart launchers

Reinforced double-layered flight suit

BOBA FETT

Long fingers to draw blood

Sensor implant

Tracker utility vest

Short-range pistol

Protective body paint

Heavy leather boots for desert travel

Long-range projectile rifle

AURRA SING

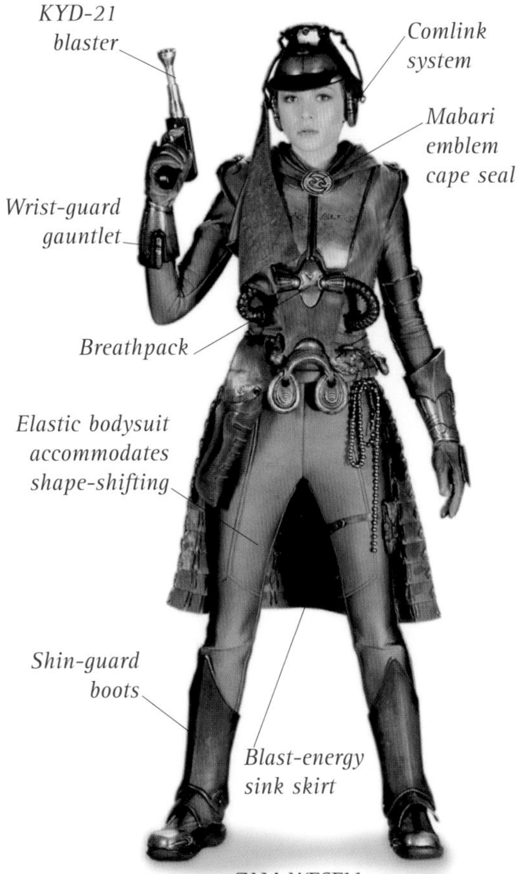

KYD-21 blaster

Comlink system

Mabari emblem cape seal

Wrist-guard gauntlet

Breathpack

Elastic bodysuit accommodates shape-shifting

Shin-guard boots

Blast-energy sink skirt

ZAM WESELL

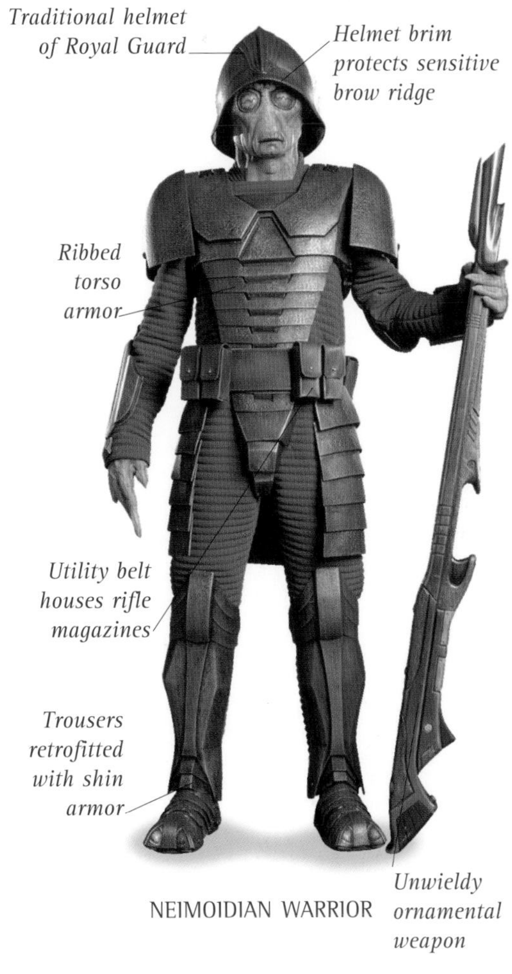

Traditional helmet of Royal Guard

Helmet brim protects sensitive brow ridge

Ribbed torso armor

Utility belt houses rifle magazines

Trousers retrofitted with shin armor

NEIMOIDIAN WARRIOR

Unwieldy ornamental weapon

Introduction

Except for a brief moment of darkness that conveys a former Jedi's final transformation into a cybernetic Sith Lord, nearly every scene in all six *Star Wars* movies displays a wealth of visual information. Heroes and villains ride in instrument-laden starships, aliens wield uniquely crafted weapons, and the histories of various cultures are indicated by distinctive architecture on numerous worlds. Although many background characters, devices, vehicles, and structures were not identified by name on screen, most have acquired names and back-stories by way of *Star Wars* novels, reference books, comics, toys, and games. Much has transpired since the publication of the first *Star Wars Visual Dictionary*, and this revised and expanded guidebook illuminates even more nooks and crannies of that far away galaxy....

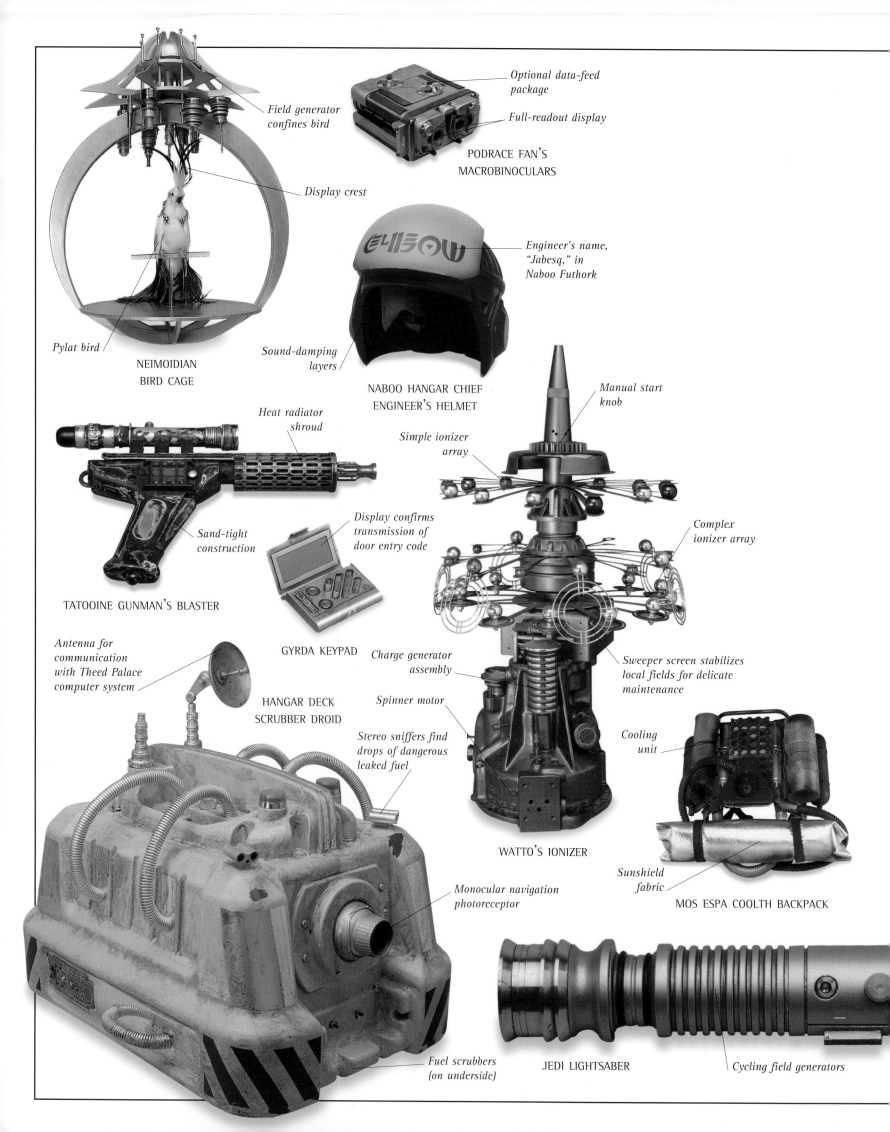

Field generator
confines bird

Display crest

Pylat bird

NEIMOIDIAN
BIRD CAGE

Optional data-feed
package

Full-readout display

PODRACE FAN'S
MACROBINOCULARS

Engineer's name,
"Jabesq," in
Naboo Futhork

Sound-damping
layers

NABOO HANGAR CHIEF
ENGINEER'S HELMET

Heat radiator
shroud

Manual start
knob

Simple ionizer
array

Sand-tight
construction

TATOOINE GUNMAN'S BLASTER

Display confirms
transmission of
door entry code

GYRDA KEYPAD

Complex
ionizer array

Sweeper screen stabilizes
local fields for delicate
maintenance

Charge generator
assembly

Antenna for
communication
with Theed Palace
computer system

HANGAR DECK
SCRUBBER DROID

Spinner motor

Stereo sniffers find
drops of dangerous
leaked fuel

WATTO'S IONIZER

Cooling
unit

Sunshield
fabric

MOS ESPA COOLTH BACKPACK

Monocular navigation
photoreceptor

Fuel scrubbers
(on underside)

JEDI LIGHTSABER

Cycling field generators

EPISODE 1
THE PHANTOM MENACE

EPISODE 1 travels back to the beginning of the *Star Wars* saga, a generation before Luke Skywalker meets Ben Kenobi and sets out on his path to destiny. In this era, Luke Skywalker's father Anakin is nine years old, and the great free Galactic Republic still stands, although its power is starting to falter. This time is populated with new characters, whose worlds are replete with gleaming spacecraft, intricate clothing, and exotic-looking robots. Just as in the real world, these artifacts tell a story. They are clues to identity. From the deathly pale appearance of Trade Federation battle droids to the tasty gorgs of Mos Espa marketplace and the fangs of the colo claw fish, the Visual Dictionary is your guide to the dazzling worlds explored in this first episode of the *Star Wars* fantasy. Because even at the beginning, there's a lot to catch up on. So jump on board.

And brace yourself.

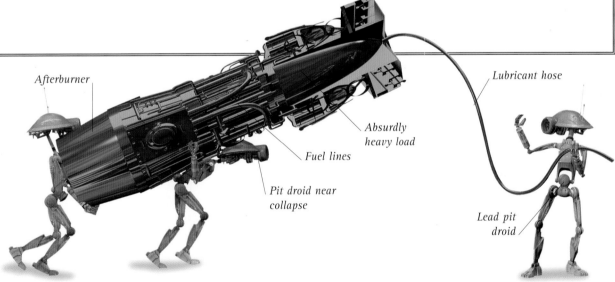

Afterburner

Lubricant hose

Absurdly heavy load

Fuel lines

Pit droid near collapse

Lead pit droid

Emitter assembly

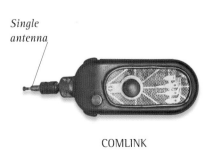

Single antenna

COMLINK

BLISSL TUNER
(MUSICAL INSTRUMENT)

SLAVE QUARTERS
BRAZIER

Hooded cloak

Hidden visage

Sith clasp

The Phantom Menace

FOUNDED LONG AGO, the Republic has united countless thousands of star systems under a single, far-reaching government. In millennia past, great sections of the Republic fought each other even as they clung to threads of unity. Peace and justice came to prevail under the protection of the wise and powerful Jedi, who draw on a mystical power known as the Force. Through the guidance of the Galactic Senate, civilization grew and the Republic became prosperous. But the price of comfort was weakness. The institutions of government became decadent and Jedi numbers dwindled to a mere ten thousand. Now, the Force itself is unbalanced and great change seems imminent...

Coruscant

A world enveloped in a single city, Coruscant is the home of galactic government and the effective center of the known universe. Representatives from all member worlds congregate here to participate in the colossal enterprise of galactic government. From among the thousands within the senate chamber, the pleas of a single voice must be heard to save the small planet of Naboo from invasion.

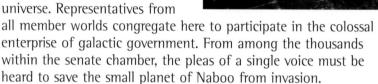

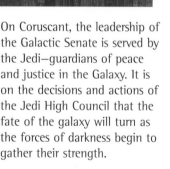

On Coruscant, the leadership of the Galactic Senate is served by the Jedi—guardians of peace and justice in the Galaxy. It is on the decisions and actions of the Jedi High Council that the fate of the galaxy will turn as the forces of darkness begin to gather their strength.

Darth Sidious

The Sith Lord Darth Sidious sets into motion the final stages of his order's 2,000-year-old plan to destroy the Jedi. Working patiently, Sidious has extended his power and influence deep into the galactic government. Using his grasp of psychology and bureaucracy to stifle justice, he brings about the crisis he needs to make his move for domination.

Coruscant provides a hiding place for the mysterious Sith. This ancient dark order has been waiting in the shadows, preparing to prey upon the Galactic Republic's time of weakness and usher in a new era of Sith rule. This phantom menace radiates outward from the center, drawing into its web individuals and worlds that lie far beyond Coruscant.

Naboo

Theed Royal Palace *Palace forecourt* *Naboo philosophers*

The provincial and little-populated planet of Naboo has benefited greatly from membership in the Republic. Within an idyll of serenity, Naboo decorative architecture expresses the planet's philosophy of arts and a harmonious way of life. The Naboo have come to regard their privilege as a birthright, and do not realize the extent to which they are dependent on the core strength of galactic government to protect them. Only when crisis descends will they face the frightening realization that the only strength they can depend on is their own.

Expressive of Naboo style in its glistening silver finish and dreamlike, artful contours, the Royal Starship is nonetheless built around a core of foreign-made engine systems. Naboo society is similarly dependent on outside industry.

Hydrostatic bubbles keep out water

Gungan-style artistic floor pattern

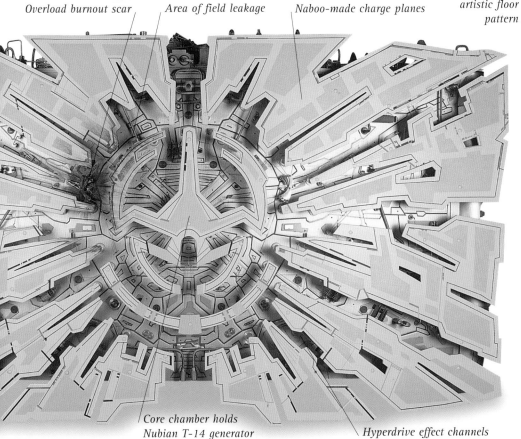

Overload burnout scar *Area of field leakage* *Naboo-made charge planes*

Core chamber holds Nubian T-14 generator

Hyperdrive effect channels improve supralight performance

Otoh Gunga

Removed from outside contact, the underwater Gungan cities of Naboo glisten like scintillating jewelry. The Gungan capital city, Otoh Gunga, prides itself on being independent of foreign influences. Nonetheless, it relies upon a quiet but vital trade with the Naboo. In this, as in the danger they face from the Trade Federation, the Gungans find that they are more connected with outsiders than they confess.

Typical Gungan design

Slave quarters *Rough adobe walls*

Hyperdrive Core

A dazzling example of Naboo style, the hyperdrive core of the Royal Starship is an intricate maze of charge planes and effect channels that allows the ship to slip smoothly beyond lightspeed. When the Nubian-made hyperdrive generator inside the core fails under the energy overloads encountered in battle, the Naboo begin to learn the realities of their dependence on the outside world.

TOUCHDOWN ON TATOOINE
The Naboo Royal Starship is forced by the broken hyperdrive core to land on the desert world of Tatooine. Queen Amidala must seek refuge in this wilderness and stake her hopes on desperate chance.

Tatooine

Beyond the reach of the Republic are the worlds of the Outer Rim, a frontier where extremes of freedom and slavery coexist. Tatooine is ruled by wealthy trading barons and gangsters. The adobe architecture of Mos Espa looks as rugged and primitive as the planet itself, but the thick walls hide sophisticated interior cooling systems. On Tatooine, not everything is what it seems—as those aboard the Naboo Royal Starship find when they encounter a slave boy named Anakin Skywalker.

Mace Windu
WISE NEGOTIATOR

SENIOR MEMBER of the Jedi Council, Mace Windu's wisdom and self-sacrifice is legendary. In a long and adventurous career, he has repeatedly risked his life to resolve great conflicts in fairness to both sides. Windu is sober and cool-minded but is also capable of dramatic actions in the face of danger. Always ready to risk himself, Mace Windu is very reluctant to risk the lives of others. In particular, he is wary of fellow Jedi Qui-Gon Jinn's headstrong belief in Anakin Skywalker, and senses great danger in the boy. These concerns weigh heavily upon him as he considers them against his friendship and respect for Qui-Gon.

Time and again, Mace Windu has stood at the center of great conflicts. His fame has only added to his negotiating skills.

Under-tunic

Tunic

Jedi robe

Utility belt

Lightsaber

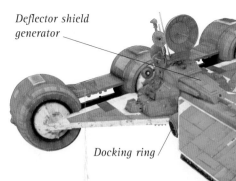

Deflector shield generator

Docking ring

Crew lounge

Color indicates diplomatic status

Cockpit

Diplomatic salon pod

Republic Cruiser

Jedi, diplomats, and ambassadors travel to trouble spots around the galaxy aboard the Republic Cruiser. This vessel's striking red color declares its political neutrality. In its well-armored salon pods, high-level negotiations take place between factions in conflict.

The Jedi High Council is secretly called upon by Supreme Chancellor Valorum of the Galactic Senate to settle the conflict with the Trade Federation. Mace Windu summons a pair of his most able Jedi for the mission. Windu little suspects the evil and danger awaiting Jedi Master Qui-Gon Jinn and his apprentice Obi-Wan Kenobi within the Trade Federation fleet.

Blade projection plate

Blade modulation circuitry

Handgrip ridges

Activator

Blade length adjust

Radiator casing segment

MACE WINDU'S LIGHTSABER

DATA FILE

◆ The Jedi use the lightsaber as a symbol of their dedication to combat in defense, not attack, and of their philosophical concern for finely tuned mind and body skills.

◆ Ambassadors, mediators, and counselors, Jedi are warriors only as a last resort.

Yoda
ANCIENT MASTER

Well into his 800s, Yoda is the oldest member of the Jedi High Council, as well as its most deeply perceptive Master. A great traveler in his younger years, Yoda has visited hundreds of worlds on his own, spending years learning different lifeways and appreciating the infinitely variable nuances of the Force. Yoda takes a personal interest in the progress of Qui-Gon Jinn and his apprentice Obi-Wan Kenobi. Yoda recognizes their strength and potential even as he disagrees with some of their "dangerously reckless" choices.

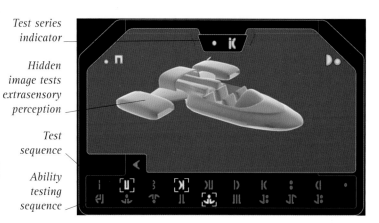

Test series indicator

Hidden image tests extrasensory perception

Test sequence

Ability testing sequence

Testing Screen

The Jedi High Council use multi-function viewscreens to test Jedi apprentices. These screens are built without buttons and are operated by Jedi mind powers. Only Force-attuned individuals can follow the high-speed series of images generated on screen. Testing screens keep the Jedi Council members in constant practice with their Force abilities.

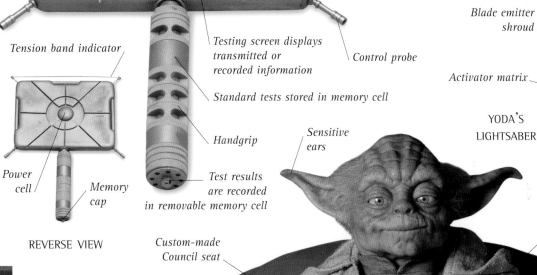

The Jedi draw their power from the Force, an omnipresent, subtle energy field surrounding all living things. The Force can lend telekinetic powers and give insights into the future, the past, or the thoughts of others.

Tension band indicator

Power cell

Memory cap

REVERSE VIEW

Testing screen displays transmitted or recorded information

Control probe

Standard tests stored in memory cell

Handgrip

Test results are recorded in removable memory cell

Blade emitter shroud

Activator matrix

YODA'S LIGHTSABER

Sensitive ears

Well-worn Jedi robe

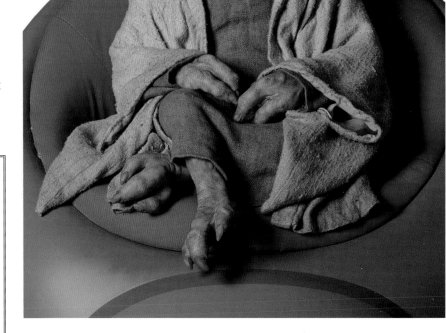

Custom-made Council seat

Having seen so much of life, Yoda views all that happens with a long perspective. Less active now than in his younger years, Yoda remains one of the two most important voices of wisdom on the Jedi High Council along with Mace Windu.

DATA FILE

◆ Yoda's gimer stick cane helps him to walk long distances and contains natural plant substances that aid meditation when chewed.

◆ It has been many years since Yoda has needed to wield his special lightsaber. Yoda takes quiet satisfaction in finding nonviolent solutions.

The Jedi High Council

THE TWELVE MEMBERS of the Jedi High Council represent a gathering of great minds who have proven themselves and their abilities in the service of peace and justice. Confident in their attunement to the Force, the Council members work together in trust, free from the petty constraints of ego and jealousy. Their Council Chamber is a place of open thought and speech, a realm of mutual respect and a haven of shared noble purpose. The Council is composed of five permanent members who have accepted a lifetime commitment to the difficult work of the Jedi. In addition, four long-term members serve until they choose to step down and three limited-term members sit for specified terms. This balance of membership keeps the Council wise and vigorous.

The Council Chamber is located atop the central spire of the Jedi Temple on the galactic capital planet, Coruscant. The 12 members sit in a ring of chairs that are spaced equally around the chamber.

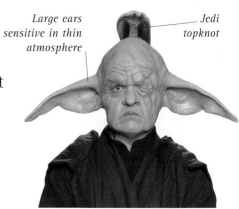

Large ears sensitive in thin atmosphere

Jedi topknot

EVEN PIELL
Jedi Master Even Piell bears a scar across his eye as a grisly trophy of a victory against terrorists who made the mistake of underestimating the diminutive Jedi Master.

Yarael Poof

The attenuated Quermian Yarael Poof is the consummate master of Jedi mind tricks. He uses Force suggestions to bring conflicts to an abrupt end, turning combatants' own fears against themselves.

Quermian upper brain

Quermians are noseless as they smell with olfactory organs in their hands

Long neck for peering above low vegetation mats

Robe hides second set of arms and chest with lower brain

Well-developed horns

Customary humanoid Jedi robes

Traditional Quermian cannom collar

Tough skin impervious to high winds of Iktotchon

Saesee Tiin

An Iktotchi pilot, Saesee Tiin is best able to focus while traveling at extremely high speeds—at the controls of the finest spacecraft. He offers a unique perspective on the Council as his telepathic mind is always racing ahead to foresee possibilities.

Large brain supported by second heart

Surcoat adapted from ancient Cerean garb

Lightsaber

Cerean cuffs

Plain trousers

Ki-Adi-Mundi

A Jedi Knight from the largely unspoiled paradise world of Cerea, Ki-Adi-Mundi's high-domed head holds a complex binary brain. Recently added to the Council, Ki-Adi-Mundi has not yet taken a Padawan learner.

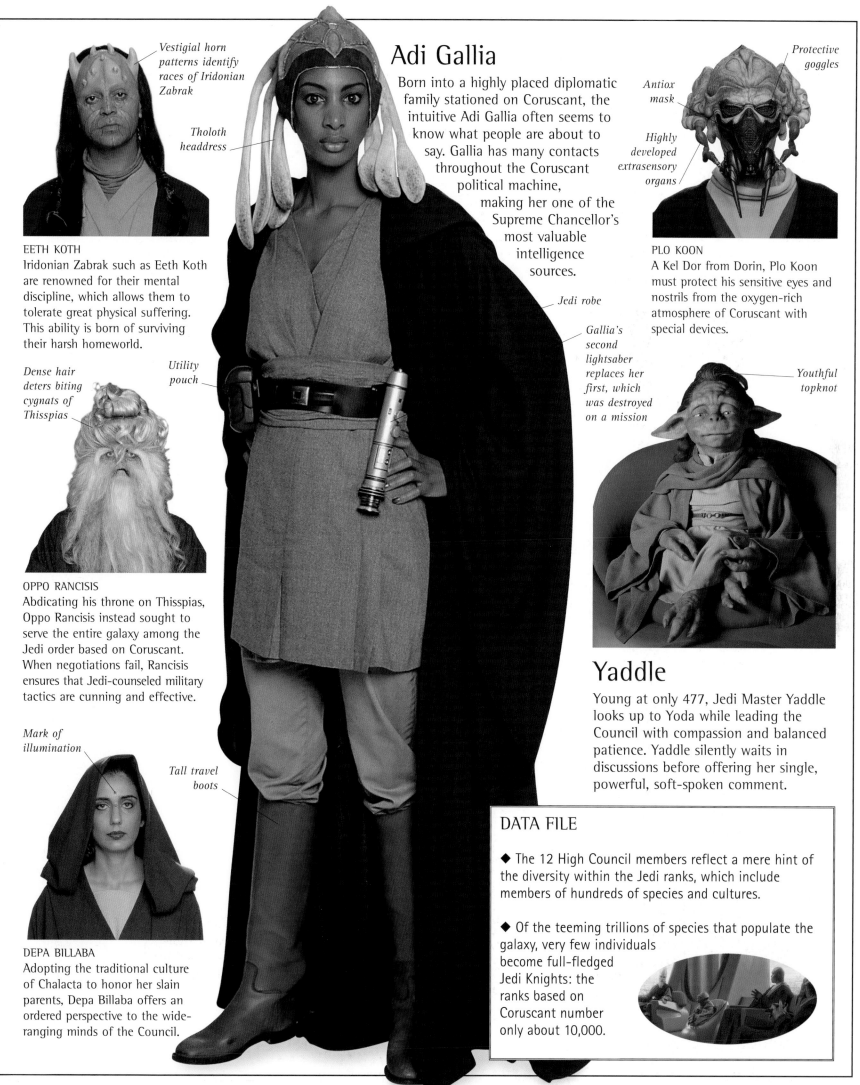

EETH KOTH

Vestigial horn patterns identify races of Iridonian Zabrak

Iridonian Zabrak such as Eeth Koth are renowned for their mental discipline, which allows them to tolerate great physical suffering. This ability is born of surviving their harsh homeworld.

Dense hair deters biting cygnats of Thisspias

OPPO RANCISIS

Abdicating his throne on Thisspias, Oppo Rancisis instead sought to serve the entire galaxy among the Jedi order based on Coruscant. When negotiations fail, Rancisis ensures that Jedi-counseled military tactics are cunning and effective.

Mark of illumination

DEPA BILLABA

Adopting the traditional culture of Chalacta to honor her slain parents, Depa Billaba offers an ordered perspective to the wide-ranging minds of the Council.

Adi Gallia

Tholoth headdress

Born into a highly placed diplomatic family stationed on Coruscant, the intuitive Adi Gallia often seems to know what people are about to say. Gallia has many contacts throughout the Coruscant political machine, making her one of the Supreme Chancellor's most valuable intelligence sources.

Jedi robe

Gallia's second lightsaber replaces her first, which was destroyed on a mission

Utility pouch

Tall travel boots

Protective goggles

Antiox mask

Highly developed extrasensory organs

PLO KOON

A Kel Dor from Dorin, Plo Koon must protect his sensitive eyes and nostrils from the oxygen-rich atmosphere of Coruscant with special devices.

Youthful topknot

Yaddle

Young at only 477, Jedi Master Yaddle looks up to Yoda while leading the Council with compassion and balanced patience. Yaddle silently waits in discussions before offering her single, powerful, soft-spoken comment.

DATA FILE

◆ The 12 High Council members reflect a mere hint of the diversity within the Jedi ranks, which include members of hundreds of species and cultures.

◆ Of the teeming trillions of species that populate the galaxy, very few individuals become full-fledged Jedi Knights: the ranks based on Coruscant number only about 10,000.

Qui-Gon Jinn
JEDI MASTER

JEDI BLOOD
TEST KIT

MASTER QUI-GON JINN is an experienced Jedi who has proven his value to the leadership of the Jedi order in many important missions and difficult negotiations. In his maturity, however, he remains as restless as he was in his youth. When Qui-Gon encounters young Anakin Skywalker on the Outer Rim desert world of Tatooine, the Jedi is deeply struck by an unshakeable sense that the boy is part of the galaxy's destiny. In boldly championing the cause of Anakin, Qui-Gon sets in motion momentous events that will ultimately bring balance to the Force—but not without great cost.

On the desert planet of Tatooine, Qui-Gon wishes to avoid being recognized as a Jedi. Accordingly, he trades his customary Jedi robe for a rough-spun poncho such as those worn by local settlers and moisture farmers.

REPUBLIC CRUISER
Dispatched by the Supreme Chancellor of the Galactic Senate to settle the Trade Federation dispute, Qui-Gon travels on board the diplomatic vessel *Radiant VII*.

As the *Radiant VII* prepares to land within the Trade Federation flagship's hangar, navigation readouts ensure precise maneuvers.

Orientation grids

Neimoidian flagship

DESTINATION NAVISPHERE

Trajectory path shows route ahead

Mode indicator

Radiant VII

Long hair worn back to keep vision clear

Jedi robe

Jedi tunic

Lightsaber

Following the custom of his day, Qui-Gon has built a lightsaber with a highly elaborate internal design. Multiple small power cells are stored in the scalloped handgrip and microscopic circuitry governs the nature of the energy blade. Simpler lightsaber designs, built outside the halls of the Jedi Temple on Coruscant, typically use a single large power cell inside a solid handgrip.

Blade projection plate

Activator

Series of micro-cells

Charging port

QUI-GON JINN'S LIGHTSABER

Qui-Gon has risen to great prominence within the Jedi order, and is well-known to the members of the High Council. Yet in spite of his outstanding service as a Jedi Knight and Master, Qui-Gon has been passed by for a seat on the Council. This is due to his bold, headstrong nature and his favoring of risk and action, which sometimes bring him into disagreement with his Jedi peers and elders.

Rugged travel boots

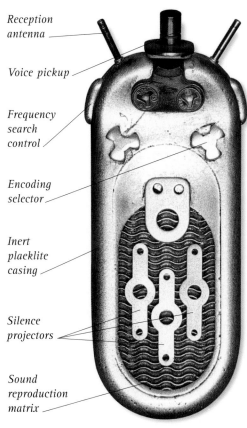

Reception antenna

Voice pickup

Frequency search control

Encoding selector

Inert plaeklite casing

Silence projectors

Sound reproduction matrix

Holoprojector

One of the utility devices that Qui-Gon carries is a small holoprojector. This can be tuned with a comlink to carry a hologram transmission for face-to-face contact, or it can be used as an independent image recorder and projector.

Qui-Gon loads his holoprojector with selected images from the technical databanks onboard the Naboo Royal Starship. He intends to use them to help obtain repair parts when the ship is grounded on Tatooine.

Tines rotate downward to plug into signal feed or to link to larger image projector

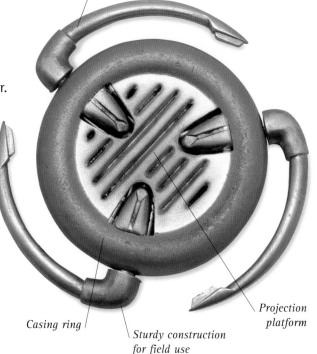

Casing ring

Sturdy construction for field use

Projection platform

TOYDARIAN TROUBLE
Some species are naturally immune to the "Jedi mind tricks" of all but the most powerful Masters. Qui-Gon Jinn has never even heard of a Toydarian before he encounters Watto on Tatooine and the Jedi soon finds that he needs more than Force-assisted "suggestions" to persuade the hovering junk dealer to cooperate with him.

Comlink

Qui-Gon's miniature comlink allows him to keep in touch with Obi-Wan Kenobi when the two operate separately. It features complex security devices to prevent unauthorized interception and is unlabeled to thwart use by non-Jedi. A silence projector lends privacy to conversations and helps Qui-Gon maintain stealth in the field.

COMLINK
REVERSE VIEW

On meeting Anakin, Qui-Gon believes he has recognized the prophesied individual who will restore balance and harmony to the Force. The Jedi feels so strongly that he has recognized this individual that he is not persuaded otherwise by members of the Jedi High Council, including the influential Yoda, who sense danger in the boy.

On Tatooine, Qui-Gon battles a Sith warrior wielding a deadly lightsaber. Since lightsabers are seldom handled by non-Jedi, the order primarily uses them as defense against blaster bolts rather than other lightsabers. However, lightsaber dueling is taught as part of classical Jedi training.

Qui-Gon earned the rank of Master when he trained his first Padawan apprentice to Knighthood, although his second apprentice failed to become a Knight. Obi-Wan is Qui-Gon's third Padawan and a worthy student of his wisdom and skill.

Liquid-cable reservoir

Grappling spike launcher

Hook for sliding down cables

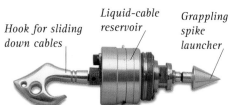

Dual-strand liquid-cable rotator

Spinner tip

JEDI FIELD GEAR

DATA FILE

◆ Th e Jedi workshops on Coruscant supply exquisite materials and tools for initiates constructing their own lightsabers. The initiates' ability to do this successfully proves their developed sensitivity to the Force.

◆ Greed and political scheming are weakening the Galactic Republic that Qui-Gon serves. In an attempt to restore lasting peace and security to the galaxy, Qui-Gon is motivated to take a more active role than that traditionally taken by the Jedi.

Obi-Wan Kenobi
JEDI KNIGHT

Short hair of a Padawan apprentice

Apprentice's long braid

Tunic

Hooded robe

OBI-WAN KENOBI has followed a responsible path on his journey toward Jedi knighthood as the Padawan apprentice to Jedi Master Qui-Gon Jinn. Strongly influenced by other leading Jedi as well as by Qui-Gon, Obi-Wan is more brooding and cautious than his teacher. He is careful to weigh the consequences of his actions and is reluctant to entangle himself unnecessarily in transgressions against the will of the Jedi High Council. A serious, quiet man possessed of a dry sense of humor, Obi-Wan strives to be worthy of his order and feels honored to be Qui-Gon's student, although he worries about his Master's tendency to take risks in defiance of the Council. Nevertheless, Obi-Wan follows Qui-Gon Jinn's example and develops an independent spirit of his own.

UTILITY BELT

Belt fastener

Fastener band

Utility belt

Traditional leather

Food and tool pouches

BREATHER POUCH

Jedi Gear

The basic Jedi clothing of belted tunic, travel boots, and robe speaks of the simplicity vested in Jedi philosophy and carries overtones of their mission as travelers. Individual Jedi keep utility belt field gear to a minimum. As initiates are taught in the great Temple, Jedi reputations are based on their spirits and not on material trappings.

UTILITY POUCHES
On field missions, Jedi carry a basic kit consisting of food capsules, medical supplies, multitools, and other essential devices.

FOOD AND ENERGY CAPSULES

A99 Aquata Breather

In this era, Jedi Knights usually carry various high-tech devices concealed in their robes or in belt pouches. On their mission to Naboo, Obi-Wan and Qui-Gon Jinn carry A99 Aquata breathers, knowing that much of the planet's surface is water. Breathers allow the Jedi to survive underwater for up to two hours. In other times, Jedi have avoided such technological devices in order to minimize their dependence on anything but their own resourcefulness.

Rugged travel boots

Regulator

Hinges for storage

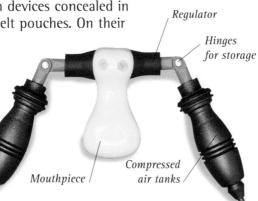

Mouthpiece

Compressed air tanks

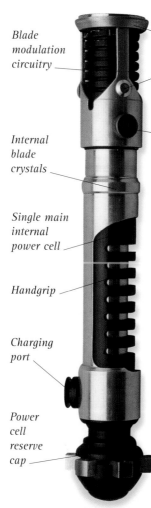

Blade
modulation
circuitry

Blade emitter

Blade length
and intensity
control

Activator

Internal
blade
crystals

Single main
internal
power cell

Handgrip

Charging
port

Power
cell
reserve
cap

Lightsaber

Lightsabers follow a
common design. Optional
elements, like blade power
and length modulators, are small
and unobtrusive. Accordingly, Jedi
lightsabers appear similar at first glance.
A closer inspection, however, reveals that
lightsabers rarely look exactly alike. All are
hand-built by the initiates themselves, making
design details a matter of individual choice.
Most Padawan apprentices build their lightsabers to
resemble those of their teachers as a mark of respect.

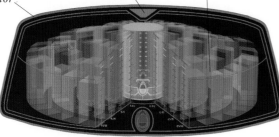

Faced with the mechanized minions of the
Trade Federation droid army, Obi-Wan
knows that he need not exercise the combat
restraint he would use with living beings. He
puts his fight training to good use, yet
maintains cool concentration.

Voice pickup

Encoder

Silencer

OBI–WAN
KENOBI'S
COMLINK

Centered
awareness

Battle
stance

Obi-Wan Kenobi views Anakin
Skywalker as an unnecessary
risk, both as a travel
companion and as a potential
Jedi. But at Qui-Gon Jinn's
request, Obi-Wan accepts
Anakin as his apprentice,
beginning a long and fateful
relationship.

Hyperdrive
diagnostic
monitor

Warning mark indicates
energy leak

Damaged priming
pylons

Blue
lightsaber
blade

Hyperdrive

When the hyperdrive
generator of the Naboo
Royal Starship is damaged,
Obi-Wan stays on board to
look after the drive core while Qui-Gon seeks
a replacement generator. Constantly
monitoring the damaged component,
Obi-Wan readies the core for repairs.

Obi-Wan is an exceptional lightsaber duelist and a formidable opponent
for Darth Maul. The Sith Lord fights with inhuman intensity, fueled by
the hateful energy of the dark side of the Force. In the heat of mortal
combat and on the brink of death, Obi-Wan faces the temptation to
draw on the same terrible strength in order to defeat his enemy.

DATA FILE

◆ Jedi robes are virtually indistinguishable from the
simple robes worn by many species throughout the
galaxy. This signifies the Jedi pledge to the service
and protection of even the most humble
galactic citizen.

◆ Obi-Wan remains loyal to
Qui-Gon even when this puts him
at odds with the Jedi High Council.

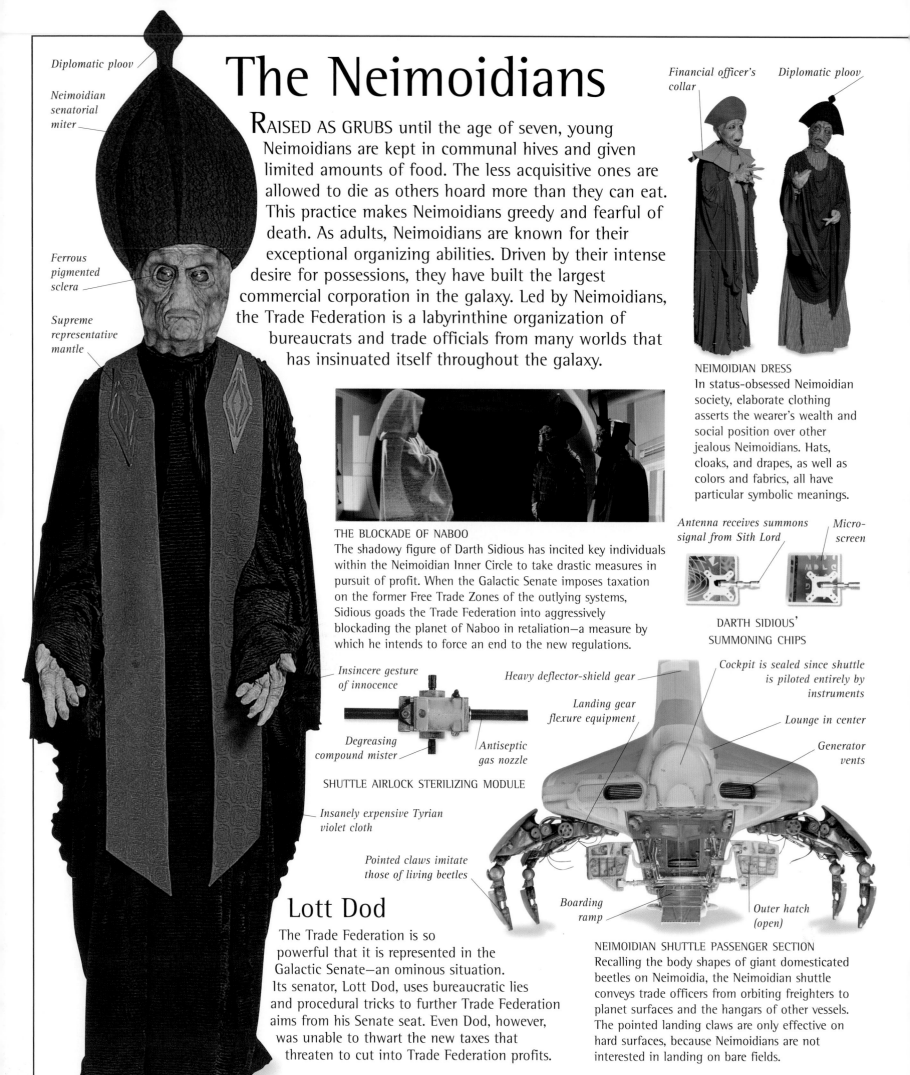

The Neimoidians

RAISED AS GRUBS until the age of seven, young Neimoidians are kept in communal hives and given limited amounts of food. The less acquisitive ones are allowed to die as others hoard more than they can eat. This practice makes Neimoidians greedy and fearful of death. As adults, Neimoidians are known for their exceptional organizing abilities. Driven by their intense desire for possessions, they have built the largest commercial corporation in the galaxy. Led by Neimoidians, the Trade Federation is a labyrinthine organization of bureaucrats and trade officials from many worlds that has insinuated itself throughout the galaxy.

Diplomatic ploov

Neimoidian senatorial miter

Ferrous pigmented sclera

Supreme representative mantle

Financial officer's collar

Diplomatic ploov

NEIMOIDIAN DRESS
In status-obsessed Neimoidian society, elaborate clothing asserts the wearer's wealth and social position over other jealous Neimoidians. Hats, cloaks, and drapes, as well as colors and fabrics, all have particular symbolic meanings.

THE BLOCKADE OF NABOO
The shadowy figure of Darth Sidious has incited key individuals within the Neimoidian Inner Circle to take drastic measures in pursuit of profit. When the Galactic Senate imposes taxation on the former Free Trade Zones of the outlying systems, Sidious goads the Trade Federation into aggressively blockading the planet of Naboo in retaliation—a measure by which he intends to force an end to the new regulations.

Antenna receives summons signal from Sith Lord

Micro-screen

DARTH SIDIOUS' SUMMONING CHIPS

Insincere gesture of innocence

Heavy deflector-shield gear

Cockpit is sealed since shuttle is piloted entirely by instruments

Landing gear flexure equipment

Lounge in center

Degreasing compound mister

Antiseptic gas nozzle

Generator vents

SHUTTLE AIRLOCK STERILIZING MODULE

Insanely expensive Tyrian violet cloth

Pointed claws imitate those of living beetles

Boarding ramp

Outer hatch (open)

Lott Dod

The Trade Federation is so powerful that it is represented in the Galactic Senate—an ominous situation. Its senator, Lott Dod, uses bureaucratic lies and procedural tricks to further Trade Federation aims from his Senate seat. Even Dod, however, was unable to thwart the new taxes that threaten to cut into Trade Federation profits.

NEIMOIDIAN SHUTTLE PASSENGER SECTION
Recalling the body shapes of giant domesticated beetles on Neimoidia, the Neimoidian shuttle conveys trade officers from orbiting freighters to planet surfaces and the hangars of other vessels. The pointed landing claws are only effective on hard surfaces, because Neimoidians are not interested in landing on bare fields.

Rune Haako

As Settlement Officer of the Trade Federation armed forces, Rune Haako serves as diplomatic attaché and legal counsel to Nute Gunray. Haako has a reputation for ruthlessly treating business partners as adversaries and conniving to wrest every last credit from them.

Neimoidians are cautious by nature and the Trade Federation has always been careful to hide its acts of extortion and manipulation behind lies and protests of good faith. Their open aggression against Naboo is new territory for them, and both Gunray and Haako are uneasy about the possibility of escalation.

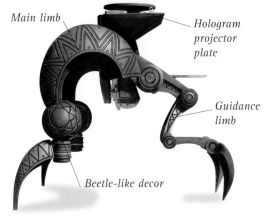

Main limb

Hologram projector plate

Guidance limb

Beetle-like decor

MECHNO–CHAIR
Walking mechno-chairs are neither comfortable nor practical. However, they are hugely expensive and express the high status of their user. They also serve as platforms for hologram transmissions of high-ranking individuals.

Nute Gunray

A Commanding Viceroy of the Trade Federation, Nute Gunray wields great authority and serves on the Trade Federation Executive Board. Deceitful and willing to kill for his far-reaching commercial aims, Gunray directs the actions of the secret army fleet from the bridge of the flagship.

Attorney's cowl

Viceroy's crested tiara

Wheedling expression

Viceroy's collar

Underhanded gesture

DATA FILE

◆ The Neimoidians' organizational skills come from running mass hives and vast fungus farms on their home world of Neimoidia.

◆ Trade Federation freighters, hauling cargo between the far-flung stars of the Republic, are a familiar sight in orbit above many civilized worlds.

The Invasion Force

WHEN THE BLOCKADE fails to intimidate the Naboo Queen into submission, the Trade Federation prepares for the next step: invasion. The Sith Lord Darth Sidious persuades Neimoidian Viceroy Nute Gunray to order the deployment of an immense secret army hidden in the cargo hangars of converted trade freighters. The Naboo little suspect the magnitude of this force, and the Neimoidian leader commits the outrage in confidence that the weak politicians of the Galactic Senate will not object. In support of his evil plans, the viceroy is aided by the cowardly captain of the war fleet command vessel, Daultay Dofine, as well as droid soldiers and powerful war craft.

Data goggles allow pilot to see constant holographic data readouts

Vessel command officer's miter

Skin mottled from self-indulgence

Comlink

Daultay Dofine reports to Neimoidian Viceroy Nute Gunray.

Daultay Dofine

Captain of the Trade Federation's flagship vessel, Daultay Dofine has climbed the ladder of rank through a combination of high birth, back-stabbing, and groveling behavior toward his superiors. Nevertheless, Dofine finds the bold plans of the Sith Lord Darth Sidious too dangerous for his tastes. However, he soon learns that his tastes are entirely irrelevant.

A fleet of specially-built C-9979 craft land the Trade Federation invasion force on Naboo. These landing craft are built to hold heavy armor and legions of troops in their bodies and repulsorlift wings. Groups of three landing craft are deployed in a pattern that cuts off all the Naboo cities from each other.

MTTs are dispatched to strategic positions, where they thunder along programmed routes.

Officer's drape

DATA FILE

◆ Wargame exercises and action against bandits threatening trade routes tested all aspects of the Trade Federation army, ensuring that the force is completely invincible ... or so it seems.

◆ The wealthy, arrogant Neimoidians tend to avoid any kind of labor, preferring to use droids instead.

Droid deployment hatch

Heavy armor plating

Repulsorlift exhaust system

Although Trade Federation war craft have only been used in exercises and skirmishes before their deployment on Naboo, their minimum-cost paint is already badly chipped. This attests to the Neimoidians' dedication to cheapness even in this profitable and long-awaited enterprise.

Protocol droid TC-14 ignores the foul play brewing against the Jedi ambassadors for the Supreme Chancellor. When the Jedi visitors are hit with poison gas, TC-14 simply wants to get out of the way, apologizing even to the battle droids outside the meeting room.

Underestimating the number of blaster turrets bristling from the Trade Federation war freighters, Naboo pilot Ric Olié takes a near-collision course in his effort to escape the deadly line of fire.

TC-14

Frequent memory erasures ensure docility

Neutral humanoid form

Serving Viceroy Nute Gunray and his lieutenant Rune Haako of the Trade Federation, TC-14 acts as servant and translator during trade negotiations with foreign cultures. TC-14 is often employed to distract official guests while legal manipulation is carried out behind their backs.

Hangar arm   *Centersphere*   *War forces carried in interior*

Triple quadlaser batteries

Armor-plated hull

Restraining bolt mount

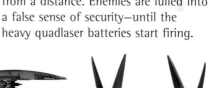

Trade Federation freighters seem harmless from a distance. Enemies are lulled into a false sense of security—until the heavy quadlaser batteries start firing.

War Freighter

To carry the forces of its army, the Trade Federation has secretly converted its commercial freighter fleet into battleships, replete with shields, blaster turrets, and military communication arrays. These disguised war freighters hide the deadly battle machines until they are right on top of their enemies—or, as the Trade Federation prefers to call them, "future customers."

SIDE VIEW

Multi-system connection wires

Walking wing in attack mode

WALK MODE

Subservient posture

Active sensor "eye"

Polished silver finish

Flight assault lasers

Reinforced knee joint

Walking limbtips

Droid Control Ship

Shinplate

Droid Starfighter

The complex, precision-engineered droid starfighters built for the Trade Federation by the Xi Char cathedral factories are variable-geometry machines. The long, wing-like claws open to reveal deadly laser cannons. On the ground, these "wings" become movable legs as the fighter shifts to walk mode for surface patrol.

Foot shell

All units of the Trade Federation droid army are controlled by the Central Control Computer onboard a modified war freighter. Without the control signal, droids shut down, making the Droid Control Ship a key target whose destruction could wipe out the entire invasion force.

Battle Droids

THE GALACTIC REPUBLIC has survived disagreements, standoffs, and even rebellion among its many member worlds, relying on the Jedi Knights to quell conflicts. In this enlightened age, few standing armies are maintained that serve anything other than ceremonial purposes, since an army could be regarded as an open threat to galactic peace. Nevertheless, as the bureaucracy of the Republic Senate indulges in endless debates and procedural bickering, the use of force has become a real threat. The wealthy Trade Federation has quietly gone far beyond any other group in assembling a massive army composed of ghostly, emotionless droid soldiers that are ready to do their masters' bidding without a touch of emotion or mercy. Their deployment upon the peaceful people of Naboo heralds the end of an age of peace and security in the galaxy.

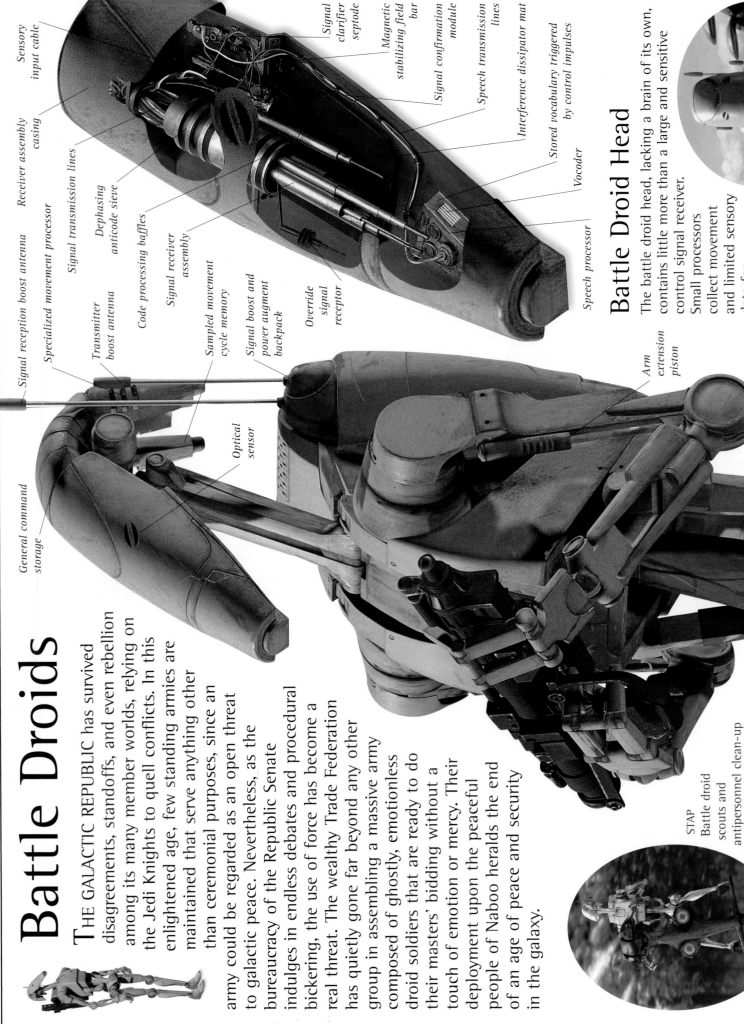

Sensory input cable

Receiver assembly casing

Signal clarifier septode

Magnetic stabilizing field bar

Signal confirmation module

Speech transmission lines

Interference dissipator mat

Stored vocabulary triggered by control impulses

Vocoder

Speech processor

Signal transmission lines

Dephasing anticode sieve

Code processing baffles

Signal receiver assembly

Signal reception boost antenna

Specialized movement processor

Transmitter boost antenna

Sampled movement cycle memory

Signal boost and power augment backpack

Override signal receptor

General command storage

Optical sensor

Arm extension piston

High-torque motors

Battle Droid Head

The battle droid head, lacking a brain of its own, contains little more than a large and sensitive control signal receiver. Small processors collect movement and limited sensory data for transmission back to the Central Control Computer, and a vocoder enables the droid to talk.

STAP
Battle droid scouts and antipersonnel clean-up snipers are swept through the air on armed Single Trooper Aerial Platforms. The repulsorlift STAP's minimal structure allows it to thread its way through dense forest that would be inaccessible to larger vehicles. The droid pilot rides exposed to enemy fire.

Command Officer

In order to streamline communication between Trade Federation officials and droid troops, certain battle droids, such as OOM-9, are designated Command Officers. Orders are conveyed to officer droids via priority channels from the Central Control Computer processors.

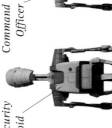

Enemy mass reading

Macrobinoculars

Enemy charge reading

Stereo image rangefinder

OFFICER'S MACROBINOCULARS

Droid type designation markings

OOM-9

Command Officer

Security droid

Pilot droid

Infantry battle droid

ᚷᚷᚷᚷᚷᚷᚷᚷᚷ
1 2 3 4 5 6 7 8 9

GALACTIC BASIC NUMERALS
IDENTIFY INDIVIDUAL DROIDS

DROID TYPES
Battle droids are structurally identical irrespective of job function. To increase efficiency, however, droids are pre-programmed with specialized subroutines. Infantry and Command Officer droids are fitted with power backpacks to boost operational range and extend recharge intervals.

Dried cartilage-shaped shin plates

DATA FILE

◆ Their lack of independent thought processors make battle droids immune to fear, cowardice, or mercy pleas.

◆ The smooth movements of battle droids are the result of pre-digitized motion-capture data taken from live soldiers and broadcast by the Central Control Computer to each droid.

Battle Droid Blaster

Waste energy conduit

Blaster gas cartridge

Power cell

Continuous-fire trigger

Entire barrel can be replaced with broad-fire pattern tip

Since battle droids are capable of wielding deadly blasters, they are designed to be incapable of independent thought. They are governed entirely by the Central Control Computer and have no ability to react to surprises or learn from experience. While battle droids can be deadly, their firing accuracy is poor.

Legs fully upright

Head is deployed last

UNFOLDING DROID
For efficient storage, battle droids are built to fold up tightly, compressing to minimal volume. In compressed configuration, 112 droids can be carried in the special deployment rack of an MTT.

Legs unfold

Blaster stored on backpack while droid is compressed

Arms unbend

Claws grip legs for stability

Skull husk head

Imitation brain sac

Bonelike arm

Generic feet can be replaced with claws or pads

Battle droids are designed to resemble skeletal Neimoidian bodies in order to look threatening. When left unburied and unburned, Neimoidian brain mantles wither to dried sacs behind the top of the skull and their noseless faces stretch and warp to a characteristic shape. This vile image of death defines the droid's features.

Droidekas

TO MAKE UP for the weaknesses of battle droids, a special contract was awarded for the creation of an altogether different combat droid that would be a much more serious weapon. The design was created by a species of chitinous Colicoids in their own image on a planet far from the Republic's core. Colicoids are known for their completely unfeeling and murderous ways, and Colla IV has been embroiled for many years in diplomatic disputes related to the death and consumption of visitors to the system. The droideka was exactly what concerned Trade Federation officers wanted: a formidable, heavy-duty killing machine to back up the battle droids in the face of determined opposition.

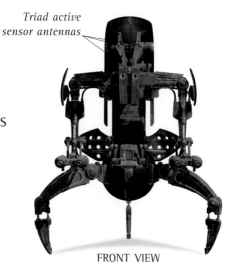

Triad active
sensor antennas

FRONT VIEW

Head-on to an attacker, a droideka presents blazing guns and a fearsome image as well as a minimal target silhouette for opponents who survive long enough to return fire.

Using a combination of momentum and repulsor effects, droidekas unfurl in a matter of seconds from wheel form into standing position, ready to attack. The dramatic transformation recalls the attack pattern of a deadly adult Colicoid, and can take unwary opponents by surprise—as the droids' manufacturers intended.

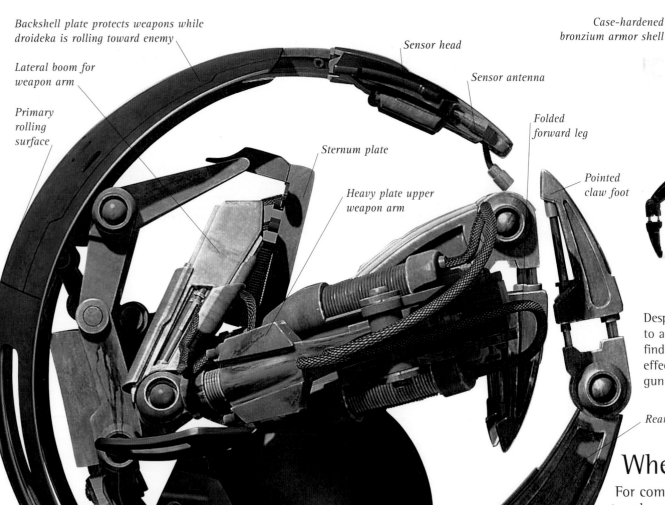

Backshell plate protects weapons while droideka is rolling toward enemy

Lateral boom for weapon arm

Primary rolling surface

Sensor head

Sensor antenna

Sternum plate

Heavy plate upper weapon arm

Folded forward leg

Pointed claw foot

Deflector shield projector flaps

Case-hardened bronzium armor shell

Reactor cooling vanes

BACK VIEW

Desperate enemies attempting to attack a droideka from behind find that its armor is extremely effective, and its moving legs and gun arms are hard to hit.

Rear leg

Wheel Form

For compact storage and optimum travel speed, droidekas retract into the shape of a wheel. Using pulsed internal micro-repulsors in sequence, they roll themselves into battle, opening at the last minute into their combat form. In transit, the wheel configuration presents a smaller and faster target to enemy gunfire.

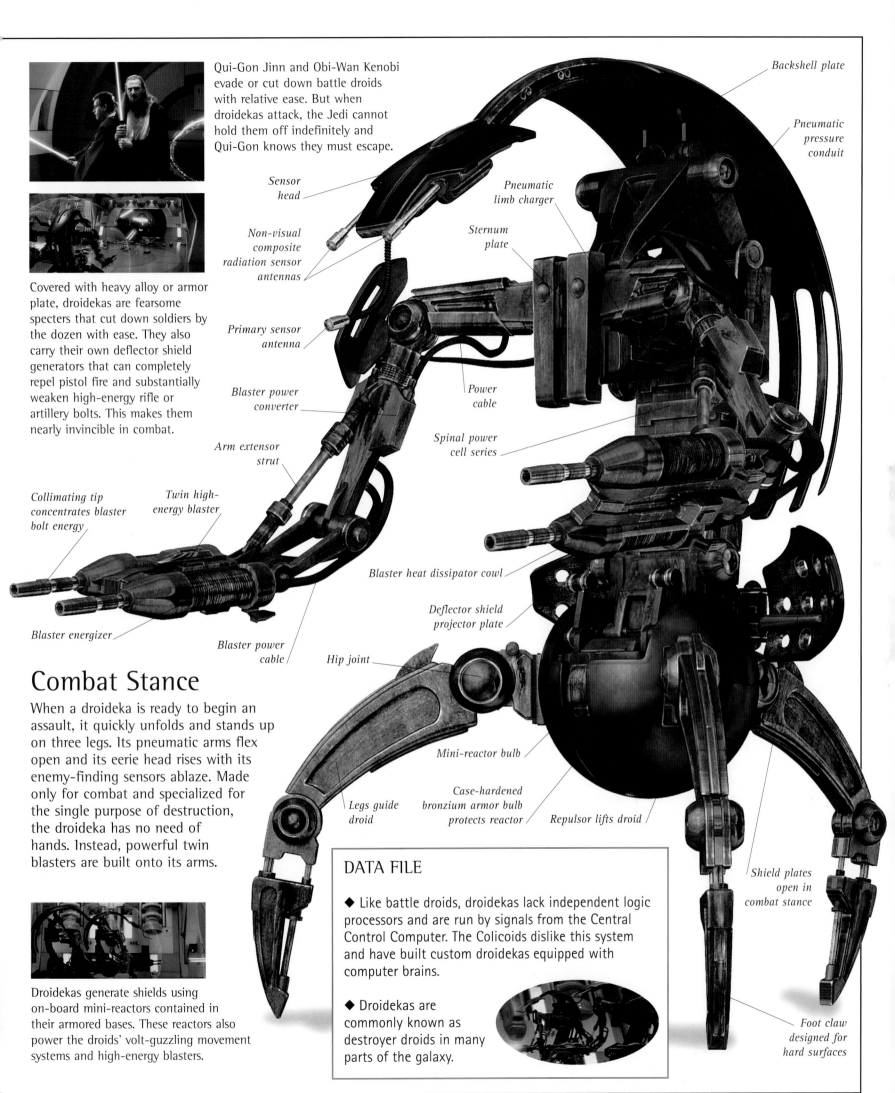

Qui-Gon Jinn and Obi-Wan Kenobi evade or cut down battle droids with relative ease. But when droidekas attack, the Jedi cannot hold them off indefinitely and Qui-Gon knows they must escape.

Covered with heavy alloy or armor plate, droidekas are fearsome specters that cut down soldiers by the dozen with ease. They also carry their own deflector shield generators that can completely repel pistol fire and substantially weaken high-energy rifle or artillery bolts. This makes them nearly invincible in combat.

Backshell plate

Pneumatic pressure conduit

Sensor head

Pneumatic limb charger

Non-visual composite radiation sensor antennas

Sternum plate

Primary sensor antenna

Blaster power converter

Power cable

Spinal power cell series

Arm extensor strut

Collimating tip concentrates blaster bolt energy

Twin high-energy blaster

Blaster heat dissipator cowl

Deflector shield projector plate

Blaster energizer

Blaster power cable

Hip joint

Combat Stance

When a droideka is ready to begin an assault, it quickly unfolds and stands up on three legs. Its pneumatic arms flex open and its eerie head rises with its enemy-finding sensors ablaze. Made only for combat and specialized for the single purpose of destruction, the droideka has no need of hands. Instead, powerful twin blasters are built onto its arms.

Mini-reactor bulb

Legs guide droid

Case-hardened bronzium armor bulb protects reactor

Repulsor lifts droid

Shield plates open in combat stance

DATA FILE

◆ Like battle droids, droidekas lack independent logic processors and are run by signals from the Central Control Computer. The Colicoids dislike this system and have built custom droidekas equipped with computer brains.

◆ Droidekas are commonly known as destroyer droids in many parts of the galaxy.

Droidekas generate shields using on-board mini-reactors contained in their armored bases. These reactors also power the droids' volt-guzzling movement systems and high-energy blasters.

Foot claw designed for hard surfaces

Queen Amidala

AMIDALA rules as Queen of the Naboo people at the age of only 14. She was raised by humble parents in a small mountain village, where her exceptional abilities were recognized early in life. Given the best training and pushed to develop her capabilities, she became Princess of Theed, the Naboo capital city, at the age of 12. Amidala was elected Queen upon the abdication of the previous sovereign, Veruna, who had become embroiled in outworld politics after a rule of 13 years. The Naboo trusted that Amidala would hold their interests close to her heart—but had no idea of the crisis looming ahead.

Beaded emblems over 240 years old, taken from an earlier queen's gown

Foreknot

Large oversleeves

Suspensas

Painted thumbnail

Feet hidden for stateliness

Black Cyrene silk fabric

FOREIGN RESIDENCE GOWN
On Coruscant, Amidala wears a dark gown befitting the gravity of her situation. This subdued foreign residence gown acknowledges Amidala's separation from Naboo and the peril her people face.

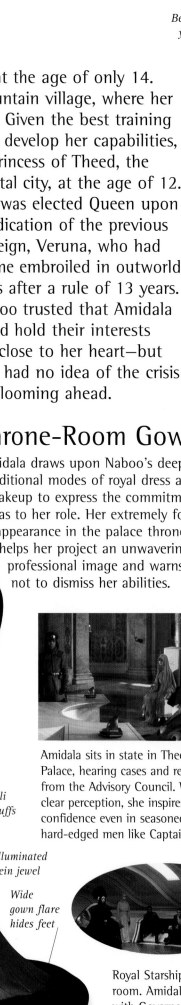

Jewel of Zenda

Gold faceframes

Hair combed over a padded form

Wide shoulders make Amidala seem larger

Hand-stitched gold embroidery

White thumbnail polish is the only tradition Amidala retains from her native village

Shed potolli fur cuffs

Illuminated sein jewel

Wide gown flare hides feet

Throne-Room Gown

Amidala draws upon Naboo's deeply traditional modes of royal dress and makeup to express the commitment she has to her role. Her extremely formal appearance in the palace throne room helps her project an unwaveringly professional image and warns others not to dismiss her abilities.

Amidala sits in state in Theed Palace, hearing cases and reports from the Advisory Council. With her clear perception, she inspires confidence even in seasoned and hard-edged men like Captain Panaka.

Antique tiara

Mauve chersilk hair veil

Full cerlin sleeves

Drapa bindings

Multilayered gown

AMIDALA'S TRAVELING GOWN

When Queen Amidala travels aboard the Naboo Royal Starship, she holds court in a spacious throne room. Amidala uses a holoprojector to communicate with Governor Sio Bibble back on Naboo.

The Queen's gowns are set off with many fine details, such as beads and suspensa ornaments. Many of these come from the palace treasure rooms.

GOLD BEADS

Amidala's stylized white makeup draws upon Naboo's ancient royal customs. The red "scar of remembrance" marks Naboo's time of suffering, before the Great Time of Peace.

Scar of remembrance divides lip

Stylized beauty marks display symmetry

NABOO VICTORY PARADE

Escoffiate headpiece

Golden hairbands

Royal Sovereign of Naboo medal

Suspensas made of delicate orichalc finework

Royal diadem

Minimal jewelry for simplicity

Jeweled finials

Aurate fan in ancient Naboo royal fashion, signifying continuity

Senate Gown

When Amidala pleads for her people before the Galactic Senate, she appears in an extraordinary gown and hairstyle that express the majesty of the free people of Naboo. The regal attire also hides Amidala's feelings and helps her stay courageous and aloof.

Grand finial hairtip ornaments balance escoffiate headpiece

Golden, triple-braided soutache

Embossed rosette

Petaled cape

Plain white gown expresses the pure happiness of new found peace

Parade Gown

After the victory over the Trade Federation, Amidala appears in a parade gown markedly different from her robes of office. The silken petals of the dress resemble huge, lovely flowers found near Amidala's home village. These flowers bloom only once every 88 years, heralding a time of special celebration.

DATA FILE

◆ Naboo's monarchy is not hereditary: rulers are elected by their people on merit. Queen Amidala is not the youngest sovereign ever to rule.

◆ Amidala can step down from the throne whenever she chooses.

The Queen's Handmaidens

DEDICATED AND LOW-KEY, the royal handmaidens shadow Queen Amidala at all times. This select group maintains Amidala's regal image, assisting behind the scenes with her elaborate gowns, hairstyles, and makeup. They also quietly protect Amidala, acting as secret bodyguards. Upon Amidala's coronation, the handmaidens were hand picked for their intelligence, courage, fitness, and resemblance to Amidala. Although the Queen has known them for just half a year, she values their company. In particular, she has become close friends with the dependable and cool-headed Sabé.

Rabé

In spite of her young age, Rabé has learned to exercise great patience in her role as handmaiden to the Queen. She soothes Amidala's nerves and helps to prepare her exotic hairstyles, which can require several hours to perfect.

Oversleeves in the Naboo style

Soft trevella cloth

Gown tinted with spectra-fade dye

Feather headdress

Gemstone and filigree ear covering

Hood to hide face

Amidala disguised as a hand-maiden

Sabé

The most important handmaiden is Sabé. First in line to become the royal decoy in times of danger, she dresses as the Queen and hides her features with white makeup. Amidala has coached Sabé in regal bearing and speech. Even so, she plays the role with apprehension, concerned that a subtle slip will give her sovereign away.

Luggage container   Wardrobe container

TRAVELING IN STYLE
The Royal Starship is equipped with wardrobe containers. From these containers, the handmaidens choose an elaborate dress for the Queen's appearance before the Senate.

Micrograv activates when container is closed

Accessory holders

Climate-controled interior

Travel luggage

The special wardrobe containers holding the Queen's wardrobe and jewelry include micrograv devices in their bases. These mechanisms ensure that clothes hang properly even if the closed container is tipped on its side.

Disguised as Queen Amidala, Sabé is flanked by handmaidens in the throne room of the Royal Starship. The still, expressionless presence of the handmaidens lends dignity to the decoy Queen as she holds court.

Battle Dress

In her guise as the Queen, Sabé wears a distinctive battle dress that allows her maximum freedom of movement. In the palace throne room, Sabé's disguise fools the Neimoidian viceroy and allows Amidala to reach a hidden pistol.

Broad waistband

Surcoat

Long skirt made of blast-damping fabric

Medium-range barrel

Snap-action trigger

Power cell in grip

ROYAL PISTOL
After being selected, the handmaidens were given bodyguard training. Each is capable of using a pistol to help defend the Queen in the unlikely event of a disturbance or emergency.

Shiraya fan headdress worn only by Queen Amidala

Wide cowl masks Eirtaé's face

Gown decorated with the royal insignia

Veda pearl beading

Glass filaments

Rabé's simple gown sets off the majesty of the Queen's appearance

Eirtaé

Handmaiden Eirtaé comes from a town in a remote river valley. Her family was wealthy and she was taught the demands of etiquette. She helps the other handmaidens—and sometimes the Queen—with royal protocol.

Sabé (disguised as Amidala)

Eirtaé

Yané

Rabé

Saché

IN ATTENDANCE
Just as Amidala wears a particular dress for each different official occasion, the handmaidens dress in matching complementary clothes.

DATA FILE

◆ Amidala has five handmaidens: Rabé, Eirtaé, Sabé, Saché, and Yané.

◆ Rabé, Eirtaé, and Sabé accompany the Queen when she escapes Theed on the Royal Starship, while Saché and Yané reluctantly stay behind.

Padmé—Disguised Queen

WHENEVER THE QUEEN is exposed to danger, she disguises herself as one of her own handmaidens, taking the name Padmé Naberrie. The identical hooded dresses and similar appearance of Amidala's handmaidens make it easy for Padmé to appear and disappear quietly from the group. When Padmé is among the attendants, handmaiden Sabé impersonates the Queen, subtly taking signals from Padmé regarding royal decisions. Captain Panaka is behind the creation of Amidala's double identity, having explained the old Palace scheme to her upon her coronation. In her guise as Padmé, Amidala accompanies Qui-Gon Jinn to Mos Espa to see for herself what the Jedi is up to.

Simple braids

Rough-spun cloth

Glass jewel of little value

Wrist bindings keep out sand and dust

Plain walking boots

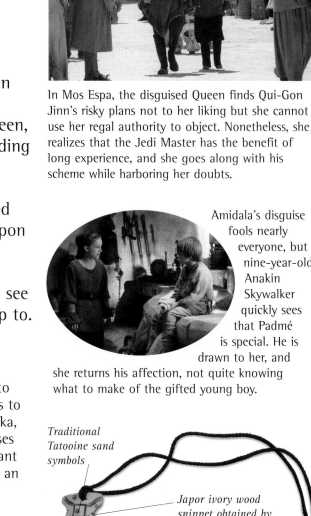

In Mos Espa, the disguised Queen finds Qui-Gon Jinn's risky plans not to her liking but she cannot use her regal authority to object. Nonetheless, she realizes that the Jedi Master has the benefit of long experience, and she goes along with his scheme while harboring her doubts.

Peasant Dress

When Qui-Gon Jinn determines to go into Mos Espa, Padmé decides to keep an eye on him. Captain Panaka, the Naboo Head of Security, promises to look after the ship. Rough peasant clothing helps Padmé blend in as an anonymous farm girl.

Amidala's disguise fools nearly everyone, but nine-year-old Anakin Skywalker quickly sees that Padmé is special. He is drawn to her, and she returns his affection, not quite knowing what to make of the gifted young boy.

Removing her white facepaint is a key element in the success of Amidala's disguise as Padmé. People are so accustomed to the Queen's formal royal appearance that they do not give ordinary-looking Padmé a second glance.

Traditional Tatooine sand symbols

Japor ivory wood snippet obtained by Anakin through trading

Jerba leather cord

LUCKY CHARM
Knowing that the future is uncertain, especially his own, Anakin carves a good-luck charm for Padmé. He hopes that she will remember him by this token in spite of what may happen to each of them.

DATA FILE

◆ Padmé and Sabé practice indirect communication in private, making a game of speaking in cryptic ways. This practice makes it easier for Padmé to guide Sabé's actions as Queen.

◆ As humble Padmé, Amidala observes things that might not be revealed to the Queen.

Being disguised as Padmé robs Amidala of her regal power, but gives her the freedom to live as a normal person. In Mos Espa, she assists with Anakin's Podracer and helps out where needed.

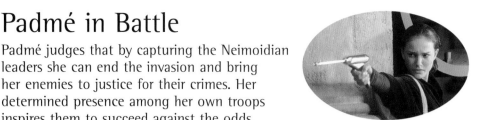

Padmé in Battle

Padmé judges that by capturing the Neimoidian leaders she can end the invasion and bring her enemies to justice for their crimes. Her determined presence among her own troops inspires them to succeed against the odds. Sabé remains disguised as the Queen to the end, providing Padmé with a critical advantage at the last minute.

MESSAGE FROM NABOO

While traveling to Coruscant, Padmé is tortured by the replay of Sio Bibble's hologram transmission, which tells of catastrophic death back on Naboo. Is it a trap? The truth? Or both? It takes great resolve for Padmé to stick to her plan of pleading Naboo's cause in the Galactic Senate when what she most wants is to be with her suffering people.

Hair pulled tightly back for action

High collar conceals blast-absorbing pad

Heavy cloth woven with energy-absorbing fibers to protect against blaster fire

Naboo royal emblem

Activator — *Encoder* — *Power cell*

Memory cell

Emitter/sensor tip

SIGNALLING UNIT

Minimal barrel makes blaster easy to hide

Smooth shell design allows blaster to be slipped out from concealment easily

Blaster gas cartridge cap

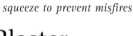

Snap trigger requires firm squeeze to prevent misfires

Energy cell in handgrip

Blaster

Padmé and the other handmaidens carry versions of the slim royal pistol. It is designed for practical use and easy concealment. The streamlined blasters pack a mild punch compared to true security guns, but they fire plasma bolts that can be deadly.

SECRET COMMUNICATION

Padmé uses a miniature device to transmit light and data signals silently to Captain Panaka during the battle in Theed.

RETURN TO THE PALACE

On her return to Naboo, Padmé dons battle dress. In the assault on her own palace, she fights alongside her troops and the Jedi allies in order to reach the throne room and confront the droid invaders. Braving onslaughts of laser bolts, Padmé is quick to return fire without qualms: she knows the battle droids are not living foes.

Small, easily concealed blaster

Short-range barrel

Calf-length coatskirt protects legs and allows easy movement

In Naboo's most desperate hour, Padmé reveals her secret identity to the Gungan ruler, Boss Nass. She knows that only a clear token of good faith such as this could win over the stubborn Gungan.

High-traction leather tactical boots

Sleeves cut for ease of movement

The Naboo

THE PEOPLE OF NABOO have prospered under the security of the Republic, advancing their society without concern for outside threats. Naboo is governed by an elected sovereign, a Governor, and an Advisory Council residing in the Royal Palace at the capital city of Theed. The Naboo live in cities and villages that are thinly scattered on the main landmass of their planet. A love of art is deeply seated in Naboo culture, taking such forms as grand architecture and elaborate clothing fashions. The Naboo regard their refined way of life as a birthright, but they will find that it is a luxury that they will have to defend.

Formal collar

Fashionable Naboo sleeves and cuffs

NABOO
The planet Naboo is small, green, and honeycombed by a curious crustal substructure that is riddled with cave passages.

THEED
The crown jewel of Naboo civilization is the city of Theed, built at the edge of a great plateau where the River Solleu winds its way toward a spectacular waterfall. Artisans, architects, and urban planners are all valued highly in Naboo culture, and their splendid city is a special testament to their efforts.

Sio Bibble

As governor of Naboo, the outspoken Sio Bibble oversees all matters brought to the Queen's attention. He also chairs the Advisory Council, and deals directly with regional representatives and town governing officials in day-to-day administration.

Domed roofs common on Naboo's buildings

CULTURAL CAPITAL
In addition to the Royal Palace, the greatest Naboo libraries, museums, shrines, theaters, and conservatories are located in Theed. The city's buildings are designed in the classical Naboo style.

Zoorif feather motif   NABOO JEWELRY   *Organic chif stone*

Sio Bibble is loath to concede to Captain Panaka's dire warnings of greater need for armament. A noble philosopher, he even refuses to change his mind during his planet's most desperate hour.

THE ADVISORY COUNCIL
The members of the Royal Advisory Council present matters to the Queen and offer her their expertise. The Council frequently changes the composition of its membership bringing a range of scholars, artists, and interested community members into the Queen's audience.

Philosopher's tunic

Governor's boots

Formal hairstyle

Robe of state

HELA BRANDES
MUSIC ADVISOR

GRAF ZAPALO
MASTER OF SCIENCES

HUGO ECKENER
CHIEF ARCHITECT

LUFTA SHIF
EDUCATION REGENT

Royal Starship

The gleaming Naboo Royal Starship conveys Queen Amidala to formal state appearances in matchless style. Built on Naboo using foreign-made engine and technology components, the ship blends the Naboo love of art with the industrial power available from other worlds.

ROYAL PERFECTION
The Royal Starship is quite unlike craft from other planets. Its distinctive interior is characterized by elegant curves and a clean, refined look. As with much Naboo design, utility is secondary to aesthetic concerns.

Hand-finished chromium finish is a royal prerogative

Starship carries no weapons

Throne room

Heat sink finial makes fuel burn cleaner

Sublight engine

High-resolution eyepiece

Talo-effect "lens" allows subatomic analysis

DAMAGE MONITOR
The Royal Starship has elaborate built-in systems to monitor equipment. When the ship suffers laser hits from the Trade Federation blockade, pilot Ric Olié can see at a glance exactly what has been damaged.

Enlarged section showing damage

View mode indicator allows different internal representations

Starship overview

HIGH-END INSTRUMENTS
High-precision diagnostic and analysis instruments onboard the Royal Starship allow the crew to conduct a variety of tests. The wide range of instruments is capable of anticipating problems before they occur.

MESON TALOSCOPE

Power cells pulse energy through equipment to be tested

Diagnostic block

Touch control

ENGINEERING ANALYSIS BOARD

DATA FILE

◆ Merchants on the fringes of Naboo's cities carry on a vital trade between their society and that of the Gungans.

◆ Onboard the Royal Starship, even simple components like this oscillation overthemister are handcrafted in the elegant Naboo style.

FORMAL FUTHARK
The Naboo alphabet has a traditional handwritten form, the futhork, and a formal form, called the futhark. The formal script, based on ovals, is used for purposes such as spacecraft identifications and control labels.

Theed Palace

Built centuries ago, the Royal Palace is the largest building in Theed. Its courts are used for meetings, dinners, parties, cultural events, and visiting dignitaries. The palace blends historic design facets with automatic doors, communications systems, and area-specific climate control.

Columns made of polished Naboo stone

Large windows lend serenity

Amidala seated before her Advisory Council

Palace Guard

Composite holoprojector built into floor

SOCIAL FABRIC
Clothing is often used as a form of social communication. During the Trade Federation blockade, citizens of Theed make subtle use of Naboo color and fashion symbolism to express their support or opposition to the Queen's policies.

Gestures of reassurance in the streets of Theed mask underlying tensions as people begin to grow hungry from the blockade. Some wonder whether their Queen will abandon them for her own safety.

Captain Panaka

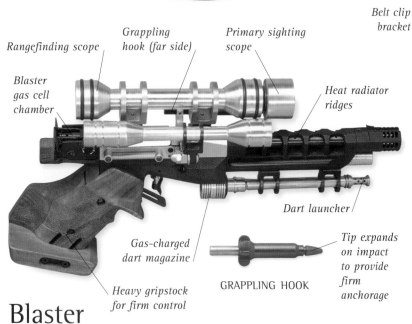

High officer headgear

Naboo Security crest

Leather jerkin covers thin anti-blast armor plates

Comlink in holster

As Head of Security for Queen Amidala, Captain Panaka oversees every branch of the volunteer Royal Naboo Security Forces and is personally responsible for the Queen's safety. Panaka was appointed after his predecessor, Captain Magneta, failed to prevent the death of the former King Veruna, who had gone into hiding upon his abdication. Veruna's "accidental" death was covered up—even from the Queen—and Magneta quietly resigned. Panaka sees the increasingly dangerous state of affairs in the galaxy and argues for stronger security measures to protect the Queen and Naboo itself. Despite this, the Advisory Council convinces Amidala to act in accordance with Naboo's traditional pacifism. Panaka foresees the outcome of this noble policy, but it takes the terror of an invasion to bring his point home.

Panaka has the confidence of an experienced man and relies on his own judgment even when Jedi Knights step in. He believes that Qui-Gon Jinn's actions risk the Queen's safety and the fate of Naboo.

COMLINK HOLDER

Comlink attachment

Sturdy casing

Belt clip bracket

Panaka's security forces use small ground craft like the Gian landspeeder for patrols and general operations. These light speeders are some of the few assets Panaka has in his effort to retake Theed Palace from the invading droids.

Blaster

Rangefinding scope

Grappling hook (far side)

Primary sighting scope

Blaster gas cell chamber

Heat radiator ridges

Dart launcher

Gas-charged dart magazine

Heavy gripstock for firm control

Tip expands on impact to provide firm anchorage

GRAPPLING HOOK

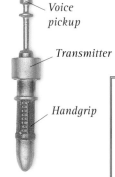

Voice pickup

Transmitter

Handgrip

COMLINK

Captain Panaka uses a master security comlink to keep in touch with his volunteer divisions, employing separate channels for command clarity.

The Royal Palace Guard use multi-function Security S-5 blaster guns. Not only do these weapons fire deadly blaster bolts, harmless sting charges, and anaesthetic microdarts, the S-5 blaster even includes a liquid-cable shooter that can coil around an enemy or let soldiers scale walls via a grappling-hook tip.

DATA FILE

◆ Captain Panaka gained combat experience in a Republic Special Task Force fighting against space pirates in the sector containing the Naboo system.

◆ The Naboo Royal Security Forces include the Security Guard, the Palace Guard, and the Space Fighter Corps. Local police answer to civilian authorities, not to Panaka.

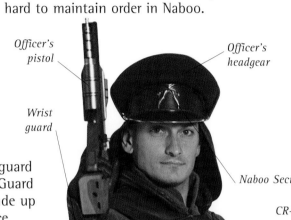

Facing the Trade Federation forces, Panaka and his Palace Guard fight with determined efficiency to return the Queen to the throne.

Security Officer

Panaka's few top officers are loyal but mostly unfamiliar with real danger. During the Trade Federation invasion, they work hard to maintain order in Naboo.

Security Guard

Marshaled under the authority of Captain Panaka, the Security Guard is the closest thing to a regular infantry on Naboo. Individual Security Guards serve primarily as sentries and patrolmen in Theed, supplementing the Theed police force on behalf of the Royal Palace. Although well-drilled by Panaka, the Security Guard is no match for the mechanized army of the Trade Federation's invasion force.

Palace Guard

The Palace Guard is the highly-trained bodyguard of the Queen and court. While the Security Guard function as a militia, the Palace Guard is made up of dedicated soldiers who typically experience battle off-planet and return to protect the Queen out of loyalty. Although few in number, the Palace Guard is the backbone of Naboo security.

Officer's pistol

Officer's headgear

Wrist guard

Naboo Security crest

CR-2 basic blaster, built to last

Resilient armor plates

Combat helmet

Chin strap

Liquid cable shooter

Un-armored joints for agility

Utility belt

Leather jerkin

Utility belt

Blast-damping armor

No leg armor for mobility

Traditional full cut thigh

Studded forearm plate for hand-to-hand combat

Shin protectors buckle over short boots

Auxiliary gear straps

High-traction, quiet-soled security boots

Uniform color denotes Security Guard

Naboo Pilots

LIKE THEIR COMRADES the Security Guard and the Palace Guard, the Space Fighter Corps is a unit of the Royal Naboo Security Forces. Its pilots are a devil-may-care lot from diverse backgrounds who fly the custom-built Naboo N-1 Starfighters with pride. Their usual missions are routine patrols, escort duties, or parade flights. Lack of combat on peaceful Naboo forces the pilots to gain experience off-planet in Republic pirate fighter groups or on the rare patrol missions that encounter troublemakers. By no means the most dangerous bunch of space pilots in the galaxy, the Space Fighter Corps are nonetheless ready for action—even in the face of the Trade Federation's overwhelming challenge.

N-1 Starfighter

Partly finished in gleaming chromium to indicate royal status, N-1 starfighters sport radial engines of Nubian make in a J-configuration spaceframe. Assisted by an astromech droid, starfighters are fast and agile, but prone to uncontrollable spins when the engines suffer damage.

Flying goggles

Anti-glare brim

Built-in communicator system

Flying jacket

Space Fighter Corps overcoat

Pilot safety harness attaches to ship's seat

Bright colors typical of Naboo style

Flying gloves

Naboo pilot-issue boots

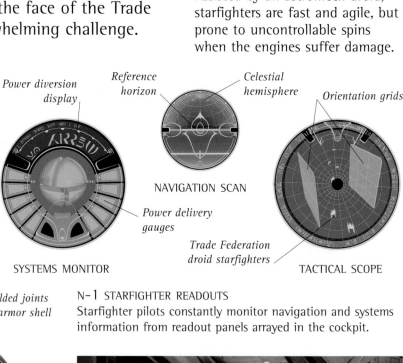

Power diversion display

Reference horizon

Celestial hemisphere

Orientation grids

Power delivery gauges

NAVIGATION SCAN

Trade Federation droid starfighters

SYSTEMS MONITOR

TACTICAL SCOPE

Welded joints of armor shell

N-1 STARFIGHTER READOUTS
Starfighter pilots constantly monitor navigation and systems information from readout panels arrayed in the cockpit.

Automatic distress beacon

FLYING HELMET

DATA FILE

◆ Naboo pilots must gain experience flying utility craft before they are permitted to take the controls of a coveted N-1 starfighter.

◆ Only a few lucky pilots have ever flown royal escort duty all the way to Coruscant, most never having left Naboo's sector.

Ric Olié

The top pilot in the Space Fighter Corps is Ric Olié, a veteran flier who answers directly to Captain Panaka. Perfectly capable of flying any craft on Naboo, it is Ric Olié's honor to captain the Queen's Royal Starship. The run through the Trade Federation blockade taxes Olié's flying abilities to the limit, and even he doubts whether they can get through alive.

R2-D2
NABOO DROID

DROID HOLD
In a small chamber on the lowest deck of the Naboo Royal Starship, R2-D2 recharges between work projects and waits with other astromech droids for assignments. A repulsorlift tube at one end of the hold conveys the droids to the outside of the ship for work on the hull during flight.

A UTILITY DROID with a mind of his own, there is more to R2-D2 than his ordinary appearance would suggest. Just one of several droids assigned to the Naboo Royal Starship, R2-D2 replaces blown fuses, installs new wiring, polishes floors, and does whatever else is necessary to maintain the gleaming vessel in perfect working condition. For a utility droid, R2-D2 is equipped with remarkable tenacity and drive to accomplish his missions. Such dedication would ordinarily go unnoticed, but when crisis envelops the Royal Starship, R2-D2 becomes a hero.

Astromech droid repair-monitor image

R2-D2 at work on the hull

Damaged deflector shield generator

IN-FLIGHT REPAIRS
Astromech droids commonly carry out a wide variety of mechanical repair and information retrieval tasks. R2-D2 does not stand out from the crowd until he singlehandedly completes repairs to the Naboo Royal Starship's shield generator.

Secondary holographic projector

Primary photoreceptor and radar eye

CO-PILOT
Standard astromech droids are used in many space fighters as onboard flight support. R2-D2 accompanies Anakin Skywalker into battle in the droid socket of a Naboo N-1 Starfighter.

REPAIR ARM
This extendible arm can clean, cut, or seal electronic components.

Hydraulic extension arm

Optional oxidizer intake

Pneumatic cleaner

Sonic welder

ROCKET THRUSTER
Accessory rocket thrusters give R2 units the ability to propel themselves through air or space.

Luminescent diagnostic display

Hydraulic arm shaft

Heat exhaust

Thrust nozzle

Deployment brace

Control impulse and power net linkage

Inference pulse stabilizers

Sand-proof joints

Extendible third leg

Swivel-mounted tread

All-terrain main drive tread

Powerbus cables

DATA FILE

◆ R2-D2 is owned by the Royal House of Naboo. He was assigned to the Queen's ship because of his outstanding performance record.

◆ Artoo's head can telescope up so that he can see out of the tight neck of a Naboo Starfighter droid socket.

Jar Jar Binks

An AMPHIBIOUS GUNGAN native to Naboo, Jar Jar is a luckless exile from his home city, Otoh Gunga. He now lives in the swamps, where he survives on his own, eating raw shellfish and other such swamp fare. His long muscular tongue helps him to scoop molluscs out of their shells and tasty gumbols out of their tree burrows. During the invasion of Naboo, Qui-Gon Jinn runs into and rescues Jar Jar. The simple Gungan's sense of honor binds him to Qui-Gon for life, even though the Jedi would much rather do without him at first.

At first, Obi-Wan Kenobi dismisses Jar Jar as an inconvenient life form to have around. However, the Gungan quickly proves useful by telling the Jedi of an underwater city where they can escape from the ground forces of the Neimoidian Trade Federation.

Gungan Survivor

Like all Gungans, Jar Jar's skeleton is made of cartilage, making him flexible and rubbery. Even his skull and jaws are elastic, giving the simple Gungan a wide range of facial expressions. Jar Jar's character, like his body, is resilient and able to bend to changes of fortune without letting his spirit break. Whether alone, in the company of Jedi, or even among royalty, Jar Jar blunders through life with light-hearted good humor in spite of his occasional panic attacks.

GUNGAN HANDCUFFS

Four-fingered hand

Cartilageous skeleton is stiff but not brittle

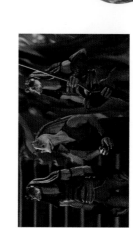

When Qui-Gon Jinn goes to Mos Espa in search of hyperdrive parts, Jar Jar accompanies him. Qui-Gon knows that this odd Gungan will help him blend into the diverse population of strange life forms inhabiting the city. Meanwhile, Jar Jar worries about exposing his amphibian skin to the heat and suns.

Partially retractable eyestalk

Nictitating membrane

Nostrils seal underwater

Large teeth for cracking shellfish

Tough skin near head for burrowing

Haillu (earlobes) for display

Tight vocal cords produce high-pitched voice

Lanky build from life in exile

Mottled skin for camouflage

Fashion statement

Mollusc and gumbol breakfast

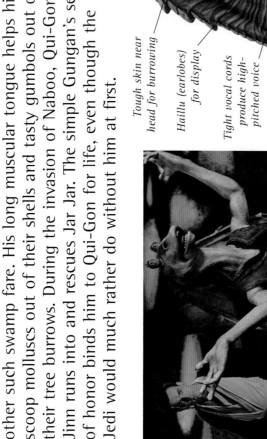

Jar Jar is reticent about the reason for his exile from Otoh Gunga, glossing over the fact that he accidentally flooded most of Boss Nass's mansion and several adjoining bubbles while working as a waiter at a high-class party. As this was not Jar Jar's first serious accident, or even his first serious flooding accident, Boss Nass was furious, and Jar Jar was exiled from his own city under pain of death.

Jar Jar is well known to the city patrol of Otoh Gunga, which has extricated him from all kinds of trouble in the past—from petty squabbles over food theft to the commotion Jar Jar caused when he inadvertently opened half of the Otoh Gunga Zoo bubbles. They know Boss Nass will not be pleased to see the infamous Gungan in his chambers again.

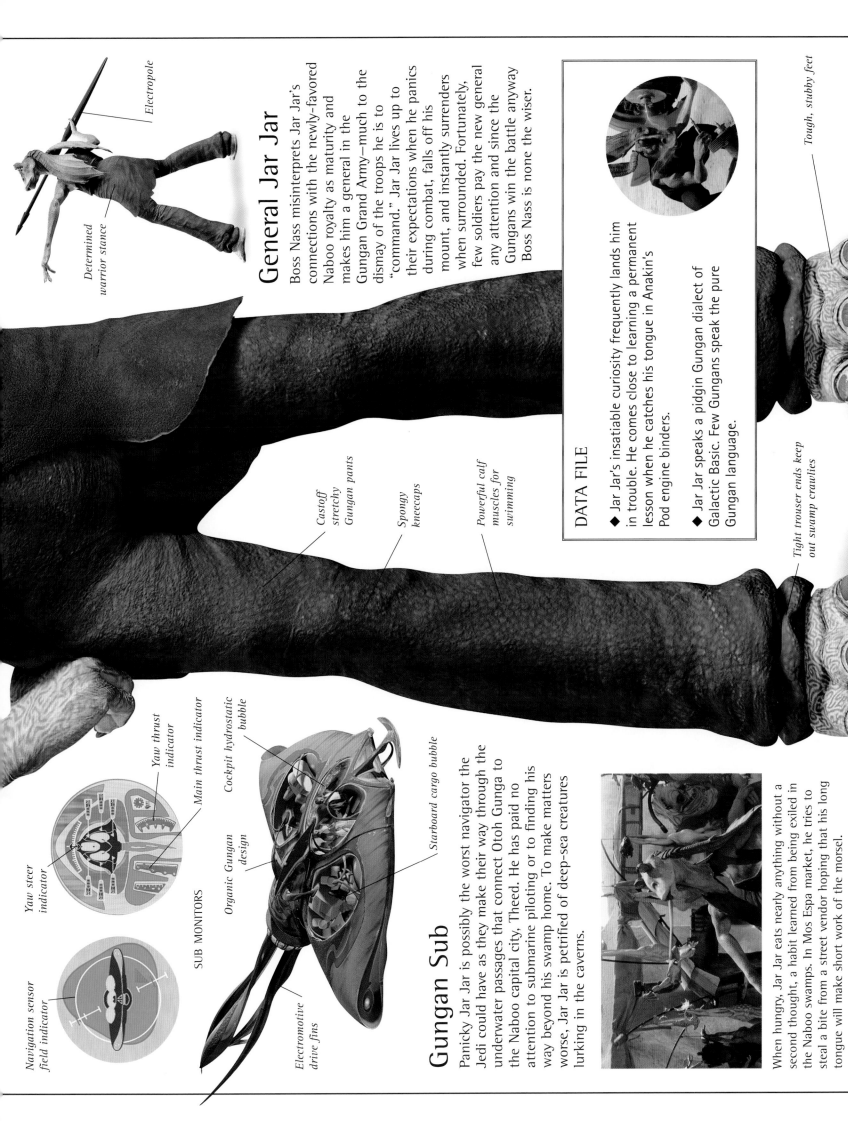

Electropole

Determined warrior stance

General Jar Jar

Boss Nass misinterprets Jar Jar's connections with the newly-favored Naboo royalty as maturity and makes him a general in the Gungan Grand Army—much to the dismay of the troops he is to "command." Jar Jar lives up to their expectations when he panics during combat, falls off his mount, and instantly surrenders when surrounded. Fortunately, few soldiers pay the new general any attention and since the Gungans win the battle anyway Boss Nass is none the wiser.

Tough, stubby feet

DATA FILE

◆ Jar Jar's insatiable curiosity frequently lands him in trouble. He comes close to learning a permanent lesson when he catches his tongue in Anakin's Pod engine binders.

◆ Jar Jar speaks a pidgin Gungan dialect of Galactic Basic. Few Gungans speak the pure Gungan language.

Castoff stretchy Gungan pants

Spongy kneecaps

Powerful calf muscles for swimming

Tight trouser ends keep out swamp crawlies

Navigation sensor field indicator

Yaw steer indicator

Yaw thrust indicator

Main thrust indicator

Cockpit hydrostatic bubble

Starboard cargo bubble

SUB MONITORS

Organic Gungan design

Electromotive drive fins

Gungan Sub

Panicky Jar Jar is possibly the worst navigator the Jedi could have as they make their way through the underwater passages that connect Otoh Gunga to the Naboo capital city, Theed. He has paid no attention to submarine piloting or to finding his way beyond his swamp home. To make matters worse, Jar Jar is petrified of deep-sea creatures lurking in the caverns.

When hungry, Jar Jar eats nearly anything without a second thought, a habit learned from being exiled in the Naboo swamps. In Mos Espa market, he tries to steal a bite from a street vendor hoping that his long tongue will make short work of the morsel.

The Gungans

GUNGANS EVOLVED in the swamps of Naboo, becoming almost equally well adapted to life on land and in water. The amphibious beings live in underwater cities hidden in deep lakes, breathing air or water with their compound lungs. Secret techniques allow Gungans to "grow" the basic structures of buildings and vehicles, which are complemented and finished by Gungan artisans in organic styles. Gungans trade with the Naboo for certain items of technology, but manufacture everything else they need from the resources of their underwater habitat. Although Gungans use mechanized vehicles, they have a close affinity with the natural world and still prefer to utilize living mounts and beasts of burden.

Older Gungans have hairlike finlets

Whiskers indicate maturity

Captain Tarpals

Kaadu patrol chief in Otoh Gunga, Captain Tarpals is usually on the lookout for thieves or dangerous water creatures that might threaten the Gungan populace. To the weary Tarpals, accident-prone Jar Jar Binks is a familiar menace who occupies his own special category.

Hydrostatic bubbles of Otoh Gunga

Kernode assembly for larger bubbles

Hydrostatic field

Field utanode assembly

Utanode

Atmospheric purifiers

Minimal utanode construction requires high power draw

Root counterphase array

Backup generator

Generators

Field wave stabilizer

Stabilizer

Utanode assembly brace

Portal zone

Habitation floor

Counterphase harmonizing struts

Otoh Gunga

The magical gleam of Otoh Gunga is hidden in the deep waters of Lake Paonga. Powerful hydrostatic membrane fields keep water out of the dwelling bubbles and give the city its characteristic jewel-like look. Special portal zones hold air in and allow Gungans to pass through without needing to use an airlock.

Field focusing element

Hydrostatic field generators

Scalefish

A variety of small fish coexist in the waters around Otoh Gunga. They are drawn to the city by its lights, but have learned by experience not to pass through to the air-filled interior.

Poison spine

RAY

TEE

LAA

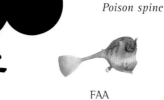

FAA

MEE

SEE

Boss Nass

Mangana aqua jewel

Crown of rulership

Prosperous face

Epaulets of military authority

Ruler of Otoh Gunga, the largest lake city, Boss Nass is a stern, old-fashioned Gungan who speaks Galactic Basic with a strong accent. He commands great authority even in communities beyond Otoh Gunga and has grown large and prosperous in his advancing years. It is in Boss Nass's power alone to summon the Gungan Grand Army, which is made up of Gungans from all settlements.

Swirl designs typical of Otoh Gungan clothing

Four-fingered hand

Rep hood

Rep robe

Otoh swirls

Long coat denotes social importance

Golden coat clasp

Gungan sandals

A fair but stubborn ruler, Boss Nass resents the arrogance of the Naboo, who regard Gungans as primitive simply because they do not embrace a technological lifestyle. He finds it best all around to minimize contact with humans.

Rep Teers

Boss Nass makes decisions with the assistance of his Rep Council. This group of appointed officers is responsible for various areas of government. Their special clothing indicates the dignity of their office. Rep Teers is responsible for the power supply that sustains the hydrostatic bubbles of Otoh Gunga.

Like all the Naboo, Queen Amidala was taught to think of Gungans as barbarians. But when the planet is faced with invasion, she realizes that her people and the Gungans must work together or die. Humbly finding the courage to ask Boss Nass for help, Amidala forges a new friendship between the two cultures. Deeply impressed with her gesture, Boss Nass changes his views as well.

DATA FILE

◆ Boss Nass has the distinctive green skin and hooded eyes of the old Ankura lineage that hails from an isolated swamp village. His distant ancestors united with the Otolla Gungans who founded Otoh Gunga.

◆ Keeper of ancient records, Rep Been knows the secrets of old Gungan hiding places.

Gungan Warfare

LONG UNITED by treaties, the Gungans do not fight the Naboo or each other. Many years ago they drove off the last invaders to threaten them. Nonetheless they maintain an armed force for tradition and defense against attack by sea monsters. The Grand Army employs both technological wizardry and traditional weaponry. Its primary focus is on defense, for which animal-mounted shield generators are used. For attack, the Gungans hurl plasmic energy balls. Soldiers of the Grand Army are inexperienced, but their resolve comes from a firm sense of duty and justice.

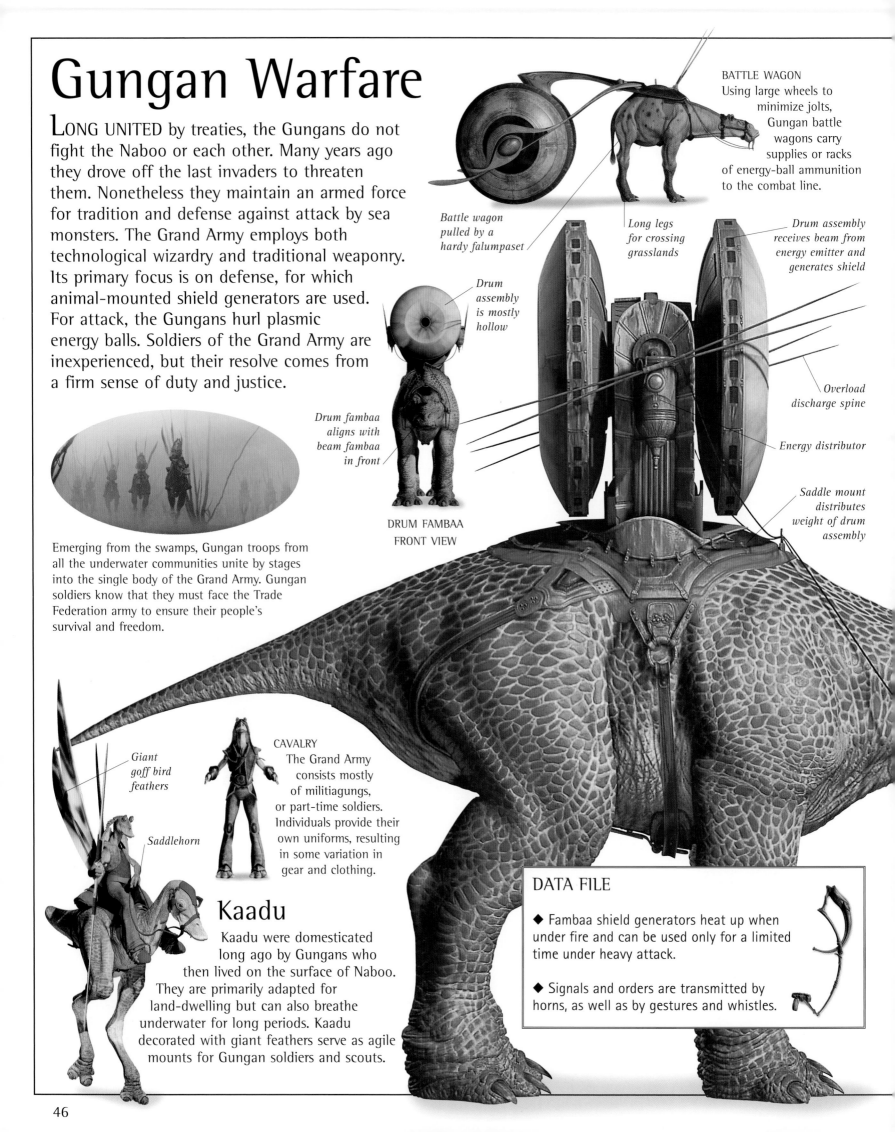

Emerging from the swamps, Gungan troops from all the underwater communities unite by stages into the single body of the Grand Army. Gungan soldiers know that they must face the Trade Federation army to ensure their people's survival and freedom.

BATTLE WAGON
Using large wheels to minimize jolts, Gungan battle wagons carry supplies or racks of energy-ball ammunition to the combat line.

Battle wagon pulled by a hardy falumpaset

Long legs for crossing grasslands

Drum assembly receives beam from energy emitter and generates shield

Drum assembly is mostly hollow

Drum fambaa aligns with beam fambaa in front

Overload discharge spine

Energy distributor

DRUM FAMBAA
FRONT VIEW

Saddle mount distributes weight of drum assembly

Giant goff bird feathers

CAVALRY
The Grand Army consists mostly of militiagungs, or part-time soldiers. Individuals provide their own uniforms, resulting in some variation in gear and clothing.

Saddlehorn

Kaadu

Kaadu were domesticated long ago by Gungans who then lived on the surface of Naboo. They are primarily adapted for land-dwelling but can also breathe underwater for long periods. Kaadu decorated with giant feathers serve as agile mounts for Gungan soldiers and scouts.

DATA FILE

◆ Fambaa shield generators heat up when under fire and can be used only for a limited time under heavy attack.

◆ Signals and orders are transmitted by horns, as well as by gestures and whistles.

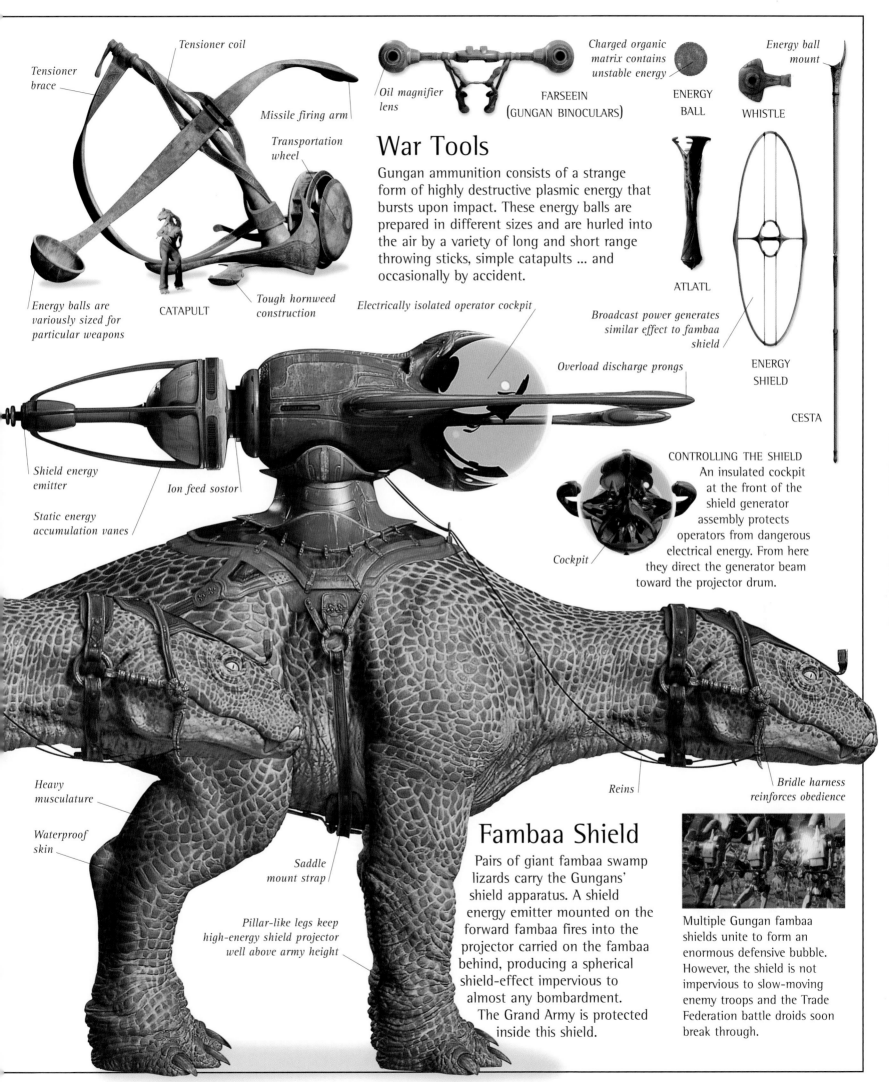

Tensioner brace

Tensioner coil

Missile firing arm

Transportation wheel

Energy balls are variously sized for particular weapons

Tough hornweed construction

CATAPULT

Oil magnifier lens

FARSEEIN
(GUNGAN BINOCULARS)

Charged organic matrix contains unstable energy

ENERGY BALL

Energy ball mount

WHISTLE

War Tools

Gungan ammunition consists of a strange form of highly destructive plasmic energy that bursts upon impact. These energy balls are prepared in different sizes and are hurled into the air by a variety of long and short range throwing sticks, simple catapults ... and occasionally by accident.

ATLATL

ENERGY SHIELD

Broadcast power generates similar effect to fambaa shield

CESTA

Electrically isolated operator cockpit

Overload discharge prongs

Shield energy emitter

Ion feed sostor

Static energy accumulation vanes

Cockpit

CONTROLLING THE SHIELD
An insulated cockpit at the front of the shield generator assembly protects operators from dangerous electrical energy. From here they direct the generator beam toward the projector drum.

Heavy musculature

Waterproof skin

Saddle mount strap

Pillar-like legs keep high-energy shield projector well above army height

Reins

Bridle harness reinforces obedience

Fambaa Shield

Pairs of giant fambaa swamp lizards carry the Gungans' shield apparatus. A shield energy emitter mounted on the forward fambaa fires into the projector carried on the fambaa behind, producing a spherical shield-effect impervious to almost any bombardment. The Grand Army is protected inside this shield.

Multiple Gungan fambaa shields unite to form an enormous defensive bubble. However, the shield is not impervious to slow-moving enemy troops and the Trade Federation battle droids soon break through.

47

Sea Monsters of Naboo

Tail highly sensitive to movement

Luminescent skin patterns help lure prey

THE WATERS OF NABOO are rich with life, the balance of sunlight and nutrients being ideal for many life forms. Microscopic plankton flourish in prodigious numbers, supporting a food chain that reaches its peak in giant predators. The sea monsters of Naboo are primarily lurkers of the deep, but some are known to drift to the surface at night or during storms—making ship travel a proverbially bad idea on the planet. Some of these monstrous creatures have been known to prey upon Gungan cities in oddly coordinated attacks, which is partly why the Gungan army stands in continued readiness. Repellent fields keep the leviathans away from the cities most of the time, but for still unexplained reasons one occasionally swims through.

Newborn colo claw fish are fully-equipped instinctive hunters

BABY COLO CLAW FISH

GUNGAN SUB TRAVELING THROUGH NABOO'S CORE

Organs of unknown purpose at end of tail

Long tail provides propulsion

Rayed tail flukes

Opee Sea Killer

A bizarre amalgam of traits ordinarily found only in a range of disparate creatures, the opee sea killer clings within dark crags, using a lure on its head to draw the attention of potential prey. It then pursues the prey using a combination of swimming legs and jet propulsion. The opee sucks in water through its mouth and emits it through openings under the plates in its skin, allowing strikingly fast swimming speeds. When the prey is near enough, the opee shoots out its long, sticky tongue.

Lure

Pectoral fins for guidance

Multidirectional eyestalks

Jet propulsion vents

Tough body plates

Gungan Sub

Tail legs drive water and help the opee cling motionless in rocky crags, waiting for prey

Opee sea killers are both aggressive and persistent. Even when attacked by large predators, these ferocious killers refuse to give up, and young opees have been known to chew their way out of a colo claw fish's belly.

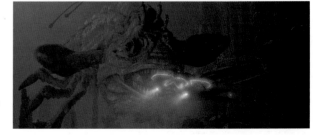

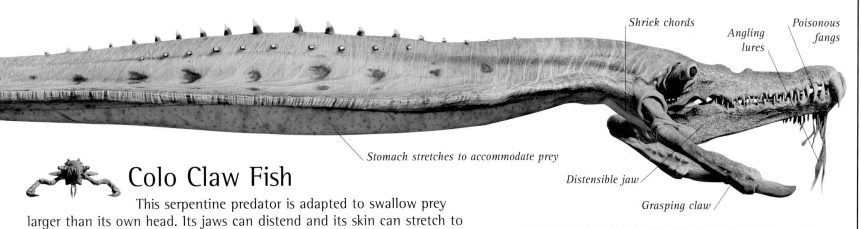

Shriek chords

Angling lures

Poisonous fangs

Distensible jaw

Grasping claw

Stomach stretches to accommodate prey

Colo Claw Fish

This serpentine predator is adapted to swallow prey larger than its own head. Its jaws can distend and its skin can stretch to engulf astonishingly large creatures. The colo seizes a prey with the huge pectoral claws for which it is named, having initially disoriented it by uttering a weird hydrosonic shriek using special structures in its throat and head. The colo digests its food slowly using weak stomach acids and must be certain to stun its prey with its venomous fangs before swallowing to avoid the creature eating its way out of the colo to safety.

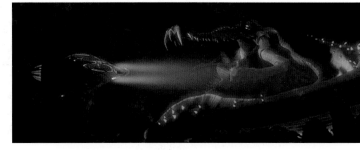

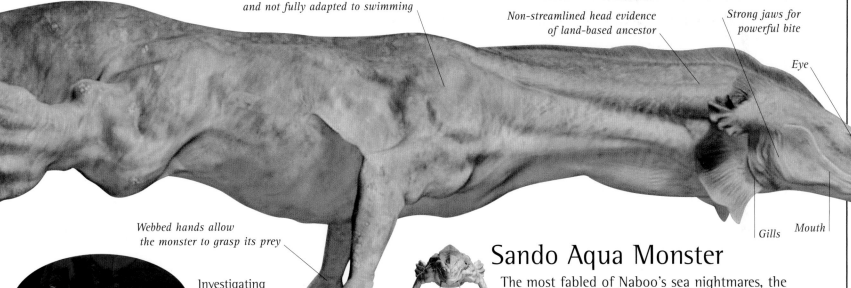

Muscular body not smoothed by fat or blubber, and not fully adapted to swimming

Non-streamlined head evidence of land-based ancestor

Strong jaws for powerful bite

Eye

Gills   Mouth

Webbed hands allow the monster to grasp its prey

Investigating the habits of the sando aqua monster would be a highly dangerous undertaking, even using the most advanced defensive equipment. The sando appears without warning and can swallow most other sea dwellers in a single gulp.

Sando Aqua Monster

The most fabled of Naboo's sea nightmares, the sando aqua monster is rarely seen. In spite of its awesome size, it is somehow capable of hiding in deep environments. The sando aqua monster's arms and legs are only partly adapted into flippers, which suggests that its recent ancestors must have been land creatures. How this gargantuan beast eats enough to support its body functions remains to be explained—as does much of Naboo's ecology.

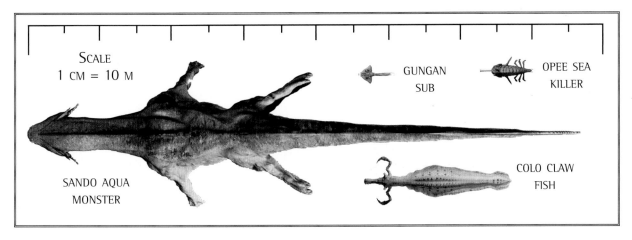

SCALE
1 CM = 10 M

GUNGAN SUB

OPEE SEA KILLER

SANDO AQUA MONSTER

COLO CLAW FISH

The opee sea killer's armored body protects it against most underwater predators, but it is defenseless against the powerful jaws of giant leviathans such as the sando aqua monster.

Darth Maul

FUELED BY THE AGGRESSIVE energies of the dark side, the Sith order began almost two millennia ago with a renegade Jedi who sought to use the Force to gain control. Both strengthened and twisted by the dark side, the Sith fought against each other to gain power and domination until only one remained: Darth Bane. To prevent internecine strife, Bane remade the Sith as an order that would endure in only two individuals at a time. Biding their time, the Sith lay in wait for the right moment to overturn the Jedi and seize control of the galaxy. The present Sith Master, Darth Sidious is the diabolically brilliant mind behind the training of one of the most dangerous Sith apprentices in history: the deadly Darth Maul.

Darth Sidious uses a clear and powerful hologram transmission to communicate with his Neimoidian minions and his apprentice field agent, Darth Maul. Fiercely demanding of high standards, Sidious has been known to dismiss individuals simply for communicating with too weak a signal.

Transmission antenna

Scan-absorbing stealth shell

Magnetic imaging device

External weapons mount

Thermal imager

Primary photoreceptor

Levitator

Electrobinoculars

Light-gathering lens

Multi-scan controls

Power cells

On Tatooine, Maul uses electrobinoculars to search for the Jedi. These electrobinoculars are equipped with radiation sensors for night vision and powerful light-gathering components for long-distance scanning.

Memory stores 360° horizon view

Filters screen out atmospheric interference

Nav-grid can be projected onto landscape

Range to target

Alarm signals energy sources or visual targets

Mode indicator

Magnification

Probe Droid

Darth Maul uses elaborate technology in his work as the Sith apprentice of Darth Sidious. One of his most useful tools is the "dark eye" probe droid, a hovering reconnaissance device that can be programmed to seek out individuals or information.

"DARK EYE" DEVICES
Probe droids locate their quarry using multispectral imaging and many kinds of scanning. The probes silently monitor conversations and eavesdrop on electronic transmissions, and can be fitted with a number of small, deadly weapons.

Scanning lens attachment

Ball detonator

Braking pedals

ELECTROBINOCULAR VIEWSCREEN
Tied to global mapping scanners in his starship, Maul's electrobinocular viewscreen displays the precise location of targets and indicates life signals or power frequencies. Specific shapes, colors, or energy types can be set as targets, and even invisible defensive fields can be detected.

Maul prides himself on his abilities as a tracker, and relishes the challenge of difficult assignments given to him by his Sith master.

Acceleration handgrips

Steering bar

Open cockpit design offers optimum visibility

SITH SPEEDER
The speeder carries no weapons, since Maul prefers the direct assault of blade weapons or the treachery of bombs to the use of blasters.

Darth Maul's speeder is powered by a strong repulsorlift engine for rapid acceleration and sharp cornering. The open-cockpit design allows Maul to leap directly from the speeder into battle.

Repulsorlift

Sith Apprentice

Darth Maul is one of the most highly trained Sith in the history of the order. Focusing on physical and tactical abilities, Maul serves his master obediently, believing that his own time for strategic wisdom and eventual domination will come. His face is tattooed with symbols giving evidence of his complete dedication to discipline in the dark side.

Vestigial horns

Hairless skull

Face tattoos

Gleaming yellow eyes

Dark robe

Double-bladed lightsaber

Beam emitter

Field cloak cut to allow fighting movement

Lightsaber blade is red due to nature of internal crystals

Heavy-action boots

Blade projection plate

Activator

Control lock

Blade modulation control

Control lock

Gauntlets

Maul's weapon is two joined lightsabers

Ribbed handgrip

Blade modulation circuitry

With his double-bladed lightsaber, Maul is equal to two Jedi who are unprepared for his powers. Since the Sith disappeared almost 1,000 years ago, Jedi are not used to facing opponents with lightsabers.

Transmission and reception antenna

Function controls

WRIST LINK
Maul's programmable wrist link allows him to remotely direct "dark eye" probe droids, arm traps, detonate bombs, and conduct other treacherous activities. It also receives signals from surveillance devices.

Maul's Lightsaber

Pushing his physical and Force-assisted abilities to the utmost, Darth Maul built and uses a double-bladed lightsaber as his primary weapon. Traditionally used only as a training device, the double-ended saber can be much more dangerous to its wielder than an enemy. In the hands of Darth Maul, however, it becomes a whirling vortex of lethal energy.

DATA FILE

◆ Maul's lightsaber contains two sets of internal components; one can act as backup to the other.

◆ Darth Maul's Sith Infiltrator spaceship is equipped with a rare cloaking device, allowing him to travel invisibly.

Anakin Skywalker

TATOOINE SLAVE

ALTHOUGH HE LOOKS like any other nine-year-old boy living on the Outer Rim planet of Tatooine, Anakin Skywalker is far from ordinary. A slave to the junk dealer Watto, Anakin lives with his mother in the spaceport city of Mos Espa. He has a natural ability with mechanical devices, quickly understanding how they work. In his spare time, Anakin repairs and builds machines, including Podracer engines and a working droid. Qui-Gon Jinn notices his keen perception and unnaturally fast reflexes, and recognizes that the Force is extraordinarily strong in Anakin.

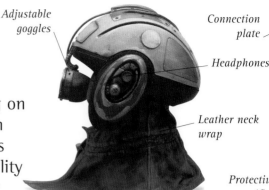

Adjustable goggles

Headphones

Leather neck wrap

Connection plate

PODRACER POWER CELL

No human has ever needed a Podracing helmet in Mos Espa, since humans ordinarily cannot ride Podracers. Anakin's extra-small helmet was made for him as a gift by Taieb, a local craftsman.

Protective magnifier eyeplate

WELDING GOGGLES

Necklace given to Anakin by his mother

Slave's simple haircut

Family and Friends

Anakin's mother, Shmi, believes in Anakin and encourages him in his dreams to escape slavery on Tatooine. His best friend, Kitster, is a fellow slave who hopes someday to become a majordomo for a wealthy Mos Espa estate. Anakin's unusual talents sometimes distance him from his friends, but Kitster has always been loyal.

KITSTER

Among Anakin's friends is Wald, a young Rodian who speaks Huttese. Wald doubts Anakin's extraordinary abilities.

Arm wraps

Anakin has his own room in the Skywalker home. Electronic and mechanical components are piled around his bed since Anakin is constantly tinkering and trying to figure things out. Working for Watto gives Anakin opportunities for picking up scrap equipment here and there.

Slave and Dreamer

Anakin has been raised by his mother to believe in himself. She has given him faith in his dreams in spite of their humble situation as slaves. Anakin looks forward to the day when he will be free to pilot starships of the mainline through the spacelanes of the galaxy. He soon finds that belief in one's dreams can have powerful results.

Rough work clothing

DATA FILE

◆ Anakin once belonged to Gardulla the Hutt, but she lost him in a bet to Watto when Anakin was about three years old.

◆ As a nine-year-old boy, Anakin would never be allowed to compete in civilized Podraces, but the Outer Rim is known for its exciting free-for-all race policies.

Tool pouch

Survival flares for use in sandstorms

Leg wraps keep out sand

Cheap, durable jumba leather

TRAVEL LUGGAGE

WUPIUPI (TATOOINE COINS)

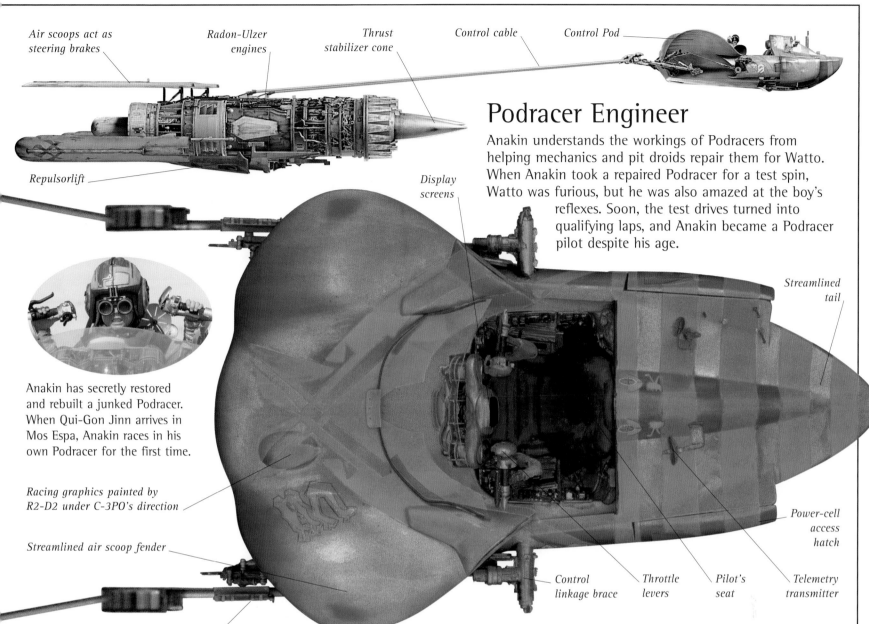

Air scoops act as
steering brakes

Radon-Ulzer
engines

Thrust
stabilizer cone

Control cable

Control Pod

Repulsorlift

Podracer Engineer

Anakin understands the workings of Podracers from
helping mechanics and pit droids repair them for Watto.
When Anakin took a repaired Podracer for a test spin,
Watto was furious, but he was also amazed at the boy's
reflexes. Soon, the test drives turned into
qualifying laps, and Anakin became a Podracer
pilot despite his age.

Display
screens

Streamlined
tail

Anakin has secretly restored
and rebuilt a junked Podracer.
When Qui-Gon Jinn arrives in
Mos Espa, Anakin races in his
own Podracer for the first time.

Racing graphics painted by
R2-D2 under C-3PO's direction

Streamlined air scoop fender

Power-cell
access
hatch

Control
linkage brace

Throttle
levers

Pilot's
seat

Telemetry
transmitter

Hydraulic pressure charging system

Schematic view of
engine mid-systems

Pressure
management
mode indicator

Starfighter Pilot

One of Anakin's dreams is to become
a starfighter pilot, and he practises in
simulator games whenever possible. Most of
Anakin's friends think his dreams are unrealistic, but
a few people realize that there is something special
about him. During the invasion of Naboo, Anakin
hides in a starfighter cockpit half-knowing that he
might try it out... just a little.

Acceleration rate
indicator

Interval
velocity scale

Highlighted
system near
critical level

ANAKIN'S PODRACER DISPLAYS

Overpressure
alarm

When the starfighter autopilot
engages, the ship flies Anakin
into the heart of the battle
raging above. He must think
furiously fast to figure out the
controls before he is killed.

When his dreams start coming
true faster than he can keep up,
Anakin finds himself standing in
the center of the Jedi Council
Chamber on Coruscant. Yoda
believes that the boy is too old,
angry, and fearful to begin Jedi
training. But Anakin is determined
not to be underestimated.

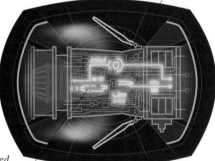

Crash-landing deep within the
Trade Federation Droid Control
Ship, Anakin accidentally fires
his torpedoes into the pilot
reactors, setting off a
cataclysmic chain reaction.

Shmi Skywalker

WHEN PIRATES CAPTURED her parents during a space voyage in the Outer Rim, young Shmi Skywalker was sold into slavery and separated from her family. During a difficult childhood, Shmi was taken from one system to another by several masters of various species while serving as a house servant. When no longer a girl, Shmi was dropped from house servant status and was forced into cleaning work. Although slavery is illegal in the Republic, laws do not reach all parts of the galaxy—and while inexpensive droids can perform menial tasks as well as humans, living slaves give great status and prestige to their owners.

Simple hairstyle typical of servants

Rough-spun tunic withstands harsh Tatooine weather

Decorative belt

WORKSTATION
When Shmi is not working at Watto's home, she is permitted to clean computer memory devices to bring in a modest income. A small area in their home where Shmi keeps her tools and equipment is devoted to this activity.

Aeromagnifier

Some of the tools at Shmi's workstation were given to Shmi in recognition of her service as a dependable servant. When Watto obtained an aeromagnifier in a large lot of used goods, he gave it to Shmi even though he could have sold it. The magnifier hovers in the right position to help her see what she is working on.

Repulsor hood

Illuminator rings

Magnifier

Mladong bracelet

SHMI'S KITCHEN
In spite of their poverty, Shmi works hard to make a good home for herself and her son, Anakin. Her kitchen includes some labor-saving devices, but lacks the more costly moisture-conserving domes and fields, which help save precious—and expensive—water.

Spicy ahrisa *Lamta* *Haroun bread* *Sidi gourd*

MOS ESPA PRODUCE

Tezirett seed

Driss pod

When the Jedi Master Qui-Gon Jinn recognizes Anakin's special qualities and offers to take him away to a greater destiny, only Shmi's selfless care for her son gives her the strength to let him go.

Slave and Mother

Tantalized several times by the false possibility of freedom, Shmi now accepts her life and finds joy in her son Anakin, whom she loves dearly. Shmi and Anakin live together in the Slave Quarter of Mos Espa, a collection of adobe hovels piled together at the edge of town.

DATA FILE

◆ Shmi learned her technical skills under a former master, Pi-Lippa, who planned to grant Shmi her freedom. However, when Pi-Lippa died Shmi was sold to a relative.

◆ Shmi can always sense when Anakin is nearby, even when she cannot see or hear him.

C-3PO
ANAKIN'S CREATION

Sᴛᴀɴᴅᴀʀᴅ ᴄʏʙᴏᴛ ɢᴀʟᴀᴄᴛɪᴄᴀ protocol droids have been in use for generations. When Anakin found the structural elements of a droid that had been stripped of parts, he restored it as a helper for his mother. Over time, Anakin scrounged the parts to complete his droid, fabricating many components himself. Anakin's droid lacks a "skin" since droid plating is valuable and the boy cannot afford it. The droid, which Anakin calls C-3PO, has yet to realize that his parts are showing.

Balance gyro

Borrowed photoreceptors

Vocoder plate

Movement sensor wiring

Photoreceptor mount frame

Composite image integrator

Image signal transmitter

Signal component collector pins

Image component lines

Photoreceptor modulation impulse carrier

Active sensing elements

Photoreceptor elements

PHOTORECEPTOR FRONT VIEW

Photoreceptor

The old droid frame Anakin started with had burned-out photoreceptors. Anakin switched these for the eyes of a used droid bought by Watto—which can now barely see. Watto still hasn't figured out how the half-blind droid managed to walk into his shop in the first place.

Rack for micro-tools

Main power recharge socket

Pelvic joint

TOOL DEMAGNETIZER

Component schematic plans

ANAKIN'S TOOLS
On Tatooine, many devices are ruined by sand and dust and then thrown away. Anakin and Shmi look out for such castoffs, which they use in their work at home.

DIAGNOSTIC SCREEN

Flexible mid-body section

Magnetic rotation assembly links to actuating coupler

While Anakin has tinkered with small devices for years, C-3PO is his first fully functional droid. Building a droid, even from standardized components, can be a challenge.

Lubricant circulation conduit

Auxiliary lubrication system pressurizer

High-torque knee joint

Rotating pin anchors into limb

HIGH-TORQUE MOTOR

Sturdy mount pole

MICRO-CIRCUIT WELDER

Welding stylus

Intermotor actuating coupler

Cleaner/ energizer

Structural limb strut

Foot angle sensor

DATA FILE

◆ Most of C-3PO's structural framework is more than 80 years old.

◆ C-3PO's programming includes memory banks that he draws upon to design the racing graphics for the cockpit of Anakin's Podracer. When he works on Anakin's machine, Threepio teams up with his future counterpart, R2-D2, for the first time.

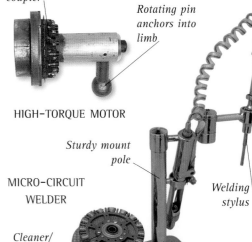

Watto

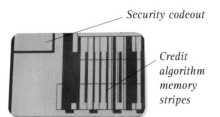

In the rugged frontier society of the Outer Rim, only hard currency counts. When Qui-Gon shows up hoping to pay with Republic credits, Watto only laughs.

Security codeout

Credit algorithm memory stripes

REPUBLIC CREDIT CHIP

Fast-beating wings allow Watto to hover

SHREWD AND POSSESSIVE, Watto is the owner of a parts shop in the Tatooine frontier town of Mos Espa. A flying Toydarian with rapidly-beating wings, Watto's pudgy body is not as heavy as it looks due to his spongy, gas-filled tissues. The junk dealer has a sharp eye for a bargain, and knows equipment merchandise inside and out. Success has allowed Watto to indulge his passion for gambling. He regularly places large bets on Mos Espa's famous Podrace competitions, matching his wits and money against the Hutts, who control the gambling world. In the past, such bets have won Watto many slaves—prized possessions and trophies of his acumen.

SERVING COUNTER TEST PANELS

Watto's Junkshop

Although Watto insists that his establishment is a parts dealership, everyone else calls it a junk shop. It cannot be denied that the range of merchandise runs from desirable rare parts and working droids to unusable scrap that he would have a hard time unloading even on desperate Jawas. Watto's droids, slaves, and staff perform repairs, obtain parts needed by clients, and do custom work with a wide range of mechanical devices.

Old-style sales register device

Protocol droid (missing some parts)

Miscellaneous scrap stuck to short-range re-grav plate in ceiling

Pit droid

Power droids handy for powering up depleted cells in merchandise

Rough adobe walls hide coolant circulating layers

Hard memory cycler (cleaned by Shmi Skywalker)

Illuminated counter surface

Electrostatic damping floor mats keep sand and dust down

Monocular photoreceptor

Equipment interface panel

Bizarre improvised equipment can be found in Watto's shop, such as the Jawa R1-type drone that assists with shopkeeping.

Serving arms

Diagnostic hookup for testing trade merchandise

Cipher converter module

Charger plug

Touch keys

Data readout screen

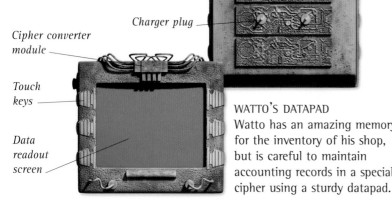

WATTO'S DATAPAD
Watto has an amazing memory for the inventory of his shop, but is careful to maintain accounting records in a special cipher using a sturdy datapad.

Power Droid

Power droids of the GNK series are mobile generators that supply power for machinery or other droids. They hover silently in the background, so commonplace that they are hardly noticed.

Monochromatic photoreceptor

Polyfeed power outlets

Ambulation gear housing

Vocoder

TALKING MAGNETITE CLEANER

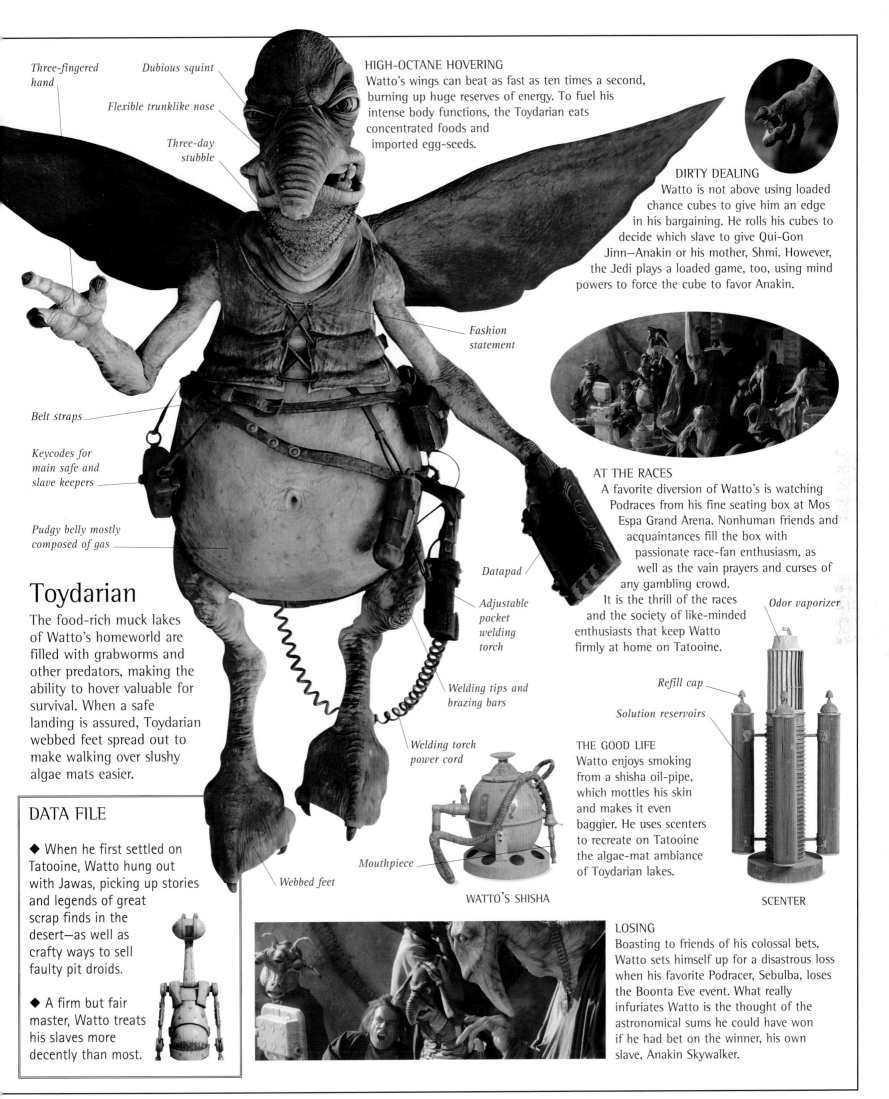

Three-fingered hand

Dubious squint

Flexible trunklike nose

Three-day stubble

HIGH-OCTANE HOVERING
Watto's wings can beat as fast as ten times a second, burning up huge reserves of energy. To fuel his intense body functions, the Toydarian eats concentrated foods and imported egg-seeds.

DIRTY DEALING
Watto is not above using loaded chance cubes to give him an edge in his bargaining. He rolls his cubes to decide which slave to give Qui-Gon Jinn—Anakin or his mother, Shmi. However, the Jedi plays a loaded game, too, using mind powers to force the cube to favor Anakin.

Fashion statement

Belt straps

Keycodes for main safe and slave keepers

Pudgy belly mostly composed of gas

AT THE RACES
A favorite diversion of Watto's is watching Podraces from his fine seating box at Mos Espa Grand Arena. Nonhuman friends and acquaintances fill the box with passionate race-fan enthusiasm, as well as the vain prayers and curses of any gambling crowd.
It is the thrill of the races and the society of like-minded enthusiasts that keep Watto firmly at home on Tatooine.

Datapad

Adjustable pocket welding torch

Toydarian
The food-rich muck lakes of Watto's homeworld are filled with grabworms and other predators, making the ability to hover valuable for survival. When a safe landing is assured, Toydarian webbed feet spread out to make walking over slushy algae mats easier.

Welding tips and brazing bars

Welding torch power cord

Odor vaporizer

Refill cap

Solution reservoirs

THE GOOD LIFE
Watto enjoys smoking from a shisha oil-pipe, which mottles his skin and makes it even baggier. He uses scenters to recreate on Tatooine the algae-mat ambiance of Toydarian lakes.

Mouthpiece

WATTO'S SHISHA

SCENTER

DATA FILE

◆ When he first settled on Tatooine, Watto hung out with Jawas, picking up stories and legends of great scrap finds in the desert—as well as crafty ways to sell faulty pit droids.

◆ A firm but fair master, Watto treats his slaves more decently than most.

Webbed feet

LOSING
Boasting to friends of his colossal bets, Watto sets himself up for a disastrous loss when his favorite Podracer, Sebulba, loses the Boonta Eve event. What really infuriates Watto is the thought of the astronomical sums he could have won if he had bet on the winner, his own slave, Anakin Skywalker.

Sebulba

AMONG THE PODRACER PILOTS of the rugged Outer Rim circuit, Sebulba has accelerated his way to the top with an unbeatable combination of courage, skill, and outrageous cheating. His murderous tactics often bring his competitors down in flames, but he knows where the race cameras are placed and manages to avoid being seen. In spite of his crimes, Sebulba has found that in Mos Espa success makes its own rules. Now enjoying the power and prestige of being a top racer, the unscrupulous Dug has just one thorn in his side—the young Podracer named Anakin Skywalker.

Sebulba's anger towards Anakin stems chiefly from fear. If the young human were ever to win a race, even by accident, Sebulba would be disgraced. The hateful Dug intends to make sure this never happens.

Sebulba is an arboreal Dug from Malastare. Swinging from tree to tree on this high-gravity planet has made Dugs strong and well coordinated. Most have no desire to leave Malastare—and this is fine with the rest of the galaxy since Dugs are notorious bullies.

Split-X radiators

Concealed flame emitter weapon

Combustion chambers

Boost afterburner

Massive engine nozzles

Control cables

Repulsor "threader" helps Podracer avoid obstacles

Control Pod

Sebulba's Podracer

Sebulba's giant Collor Pondrat Plug-F Mammoth Split-X Podracer would be classified as illegally large if race officials were ever able to take a close enough look at it. Concealed weapons like Sebulba's flame emitter lend that special winning edge during a race.

Compressor

Sebulba's race graphics

Stabilizing vane

Podracer cockpits are customized to suit the particular driver's anatomy. Sebulba's complex array of control pedals and levers is woven into an even more complicated automatic data transmission bank that provides readouts of all engine conditions during the race.

Main combustion pyrometer readout

Pre-feed pyrometer readout

Throttle lever

Aeration mix gauge

Second-stage fuel flow rate indicator

The race crowds love a winner, and Sebulba delivers victories time and again. The odious Dug plays to the crowd when in their sight, and has become the heavy favorite in the betting pits.

Crowd-pleasing grin

Wattle

Sebulba, Podrace Anarchist

Sebulba is a highly skilled Podracer, but he was not quite good enough to make it to the top on ability alone. When he found that intimidation and race violations were quite effective in gaining victory, he refined these abilities and began to add secret weapons to his racing machine. Dispatching opponents without getting caught is now the chief sporting aspect of Podracing for the malevolent Dug.

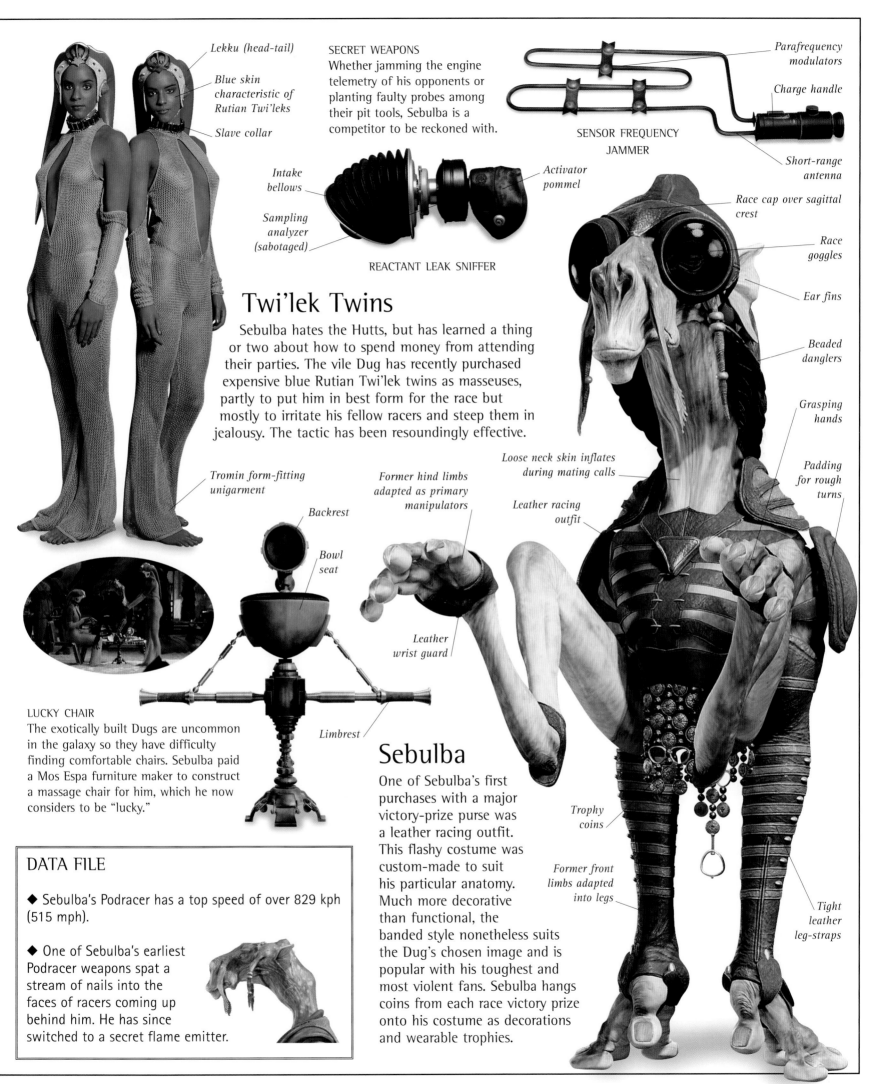

Lekku (head-tail)

Blue skin characteristic of Rutian Twi'leks

Slave collar

SECRET WEAPONS
Whether jamming the engine telemetry of his opponents or planting faulty probes among their pit tools, Sebulba is a competitor to be reckoned with.

Parafrequency modulators

Charge handle

SENSOR FREQUENCY JAMMER

Short-range antenna

Intake bellows

Activator pommel

Sampling analyzer (sabotaged)

REACTANT LEAK SNIFFER

Race cap over sagittal crest

Race goggles

Ear fins

Beaded danglers

Grasping hands

Twi'lek Twins

Sebulba hates the Hutts, but has learned a thing or two about how to spend money from attending their parties. The vile Dug has recently purchased expensive blue Rutian Twi'lek twins as masseuses, partly to put him in best form for the race but mostly to irritate his fellow racers and steep them in jealousy. The tactic has been resoundingly effective.

Loose neck skin inflates during mating calls

Padding for rough turns

Tromin form-fitting unigarment

Former hind limbs adapted as primary manipulators

Leather racing outfit

Backrest

Bowl seat

Leather wrist guard

LUCKY CHAIR
The exotically built Dugs are uncommon in the galaxy so they have difficulty finding comfortable chairs. Sebulba paid a Mos Espa furniture maker to construct a massage chair for him, which he now considers to be "lucky."

Limbrest

Sebulba

One of Sebulba's first purchases with a major victory-prize purse was a leather racing outfit. This flashy costume was custom-made to suit his particular anatomy. Much more decorative than functional, the banded style nonetheless suits the Dug's chosen image and is popular with his toughest and most violent fans. Sebulba hangs coins from each race victory prize onto his costume as decorations and wearable trophies.

Trophy coins

Former front limbs adapted into legs

Tight leather leg-straps

DATA FILE

◆ Sebulba's Podracer has a top speed of over 829 kph (515 mph).

◆ One of Sebulba's earliest Podracer weapons spat a stream of nails into the faces of racers coming up behind him. He has since switched to a secret flame emitter.

Podrace Crews

PODRACERS are complex machines that require extensive maintenance and frequent repair. The mechanical stress of running high-performance engines at up to 800 kilometers per hour takes a heavy toll on any Tatooine Podracer. The pit crews rebuild the battered machines and prepare them for the next big race. Assisted by frantic pit droids and pestered by race officials citing violations, Podracer crews must also put up with the egos of the racers themselves. In spite of it all, the crews take great satisfaction in knowing that they make all the action possible.

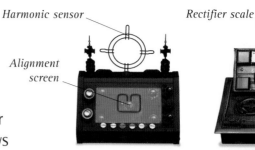

Harmonic sensor

Alignment screen

Rectifier scale

Output sampler

POWER OUTPUT ANALYZER

INSTRUMENT CALIBRATOR

Podracing crews use specialized instruments to analyze engine performance and diagnose faults. Tools should be standardized for safety and fairness, but in practice no two crews have the same gear.

Overhead crane track

Heavy cranes move Podracer engines

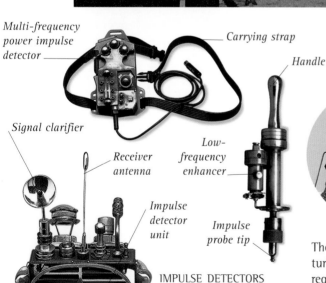

Skylights muted with cloth

Massive Podracer engines

Lubricant hoses provide many kinds of oil

Reactant pressurizers

Pit droid

Power cell chargers

Sebulba and his slaves on display

Pit Hangar

In the huge Podracer hangar at Mos Espa Grand Arena Podracers are tuned to their best by busy pit crews until the last minute before a race. Heavy-duty overhead cranes help with maintenance and repair. Race officials attempt to certify the vehicles, but the crews use every tactic imaginable to distract, threaten, or bribe them.

Multi-frequency power impulse detector

Carrying strap

Handle

Signal clarifier

Receiver antenna

Low-frequency enhancer

Impulse detector unit

Impulse probe tip

Polarizing field insulator

Pacithhip mechanic

Welding goggles

Utility tool vest

IMPULSE DETECTORS
Key parts of every pit mechanic's kit are impulse detectors, which monitor the dangerous power outputs of Podracers.

The mammoth, deafeningly loud turbines of Podracer engines require fine-tuning to make it through a race. The delicate work can often be dangerous, and mechanics must be careful when they are near the engines whether they are ignited or not.

PODRACE MECHANICS
Humans, who cannot safely pilot the blindingly fast Podracers, often become expert mechanics in Podracer crews. These largely unsung geniuses build some of the best engines for species that can exploit the powerful machines to their fullest capacities.

Pit droids are such a common sight near Podracers that they go mostly unnoticed, in spite of the bizarre antics they sometimes engage in when trying to get a job done. The real mechanics are left to make the complex decisions and oversee customized engine modifications.

Ion baffles

CURRENT FLOW FILTER

Vanadium alloy

Insulating sleeve | Firing terminal

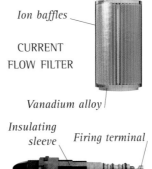

PODRACER POWER PLUG

DATA FILE

◆ The fatality rate in the frontier-world Boonta Eve Classic is higher than in any other Podrace in the Outer Rim.

◆ A tap on the "nose" of a pit droid causes it to deactivate and collapse into a compressed form for easy storage (and to keep it out of trouble).

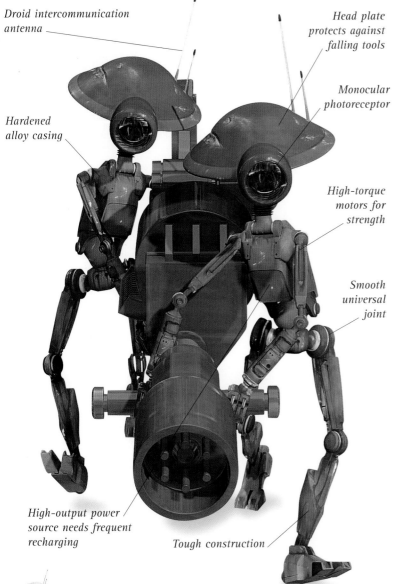

Droid intercommunication antenna

Head plate protects against falling tools

Monocular photoreceptor

Hardened alloy casing

High-torque motors for strength

Smooth universal joint

High-output power source needs frequent recharging

Tough construction

Pit Droids

Programmed to have a permanent sense of urgency, pit droids are utility mechanics that assist with Podracer maintenance jobs. Their compact form allows them to reach small parts and linkages in and under the big engines. Pit droids are built with minimal logic processors so they take orders without asking personal or superfluous questions. However, this also leaves them easily confused and apt to get into trouble when left to their own devices.

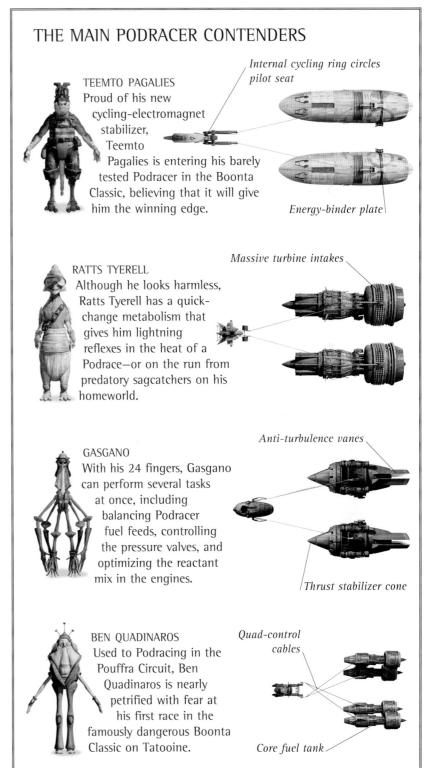

THE MAIN PODRACER CONTENDERS

TEEMTO PAGALIES
Proud of his new cycling-electromagnet stabilizer, Teemto Pagalies is entering his barely tested Podracer in the Boonta Classic, believing that it will give him the winning edge.

Internal cycling ring circles pilot seat

Energy-binder plate

RATTS TYERELL
Although he looks harmless, Ratts Tyerell has a quick-change metabolism that gives him lightning reflexes in the heat of a Podrace—or on the run from predatory sagcatchers on his homeworld.

Massive turbine intakes

GASGANO
With his 24 fingers, Gasgano can perform several tasks at once, including balancing Podracer fuel feeds, controlling the pressure valves, and optimizing the reactant mix in the engines.

Anti-turbulence vanes

Thrust stabilizer cone

BEN QUADINAROS
Used to Podracing in the Pouffra Circuit, Ben Quadinaros is nearly petrified with fear at his first race in the famously dangerous Boonta Classic on Tatooine.

Quad-control cables

Core fuel tank

The Podrace Crowd

NOTHING COMPARES to the sheer spectacle of Podracing as witnessed in the worlds of the Outer Rim. Racers tear through rugged landscapes driving all manner of non-standardized machines in a contest of raw nerve and razor-edge calculation. Each racer has fought blistering competition to get on the circuit, rules are seen as guidelines, and safety concerns are thrown to the wind. To witness an all-star event like the Boonta Eve Podrace on Tatooine is to live the thrill of racing at its most intense.

Race course through desert wilderness • Pit hangar • North stands • Starters' box and finish line

Arena citadel with betting floors

Concessions concourse

Starting grid

Shuttle terminal

West stands

Parade of racers' flags

Patches repair damage from being shot down

Jawa-built envelope

Cheap channel race omnicam

SIDE VIEW

Transmission antenna

Mos Espa Arena

The atmosphere before a Podrace is electric. Spectators take their seats in the stands; the rich enter their boxes or elevating platforms for an aerial view; Podracers are prepared in the pit building and the betting floors are scenes of feverish activity as the odds are updated every few seconds.

The system for determining the starting lineup of the Boonta Eve race involves an apparently baffling combination of performance statistics, outright bribery, and random chance.

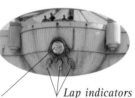

The starters' box holds race officials, the starting light, and three lap indicators.

Starting light • Lap indicators

FLOONORP
SABRIQUET
DRIXFAR

Race cameras used to be built into the rocks along the course to help spectators catch every thrill, but these were all stolen or shot to pieces. Now, a fleet of hovering cam droids is used.

Repulsorlift wing

Multiple lenses catch a range of angles on key turns and speed flats

PODRACE CAM DROID

FANATICAL SPECTATORS
Thousands of race fans fill the vast capacity of Mos Espa Grand Arena for the big races such as the Boonta Eve. Every language in the galaxy is heard from the Podrace enthusiasts as entire fortunes are wagered on current favorites and hopeless longshots.

MUSICAL INSTRUMENTS
Musicians stroll the stands on race day, entertaining the crowds for contributions. Many of the improvised instruments they play are made from engine parts.

DATA FILE

◆ Mos Espa Arena holds more than 100,000 spectators.

◆ Race contestants are granted seating for chosen supporters. Anakin's mother and friends watch the race from an elevating platform.

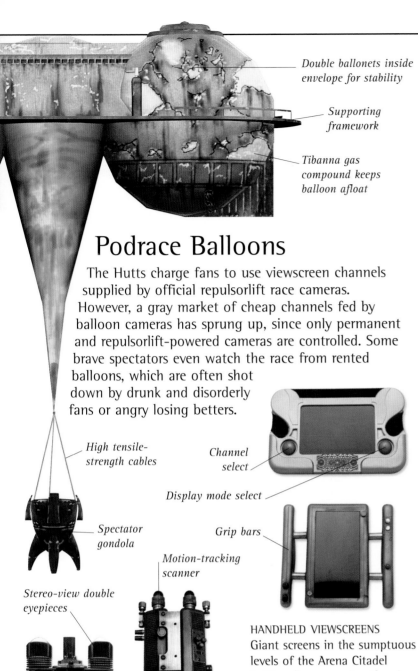

Podrace Balloons

The Hutts charge fans to use viewscreen channels supplied by official repulsorlift race cameras. However, a gray market of cheap channels fed by balloon cameras has sprung up, since only permanent and repulsorlift-powered cameras are controlled. Some brave spectators even watch the race from rented balloons, which are often shot down by drunk and disorderly fans or angry losing betters.

Double ballonets inside envelope for stability

Supporting framework

Tibanna gas compound keeps balloon afloat

High tensile-strength cables

Spectator gondola

Stereo-view double eyepieces

Channel select

Display mode select

Motion-tracking scanner

Grip bars

RACE ELECTROBINOCULARS

HANDHELD VIEWSCREENS
Giant screens in the sumptuous levels of the Arena Citadel betting floors monitor the views from the race cameras. However, most fans prefer to to watch the race in the stands using rented screens or electrobinoculars.

THE PODRACERS

BOLES ROOR
Racing his near-stock Podracer, Boles Roor is out of his league on Tatooine, where they don't make allowances for sub-par skills. He will be lucky to finish the race.

Poor-quality welding

Racing insignia

MARS GUO
A loudmouthed braggart, Mars Guo is a Phuii with a chip on his shoulder and an eye for blue masseuses in skimpy outfits. Guo will find that it doesn't pay to chat up a Dug's slave girl when the Dug is a fiend for revenge.

Triocular vision

Neural bundles process sensory input at high speed

Electrostatic repeller visor

MAWHONIC

ARK "BUMPY" ROOSE

NEVA KEE

ELAN MAK

CLEGG HOLDFAST

Thermoregulator flaps

ALDAR BEEDO

EBE ENDOCOTT

WAN SANDAGE

DUD BOLT

ODY MANDRELL

Jabba the Hutt

Somewhere in Mos Espa there is a little-known official who legally rules the city, but the wealthy gangster "First Citizen" Jabba the Hutt is really in control. Jabba presides over the Boonta Eve race from the best box seats in the arena, thinking only of the profits he will reap through his gambling organizations. His major-domo Bib Fortuna attends to every arrangement, keeping Jabba's entertainment running as smoothly as his criminal operations.

Jabba the Hutt

Bib Fortuna, Jabba's Twi'lek major-domo

Diva Shaliqua, one of Jabba's slaves

Jabba's shisha

Chokk, an armed bodyguard

R5-X2 computes betting odds and Jabba's winnings

Huttese glyphs of good fortune

Diva Funquita, Gardulla's assistant

Gardulla the Hutt, Jabba's guest and sometime rival

Dwarf nunas brought back by one of Jabba's assassins from a recent mission

Tatooine Inhabitants

A FRONTIER WORLD, the desert planet Tatooine lies on an important hyperspace route between the civilized planets of the galactic core and the distant star systems of the Outer Rim. Traders and smugglers run all manner of goods through Tatooine's spaceports, answering to few authorities besides the gangster Hutts. On the desert surface, inhabitants include desperate settlers, impoverished spacers, aliens of dubious reputation, droids of all kinds, along with the scattered representatives of Tatooine's native populations, who are best adapted to life on this difficult world.

The slave Erdan was chemically enlarged by his owner to increase his work-rate. His face was patterned as a mark of ownership.

Spacers willing to run routes into the risky areas beyond Tatooine wait for work in a streetside café, where cooled table slabs offer some respite from the heat. Games like triga help to pass the time.

Drann player markers

Sett player home

TRIGA GAME

Spacers' café

Cheap imitation chiller tables offer no coolth

Teguar deal-maker | *Retractable awning* | *Amphibious gorgs cooked at street stalls* | *Non-indigenous species recovered from freighter bilge*

Locals keep a low profile

Gorg dipping sauces | *R2-D2*

Broken antenna

Marketplace

In the crowded marketplace alleys of Mos Espa, various quarters specialize in particular types of trade. Some serve the day-to-day needs of local inhabitants, while others house droid mechanics, engine repairers, and—if you know where to look—illegal weapons dealers.

GORGMONGER
Gragra claims to keep her amphibian food stock in a large basement culture pool, but she actually grows them in a sewer zone under Mos Espa.

Intensity controls

Compressor

Coolth emitter vents

COOLING UNIT
Many street vendors in Mos Espa keep cooling units near their wares to draw potential customers from the hot streets.

Head salvaged from Temirca droid

Montoro serving drone body

Repair worker arms

Welding droid

Podracer engine shroud

Droids

In the Outer Rim, ancient and heavily repaired droids can often be seen lurching through back alleys. Also common are exotic hybrids made of parts combined from dissimilar droids. The resulting machines tend to have either limited mentalities or personalities as bizarre as their origins.

Ignored or derided by the gangster and spacer classes, Mos Espa settlers try their hardest to avoid involvement in local disputes or gunfights.

Beasts of Burden

Tatooine's heat, dust, and sandstorms can damage mechanical transport, but animals make ideal beasts of burden. Dewbacks are used all over Tatooine, eopies are common only around Mos Espa, and banthas are the exclusive mounts of the Sand People.

Suspicious-looking luggage

White skin pigmentation reflects sunlight

Scaly skin retains moisture

DEWBACK

Flexible snout for uncovering sand lichen that grow just beneath the planet surface

Broad feet for sand travel

EOPIE

Natives of Tatooine, eopies are able to carry heavy loads in intense heat without tiring.

Long barrel for accuracy

Gaffi stick

Stolen projectile rifle

Sandproof bindings

Protective eye lenses

Filtering sandmask

Bound hands

Heavy cloak and bindings protect against sand and sun

Ammo bandoleer

Clan-crafted leatherwork

At times, Sand People steal guns but strongly favor traditional club and ax weapons for close quarters combat.

Indigenous to Tatooine, Jawas have become used to contact with space travelers. Many Jawas act as metal scavengers and equipment-repair craftworkers.

Long robe allows free movement and ventilation

Sling

Power cell

Sand People take pot shots at fast-moving Podracers from remote sections of the Podrace course, hoping to strand and attack race pilots.

DATA FILE

◆ Jawa clans can be distinguished by subtle differences in their cloak designs.

◆ Children in Mos Espa play with fortune-telling "Eyes of Mesra," an old desert tradition.

BACKPACK COOLERS
Twin suns make for searing hot middays, so pedestrians in Mos Espa often wear personal cooling units.

Sand People

Unlike the Jawas, the native Tatooine Sand People have not adapted to easy contact with outworld settlers. Resentful of incursions in their territory, Sand People prey upon travelers and are known as Tusken Raiders. Renowned for their savagery, Tusken Raiders are lethally dangerous and not to be trifled with.

Handle

Ion charger exhaust

Collector

Intake

SANDSTAT
Sand and dust blows into every corner of Mos Espa; the fastidious clean up with electrostatic sandstats.

Bandaged feet

Chancellor Valorum

Distinguished gray hair

Premature aging from pressures of governing

Veda cloth robe

Ornate overcloak

A LIFETIME OF PREPARATION led to Finis Valorum's election as Supreme Chancellor of the Galactic Senate. Valorum inherited the legacy of a family whose greatest members had each represented more than 1,000 worlds. Centuries ago, a Valorum served as Supreme Chancellor. Finis Valorum has now equalled this achievement, ruling the entire Republic from the galactic seat on Coruscant. However, he has also inherited a government grown weak from its own success: the galactic representatives have become distanced from their people and now the entire system is degenerating.

Blue band symbolic of Supreme Chancellor

Coruscant

The galactic capital, Coruscant, is almost entirely covered with skyscrapers. These kilometers-high buildings provide living space for more than a trillion inhabitants, including the thousands of representatives in the Senate Chamber. The planet is entirely dependent on outside support to survive, consuming resource shipments from a steady stream of vast freighters.

Sei Taria

Septsilk robe signifies wealth

Chancellor Valorum's administrative aide, Sei Taria assists him in confirming the fine details of necessary procedural regulations. She has learned much from Senator Palpatine.

Blue skin screens out harmful radiation

Chagrian horns used for intimidating display

Lethorns

DATA FILE

◆ Coruscant has been the center of galactic government for tens of thousands of years. Its early history is shrouded in legend.

◆ Increasingly, Supreme Chancellor Valorum has been influenced by senators such as Palpatine to compromise what he knows is right for the sake of approved procedure.

Mas Amedda

The stern Chagrian Mas Amedda is responsible for keeping order in the Senate. Accused of misusing his parliamentary powers for bribes, Amedda stands firm to his own code of honor.

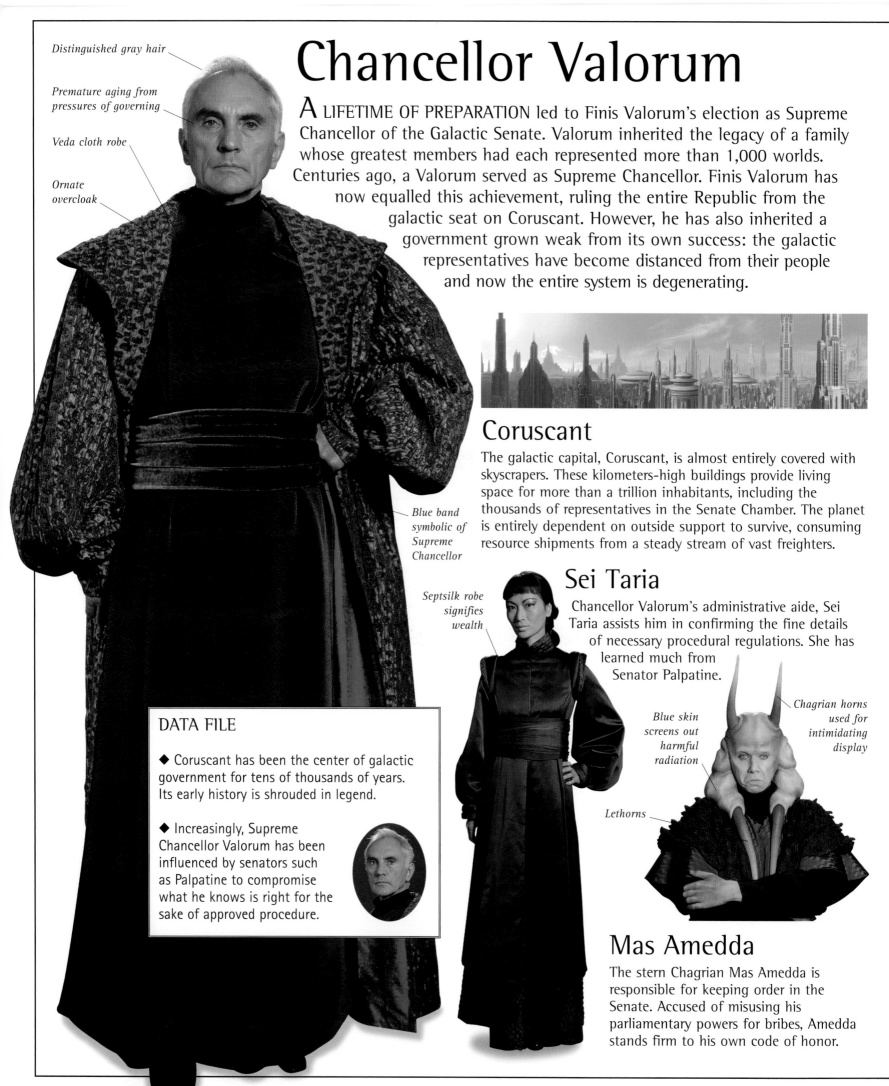

AIR TAXIS

Multi-spectrum headlights

Communications antenna

Air taxis carry passengers throughout the bewildering maze of canyons and pinnacles in Coruscant's skyscraper landscape.

High altitude repulsors

Senate Guard

The guards of the Galactic Senate wear striking robes of blue, symbolizing the Senate's supreme authority and the long tradition of its wise and just rule. The large crest and simple drape are ceremonial effects rather than functional designs.

Highly visible crest

Muzzle brake dampens rifle blast

Large, unwieldy ceremonial rifle

Platform seating

Senate guard

SENATE PLATFORMS

The vast amphitheater of the Senate Rotunda is lined with 1,024 platforms. The majority are used by sectorial senators, who represent their own planet and hundreds of others in a galactic sector. The remaining platforms are available for limited periods to alliances, commercial powers, or individual planets with special causes to bring before the senate.

Repulsorlift

HOVERCAM
SIDE VIEW

When a senate representative is recognized for official speech, their senate platform detaches itself from the rotunda and flies out into the open chamber for prominence.

Rodian representative on senate platform

Control antenna

Wide angle lens

Telephoto lens

Hovercam

A squadron of flying hovercams patrols the Rotunda to record the speeches and votes of the Senate representatives. Some hovercam operators abuse their responsibility and omit to record certain individuals, while others allow unscrupulous senators to alter the record of their words after they are spoken.

Repulsor floaters

THE DIVERSITY OF THE SENATE

A vast range of alien species populates the Senate Rotunda, hailing from every corner of the Republic. Among them can be seen the traditional costumes of hundreds of planets, as well as many fashions particular to Coruscant.

Dual mouths for stereo language

Brain in neck hump

SENATOR
YARUA FROM
KASHYYYK

Alderaan aides

LIANA
MERIAN

AGRIPPA
ALDRETE

TENDAU BENDON

Renowned for their tempers, Wookiee senators are nonetheless possessed of a firm sense of fair justice. Senator Yarua finds commercial power within the senate reprehensible and is determined to restore justice to galactic government.

Senator Palpatine

ENDLESS PATIENCE has been Palpatine's key to success. Passed over as a young politician and repeatedly turned down for office and appointment, he has learned the value of quiet persistence. Palpatine has risen through the ranks to attain the powerful office of sectorial representative to the Galactic Senate on Coruscant. Palpatine represents some 36 worlds in a backwater sector, of which his provincial home planet of Naboo is typical. Turning this background to his advantage, Palpatine has been ever-present in the halls of galactic politics, impressing friend and opponent alike with his unassuming demeanor and simple but powerful insights into how the galaxy could be better run.

Blue color hints at Palpatine's interest in the Chancellorship

Elaborate cloak asserts sectorial authority

Naboo-style bloused sleeves with long cuffs

Palpatine's apartment is modest compared to the stunning palaces of other sectorial representatives

Over time Palpatine has developed a reputation as someone apart from intrigue and corruption, as he patiently condemns the many abuses of bureaucracy that come to his attention. It is little surprise to insiders that he is nominated for the office of Supreme Chancellor.

PALPATINE'S APARTMENT
Few outsiders are welcomed into Palpatine's scarlet chambers. They are the exclusive haunt of his trusted confidants until Amidala arrives on Coruscant to plead her case.

Queen Amidala

Royal handmaiden

Strange red decor

Diplomat

Palpatine never favored Naboo's previous sovereign, King Veruna, even after the stubborn ruler heeded Palpatine's suggestions to become more involved in foreign affairs. Queen Amidala suits Palpatine, since he believes she will better follow his directions.

Before they meet at the Senate, Queen Amidala has only seen Palpatine in person once, at her coronation. She half-suspects that his concern for Naboo is secondary to his political ambitions.

DATA FILE

◆ Senator Palpatine's unusual choice of art objects reveals to Queen Amidala that he has left his Naboo heritage far behind and has adopted a more worldly point of view.

ROUTE TO SUCCESS
Palpatine consistently favors less concern for senatorial legality and procedure and more attention to simply doing what he considers needs to be done. It is as

a result of this practical attitude that many look forward to the clear-minded leadership that Palpatine promises to provide.

The Senate
GALACTIC POWER

The POWER of sectorial senators is immense, as they control access to the Senate for hundreds of planets. The temptations that go with such power are equally great. Corrupt senators are no longer unusual, even at the highest level, and few Republic citizens expect anything but empty promises and word games from anyone who sets foot on Coruscant. In truth, many senators are lazy and greedy, but by doing nothing to stop the spread of evil they become some of its greatest supporters.

Gesture showing objection

MOT-NOT RAB

Gesture denying guilt

AKS MOE

Gesture blaming others

PASSEL ARGENTE

Gesture of reassurance

HOROX RYYDER

Consorts

Senators are attended by assistants, aides, and consorts according to customs and traditions of their home planets and sectors. Many young aides are repulsed by the abuses of government they see on Coruscant, but they stay on, reluctant to lose their positions of power.

Rare red-skinned Lethan Twi'lek

Lekku (head-tail)

Ear flaps store fat

Gaudy robe

SENATORIAL POLITICS

Many senators have become known for judicious nonalignment, allowing their worlds to profit from supplying both sides in conflicts. Critics comment that three-eyed Malastarians like Baskol Yeesrim can not only see both sides of an issue, but can always spot their position of advantage right in the center.

CONSORT TO TONBUCK TOORA

Senator Tonbuck Toora's last traces of idealism have been eradicated by watching the downfall of the just and from counting the profits that flow from finding loopholes in the law. She now counts as friends criminal senators she once held in contempt and rewards loyal supporters with well-paid appointments as consorts or aides.

DATA FILE

◆ Lavender was chosen for the color of the Senate interior because it was the only hue that had never been associated with war, anger, or mourning in any culture in the Republic.

◆ Senator Tikkes moved from business to Coruscant politics to make some *real* money.

Senator Orn Free Taa

Indulgent lifestyles are nowhere more extreme than on Coruscant. Senator Orn Free Taa has found possibilities beyond his wildest dreams. He views galactic government as merely the sport of the mighty like himself. In his excesses he has grown vile and corpulent, but he is confident that money and power will always make him attractive.

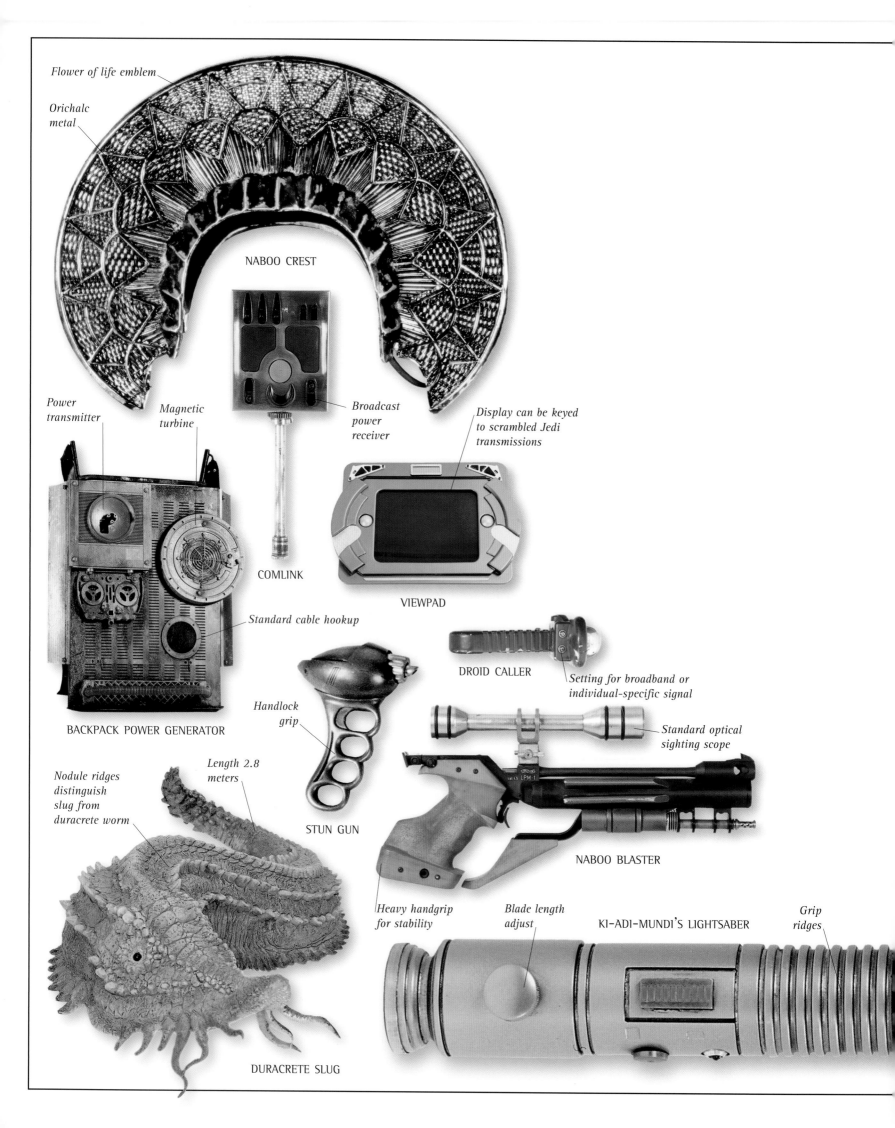

Flower of life emblem

Orichalc metal

NABOO CREST

Power transmitter

Magnetic turbine

Broadcast power receiver

COMLINK

Display can be keyed to scrambled Jedi transmissions

VIEWPAD

Standard cable hookup

BACKPACK POWER GENERATOR

DROID CALLER

Setting for broadband or individual-specific signal

Handlock grip

Standard optical sighting scope

Nodule ridges distinguish slug from duracrete worm

Length 2.8 meters

STUN GUN

NABOO BLASTER

Heavy handgrip for stability

Blade length adjust

KI-ADI-MUNDI'S LIGHTSABER

Grip ridges

DURACRETE SLUG

EPISODE II
ATTACK OF THE CLONES

In A TIME OF INSTABILITY, the galaxy stands on the brink of rupture as powerful forces threaten to tear the Republic apart. The small numbers of peacekeeping Jedi cannot quell outright rebellion, and the great commercial powers are increasingly lured by the temptations of greed. Disruptive changes are at hand and the lines between good and evil are becoming unclear. Amid these epochal events, the galaxy's fate will turn upon the choices of only a few individuals, whose destinies are clouded. The Jedi have already lost a great leader with the defection of Count Dooku—will they now be forced to engage in the first full-scale war since the inception of the Republic? Where lies the path of honor in this uncertain time? When the valiant must choose between love and duty, peace and war, danger waits in every breath.

Trace in these pages the faces of legend, the shadows of inner turmoil, and the instruments of fate as one by one the final elements of a terrible destiny unfold.

Blade projection plate

Body heat detector

Jedi tunic

Action bodysuit

Parry 4 position

Attack 5 position

Synthetic leather surcoat

Metal-cutting pincer

Ancient demagogue

Reversed attack stance

SECURITY MONITOR   DEFENDERS OF JUSTICE   STONE MITE   SISTROS STATUE

The Growing Darkness

LONG AGO, a prophesy foretold the coming of an individual who would "bring balance to the Force," ushering in a new era of peace following one of great instability. With the Separatist crisis, the future of the great Galactic Republic is clouded with uncertainty and the peace-keeping Jedi are too few to hold together an entire galaxy. In this age, the Sith have reappeared, their evil hidden perhaps in the heart of liberty's citadel—and while the prophecy is looked upon anew, many of the galaxy's denizens have no choice but to fend for themselves.

Beyond the vision of the Jedi Knights, somewhere within the darkness, the greatest master of evil ever to use Sith power bides his time. As his strength grows, his plans begin to shape the course of the galaxy, and his snares await the unsuspecting.

A Time of Change

Below the spires of Coruscant where the Jedi High Council and the Senate debate how to resolve the Separatist crisis, ordinary people struggle through a period of growing unrest. Ancient patterns are in upheaval and vast populations are on the move. In such a time, individuals must learn self-reliance and trust in what they can carry.

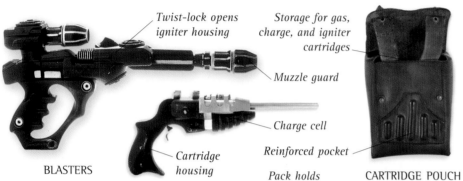

Twist-lock opens igniter housing

Muzzle guard

Charge cell

Cartridge housing

BLASTERS

Storage for gas, charge, and igniter cartridges

Reinforced pocket

CARTRIDGE POUCH

PROBES

Reinforced covering

MESH GLOVES

Enhanced parallax sensors

Holographic display

SCANNER

Anti-microbe field plate

Antithermic frame

WATER POD

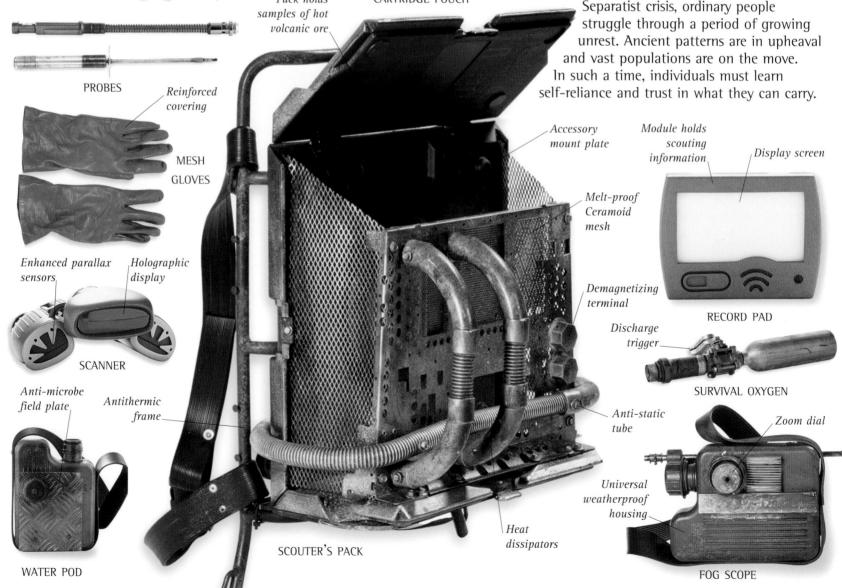

Pack holds samples of hot volcanic ore

Accessory mount plate

Module holds scouting information

Display screen

Melt-proof Ceramoid mesh

Demagnetizing terminal

RECORD PAD

Discharge trigger

Anti-static tube

SURVIVAL OXYGEN

Heat dissipators

Universal weatherproof housing

Zoom dial

SCOUTER'S PACK

FOG SCOPE

71

Private spire of Raith Seinar, military spacecraft engineering genius

Jedi Padawan learner's braid reveals true identity to a Jedi initiate

Thousand Moons young matron's dress

Pattern common in Thousand Moons system

Hidden Demons

Anakin Skywalker's fate has made him a Jedi and brought him to the center of events at the galactic capital. Senior Council members suspect he is the Chosen One. But like Coruscant itself, Anakin contends with inner demons against which an ancient prophecy seems little help.

Squad of clone troopers

Since its inception, the Republic has been protected by its system of law rather than by the force of armies. But the law is only as strong as its people, and when their vigilance fades, armies may regain the upper hand.

Jedi boots in altered color

DATA FILE

◆ Many Coruscant freighters designed for hauling cargo are now forced by necessity to carry many hundreds of passengers as well.

◆ Military expenditures in the Republic are dramatically rising during this troubled period.

Refugees

Anakin Skywalker and the woman he is protecting flee Coruscant in disguise, but they cannot hide from the Sith. In the time of greatest crisis, they are caught within the plans of the powerful, and like all galactic refugees, find they must rely on their inner resources.

Senator Padmé Amidala

Severe hairstyle conforms to diplomatic etiquette

Neckband is gift from Naboo Council

As ELECTED QUEEN of Naboo, Padmé Amidala won the lasting devotion of her people by showing extraordinary strength of character during the Trade Federation invasion. On the expiration of her second and final term of office, she yielded her authority in spite of popular demand for a change in the law that would have allowed her to rule longer. She was soon elected Senator to represent the 36 Naboo regional star systems; Padmé now travels widely to build support for her causes, returning to the galactic capital of Coruscant when necessary.

Senator Amidala's retinue returns to Coruscant in the sleek Naboo Cruiser to speak against a vote on the Military Creation Act. Padmé lands amidst high tensions and an invisible web of intrigue.

Cordé (disguised as Padmé)

Dormé

Like the Naboo Queen, Padmé is served and protected in vulnerable situations by loyal handmaidens who can act as decoys, assuming Padmé's identity, appearance, and dress.

Streamlined body for easy deployment from within garments

Naboo chrome finish

BLASTER

New tactical pilot suit

N-1 Camouflage

For security, Padmé sometimes travels disguised as a Naboo starfighter pilot. Other planetary Senators would never condescend to yield the trappings of their status, so the simple ruse is effective.

Senatorial gown more low-key and practical than royal display garments Padmé wore as Queen

Auto-encrypting comm unit

Starfighter pilot emblem

Anti-glare goggles

Supplementary oxygen hookup

STARFIGHTER HELMET

Senatorial Dress

Padmé dresses with decorum when speaking in the Senate on important issues. A tireless champion of peace and freedom, she has worked for years against a much-debated proposal to create a great army of the Republic, which she believes might be the catalyst for war.

Senatorial Accomodation

While on Coruscant, Padmé and her retinue reside in quarters atop one of the ancient skyscrapers. Living in anything less than a penthouse would diminish Padmé's standing on the status-obsessed world and impede her diplomatic efforts. While the quarters are comfortable, Padmé loathes Coruscant's gray, artificial environment.

Padmé's modest rooms do not have the fortress-like security systems used by more sophisticated politicians. The Senator sleeps exposed to many unseen dangers.

Padmé's apartment

UNTIMELY RETREAT

It takes two assassination attempts to convince Padmé to leave Coruscant for the safety of Naboo. Her retreat is a bitter one, for she will likely be absent during the vote on the army proposal and flight is alien to her character.

Subdued colors express grave mood

Synthetic leather gauntlets for hand-to-hand combat

Naboo blaster

Captain Typho oversees security for Senator Amidala and her retinue. He is the nephew of Captain Panaka, who served Padmé while she was Queen of Naboo.

Captain Typho

Raised to his Senatorial post because of his uncompromising loyalty and his ties to Panaka, Captain Typho is a relative novice to the world of lethal subterfuge that most galactic representatives in the Senate take for granted.

Corset of light armor that doubles as protection

Traditional security tunic

Fabric hides uncomfortable blast-damping underskirt

Naboo military boots

Positive traction grip soles

DATA FILE

◆ Naboo soldiers compose most of Captain Typho's security force on Coruscant.

◆ Captain Typho's eye patch is a mark of dedication, since he lost his eye in the line of duty.

Supreme Chancellor Palpatine

PALPATINE IS CAREFUL TO present himself as a mild-mannered servant of the public good, avoiding ostentation and ever protesting the limits of his abilities. Palpatine ascended to office amid mass frustration with the previous Supreme Chancellor—but there is increasing evidence that Palpatine himself quietly built much of this opinion behind the scenes. It also seems that a pattern may be emerging in Palpatine's work as Supreme Chancellor: Always citing the best interests of the Republic, he has consistently increased his own power, from legal authority to his institution of the Chancellor's Red Guard, who now attend every committee meeting. For some, his true intentions remain unclear.

Sleeves of ancient design

Subdued color and simple style convey gravity without pompous exhibitionism

Security Innovator

The Supreme Chancellor has placed the new Red Guard under his direct authority, while a Senatorial committee oversees the old Blue Guard. Palpatine calls this an efficient streamlining of cumbersome bureaucracy. Objectors have called it an illegal personal bodyguard, but such talk runs the risk of violating Palpatine's new security laws.

Face shield protects Red Guard's identity

Blue Guard

Although he prefers to avoid ostentation, Palpatine heeds the tradition for high political officials to maintain impressive audience chambers. During meetings, the large, scenic window reminds those involved that their decisions have wide repercussions.

Red Guard summoner

Ultra-dense lanthanide alloy armor

Red Guard force pike

Hidden shield generator

SEAT OF OFFICE
Palpatine has bowed to the concerns of his aides by accepting a special chair of office that affords him secret shielding and cunning protection. This chair also provides direct, secure communication with Palpatine's aides and with the Red Guard.

Blue Guard rifle

Ceremonial stylings

The Red Guard

Palpatine has kept the details of the Red Guard's training secret, citing security concerns. No one seems to know where this protection force and its trappings come from. Instead of stun rifles, the Red Guard use force pikes, which are more likely to be lethal.

Eyes see only in ultraviolet light

Umbaran shadowcloak is patterned in ultraviolet colors

Attack and display horns

Lethorns

The Jedi Council often discusses political opinions with Supreme Chancellor Palpatine. The support of the great Jedi reassures many who might otherwise doubt the Chancellor's motives.

Sly Moore and Mas Amedda

Sly Moore is Palpatine's Staff Aide. She controls access to the Chancellor, which gives her tremendous power. Moore comes from the shadowy world of Umbara, deep within the dark reaches of the Ghost Nebula. Umbarans are known for their abilities to subtly influence, and even control, others.

As Speaker of the Senate, Mas Amedda is responsible for keeping order in debates. He is a stern and stoic Chagrian, who refuses to comment on the changes he has witnessed during Palpatine's tenure.

While the average citizen has grown weary of politics, momentous events are afoot. Separatists foment unrest, and rumors are rife of secret armies. In ages past, safeguards limited the power of the Supreme Chancellor—but Palpatine calls them impediments to effective leadership, and may soon overturn them, with substantial support.

DATA FILE

◆ Palpatine's term ended several years ago, but a series of crises has allowed him to stay in office beyond the Senate's legal limit.

◆ Close aides say that Palpatine sometimes works for days without sleeping.

◆ Palpatine has revived the old tradition of appearing before the masses to accept their applause and vocal support.

OFFICE IDOLS
Palpatine's statues honor obscure figures from the past who possessed much arcane wisdom and law, but whose actions are shrouded in controversy.

The Corrupt Senate

Epaulettes signify military service

Amulet of Trust from Gungan Sacred Place

Mantle of office

STAR SYSTEMS are starving under heavy taxation. Pirates plague the spacelanes, corporations consume worlds, bureaucracy stifles justice—and yet the Senate can do little. Power and wealth are corrupting this once-noble gathering until it seems that soon only money will have a voice. Honest Senators who speak out are becoming rare. Few leaders light the way in this troubled era, and even the Jedi are beginning to be unsure whom to trust.

In Padmé's absence, Jar Jar represents Naboo in the Senate. With the best of intentions, Jar Jar sets in motion a new galactic era as he proposes a motion for the Supreme Chancellor to accept emergency powers.

Orthodox Halbara hairstyle

Sybarion gown

Some Senators adopt the fashions of Coruscant, while others maintain the traditions of their homeworlds. Senators' clothing, styling, and mode of conduct can offer clues to their political sympathies.

ISTER PADDIE   LEXI DIO   SUPI

Representative Binks

After the Battle of Naboo, Jar Jar Binks rode a wave of Naboo goodwill to become Associate Planetary Representative in the Galactic Senate. The Naboo value purity of heart over other qualifications to govern, often electing juveniles as their rulers. In the case of Jar Jar, they elevate a simple, well-meaning soul to a position that may be beyond his abilities.

Traditional banner

Few Senators can completely resist the temptation to indulge themselves. Nations, worlds, systems, and staggering wealth can be had in illicit exchange for votes or strategic abstentions on critical legislation.

DATA FILE

◆ The motion for emergency dictatorial powers—the Military Creation Act—is one of the few proposals that demand an immediate vote by the Senate.

◆ The Anx Senators are among the small number who openly support Bail Organa's uncompromising moral code.

Bail Organa

Bail Organa of Alderaan is a noble Senator in an ignoble time. In ages past, he would have been revered as a great leader. Amid the current moral decay, Bail's colleagues demean him as simplistic for his eloquent and impassioned support of the value of civic virtue.

Alderaanian patrician boots

Droid Types

DROIDS RANGE FROM simple machines to complex, sentient artificial beings. They are generally treated as mere utility devices regardless of their level of intelligence, and most citizens hardly notice them. Memory wipes, which are customarily performed when a droid acquires a new owner, can delete filed information or completely erase a droid's stored experiences. When "zeroed" this way, even sophisticated droids may be rendered barely self-aware. If allowed to build experience between memory wipes, some droids seem to develop individual identities and even idiosyncratic personalities.

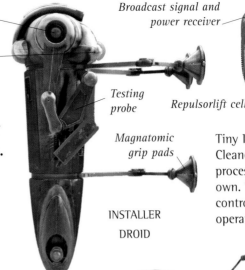

Probe servo

Signal receiver

Testing probe

Magnatomic grip pads

Broadcast signal and power receiver

Repulsorlift cell

INSTALLER DROID

Electrostatic polisher

CLEANER DROID

Tiny Installer Droids and Cleaner Droids have no processor power of their own. They are tied to master control systems that broadcast operating commands.

Added memory housing

Standardized body

Treaded drives

Retractable third leg

Tools behind panels

Astromech Droids

"Astro Droids" are multipurpose computer repair and information retrieval systems. They are given just enough processor power to do their jobs, communicating only via electronic beeps and whistles. Astro Droids have an inclination to exceed their programming if their stored experiences develop far enough.

Location transmitter

Retrieval signal receptor

Vocoder

Audio pickup

Processor housing

Extensible neck

Heavy casing

Light-duty manipulator arm

Balance gyro

Low-dexterity graspers

Drive wheel

DATA FILE

◆ Droids are frequently misused because galactic law treats them as machinery regardless of their self-awareness.

◆ Droids are banned on some worlds where their ultrasonic frequencies irritate sensitive species.

On Tatooine, Unipod Droids pull rickshaws that float on unlicensed broadcast-power repulsors.

Unipod Droid

Compact, semi-humanoid Unipod Droids are an ancient model that has seen little change for centuries. These stoutly built droids are highly reliable, but their minimal processors suit them for little more than simple manual labor.

HYPERDRIVE RING

Obi-Wan Kenobi
JEDI MENTOR

A DEDICATED JEDI KNIGHT facing a time of great crisis, Obi-Wan Kenobi finds himself at the heart of galactic turmoil as the Republic begins to unravel. Kenobi has witnessed the death of his Master, Qui-Gon Jinn, and knows the challenges the Jedi face in the defense of justice. He is cautious where his apprentice, Anakin Skywalker, is impulsive. Kenobi strives to train Anakin in the discipline that will make him a pillar of strength against the dark side. As dangers unfold, Kenobi's abilities and judgment form one of the last bulwarks against the collapse of the Republic.

SCANNER

COMLINK

Traditional leather utility belt

Lightsaber

Obi-Wan's Jedi apprentice is Anakin Skywalker, the boy suspected of being the prophesied individual who can "bring balance to the Force." Anakin's independence, born of his late induction into the Order, has brought Kenobi reprimands from Jedi elders Yoda and Mace Windu.

Trailing a would-be assassin into a nightclub on Coruscant, Kenobi steps casually to the bar "to have a drink." As planned, his apparent relaxation draws out his quarry, who finds that the Jedi's extraordinary powers give him a lightning edge—it is virtually impossible to take Obi-Wan by surprise.

Utility pouch

Food and energy capsules

Jedi tunic layered to adapt to different environments

Jedi robe

Rugged travel boots

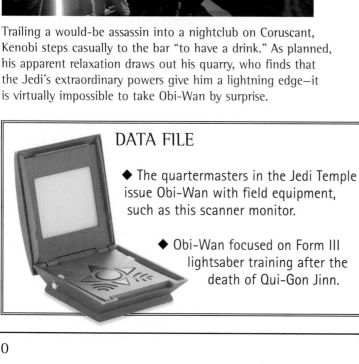

DATA FILE

◆ The quartermasters in the Jedi Temple issue Obi-Wan with field equipment, such as this scanner monitor.

◆ Obi-Wan focused on Form III lightsaber training after the death of Qui-Gon Jinn.

Long hair of Jedi Knight

Two-handed grip for full saber control

Kenobi specializes in Form III lightsaber combat, which maximizes defensive protection. Invented ages ago when blaster weapons first became common in the hands of Jedi enemies, Form III began as high-speed laserblast deflection training. Over the centuries, it has been refined into an expression of nonaggressive Jedi philosophy.

Form III brace-ready stance

Blade emitter

Blade modulation circuitry

Blade length and intensity control

Activator

Blade power adjust

Internal blade crystals

Handgrip

Power cell housing

Piloting a Delta-7 starfighter on his field mission, Obi-Wan relies on a built-in Astromech Droid called R4-P17 to manage shipboard systems independently.

Captured on Geonosis, Kenobi comes face-to-face with Count Dooku, who once trained Qui-Gon Jinn. The Count tempts Obi-Wan with an offer of power in the Separatist regime, but Kenobi's dedication to justice is incorruptible.

Field Agent

Accomplished in a wide variety of skills ranging from diplomacy and psychology to military strategy and hand-to-hand combat, Obi-Wan has to be ready for anything on his field assignments. On Kamino, his investigation bursts into explosive conflict when bounty hunter Jango Fett resists arrest. Covered in armor and weaponry, Fett is a professional at the top of his field, but he cannot overcome Obi-Wan. The best Fett can manage is escape—with a powerful tracer beacon attached to his ship.

Signal port

TRACER BEACON

Star Tracker

Pursuing Jango Fett across the galaxy, Obi-Wan engages in a space duel with Fett and his deadly spacecraft, *Slave I*. Obi-Wan proves his abilities as an expert pilot and tactician, sacrificing his spare parts in a ruse to put Fett off his trail with apparent explosion debris. From high in orbit, Obi-Wan's top-of-the-line starfighter sensor suite then traces Fett down to the weird planet surface of Geonosis.

Wide-band sensor scan

Sensor select monitor

Systems impedance monitor

STARFIGHTER DISPLAYS

Graphic damage monitor

Facing off against Count Dooku, Kenobi wisely exercises restraint where his apprentice rushes in headlong. A Jedi of powerful inner focus, Obi-Wan nevertheless finds he is unprepared for the Count's specialist techniques. Against Kenobi's Form III moves, the Count demonstrates the ancient and elegant precision of Form II lightsaber combat.

Anakin Skywalker

JEDI APPRENTICE

Twenty-Year-Old Jedi Padawan Anakin Skywalker is gifted with extraordinary Force skills and piloting abilities. His talents make him impatient with Jedi traditions that seem to hold him back and he often disagrees with the more cautious Obi-Wan Kenobi. Skywalker was accepted into the Order at the age of ten, far later in life than its rules allow, and his emotional bond with his mother was already strong. Anakin still struggles with the pain of this separation. Jedi Council members suspect Anakin of being the prophesied One who can bring balance to the Force. But Anakin must face ever steeper challenges to master the dangerous force that is himself.

Padawan's short hairstyle with learner braid

Standard Jedi tunic

Synthetic leather surcoat offers more protection than traditional cloth garment

Anakin is capable but not yet professional, criticizing his Master Kenobi in front of their charge, Senator Amidala. Anakin prefers to exceed his and Obi-Wan's mandate to only protect Padmé by trying to discover who is after her.

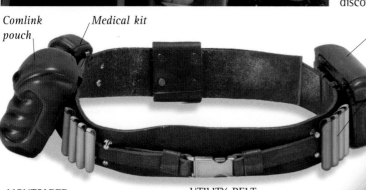

Comlink pouch

Medical kit

Mechanical tool pouch

Food and energy capsules

LIGHTSABER

UTILITY BELT

Most Jedi Padawans build their lightsabers to resemble those of their Masters as a gesture of respect. Anakin constructed his own lightsaber while in a trance-like state, resulting in a design that favors maximum strength.

Heavy duty body cylinder

Activator and power indicator

Power-cell housing

Blue lightsaber blade generated via traditional Jedi crystals is more maneuverable but slightly less powerful than blade using synthetic Sith crystals

Unconventional tunic color expresses Anakin's independence

Synthetic leather protective boots

Dark Knight

The tunics, robes, and cloaks worn by Jedi are honored traditions, but not uniforms. From the time they become Padawans, Jedi are free to dress as they choose. Anakin Skywalker breaks with tradition in his garments, both in their color and material. His distinctive dark clothing makes him stand out at the Jedi Temple and draws concern from Jedi elders.

Field boots weighted for training

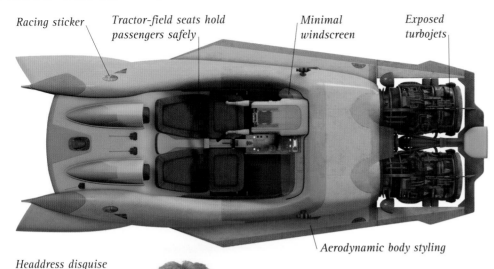

Racing sticker *Tractor-field seats hold passengers safely* *Minimal windscreen* *Exposed turbojets*

Aerodynamic body styling

Airspeeder

Anakin is possibly the best pilot ever to train within the Jedi Temple. When he commandeers an airspeeder in pursuit of an assassin on Coruscant, his abilities are phenomenal. Anakin violates Jedi policies on vehicular speed and risk—guidelines intended to safeguard other craft, but not designed with so gifted a pilot in mind. Anakin's antics prompt the remark from Obi Wan, "Why do I get the feeling you're going to be the death of me?"

Headdress disguise for Padmé

Forbidden Feelings

Only 20 Jedi have ever left the Order, but Anakin is coming perilously close. When he is assigned to protect the woman he has loved since childhood, he is torn between love and duty. The Jedi discipline does not seem to help him as it does the others, so his loyalties are put to the test: Will he insist on being an exception to the rules of the Jedi Order?

On Coruscant, Anakin suspects that Padmé has feelings for him. On Naboo, where Anakin's charm is in full force, Padme's feelings become transparent—but the inherent danger of their passions frightens both Senator and Jedi.

When Anakin senses his mother in terrible pain, Padmé goes with him to Tatooine in search of her. After Anakin fails to rescue Shmi in time, Padmé must alleviate the Padawan's anger, resentment, and despair.

In Anakin's mind, it is his own lack of resolve and strength that has failed his mother and cost him so much pain. At his mother's grave, marked by a black stone, Anakin makes a silent vow to build his strength until nothing can withstand his power.

Sensory impulse lines *Electromotive power lines* *Interface module links wiring to nerves*

Fingertips electrostatically sensitive to touch

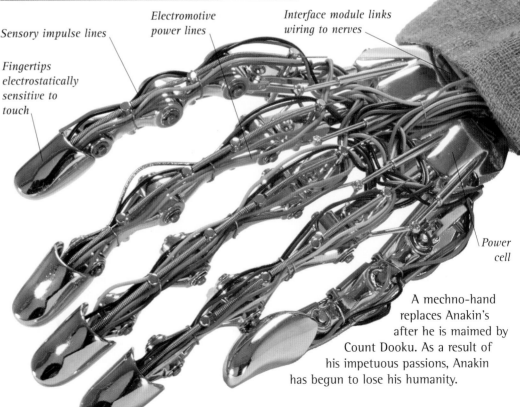

Power cell

DATA FILE

◆ Anakin has started the study of lightsaber Form IV, known for its power.

◆ The pain of life-draining Sith lightning is an experience of evil that Anakin will never forget.

A mechno-hand replaces Anakin's after he is maimed by Count Dooku. As a result of his impetuous passions, Anakin has begun to lose his humanity.

Zam Wesell

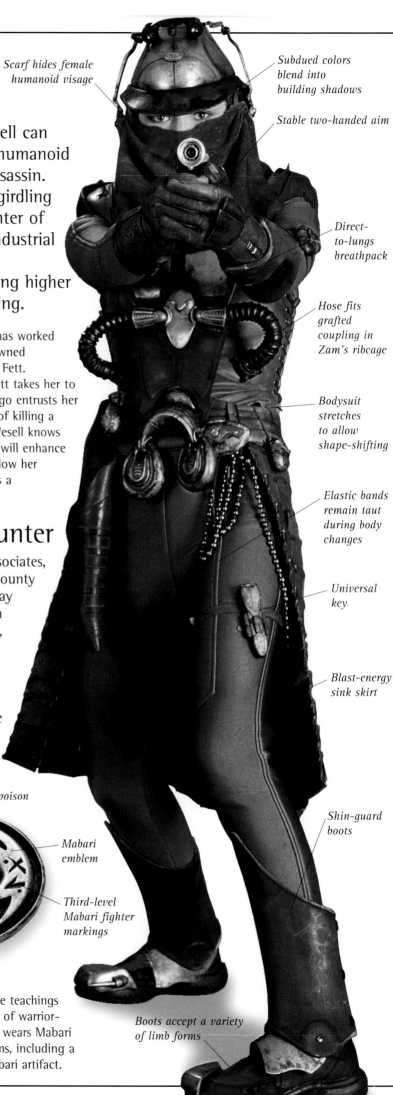

Scarf hides female humanoid visage

Subdued colors blend into building shadows

Stable two-handed aim

As A CLAWDITE SHAPE-SHIFTER, Zam Wesell can change her appearance to mimic a range of humanoid forms, giving her a special edge as a hired assassin. Zam learned her trade on Denon, the globe-girdling metropolis second only to Coruscant as a center of galactic business. In the high-risk world of industrial espionage, Zam rose from corporate security sergeant to executive bodyguard before seeking higher fees for contract execution and bounty hunting.

ASN-121
ASSASSIN DROID

Direct-to-lungs breathpack

Hose fits grafted coupling in Zam's ribcage

For some years Zam has worked on and off with renowned bounty hunter Jango Fett. Her latest job with Fett takes her to Coruscant, where Jango entrusts her with the assignment of killing a prominent Senator. Wesell knows that this opportunity will enhance her reputation and allow her to return to Denon as a master in her field.

Bodysuit stretches to allow shape-shifting

Bounty Hunter

A loner with few close associates, Zam Wesell is typical of bounty hunters. She inhabits a gray zone that extends to both sides of the law. Arrogant, highly skilled, and feeling unchallenged by legal bodyguard and security work, Wesell regards bounty hunting as a more suitable channel for her superior talent.

Elastic bands remain taut during body changes

Universal key

Blast-energy sink skirt

Stinger painful but not fatal

Bite delivers lethal nerve poison

Shin-guard boots

KOUHUNS

Zam uses two deadly kouhuns for her Senatorial assassination job. Small, silent arthropods like the kouhuns of Indoumodo can evade even tight security. Unlike projectiles or energy weapons, they are virtually impossible to trace back to their users. Kouhuns are starved in advance, so they head straight for warm-blooded life forms when released, and use a fast-acting nerve toxin to kill their prey.

Mabari emblem

Third-level Mabari fighter markings

CAPE SEAL

Zam's discipline derives from the teachings of the Mabari, an ancient order of warrior-knights on her homeworld. She wears Mabari inscriptions and stylized emblems, including a cape seal that is an ancient Mabari artifact.

Boots accept a variety of limb forms

To prevent being traced, Zam Wesell prefers to steal a new vehicle for each new job. But when her security depends on performance she uses her own airspeeder.

Streamlined with enclosed cockpit for high speeds

Cleaning rod

Electromagnetic pulse barrel

Secret compartment for sniper rifle

Waste heat and radiation radiator

Zam favors her KYD-21 blaster pistol for both attack and defense, though Jango has begun teaching her that projectile weapons can be useful when working invisibly in the dark.

Igniter pin

Hadrium alloy

Muzzle brake absorbs emitter flash

Embedding prongs

Blaster gas capsule loading port

Injector needle

Poison chamber

Stabilizing fins

Guardless trigger for fast action

KYD-21 Blaster

Handle holds power cell

Though she carries a projectile rifle at Jango's insistence, Zam's primary weapon is a compact, precise KYD-21 pistol. She finds she can hide a pistol more easily when she needs to disguise herself as a non-threatening presence in order to close in on her mark.

Under intense Jedi mind-pressure, Zam begins to reveal her employer... until she is silenced by an assassin.

SABERDART

Preferring to leave no trace, Zam dislikes projectile weapons. A saberdart such as Jango might use may be silent and highly lethal, but has the potential to lead pursuers back to its source.

Visor cuts glare

Light helmet

Comlink system

Scrambled direct comlink pickup to Jango Fett

Clawdite shape-shifters, or "changelings," evolved on a world inhabited by warring humanoid subspecies. Shape-shifters developed the ability to mimic the appearance of other species in order to blend in without being killed. As a changeling dies, its ability to shape-shift fades and it returns to a neutral Clawdite configuration.

Flexible armorweave jerkin

PROJECTILE RIFLE

Simple optical scope

High Stakes

Zam knows that in accepting a risky assignment from Jango Fett, she is in danger of being used as an expendable pawn. Such are the risks of the high-stakes trade in death, and Zam is prepared to take them... though she will find that she is not equipped to outrun two Jedi.

Power amplifier circuitry

DATA FILE

◆ Shape-shifting takes effort, and it is only through long practice that Zam has learned to rest in a mimicked form.

◆ Although shape-shifters are most effective at a limited range of shapes they imitate often, medical assistance can enhance their abilities much further.

Recoil-damping stock

Coruscant Underlevels

Eye threads

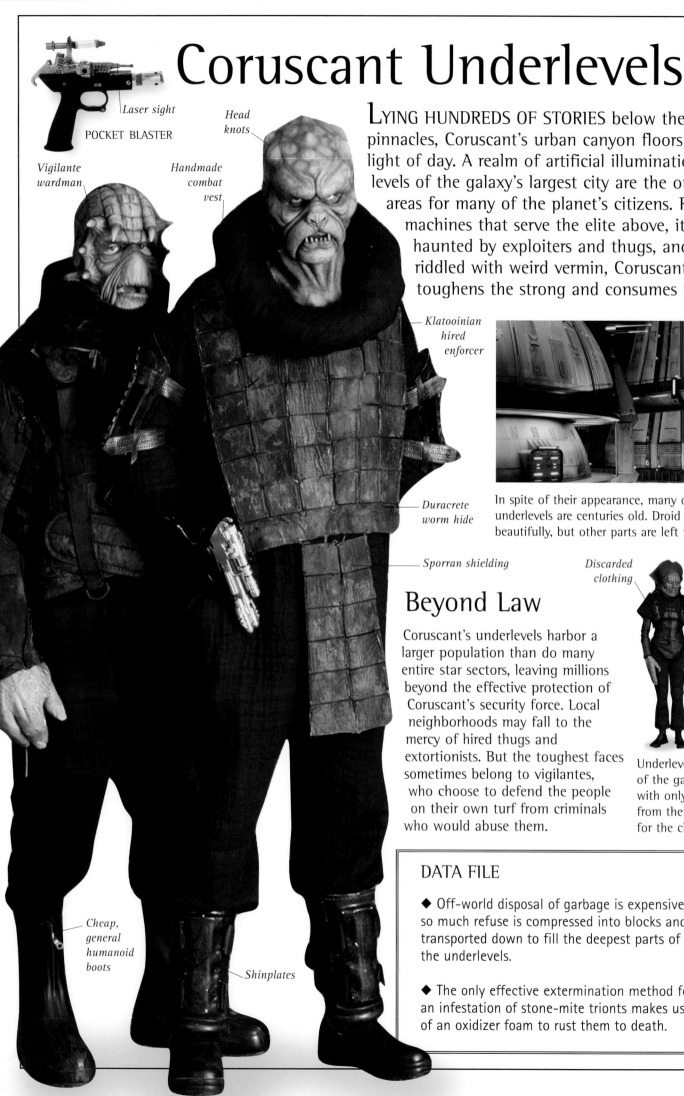

Laser sight

POCKET BLASTER

Head knots

Vigilante wardman

Handmade combat vest

Klatooinian hired enforcer

Duracrete worm hide

Sporran shielding

Cheap, general humanoid boots

Shinplates

LYING HUNDREDS OF STORIES below the skyscraper pinnacles, Coruscant's urban canyon floors never see the light of day. A realm of artificial illumination, the lower levels of the galaxy's largest city are the only affordable areas for many of the planet's citizens. Rumbling with machines that serve the elite above, its streets haunted by exploiters and thugs, and its walls riddled with weird vermin, Coruscant's underworld toughens the strong and consumes the weak.

In spite of their appearance, many of the buildings in Coruscant's underlevels are centuries old. Droid crews maintain some sections beautifully, but other parts are left to decay.

Impoverished Bith

Discarded clothing

Beyond Law

Coruscant's underlevels harbor a larger population than do many entire star sectors, leaving millions beyond the effective protection of Coruscant's security force. Local neighborhoods may fall to the mercy of hired thugs and extortionists. But the toughest faces sometimes belong to vigilantes, who choose to defend the people on their own turf from criminals who would abuse them.

Underlevel Coruscanti hail from all parts of the galaxy. Many immigrants arrive with only a small case of belongings from their homeworlds, little prepared for the challenges they find.

DATA FILE

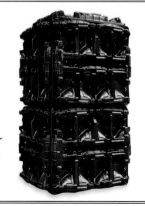

◆ Off-world disposal of garbage is expensive, so much refuse is compressed into blocks and transported down to fill the deepest parts of the underlevels.

◆ The only effective extermination method for an infestation of stone-mite trionts makes use of an oxidizer foam to rust them to death.

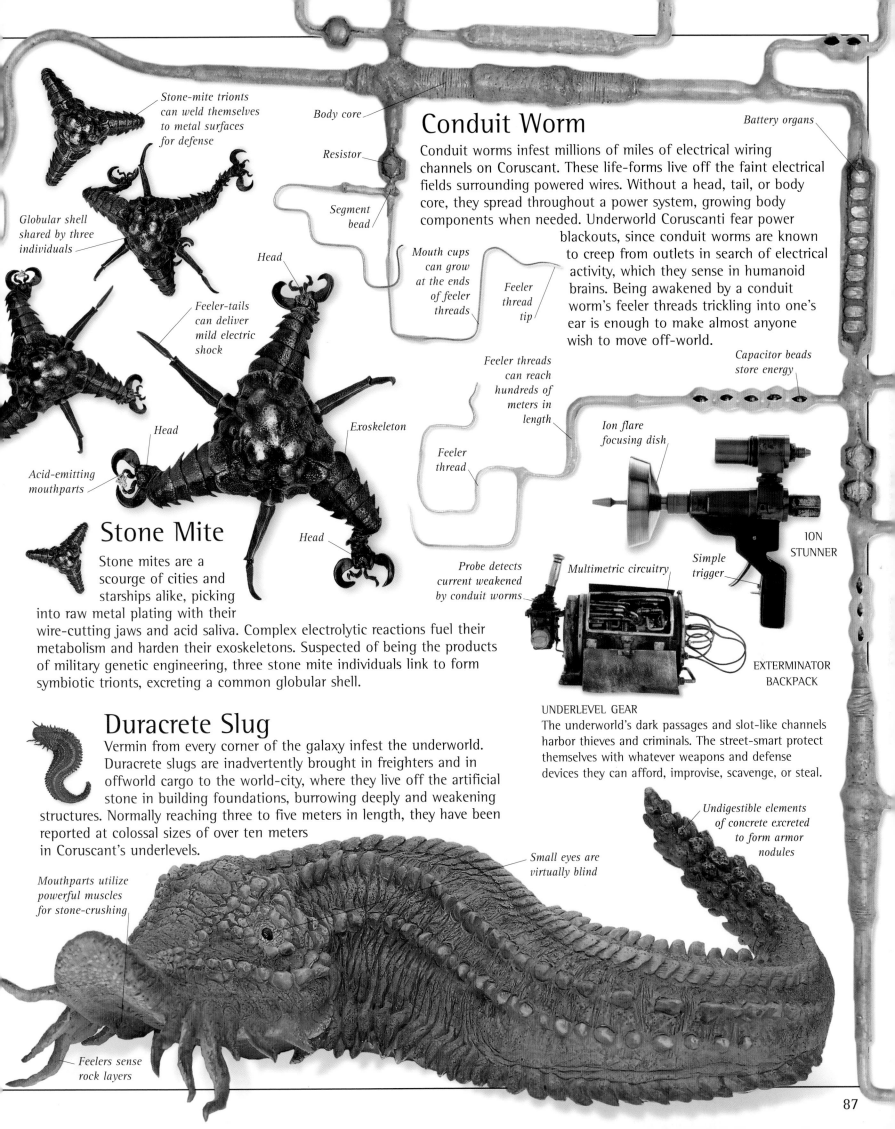

Stone-mite trionts can weld themselves to metal surfaces for defense

Body core

Resistor

Segment bead

Globular shell shared by three individuals

Head

Feeler-tails can deliver mild electric shock

Head

Acid-emitting mouthparts

Head

Exoskeleton

Mouth cups can grow at the ends of feeler threads

Feeler thread tip

Conduit Worm

Conduit worms infest millions of miles of electrical wiring channels on Coruscant. These life-forms live off the faint electrical fields surrounding powered wires. Without a head, tail, or body core, they spread throughout a power system, growing body components when needed. Underworld Coruscanti fear power blackouts, since conduit worms are known to creep from outlets in search of electrical activity, which they sense in humanoid brains. Being awakened by a conduit worm's feeler threads trickling into one's ear is enough to make almost anyone wish to move off-world.

Battery organs

Capacitor beads store energy

Feeler threads can reach hundreds of meters in length

Feeler thread

Ion flare focusing dish

ION STUNNER

Stone Mite

Stone mites are a scourge of cities and starships alike, picking into raw metal plating with their wire-cutting jaws and acid saliva. Complex electrolytic reactions fuel their metabolism and harden their exoskeletons. Suspected of being the products of military genetic engineering, three stone mite individuals link to form symbiotic trionts, excreting a common globular shell.

Probe detects current weakened by conduit worms

Multimetric circuitry

Simple trigger

EXTERMINATOR BACKPACK

UNDERLEVEL GEAR

The underworld's dark passages and slot-like channels harbor thieves and criminals. The street-smart protect themselves with whatever weapons and defense devices they can afford, improvise, scavenge, or steal.

Duracrete Slug

Vermin from every corner of the galaxy infest the underworld. Duracrete slugs are inadvertently brought in freighters and in offworld cargo to the world-city, where they live off the artificial stone in building foundations, burrowing deeply and weakening structures. Normally reaching three to five meters in length, they have been reported at colossal sizes of over ten meters in Coruscant's underlevels.

Undigestible elements of concrete excreted to form armor nodules

Small eyes are virtually blind

Mouthparts utilize powerful muscles for stone-crushing

Feelers sense rock layers

Outlander Nightclub

AGAINST THE SPECTACULAR BACKDROP of the largest city in the galaxy, the Outlander provides a setting for a wide variety of purposes. While some patrons pass through its doors just to have a good time, most are in search of something else: a companion, a sale, or someone to con. Weaving among the would-be glitterati are low-lifes and criminals searching for gullible victims to exploit. For all of them, the gambling club is a place that makes the rest of the world fade away. To an assassin on the run, the Outlander is a potential haven—if Zam can somehow lose the pursuing Jedi among the crowd.

Obi-Wan and Anakin exercise subtle teamwork when they trail Zam to the Outlander. Anakin enters the crowd to flush out the target while Obi-Wan bides his time, waiting for Wesell to make her move.

Human hair wig

Thoadeye-style makeup

"Starshine special" additive given only for the right wink

Color-coded basic drink components

Central liquid-processing unit

Aludium pu-36

Polyquaternium-7 multicarbonator

Insecticide

Height-enhancing shoes of hired dancer

The Right Mix

What one species might find a good drink may be a lethal poison to the next creature who steps up to the bar. To avoid a lawsuit on the lawyer-ridden planet of Coruscant, most small nightclubs play safe by serving minimum-risk, watered-down drinks. Trusted regulars receive much better service and far more interesting concoctions.

Patrons

The Outlander attracts a mostly humanoid clientele. Pan-species clubs are only for the truly determined and stout of heart, as humans tend to feel uncomfortable at clubs designed for quasi-ambulatory plant wads accustomed to living in shallow water—and vice-versa.

Solloops
hairstyle

Flexible antenepalps
concealed under hair

The pursuit of
fashion can be
desperately
confusing amid the
vast populations of
Coruscant, and even
a Jedi's ancient
traditional tunic does
not stand out in the
Outlander crowd.

Petrified hairstyle

Surgically
altered eye color

Gesture of influence

Cult tattoo
betrays affiliation

Slythmongers

Low-lifes who peddle cheap narcotics manufactured by disbarred
pharmacists are called slythmongers on Coruscant. A few are
likely to show up at any average club. Slythmongers must
be prepared for a quick exit when customers have a bad or
fatal reaction to the latest, most fashionable concoction.

Cilona-extract "death
sticks" are powerful
narcotics. Each
successive dose literally
shortens the user's
lifespan in increasingly
large intervals.

Two grades of cilona
for adding to drinks

DEATH STICKS

Accent gas
emitter

Faytonni

Masked
Weequay

Chiller
surface

Hidden
knockout
drops

Long
overcoat
conceals
illegal
chemicals
for sale

Heat
exchange
vanes

Soluble
zoosha
fabric

Con artists merge into the
crowd at the nightclub.
Tonight's miscreants
include a professional kidnapper,
a crime lord's enforcer, and the
unconvincing "Lieutenant"
Faytonni dressed in a stolen
military uniform.

Refrigeration
tubes

DRINKS CHILLER

Shoes contain
secret storage
for contraband

DATA FILE

◆ When club owners spike drink-
synthesizer tanks with liquids such
as medical sterilizers or hydraulic
fluid, the "unique" resulting
concoctions can bring a flood of new
customers—or a deluge of lawsuits.

Dexter's Diner

AFTER BOUNTY HUNTER Zam Wesell is killed by a mysterious toxic saberdart, Obi-Wan Kenobi heads for the haunt of a four-armed Besalisk named Dexter Jettster. Dexter's unassuming diner serves more than hearty food—favored diners can also obtain nuggets of precious information. The brusque but good-hearted Jettster has a checkered past with expeditionary oil-harvesting crews across the galaxy. He spent many years manning rigs, tending bar, cooking chow, brawling, dealing in contraband, and running weapons on the side to disaffected locals. On Coruscant, Dexter has made a fresh start with his diner and enjoys his stable and straightforward new employment.

Within the endless metropolis of Coruscant, the "world of worlds," one can find nearly anything if one knows where to look. Well off the fashionable dining routes, in a business and manufacturing district, lies the small installation known as Dexter's Diner.

The spirited antique Droid Waitress, WA-7, serves Dexter and his clientele with officious precision.

Four large arms require hearty metabolism

Hermione's belt

Voice reader

Decorative skirt

Built-in order transmitter

Upper-hands are dominant manipulators

Retaining cord

Record stylus

Repulsor stabilizer

ORDER COMM

Diner logo

Agile unipod wheel

Lower-hands are secondary graspers

Lucky washrag

Dress style harks back to earlier time

Dexter's cooking provides an alternative to Coruscant's often bizarre menus. It was the unidentifiable "vercupti of sgazza boleruueé" on the Jedi Temple Main House menu one day that drove Obi-Wan to try the diner, and rekindle his friendship with Dexter Jettster.

Hermione Bagwa

Boots offer protection from toxic kitchen slops

Dexter's waitress, Hermione Bagwa, duels with WA-7 for mastery of the dining room. Each is convinced that she has the superior position. Hermione grew up in the Coruscant underlevels and feels very fortunate to work on the surface now.

DATA FILE

◆ Regulars at Dexter's Diner debate the degree to which the menu's distinctive "special recipes" are influenced by Dexter's background in mining sluices and industrial lubricants.

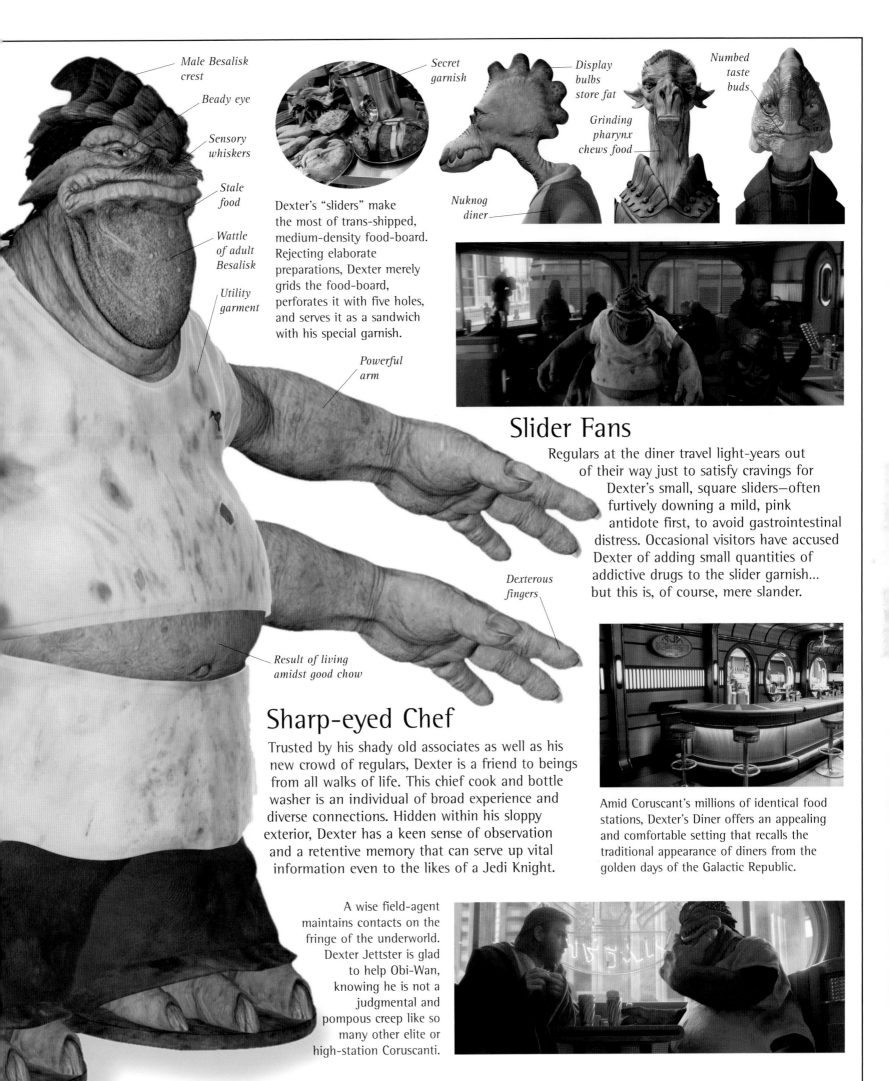

Male Besalisk crest

Beady eye

Sensory whiskers

Stale food

Wattle of adult Besalisk

Utility garment

Powerful arm

Dexterous fingers

Result of living amidst good chow

Secret garnish

Dexter's "sliders" make the most of trans-shipped, medium-density food-board. Rejecting elaborate preparations, Dexter merely grids the food-board, perforates it with five holes, and serves it as a sandwich with his special garnish.

Display bulbs store fat

Grinding pharynx chews food

Numbed taste buds

Nuknog diner

Slider Fans

Regulars at the diner travel light-years out of their way just to satisfy cravings for Dexter's small, square sliders—often furtively downing a mild, pink antidote first, to avoid gastrointestinal distress. Occasional visitors have accused Dexter of adding small quantities of addictive drugs to the slider garnish... but this is, of course, mere slander.

Sharp-eyed Chef

Trusted by his shady old associates as well as his new crowd of regulars, Dexter is a friend to beings from all walks of life. This chief cook and bottle washer is an individual of broad experience and diverse connections. Hidden within his sloppy exterior, Dexter has a keen sense of observation and a retentive memory that can serve up vital information even to the likes of a Jedi Knight.

Amid Coruscant's millions of identical food stations, Dexter's Diner offers an appealing and comfortable setting that recalls the traditional appearance of diners from the golden days of the Galactic Republic.

A wise field-agent maintains contacts on the fringe of the underworld. Dexter Jettster is glad to help Obi-Wan, knowing he is not a judgmental and pompous creep like so many other elite or high-station Coruscanti.

Jedi Temple

F OR MILLENNIA the Jedi Temple on Coruscant has served as the training ground and home base of the Jedi Knights, peacekeeping defenders of justice throughout the galaxy. At the Temple, Jedi initiates learn the ways of the Force, a mystical energy field created by all living things. Hundreds of other individuals who are not Jedi Knights provide vital support in everything from operations management to technical analysis. The galaxy is so large that complete law enforcement is impossible; so most Jedi rove through assigned regions on "journey missions," empowered to support justice as they see fit. Jedi based at the Temple travel on special assignments.

The Jedi Temple on Coruscant occupies hallowed ground sanctified by the noble efforts of Jedi dating back many thousands of years into remote antiquity.

Jedi Padawan with learner braid

Traditional Jedi robes

Natural skin coloration

The Jedi eschew materialism as they do any attachments that could cloud their judgment. Yoda's years of dedication have raised him to power and influence, but he meets his colleagues in a simple cell.

Visually disruptive patterning

Active Jedi

Jedi begin their lifelong training when they are recognized as gifted children. They accept a life of total dedication and self-sacrifice to become diplomat-warriors. As initiates, they train together until they are accepted as Padawans, or apprentice learners. They must then face the Trials to become Jedi Knights, who are allowed in turn to take on an apprentice and earn the title of Master.

Gesture of patience

Diplomatic boots less rugged than field-agent boots

Shaak Ti

Jedi come from every corner of the galaxy. Jedi Master Shaak Ti is a Togruta, a species which lives in dense tribes on the planet Shili, where the disruptive coloration of their long lekku (head-tails) serves to confuse predators. Unlike most of her kind, Shaak Ti is a highly independent spirit.

Yoda—Jedi Instructor

THE WISE YODA is the sole member of the Jedi Council to recognize the present danger of Jedi complacency. Yoda sees that, in these troubled times, the greatest challenge may come from within the system itself. Even at his advanced age and with his formidable reputation and responsibilities, Yoda still trains young initiates. His students are taught to take nothing for granted and to keep their minds open to every possibility, avoiding the pitfalls of overconfidence.

Obi-Wan Kenobi has grown close to Yoda since the death of Kenobi's Jedi Master, Qui-Gon Jinn. Facing a difficulty in his current assignment, Obi-Wan does not hesitate to consult with his wise friend and colleague, who in turn uses the opportunity as an exercise for his young Jedi initiates.

Short Padawan haircut

Bear Clan member

Low-power "safety blade" generator

TRAINING LIGHTSABER

Sensitive ears complement Yoda's habit of listening more than talking

Hand gestures help focus mental use of the Force

Adjustable-opacity faceplate

NOVICE HELMET
Young initiates wear helmets that mask their vision, training them to see using the Force rather than their bodily senses alone.

JEDI INITIATES

Hidden Strengths

Yoda's capabilities with the Force give him amazing strength and speed, as well as the ability to levitate. These special powers, combined with his knowledge of fighting tactics, allow him to overcome virtually any opponent, though times are few indeed that Yoda has actually used his lightsaber in combat.

Simple robe is a sincere expression of humility, despite Yoda's great power and reputation

DATA FILE

◆ More than 9,000 fully trained Jedi are scattered throughout the galaxy, with a further 200 available at the Jedi Temple for emergency missions.

◆ Yoda has never revealed his homeworld, and his species is rarely seen anywhere in the galaxy.

Jedi Archives

EVER SINCE the ancient origins of the Jedi Order, knowledge and its mastery have been vital to the Jedi mission of supporting peace and justice throughout the Republic. The great Archives Library in the Jedi Temple safeguards the accumulated knowledge gathered by millions of individuals over hundreds of generations. It is a repository of seemingly infinite information on every part of the known galaxy and on billions upon billions of its inhabitants. The Archives is the greatest library in the Republic, and an incomparable asset to the Jedi, whether they are acting as diplomats, counselors, or fighters.

Traditional Ansata pattern symbolizing knowledge and learning

Lightsaber still worn as testament of field service

The Main Hall of the Jedi Archives holds most of its information in holobooks to prevent electronic access by overly curious outsiders. Some of the holobooks date back many thousands of years to the earliest days of the Galactic Republic.

Chon Actrion, "Architect of Freedom"

The Archives offers many opportunities for reflection. Statues remind Jedi not only of the great and the good, but also of the "Lost 20"—the only Jedi to leave the Order voluntarily.

Simple plinth

Jocasta Nu

Madame Jocasta Nu is Archives Director and a former active Jedi Knight. Her astonishing memory seems to rival the Archives itself, which she runs as a tool rather than a service, expecting Jedi and support personnel to do their own research. Her pride sometimes blinds her to the Archives' limitations, however.

Full robe worn by Nu in elder years

DATA FILE

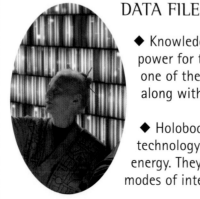

◆ Knowledge has been a key source of Jedi power for thousands of years. It is considered one of the three pillars of Jedi strength, along with the Force and self-discipline.

◆ Holobooks are an ancient self-contained technology requiring only small amounts of energy. They are easy to use and offer many modes of interaction with their users.

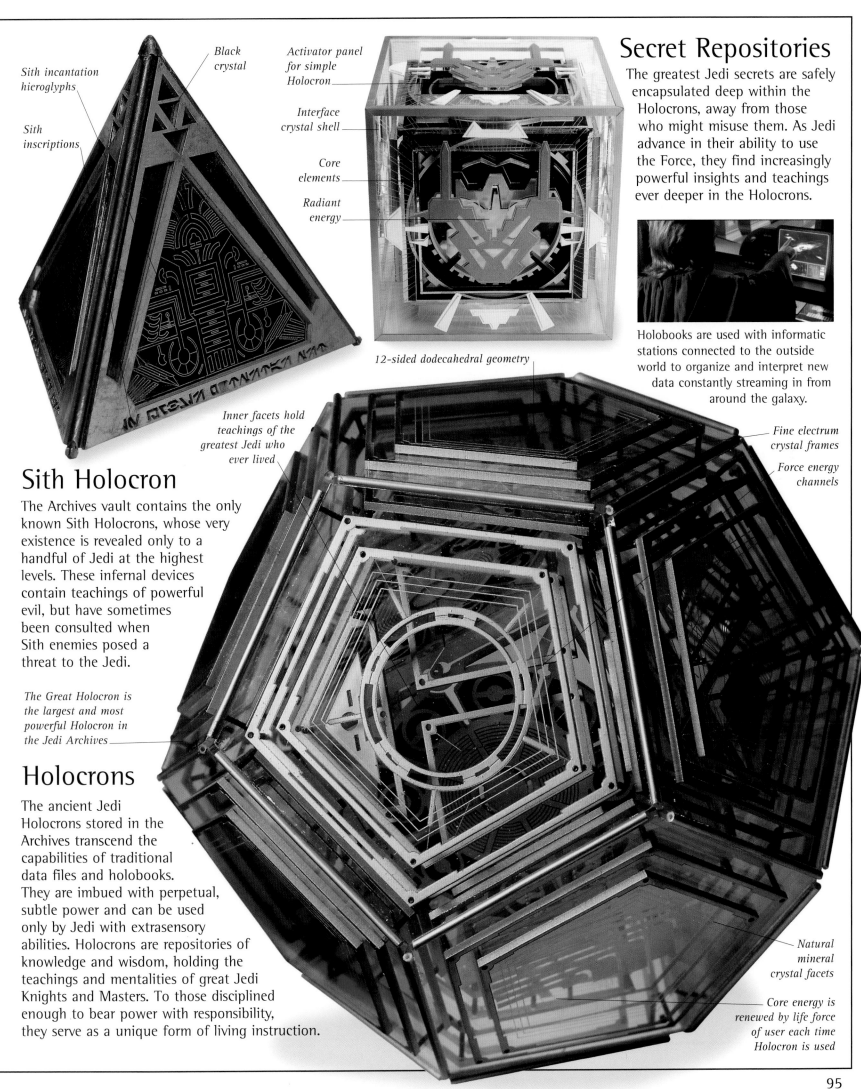

Sith incantation hieroglyphs

Sith inscriptions

Black crystal

Activator panel for simple Holocron

Interface crystal shell

Core elements

Radiant energy

Secret Repositories

The greatest Jedi secrets are safely encapsulated deep within the Holocrons, away from those who might misuse them. As Jedi advance in their ability to use the Force, they find increasingly powerful insights and teachings ever deeper in the Holocrons.

Holobooks are used with informatic stations connected to the outside world to organize and interpret new data constantly streaming in from around the galaxy.

12-sided dodecahedral geometry

Inner facets hold teachings of the greatest Jedi who ever lived

Sith Holocron

The Archives vault contains the only known Sith Holocrons, whose very existence is revealed only to a handful of Jedi at the highest levels. These infernal devices contain teachings of powerful evil, but have sometimes been consulted when Sith enemies posed a threat to the Jedi.

The Great Holocron is the largest and most powerful Holocron in the Jedi Archives

Holocrons

The ancient Jedi Holocrons stored in the Archives transcend the capabilities of traditional data files and holobooks. They are imbued with perpetual, subtle power and can be used only by Jedi with extrasensory abilities. Holocrons are repositories of knowledge and wisdom, holding the teachings and mentalities of great Jedi Knights and Masters. To those disciplined enough to bear power with responsibility, they serve as a unique form of living instruction.

Fine electrum crystal frames

Force energy channels

Natural mineral crystal facets

Core energy is renewed by life force of user each time Holocron is used

Freighter Trampers

Cramped quarters

FOR CENTURIES, Coruscant has attracted immigrants in search of seemingly infinite opportunities. As the present turmoil leaves individuals uncertain of their future, many are now heading back to their homeworlds or further out into the galaxy in search of new employment. Among these migrants are the freighter trampers, so-called because they commute from job to job on the freighter lanes. The trampers form a community of their own, and such a diverse mix forms an ideal environment in which Anakin and Padmé may travel unnoticed.

On the freighter, Padmé travels with a minimum of belongings, as she is no longer required to wear the formal attire of political office.

Concealed stun baton

Steerage overseers have the authority to strand miscreants on any passing star system. These harsh measures serve to keep the freighter trampers in line.

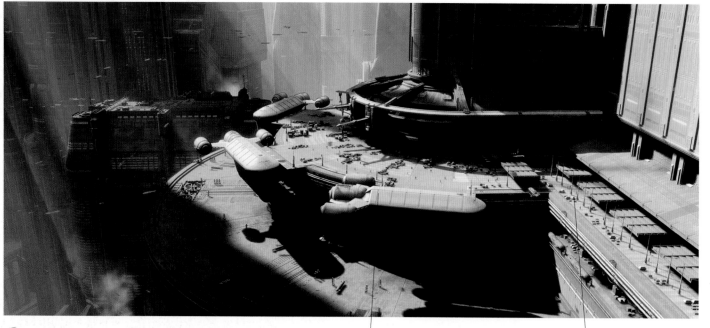

Space freighter at docking bay

Crowded platform

Coruscant Spaceport

On Coruscant, space freighters with heavy drive engines are allowed to land only at spaceports. Coruscant's stiff engine-maintenance regulations and powerful damper fields make its docking bays less radioative than those on less-developed planets. Always heavily traveled, the Coruscant spaceports are beginning to strain toward capacity as more passengers sign on for transit off-world.

Filter for polluted air in steerage

Backpack transponder for mining scout

Housing made of bedpan

Donovian rainmen wear distinctive rain hoods. The rainmen service signal towers over the rugged terrain of Donovia, a planet mined for many precious materials.

Welder made from diatomic bomb igniter

TRAMPER GEAR
Freighter trampers barter with each other for the goods in their possession, and often recombine components of disparate origins into workable equipment, or "tramper gear."

Hood allows close work in rain

Tired electrician awaiting next job

Journeyman-team foreman signaling availability for work

Sealer's kit

Traveling in disguise aboard the freighter *Jendirian Valley*, Anakin and Padmé mix with ordinary people, unhindered by their usual professional personae.

C00-series cookdroid

Freighter food is the epitome of utility nourishment. Cookdroids are programmed to use the most basic and inexpensive recipes, which ensures that a wide variety of humanoids and aliens will find the food edible.

Economic Refugees

Many freighter trampers indenture themselves to corporations in order to earn the cost of their passage to new worlds in search of work. However, many find that when they arrive, the long-hoped-for employment has disappeared. They then have to indenture themselves for a second passage to another world, starting a cycle in which millions live in a form of bondage little different from slavery.

Raddan vermin-killer's vest

Spellsayer's teardrop emblem

Pants cover protective undergarments

TRAMPER DRESS
Freighter trampers sport a bewildering array of clothing, indicating various specialized professions, callings, or cultures.

Reactor tender's gear

Breath mask filters out radioactive gases

Coverings expose as little flesh as possible

Lead-impregnated clothing acts as shielding

Mutant Aqualish with second pair of eyes

Nuclear-waste technician's garb

DATA FILE

◆ Seasoned freighter trampers can quickly spot a batch of fresh synthetic vegetables on a tray of preservative-loaded food that may be years old.

◆ Freighter passengers are now leaving Coruscant at a rate that would depopulate an ordinary planet in one standard month.

Padmé–Naboo Senator

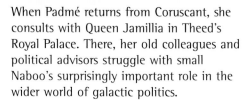
Formal court hairstyle

WHEN PADMÉ NABERRIE last saw Anakin Skywalker, he was just a boy, though she sensed something special about him even then. Now that Anakin has re-entered her life, Padmé is amazed at the effect the young Jedi has on her. She senses a connection that overcomes all her efforts to deny it, a feeling in conflict with her dedication and determination to serve her people. Her increasingly dangerous life and her exposure to the death of loved ones force Padmé to realise how precious every minute is. At the crucial moment, she becomes determined to live as fully as possible no matter what the consequences—and if she is to be destroyed, she will go down fighting.

After her years in political service, the planetary government complex on Naboo serves as a familiar walking place for Padmé.

Padmé's family home in the Lake Country is called Varykino. It is here that she feels safest and can most be herself.

Symbol

All high offices on Naboo are elective, yet they carry with them the complex dress codes associated with hereditary nobility. Padmé accepts the symbolic value of such trappings but would prefer to wear clothes that express her own identity.

Processor status indicators

Camera eye

Spotlight and holoprojector

Gas cartridge *Valve assembly* *Welding tip*

GAS TORCH

Mechanical grasper

Astromech Droids are built for versatility and are easily fitted, and re-fitted, with a range of standardized parts and equipment.

Rocket assembly

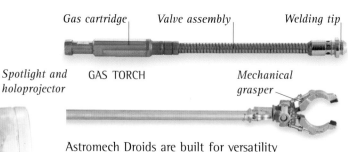
Actuator *Capacitor* *Extensor rod*

Polydigital grasper

R2-D2

Padmé is faithfully attended by R2-D2, an Astromech Droid that regularly exceeds its programming in loyal service. While droids are disregarded through most of the galaxy, on open-hearted Naboo, Padmé is not unusual in feeling an affection for a mechanical servant who seems so spirited.

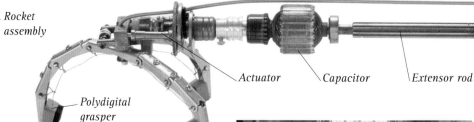

When Padmé returns from Coruscant, she consults with Queen Jamillia in Theed's Royal Palace. There, her old colleagues and political advisors struggle with small Naboo's surprisingly important role in the wider world of galactic politics.

Retractable third leg

Sensory impulse cable

Headband for decoration

At Varykino, Padmé talks with Anakin about the difficult situation they face: Their demanding careers do not allow either of them to fall in love.

The Jedi and the Senator share their views on how galactic politics ought to run. Both are in positions to affect such matters.

Armband signifies political service

Practical hairstyle for travel and action

Enhanced targeting-gear mounting bracket

Collimating tube and heat radiators

Military blaster

Trigger guard

Difficult one-handed grip

Utility belt

Padmé takes Anakin to Tatooine to help him find his mother, Shmi Skywalker. A decisive woman, she acts quickly when she realizes that time is short.

Individual

In her family home, Padmé is at last free to wear non-official clothing. Deeply affected by the presence of Anakin Skywalker, she tells herself that she cannot and will not fall in love with him, but unconsciously she wears a gown expressive of her true feelings.

Spare energy magazines for blaster

Customised H-type Nubian yacht

Pilot station

After stepping down from the throne of Naboo, Padmé continues to use starships sheathed in regal mirrored chromium. The honor was awarded in respect of her pivotal role in repelling the Trade Federation's invasion of her planet.

Light shin armor

Fighter

Accompanying Anakin on his journey across the galaxy, Padmé plunges into the heart of the Separatist crisis. She faces extraordinary danger with the same determination that made her a successful Queen. Nothing can overcome her will.

DATA FILE

◆ Padmé served as Queen for the maximum two four-year terms and was elected Senator upon the conclusion of her reign.

◆ Padmé has had only limited weapons training but demonstrates natural skill at aiming a blaster.

◆ Free of the symbolic requirements of monarchy, Padmé can wear practical clothing on Geonosis.

Having survived great calamity together, Padmé and Anakin surrender to their feelings and marry. The marriage of a Jedi is a grave portent, violating a sacred code of honor in the Order.

Action boots with firm grip

Kaminoans

WHEN A GLOBAL CLIMATE SHIFT flooded their planet, the Kaminoans were forced to adapt. They developed cloning technology and practised selective breeding to keep their race alive. As a result of the hardships endured during the Great Flood, the Kaminoans have an austere, non-materialist outlook. They are outwardly polite, yet behind this lurks an extreme intolerance of physical imperfection. The Kaminoans are reliant on certain outworld technologies and raw materials to maintain their advanced society, so they use their cloning abilities to produce goods for export. When a Jedi named Sifo-Dyas placed an order for a massive clone army a decade ago, the Kaminoans embarked upon the largest human cloning project ever undertaken.

Large eyes see well in murky conditions

KO SAI

Elongated bones allow limited flexibility in neck

TAUN WE

Long neck consists of seven elongated bones

Female Kaminoans lack headcrest

The planet Kamino once had extensive land areas, but the melting of inland continental glaciers sank all land beneath the waves. Today, only the Kaminoan stilt cities project above the water, forming colonies of varying sizes around the planet.

Black body-glove underlayer

Clone serum test probe

Clone science emblem

Serum sample pouch

Black cuff is a mark of honor; scientific rank indicated by thickness

Spongy wings

Kaminoan saddle rig

Skull contains buoyancy chambers

Sieve plates filter plankton underwater or in flight

Kaminoans use domesticated aiwhas for sport and transportation between close-sited colonies. These animals can fly and swim with equal ease, controlling their density using a water-vascular system. This system allows the aiwhas to fill their spongy tissues with seawater when they want to swim underwater, and to wring the water out and shed it to lighten themselves for flight.

Obi-Wan Kenobi identifies himself as a Jedi to Kamino Space Traffic Control on his way in and, upon landing, is met by the Prime Minister's assistant.

Project Leaders

Ministerial assistant Taun We serves as a Project Coordinator for the clone army. Taun We has studied human emotional psychology to ensure that the clones are developed into mentally stable individuals. Chief Scientist Ko Sai, serene yet exacting, oversees the clone-army project's biological aspects, ensuring that clones are of the highest quality. She also supervizes the delicate redesign of the genetic codes that make the clones independently intelligent, but preconditioned for obedience. No other scientist in the galaxy could so capably manipulate the genes of another species.

Dexterous fingers

White form-fitting clothing

Cloak of office

Kamino's prime minister, Lama Su, is well aware of the clone army's importance to his economy. He personally meets the Jedi whom he thinks has come to inspect it.

Lama Su is unsure whether Obi-Wan Kenobi's seeming ignorance of the tremendous clone army is a devious test or a complex form of politeness. Regardless, his overriding concern in meeting with Kenobi is to ensure that the Kaminoans will obtain their first shipment bonus payment, so he makes nothing of the Jedi's odd behaviour.

Kaminoan stilt cities echo the Kaminoans' former land colonies. These were communal dwellings constructed of wattle and daub, which shed water easily in the long storm seasons.

DATA FILE

◆ Kaminoans see color only in the ultraviolet spectrum. Their seemingly white dwellings are suffused in many shades that humans cannot see.

◆ Prime Minister Lama Su is the head of the ruling council of Kamino colony governors. He is aware of the larger arena of galactic events, but is nonetheless little interested in outworld politics.

TIPOCA (KAMINOAN CAPITAL CITY)

Communications tower

Static discharge towers vital during electrical storms

Streamlined outer shell sheds water and wind

Pylons present minimal silhouette to avoid wave battering

Pylons embedded in shallow continental shelf below

Digitigrade configuration of feet adds height

Small feet adapted to firm Kaminoan seabeds and now to hard flooring

Clone Trooper Growth

CLONE ARMY PROJECT EMBLEM

THE MYSTERIOUS Jedi Sifo-Dyas ordered from the Kaminoan cloners a secret army created from a single individual. An agent named Tyranus selected the clone-source: Jango Fett, a man whose natural combat ability and high endurance level would produce the ideal soldier. Under Kaminoan Chief Scientist Ko Sai, the clones' genetic code was altered to accelerate their growth to twice the normal human rate, and their mental structure was subtly reconfigured to make them obedient to authority. Comprehensive training shapes the identity and abilities of the clones throughout their development. The result of this colossal project is an army of identical soldiers produced in a world of clinical efficiency.

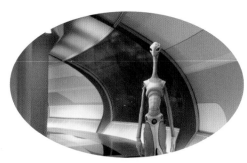

Most Kaminoans regard the clones as laboratory specimens but Taun We feels some affection for the young cadets.

The clones begin life as artificially created embryos that are mass-produced in the Egg Lab.

Durable inert plastoid helmet

Odd-class helmet has gold plating

Broadcast signal receiver

Broadcast power receiver

Anodized-color equipment for even-class helmet

ODD-CLASS HELMET
The clones wear special learning helmets, which are color coded to reflect odd or even numbering. Odd or even is the only identity distinction the clones are allowed.

EVEN-CLASS HELMET

Mental receptivity enhancer

Biorhythm synchronizer

Earphone silences external sounds to provide isolated audio environment for learning

Accelerated Learning

Clone youths grow at twice the rate of ordinary humans, so they crave information but receive only half the normal time to assimilate it. This loss of life-experience is compensated for by a learning program that focuses more on military knowledge than on academics. In addition, special equipment modulates brainwaves and enhances the clones' ability to retain instruction.

Pickup reads vocal responses

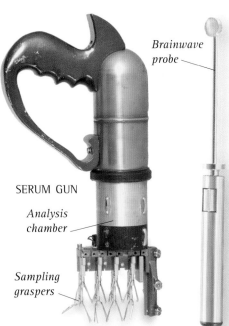

Brainwave
probe

Brainwave
canceler

SERUM GUN

*Analysis
chamber*

*Sampling
graspers*

Clone birth pod

*Reorientation
unit*

Maintaining Perfection

The Kaminoans strive to control every aspect of the clones' existence for perfect regularity, but slight deviations occur in the development of any living individual's biochemistry. Chief Scientist Ko Sai inspects the clones at every stage of life to identify those who have drifted from the standard. Aberrant clones are given extra conditioning to regularize them.

*Cord used for symbolic
honor training*

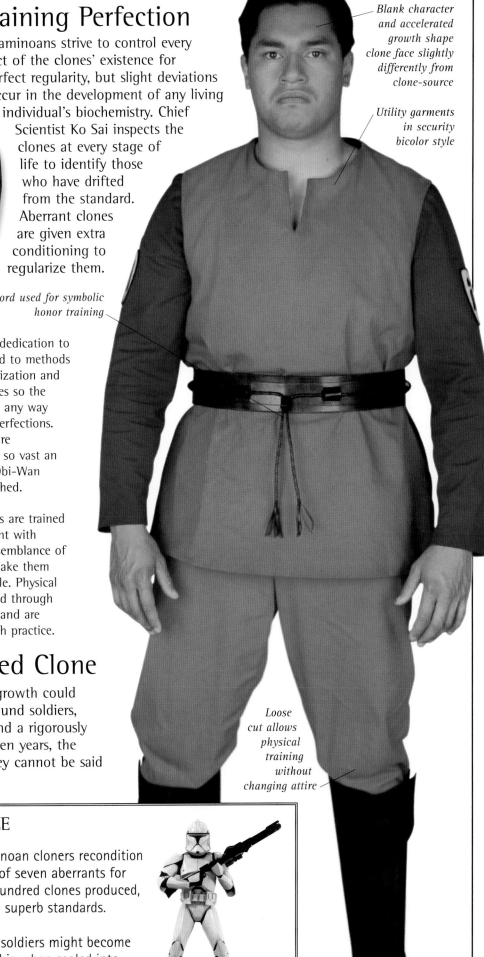

*Blank character
and accelerated
growth shape
clone face slightly
differently from
clone-source*

*Utility garments
in security
bicolor style*

The Kaminoans' dedication to perfection has led to methods of absolute sterilization and ultraclean surfaces so the clones are not in any way tainted with imperfections. Such standards are extraordinary for so vast an enterprise, and Obi-Wan Kenobi is astonished.

Batches of clones are trained in an environment with exactly enough semblance of community to make them emotionally stable. Physical skills are imparted through learning devices and are perfected through practice.

Developed Clone

The stress of accelerated physical, mental, and emotional growth could easily drive a clone insane. To counter this and produce sound soldiers, the Kaminoans provide a highly disciplined environment and a rigorously balanced development program. At a physical age of just ten years, the clones are fully developed and ready for battle, though they cannot be said to have normal personalities.

*Loose
cut allows
physical
training
without
changing attire*

As "adults," the clone troopers resemble their source, Jango Fett. Fett lives on Kamino and helps train the troopers, knowing better than anyone how to guide their development and impart military skills to the copies of himself.

DATA FILE

◆ The Kaminoan cloners recondition an average of seven aberrants for every two hundred clones produced, maintaining superb standards.

◆ Ordinary soldiers might become claustrophobic when sealed into armor, but clone troopers are trained to wear it for extended periods.

Clone Trooper Equipment

CLONE TROOPER armor and equipment is based in part on the battle gear of the Mandalorian "shocktrooper" supercommandos, of whom Jango Fett is a survivor. Fett's light armor inspired the heavy-duty shell completely covering the clone trooper. Replacing the Mandalorian flightsuit is a pressurized black body-glove that protects against acrid vapors or even the vacuum of space. The distinctive shocktrooper "T" visor plate is adapted with an enhanced breath filter for optimal operations under the often poor environmental conditions of battle. Together with their superb training and conditioning, clone troopers feel virtually invincible with this panoply.

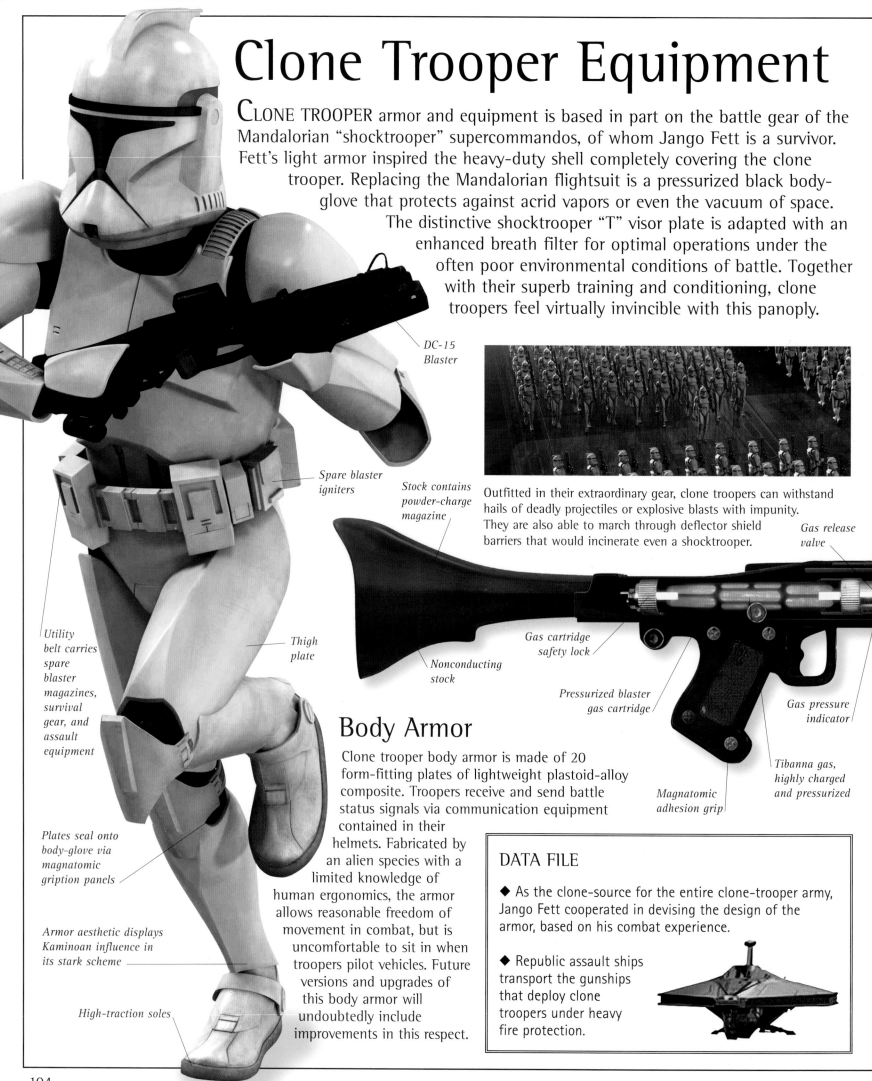

DC-15 Blaster

Spare blaster igniters

Stock contains powder-charge magazine

Outfitted in their extraordinary gear, clone troopers can withstand hails of deadly projectiles or explosive blasts with impunity. They are also able to march through deflector shield barriers that would incinerate even a shocktrooper.

Gas release valve

Utility belt carries spare blaster magazines, survival gear, and assault equipment

Thigh plate

Nonconducting stock

Gas cartridge safety lock

Pressurized blaster gas cartridge

Gas pressure indicator

Body Armor

Clone trooper body armor is made of 20 form-fitting plates of lightweight plastoid-alloy composite. Troopers receive and send battle status signals via communication equipment contained in their helmets. Fabricated by an alien species with a limited knowledge of human ergonomics, the armor allows reasonable freedom of movement in combat, but is uncomfortable to sit in when troopers pilot vehicles. Future versions and upgrades of this body armor will undoubtedly include improvements in this respect.

Plates seal onto body-glove via magnatomic gription panels

Armor aesthetic displays Kaminoan influence in its stark scheme

High-traction soles

Magnatomic adhesion grip

Tibanna gas, highly charged and pressurized

DATA FILE

◆ As the clone-source for the entire clone-trooper army, Jango Fett cooperated in devising the design of the armor, based on his combat experience.

◆ Republic assault ships transport the gunships that deploy clone troopers under heavy fire protection.

Enhanced breath filter for battle conditions

Comlink antenna built into helmet

"T" visor derived from shocktrooper helmet

Laser turret

Heavy-lift agrav drive

AT-TE

Armored hull

REPUBLIC GUNSHIP

AT-TE CARRIER

All-terrain walking legs

AT-TE WALKER

Spare blaster magazine

Grappling hook

Knee plate

Battle Gear

Vital combat transports and fighting machines have been developed alongside the clone troopers. This new equipment expresses the battle philosophy of the clone army: It is built for heavy use and the unleashing of maximum-effort assaults without warning. These approaches differ from the forms of battle seen throughout the galaxy for thousands of years, in which armies deployed their strength cautiously over long periods.

Troop deployment hatch (raised)

Command bridge

WHITE TERROR
Clone trooper uniforms are not camouflaged, because troops fear no one and want their enemies to see them coming from afar.

Walking legs

SPHA-T

Power amplifier circuitry

Ignition chamber

Expansion chamber

Power setting adjust

Electromagnets

Accelerator

Galven circuitry

Collimating tube

Flip-up optical sight for open combat

Igniter

Pre-ionizer

Hyper-ionizer

Magnetic pulse stabilizers

Sniper scope in storage position doubles as handhold

DC-15 RIFLE

Heat-exchange elements

Radiator fins

Weaponry

Clone troopers are issued plasma guns of two types. Like all standard blaster weapons, these guns create a charged plasma bolt using a small amount of Tibanna gas. Blaster weapons free clone troopers from the need to carry projectile ammunition but are notoriously hard to aim due to the inherent instability of plasma bolts.

Heat radiator fins

Rifle break point for replacement of gas cartridge

Weighted stock improves balance of rifle

Heavy duty fasteners

Heat exchange elements in muzzle reduce danger of damage from overheating

Charge magazine locks in on opposite side

Tibanna gas is carried in a replaceable cartridge that lasts about 500 shots, depending on the weapon's settings and traits. Power-charge magazines supply the gun with energy to hyper-ionize the gas into charged plasma in an igniter chamber. The resulting bolt is accelerated out of the gun electromagnetically.

Charge magazine

Spare igniter

DC-15 BLASTER

Blaster lacks rifle's enhanced power control components, limiting range

Folding stock for braced firing

Lock-in charge magazine

Jango Fett–Bounty Hunter

AFTER THE MURDER of his parents, Jango Fett was adopted and raised by the legendary Mandalorian warrior army, a mercenary group who earned a reputation as the most formidable supercommandoes in the galaxy. The Jedi destroyed this dangerous force, but Fett survived and continues to wear the armored, weapon-filled uniform that helped make the Mandalorians a dreaded name. Keeping himself in top condition and training often with his equipment, Jango Fett combines physical and tactical skill with a prudent intelligence that is a rare attribute in the bounty-hunting community.

Jango's reputation enables him to hire stringers, wisely minimizing his own risk. He often works with Zam Wesell, to whom Jango assigns the dangerous job of assassinating the Senator for Naboo.

Explosive/grappling missile

Fuel tank

Gauntlets can mount various weapon systems

Jetpack

Jetpack activator

Gimbaling servo

Rocket thrust vectoring nozzle

Segmented armor plate allows flexibility

Traditional sash binding of journeyman protector

Holster design holds and protects custom-made pistols

Pineal eye sensor allows Jango to see behind him

Helmet design balances protection with tactical visibility

WESTAR-34 blaster

Gauntlet projectile dart shooter

Whipcord thrower

Utility pouches

Waterproof layered flight suit

Tactical boots with magnatomic adhesion soles

Kneepad rocket-dart launchers

Even the surprise appearance of a Jedi Knight is not enough to overcome Fett's topnotch combat skills. When Obi-Wan Kenobi tries to capture him, Jango is well-prepared and instantly launches a volley of blasts that would annihilate an ordinary opponent.

In battle with Kenobi, Fett soon appreciates the seemingly supernatural abilities of the Jedi. Jango must quickly re-assess his tactical situation before Kenobi gains the upper hand.

Walking Armor

Mandalorians who could afford it commissioned backup suits of their armor. Fett has replacement armor for much of his suit, with additional items that can be fitted for particular mission profiles. Some configurations stress brute-force armament, while others maximize nonlethal weapons used for capturing quarry.

Ultrasonic emitter

FIELD SECURITY OVERLOADER

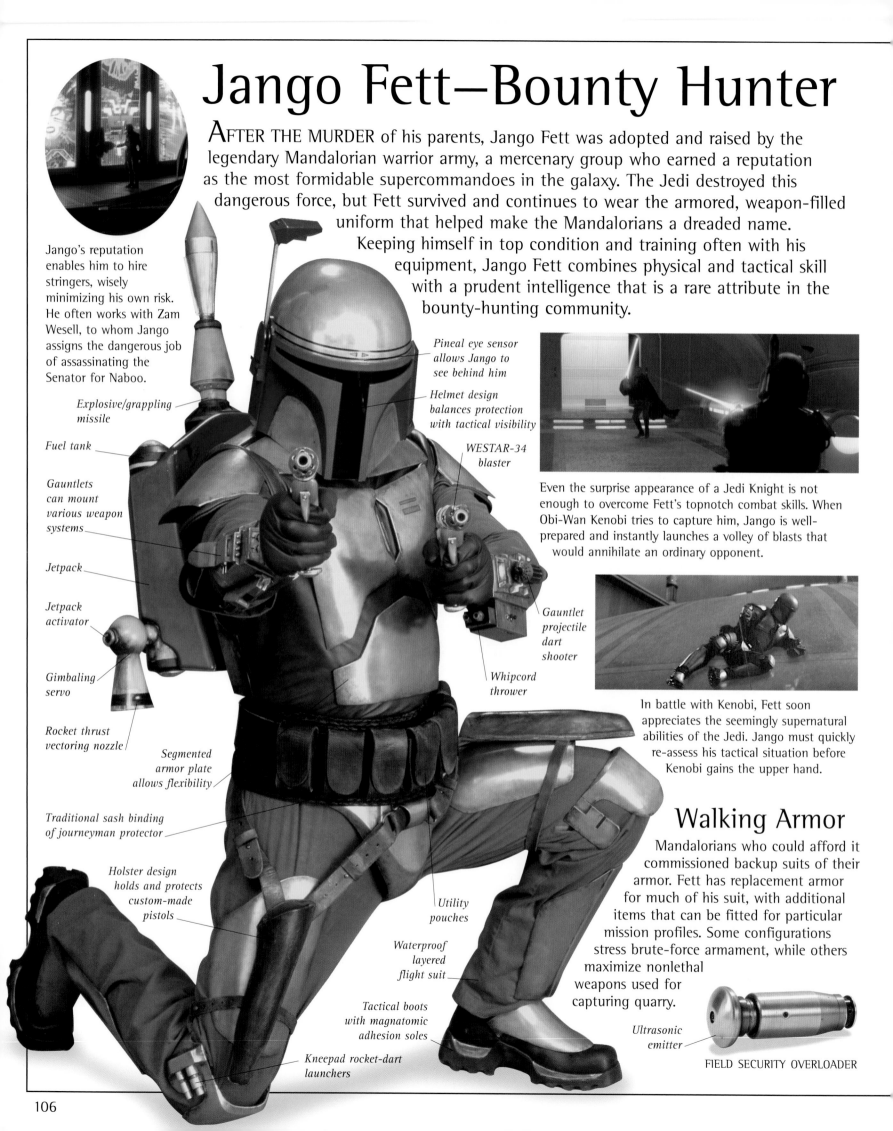

WESTAR-34 Blaster

Gas and power cell cartridge

Trigger

Weight-minimizing cutout handle

Low-power pulse indicator

Overload flash dissipator port

Favoring agility and precision over high capacity, Fett had a set of compact WESTAR-34 blasters custom-made. Designed for brief but intense surprise attacks at close range, the pistols are made of an expensive dallorian alloy, which can withstand sustained-fire heating that would melt an ordinary gun.

Code algorithm selectors

Signal projector

Activator

LOCK BREAKER

Targeting rangefinder swings down for sighting

Mandalorian helmet

Concussion missile

Never governed by passions or panic, Fett coolly calculates his every move, always playing to win or survive. He knows when to make use of evasion and thus outlasts both rivals and opponents.

Blades deploy from gauntlet for surprise in unarmed combat

Energized blast dissipation vest

Secondary jetpack

Warhead missile

Holstered WESTAR-34 blaster

Missile thrust vent

Realizing that Kenobi is a formidable opponent, Fett launches his jetpack missile set for explosive charge. The missile can be optionally locked dead as a grappling hook. Set to explode, it would kill any ordinary humanoid, but will it kill a Jedi?

JETPACKS
Fett's gear includes two models of jetpack, one more heavily armored and carrying a larger-bore missile.

Fine-bore missile

Missile targeting rangefinder

Missile charge boost

DATA FILE

◆ Ten years ago, Darth Tyranus recruited Jango as the clone-source for the Kaminoans' secret clone-army project.

◆ Jango's Mandalorian armor is one of the only surviving sets of this feared and elusive panoply.

Professional

Raised in a brutal frontier environment on Concord Dawn, Fett is tough and self-reliant. He has worked out his own sense of morality which is honorable by his standards. He keeps his bargains and he earns his pay. As a bounty hunter, Fett has become so professionally formidable that planetary governments are known to hire him.

Jango and Boba Fett

ENTRY KEYPAD

THE MANDALORIAN WAY lives on in the bond between Jango Fett and his son Boba. Growing up at his father's side, Boba has learned the value of superior training, judgement, and weaponry. To Boba, Jango stands above the greed and betrayal encountered in the underworld, and is a man of honor who is unfailingly truthful with him. To young Boba, Jango Fett is father, family, ideal, and hero, the greatest of the Mandalorians and the image of his own destiny.

Jango maintains a Spartan apartment on Kamino. He uses it as a safe house for himself and his son, far from the dangerous entanglements of his professional life.

Like Father, Like Son

In Mandalorian tradition, fathers were responsible for training their sons in combat skills. At age 13, boys had to face the trials of manhood. Although these rites could be fatal, actual deaths were extremely rare because candidates were so well prepared. The close father-son bond, built on respect, trust, and discipline, produced highly capable and confident individuals.

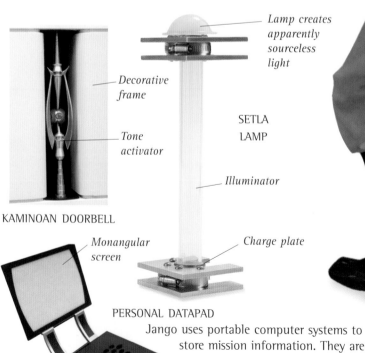

Decorative frame

Tone activator

KAMINOAN DOORBELL

Lamp creates apparently sourceless light

SETLA LAMP

Illuminator

Charge plate

Monangular screen

PERSONAL DATAPAD

Jango uses portable computer systems to store mission information. They are programmed to erase all stored information if not handled correctly.

Earpiece receives signals from Slave I and protects Jango from enemy sonic weapons

Jango teaches Boba by example

Bicolor tunic in traditional security style

Practiced fighting stance

Utility pouches

Armored kneepad

Military-grade cloth pants

Shinplate

Mandalorian youth boots

Reinforced boot

Boba Fett

Young Boba Fett is perceptive and intelligent. He has learned to assess situations carefully, and to listen more than he talks. When Obi-Wan Kenobi appears at the Fetts' apartment, Boba immediately senses trouble, but betrays none of his concern.

Disciplined posture

Rain cloak

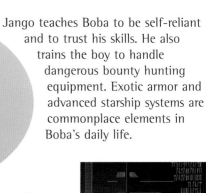

Jango teaches Boba to be self-reliant and to trust his skills. He also trains the boy to handle dangerous bounty hunting equipment. Exotic armor and advanced starship systems are commonplace elements in Boba's daily life.

Jango's stored armor

Darien lava-skimmer color scheme

Air scoop

BOBA'S AIRSPEEDER MODEL

Oovo security force markings

Systems status readouts

Energy shield generator

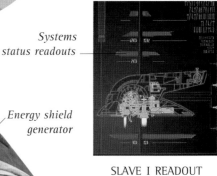

SLAVE I READOUT

Boba knows when to stay in the background. Jango trusts his son's discretion and keeps him around even during critical meetings.

Large, variable-opacity windshield allows superb range of vision

Wing rotation axis

Repulsorlift wing

Wing extension struts

DATA FILE

◆ Boba Fett is a perfect, unaltered clone of his father, part of Jango's compensation from the Kaminoans.

◆ Jango knows that Darth Tyranus, who recruited him for the clone-army project, is actually the Separatist leader, Count Dooku.

Even in combat, Boba Fett stays at his father's side. He trusts in his father's abilities and learns from Jango's skillful actions in every encounter.

Main hatch

Boarding ramp

Target scanner (under outer plating)

Slave I

Missile launcher

Jango Fett pilots a prototype Kuat Systems *Firespray*-class interceptor of the kind made for patrolling the prison moon of Oovo 4. Fett reasoned that a starship designed to thwart some of the galaxy's most hardened criminals would be excellent for his unusual line of work.

Charge balance readout

WEAPONS MONITOR

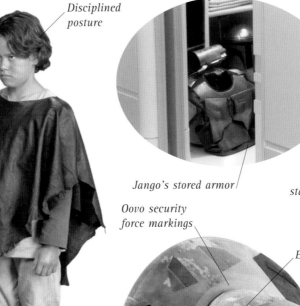

The Lars Family

Settler's simple hairstyle

Rough clothing made in Anchorhead

Tunic

Desert robe

MUSHROOM JAR

TATOOINE'S moisture farmers survive in territories most other people consider uninhabitable. In their search for an independent existence away from the overcrowding and often slave-like employments of the Core Worlds, the Lars family have made Tatooine's barren desert their home. Rendered close-knit by the dangers and hardships they all face, the Lars family and the moisture-farming community band together against the native Tusken Raiders. Pioneer settler Cliegg Lars earned his farm by a homestead claim, raising his son Owen on the great salt flats, together with his second wife, a former slave named Shmi Skywalker.

Moisture farms on the salt flats of Tatooine use arrays of vaporator towers spread out across vast distances to extract minute amounts of water from the atmosphere. A precious commodity on the desert world, water can be used for barter, for sale, or for hydroponic gardens. Homesteads are dug into the ground to provide respite from extreme temperatures.

Owen never expected to meet his step-brother, Anakin, knowing that Jedi must sever their family ties. When Anakin arrives, Owen has mixed feelings about his more worldly relation who left his own mother to become a Jedi.

Owen and Beru

The small town of Anchorhead provides a nexus for the moisture-farming community of the Great Chott salt flat. There, Owen Lars met Beru Whitesun, his girlfriend. Beru's family have been moisture farmers for three generations, making them among the settlers most thoroughly adapted to Tatooine life.

The Lars' kitchen is a simple, functional space built around the basic concern of conserving moisture. Food is never left out for long, and moisture traps are built into the self-sealing cabinets.

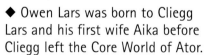

DATA FILE

◆ Owen Lars was born to Cliegg Lars and his first wife Aika before Cliegg left the Core World of Ator.

◆ The Lars family maintains an array of some 63 water vaporators spread out across the flat desert around the homestead, making their farm a relatively small one by Tatooine standards.

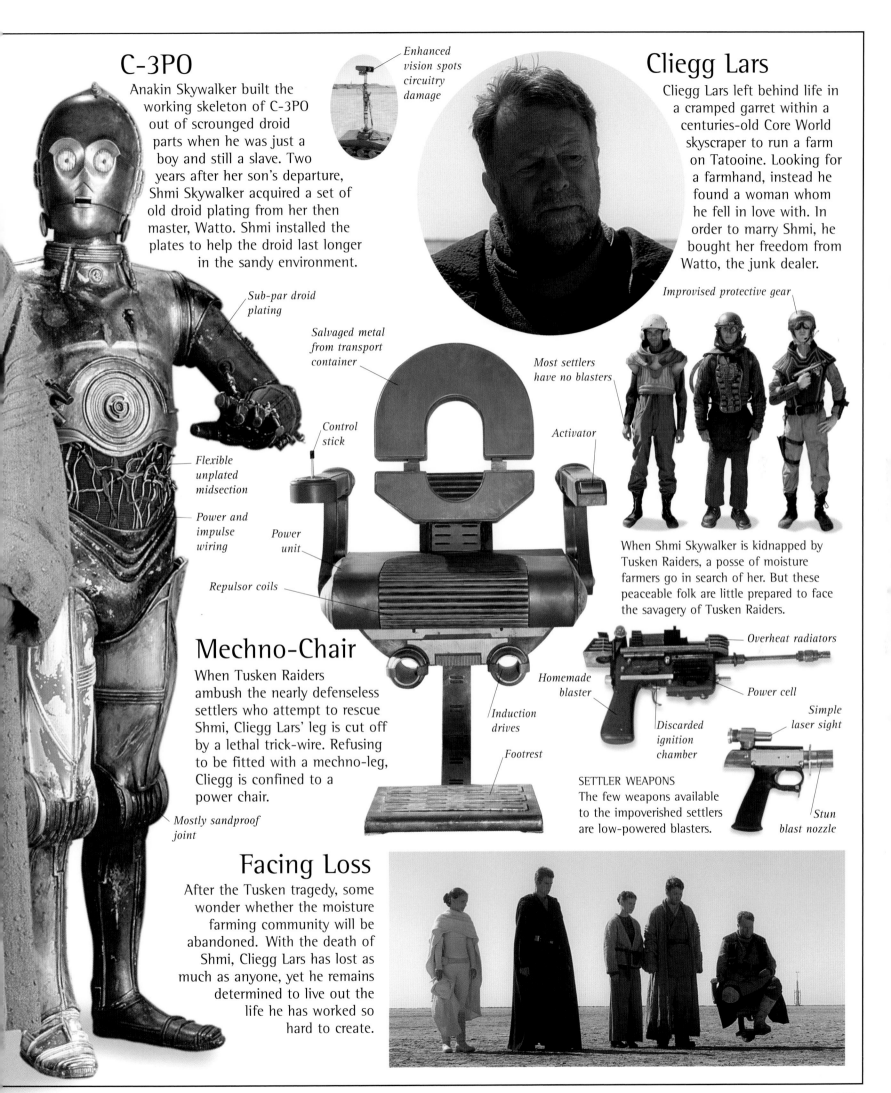

C-3PO

Anakin Skywalker built the working skeleton of C-3PO out of scrounged droid parts when he was just a boy and still a slave. Two years after her son's departure, Shmi Skywalker acquired a set of old droid plating from her then master, Watto. Shmi installed the plates to help the droid last longer in the sandy environment.

Enhanced vision spots circuitry damage

Sub-par droid plating

Flexible unplated midsection

Power and impulse wiring

Cliegg Lars

Cliegg Lars left behind life in a cramped garret within a centuries-old Core World skyscraper to run a farm on Tatooine. Looking for a farmhand, instead he found a woman whom he fell in love with. In order to marry Shmi, he bought her freedom from Watto, the junk dealer.

Improvised protective gear

Most settlers have no blasters

Salvaged metal from transport container

Control stick

Activator

Power unit

Repulsor coils

Mechno-Chair

When Tusken Raiders ambush the nearly defenseless settlers who attempt to rescue Shmi, Cliegg Lars' leg is cut off by a lethal trick-wire. Refusing to be fitted with a mechno-leg, Cliegg is confined to a power chair.

Mostly sandproof joint

Induction drives

Footrest

When Shmi Skywalker is kidnapped by Tusken Raiders, a posse of moisture farmers go in search of her. But these peaceable folk are little prepared to face the savagery of Tusken Raiders.

Overheat radiators

Homemade blaster

Power cell

Discarded ignition chamber

Simple laser sight

Stun blast nozzle

SETTLER WEAPONS
The few weapons available to the impoverished settlers are low-powered blasters.

Facing Loss

After the Tusken tragedy, some wonder whether the moisture farming community will be abandoned. With the death of Shmi, Cliegg Lars has lost as much as anyone, yet he remains determined to live out the life he has worked so hard to create.

Eyeslit

Sandshroud

Tusken Raiders

Tatooine's native Tusken Raiders, or Sand People, are violent enemies of the moisture farmers, with whom they compete for precious water sources on the desert planet. These fearsome creatures are often larger than humans yet they blend into the landscape with baffling ease, allowing them to move almost invisibly. Sand People live in tribal clans loosely scattered across the dunes and canyonlands of Tatooine. They travel lightly and possess few objects, the most treasured of which are the skulls of their ancestors and krayt dragon pearls.

Sand People are reputed to slay anyone foolish enough to come near their sacred wells.

Jewelry made of metal taken from slain captives

Female Tusken's pouch

Sand People live in Tatooine's most barren wastes, where no human settlers could survive. For most of the year, Tusken Raiders rove the desert, but during the height of the hot season, many tribes live in semi-permanent camps.

Womp-rat tusks

Even hands must always be covered

Only someone with the powers of a Jedi could enter a Tusken camp unnoticed. Sand People are uncannily skilled sentries, and can detect humans entering their territory long before they themselves are seen by the intruders.

Desert cloak

DATA FILE

◆ Many gruesome legends surround Tusken Raiders, who are even known to spit streams of blood at their victims during attacks.

◆ Sand People fashion spirit masks from natural materials for use in rituals.

Shrouded In Mystery

Tusken Raiders are strongly divided along gender lines. Females maintain the camps while the males hunt and fight. Sand People keep their flesh carefully covered, only revealing it on their wedding night. For any other exposure of skin, even accidental, Tusken Raiders are banished or killed, depending on the tribe.

Bandaged feet

Gaffi stick

Sandbat venom

Blood spitter

Simple charged-projectile rifle for long-distance shooting

Ammo pouches

Typical double-axe

Sand Gear

Throughout their desert range, Sand People wear similar gear, although each tribal clan has its own distinctive details. Some groups wear a kind of sand-repelling capsule around their necks, while others use simple scarves. Raiders reject most advanced technology, but will take horrific advantage of a stolen blaster gun until its power is spent.

WARNING POSE

Krayt dragon horn

Tools and rations

GADERFFI
The Sand People's traditional weapon is the gaderffi, or "gaffi" stick. These dreaded axes are made from krayt dragon horn and spacecraft plating salvaged from desert wrecks.

Tusken Raiders can hide even in the featureless landscape of the salt flats, where they sometimes lie in wait to kidnap or kill moisture farmers who come out to tend their vaporators.

Full-length sandshroud

Tusken Uli-ah

Unisex youth helmet

Eye and mouth slit

Sand People children, called Uli-ah, wear unisex garments that hide all flesh. These traditional clothes protect Uli-ah from sun, sand, and wind, and conserve precious moisture. Young Tusken Raiders lack full tribal acceptance until they complete a rite of passage at age 15.

Sandcloak

Sand People make a few basic items such as stoves from scavenged and stolen metal. More complex devices are usually taboo.

Ancient wood poles

Skin covering hardened for use at seasonal camp

Tent carried on bantha for travel

Spiked club

Entry forbidden to non-family

Carryall pouch

URTYA TENT
Sand People travel with light tents called urtya. These dwellings are made from skins, tendons, and sticks gathered from occasional exposures of Tatooine's sand-flooded, long-dead forests.

Urtah (Tusken Raider carrying pack)

Sacred ancestor skulls kept inside

Hardener made from bantha spittle

Sandrobe

113

Count's gaze immobilizes weak-minded individuals

In the droid foundries of Geonosis, the Count hopes to have found the anvil upon which he can forge the sword of the Republic's undoing.

Cape is emblem of Count of Serenno

Curved lightsaber hilt allows precise crossparry moves

Count Dooku

THE DANGEROUS AND ELEGANT Count Dooku was once a Jedi Master of great repute. He left the Jedi Order after the Battle of Naboo, returning to his homeworld of Serenno and his family title of Count. By protesting the failure of galactic government, Dooku has swayed many systems to the Separatist movement, which seeks independence from the Republic, but his real motives lurk in darkness. The Count has always wielded considerable power—by natural authority, by lightsaber, and now by wealth and persuasion. This double-dealing master of the Force has taken a place at the heart of galactic events and he threatens the very survival of the Republic.

Cape enlarges Count's silhouette to intimidating effect

Dark Alignment

Although Dooku joined the Order at the usual age, he never fully gave it his inmost allegiance. He maintained a streak of independence, which he transmitted to his pupils, including the late Qui-Gon Jinn. Dooku's considerable strength in the Force made him enigmatic even to Yoda, and there were whispers that he experimented with Sith teachings, using a dark Holocron kept in the Jedi Archives. The Council underestimated Dooku's interest in power.

Underlayer made of costly, fine-grade armorweave fabric, which drapes like silk and helps dissipate blast or lightsaber energy

Elegant, tall dress boots

DATA FILE

◆ The Count is master of his family's fortune and one of the wealthiest men in the galaxy. He could field an army on his own resources.

◆ As a youngling, Dooku trained under Yoda. The great Jedi Master hoped, with careful teaching, to overcome the effects of Dooku's persistent independent spirit.

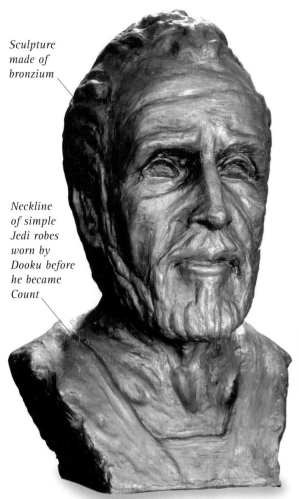

Sculpture made of bronzium

Neckline of simple Jedi robes worn by Dooku before he became Count

Dooku's Lightsaber

As a Jedi Master, Count Dooku set aside the lightsaber he built as a young Padawan and created a superior one, as Jedi sometimes do. In creating his personalized design, he chose a configuration that had no connection to that of his master, Yoda, nor to the style in fashion at the time. Instead, he studied Jedi Archives records to create a lightsaber of the type that was standard in the heyday of Form II lightsaber combat. Form II is an ancient technique that favors long, elegant moves and incredible deftness of hand.

Dooku tempts the captured Obi-Wan Kenobi with an offer to join him in the Separatist movement. The Count subtly uses the Force to probe Obi-Wan's spirit for inner weaknesses.

Emitter guard

Blade emitter

Thumb trigger can shorten blade instantly for short-range surprise attack

Inclined blade focusing chamber

Thermal radiator grooves

Sith synthetic crystals (inside saber) replace original ones for greater power

The Lost Twenty

Only 20 individuals in the history of the Jedi Order have ever renounced their commissions. Their leave-taking is sorely felt among the Jedi, who memorialize them with portrait busts in the Archives. Count Dooku is the most recent of the "lost" ones. He is considered the most bitter loss because the Force was so strong in him.

The curved hilt of Dooku's lightsaber allows for superior finesse and precise blade control. This design gives Dooku an edge when facing Jedi, who have mostly trained to use lightsabers to deflect blaster bolts.

Projector

Cells given by Sith Master

HOLOPROJECTOR
After he left the Jedi Order, Dooku was no longer able to use the Sith Holocron in the Archives. He now studies holographic cells containing mystic teachings of shadowy power.

When the arrival of the Jedi forces spoils his primary plans, Dooku uses one of his several means of escape—a small, open-cockpit speeder bike.

Activator

Fastener

Magnatomic adhesion plates

Dooku reveals the full measure of his dark nature when he casts legendary Sith lightning. Virtually impossible to deflect, Sith lightning causes excruciating pain and weakens life. The Jedi possess no exact equivalent to such an evil use of the Force.

Compound power cell

Reserve power cell

Phase A power cell

The Separatists

COUNT DOOKU'S CALL for independence from the decaying and increasingly corrupt Republic is answered by some of the most significant and authoritative factions in the galaxy. Among them stands a sinister gathering of commercial empires and megaconglomerates, whose power could rival that of the Republic itself. Disaffected and opportunistic Senators also support the Separatist movement. The political system was never constructed to deal with the rise of corporate superpowers, whose motives and morals focus on profit alone. Without decisive support from the Galactic Senate, the Republic's very structure is in danger of being undermined.

The Corporate Alliance

The Corporate Alliance is the negotiating body for the galaxy's major commercial operations. As head of the largest corporation, Passel Argente commands the office of Alliance Magistrate. Argente has risen to great heights of wealth and power as chairman of the merchandising conglomerate called Lethe. Workers and consumers are encouraged to identify with the company in a near-religious way.

RUNE HAAKO

NUTE GUNRAY

Large, pompous miter

Elaborate Neimoidian headdress

Conniving gesture

Oath-taking gesture

Sign of insincerity

Command control reception antenna

Tracking transmitter

Stereoscopic visual sensor

Drive axis hub

Weapons outrigger

Stabilizing outrigger

High-traction drive tread

Robust male cranial horn

PASSEL ARGENTE

Oily cloak

CORPORATE ALLIANCE TANK DROID
When Alliance corporations face resistance to their development plans, Tank Droids are used to clear the way. The wheel-like machines are widely feared.

Grasping hands

The Trade Federation

The Trade Federation controls freighters, ports, and way stations on the galactic commerce routes. Its power is profitably supported by a droid army, which operates under the guise of "securing the lines of trade." Trade officials appear immune to prosecution for their brutal intimidation.

Communications tower

TRADE FEDERATION CORE SHIP
Large Trade Federation freighters are not designed for planetary landings. However, the core ships can detach from the freighters and descend on their own.

The Commerce Guild

The Commerce Guild seeks to control any large corporation involved in raw materials. Increasingly, it enforces tribute payments with its private army. The Guild maximizes profit by stifling alternative technologies and bribing corrupt officials and Senators to control market forces with tariffs.

Traditional skullcap

Gossam rings elongate neck

PRESIDENT SHU MAI

HOMING SPIDER DROID

Armored body core

Extension hydraulics

All-terrain legs

Gracile female cranial horn

Homing laser

Parallax signal tracing dish

Ambulation motors

Tracing antenna

Koorivan matron's hood

DENARIA KEE
(AIDE)

Infrared photoreceptor

Formal breastplate of office

DWARF SPIDER DROID
Commerce Guild army droids are built with striding legs for roadless terrain on rugged mining worlds. These destructive droids hunt down operations attempting to evade tribute payments.

Subservient gesture

Robe made of shimmerbird tongues

The IG Banking Clan

The InterGalactic Banking Clan is headquartered on Muunilinst. It is vastly powerful, with most influence shared by a few old banking families. The fiscally prudent chairman San Hill views the galaxy in purely monetary terms, so he naturally finances both sides of a major conflict.

Pale skin from indoor living

Palo Banking garb

SAN HILL

Hailfire missile launcher pods

Hoop wheel

HAILFIRE DROID
Hailfire Droids roll rapidly into action to discourage those who might default on IG Banking Clan loans. Murderous explosive missile launchers dispatch "late payment notices."

Cyclopean photoreceptor

Sequenced magpulse drive

PO NUDO

AIDE

Shi'ido changeling in disguise

TIKKES

Large aural chamber

Food manipulation tentacles

Senators

Demoralized by bureaucratic inaction and corruption, some Senators see Count Dooku's bid for independence as a brave and noble cause. Others align themselves with the Separatists merely for greater personal gain.

DATA FILE

◆ Count Dooku leads the Separatists and knows every faction's weak points.

◆ Most commercial armies are legally licensed even though they violate the spirit of the laws against private armies.

Geonosian Aristocracy

THE GREAT HIVE COLONIES of the sentient Geonosians teem beneath the surface of Geonosis and extend upward from the barren landscape like strange towers. The quasi-insectoid Geonosians are a completely caste-segregated society. The arrogant upper class rules with savage authority, while the masses labor in great swarms at large-scale industrial operations. Workers are conditioned to loathe the thought of separation from the hive and its systems of complete control. The Geonosian aristocrats' ability to harness the populace for harsh industrial work has made Geonosis a very profitable society for its rulers. The planet has become known particularly in recent years for its huge Battle Droid foundries.

Sentry house

Hive form imitates Geonosis's natural rock spikes

A ring system of small asteroids surrounds the planet Geonosis. The asteroids are rich in metals, forming a huge resource of raw materials for the manufacturing operations on the planet below.

Hive Colonies

To escape the notice of rival tribes and the huge, lanky insectoid predators on Geonosis, the Geonosians live in underground hives. The hives were traditionally concealed within the landscape and blended into it with naturalistic forms.

Structure formed in organic style

Exhaust vent

Dense high-altitude fog on Geonosis produces gloomy, night-like conditions that may last for weeks. Geonosian life is adapted to these circumstances, and many creatures are bioluminescent.

Geonosian society exists for the benefit of the few in the upper caste. Ruling members think nothing of forcing thousands of workers to labor for their whims. They have overseen the creation of the spectacular architectural realm in which they all live, adapting forms they once built by instinct into more refined, spire-like structures.

DATA FILE

◆ Traditional "free-formed" Geonosian architecture is sculpted in rock paste, a material mixed from domesticated phidna parasite excretions and stone powders.

◆ Geonosian phidna are cultivated in hydroponic gardens to supply the hive construction industry.

Sun Fac

Upper-caste wings

Poggle's chief lieutenant, Sun Fac, ensures that his master's will is done throughout Geonosis. Unusually intelligent and creative for a Geonosian, Sun Fac is adept at playing whatever role will best accomplish the needs of the moment. He may be a sympathetic listener or a heartless executioner, depending on which will increase productivity.

Poggle the Lesser

The Stalgasin hive colony ruled by Archduke Poggle the Lesser currently controls all the other major hives on Geonosis. Poggle has negotiated with outworld interests and coordinated widespread planetary hive efforts on the largest industrial projects ever undertaken by Geonosian society—the building of colossal numbers of Battle Droids for the Trade Federation and their Separatist allies. The tremendous income from these projects has secured Poggle's power, but this situation could change, as it has done in the past. The infighting rife in Geonosian society usually makes clients reluctant to place large orders.

Spider emblem of office

Long wattles favored by high-caste Geonosians

Trappings of aristocracy

Bracelets represent number of prime hives under Poggle's control

Command staff

Expensive visgura thread made from extinct cave spider's giant egg cases

Wings not used after youth

Additional pair of antlers grow each standard year

Armored hide

Exoskeletal flexibility joint

Blade-like images are common in Geonosian art, reflecting the violence of Geonosian society. Poggle is rumored to have had his political opponent murdered in a coup and to carry the rival's limb bones as a staff.

Toe structure allows Geonosians to cling to rock crags

Common on both Geonosis and neighboring Tatooine, massiffs are emblems of authority for Geonosian aristocrats, who keep them as pets. Massiffs also rid the hives of vermin in return for safety from predators outside.

Sharpened tip used to prod inferiors

119

Trade Federation Battle Droids

THE WEALTHY TRADE FEDERATION is a key faction in the Separatist movement, supplying its army of Battle Droids. The Trade Federation's defeat in the Battle of Naboo made clear the need for stronger, more independent infantry forces, and thus the Super Battle Droids were commissioned as improvements on their standard, skeletal-form predecessors. Like the terrifying droideka, these military-grade robots violate Republic regulations on private security forces, but the Neimoidians have too much influence to fear the galactic courts. Count Dooku himself arranged the deal in which a large force of Super Battle Droids are being secretly manufactured within the droid foundries of Geonosis, building even greater power for the Separatists.

Neimoidians are too fearful to fight their own battles and too deceitful to trust living soldiers, preferring to use Battle Droids for their nefarious purposes. Often criticized for their cowardliness, they have found Count Dooku surprisingly supportive of their mechanized army.

Main signal receptor unit buried in reinforced armor

Arms stronger than Battle Droid limbs

Thick acertron armor protects primary power unit in chest

Enhanced signal receptor package

Broad areas most heavily armored

Dehumanized silhouette increases intimidation effect

Limbs remain narrow in forward silhouette for target minimization

High center of gravity balanced by movement algorithms

Super Battle Droid

The tough and durable Super Battle Droid's armor and reinforced joints sacrifice some mobility for improved protection. For economy, the design makes use of standard Battle Droid internal components, but packages them in a much stronger shell.

Flexible armored midsection

Cryogenically-tempered body-shell elements are hardened, but flex slightly under stress to reduce breakage

Standard Trade Federation Battle Droids are still in use, having proven effective at policing subject populations.

Heavy shoulder armor protects command signal receptor

DATA FILE

◆ The droidekas' superior construction and design explains their high cost, which is over 200 times the price of a Battle Droid.

◆ Unlike droidekas, humans cannot carry personal shield generators because of the technology's high radioactivity.

Heavy droideka can project its own defensive shield

Complex form can fold up into a ball shape for movement to battle site

Custom-made blaster units use high-pressure blaster gas

Handtip contains firing impulse transmitter to trigger standard blaster weapons

Blaster hands built only for battle

Droideka

Heavy-duty droidekas are invulnerable to standard blaster weapons and Jedi lightsabers. These fearsome and illegal assault robots have been known to blast even their owners if not perfectly operated. Neimoidian lawyers have helped the Colicoid manufacturers of the droideka evade costly death and damage lawsuits.

Recess on hidden inner surface to reduce weight

High-torque motors

Firing impulse generators

Excess heat radiated through calf vanes

Shinplate hard-forged in one piece

Reinforced ankle joint

Strap-on foot tips can be replaced with claws or pads suited to different terrain

Monogrip hands lack dexterity but are hard to damage

Knee joint bearings hermetically sealed

Geonosian Drones

LEGIONS OF DRONES serve the Geonosian aristocracy and live within the rigid dictates of hive society. The three biologically distinct castes of drones have been further altered by genetic modification and selective breeding to produce drones specialized for many roles inside the hive. Drones have few rights, limited exercise of free will, and are executed with little concern if they prove aberrant, as there are always more to take their place. For the average drone, with its limited mentality, such a life of communal work is the only one it would want.

Drones have no rooms, possessions, or personal space of their own. To conserve resources for Geonosian rulers, drones may be ordered into sleep-like stasis when they are not needed, reducing their requirements for food and space.

Geonosian sentries stand guard against hive invaders, which may be large verminous creatures or drones from rival hives. Geonosian intruders may be seeking to raid them, sabotage their works, or shift the balance of power by assassinating rulers.

BINDERS WORN BY CAPTIVES

Charged tip delivers shock

Insulated grip

Electronic release mechanism

Pulse lock points weld hasp tight

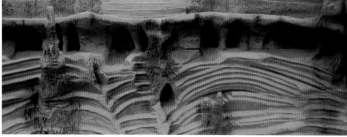

Rather than sacrifice hive resources to support prisoners, Geonosians make captives serve as public entertainment in the arena, where they are subjected to combat against vicious beasts or each other. These entertainments reinforce the power of Geonosian rulers and pacify the drone masses with violence.

Vestigial wings of service drone

Tether tie-offs

Saddle horn provides grip for rider

Saddle rig

Rim beading decoration

Strong neck vertebrae carry heavy head

Small braincase of drone

Elongated snout for digging into egg caches

Tail stinger amputated

Drone harness styles vary little

Blunt teeth for mashing eggs

ORRAYS

Tame orrays carry picadors in the arena. In antiquity, orrays hunted for the mass deposits of Geonosian eggs laid to start a new hive, devouring thousands of larvae in a single meal.

Picador

The picadors control the creatures and criminals in the arena. The position is one of the few of note to which a drone can aspire. Drones of any caste may become picadors if they prove themselves in the arena, after which they are allowed to learn the work of goading beasts and removing bodies.

Anodized staff

STATIC PIKE

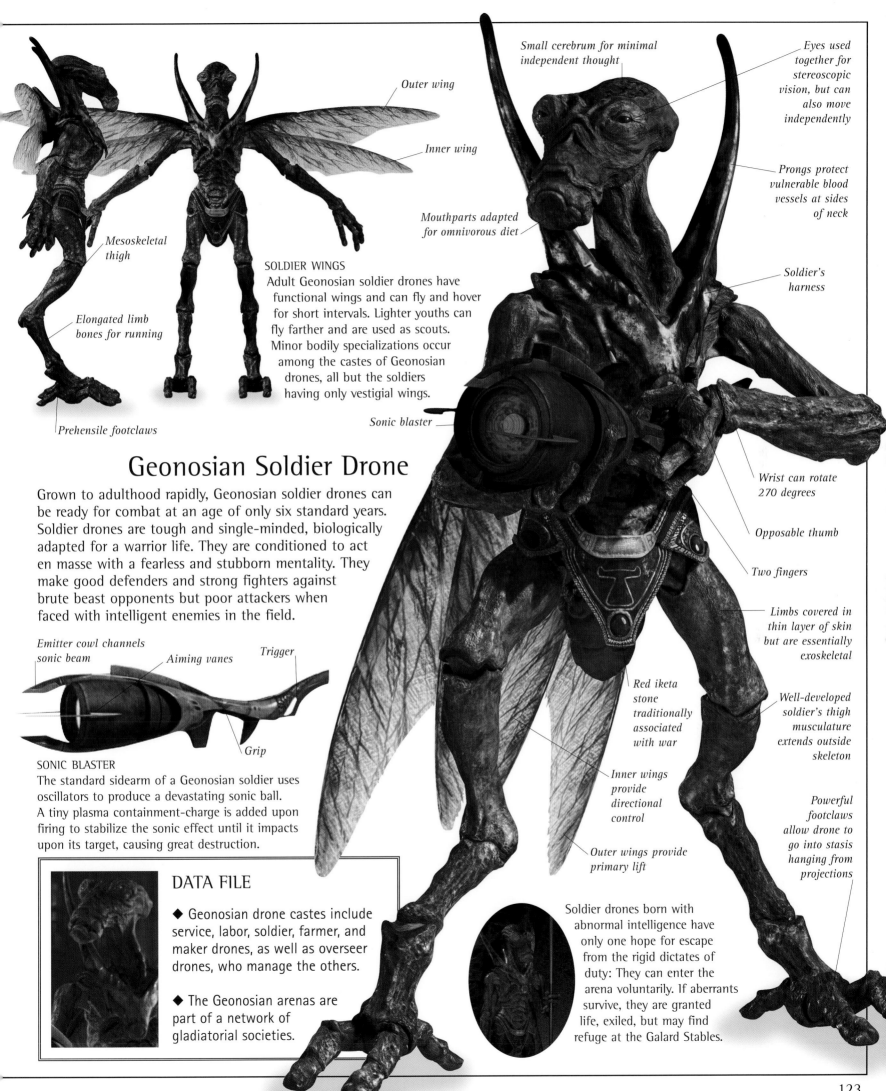

Outer wing

Inner wing

Mesoskeletal thigh

Elongated limb bones for running

Prehensile footclaws

SOLDIER WINGS
Adult Geonosian soldier drones have functional wings and can fly and hover for short intervals. Lighter youths can fly farther and are used as scouts. Minor bodily specializations occur among the castes of Geonosian drones, all but the soldiers having only vestigial wings.

Small cerebrum for minimal independent thought

Eyes used together for stereoscopic vision, but can also move independently

Mouthparts adapted for omnivorous diet

Prongs protect vulnerable blood vessels at sides of neck

Soldier's harness

Sonic blaster

Wrist can rotate 270 degrees

Geonosian Soldier Drone

Grown to adulthood rapidly, Geonosian soldier drones can be ready for combat at an age of only six standard years. Soldier drones are tough and single-minded, biologically adapted for a warrior life. They are conditioned to act en masse with a fearless and stubborn mentality. They make good defenders and strong fighters against brute beast opponents but poor attackers when faced with intelligent enemies in the field.

Opposable thumb

Two fingers

Emitter cowl channels sonic beam

Aiming vanes

Trigger

Grip

Limbs covered in thin layer of skin but are essentially exoskeletal

Red iketa stone traditionally associated with war

Well-developed soldier's thigh musculature extends outside skeleton

SONIC BLASTER
The standard sidearm of a Geonosian soldier uses oscillators to produce a devastating sonic ball. A tiny plasma containment-charge is added upon firing to stabilize the sonic effect until it impacts upon its target, causing great destruction.

Inner wings provide directional control

Outer wings provide primary lift

Powerful footclaws allow drone to go into stasis hanging from projections

DATA FILE

◆ Geonosian drone castes include service, labor, soldier, farmer, and maker drones, as well as overseer drones, who manage the others.

◆ The Geonosian arenas are part of a network of gladiatorial societies.

Soldier drones born with abnormal intelligence have only one hope for escape from the rigid dictates of duty: They can enter the arena voluntarily. If aberrants survive, they are granted life, exiled, but may find refuge at the Galard Stables.

Arena Beasts

CONDEMNED PRISONERS and gladiators face a terrifying array of monsters in the Geonosian arenas. Common criminals are strung up or let loose with the beasts, which are released from underground hive pens. Many of these creatures behave in predictably gruesome and crowd-pleasing ways, and some are trained by their keepers to maximize their more hideous behaviors. The most crowd-pleasing spectacle is saved for last, when rare beasts from far-flung star systems are released into the arena to savage criminals deserving of special attention.

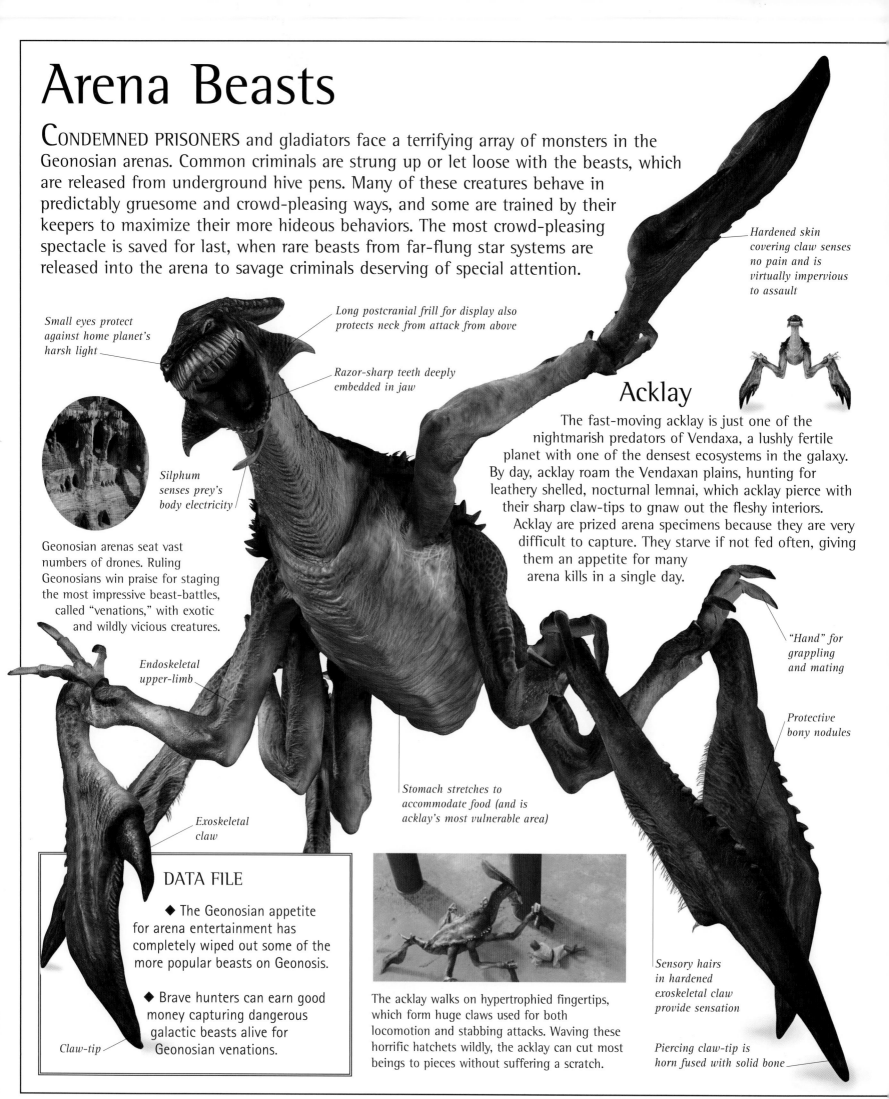

Hardened skin covering claw senses no pain and is virtually impervious to assault

Small eyes protect against home planet's harsh light

Long postcranial frill for display also protects neck from attack from above

Razor-sharp teeth deeply embedded in jaw

Silphum senses prey's body electricity

Acklay

The fast-moving acklay is just one of the nightmarish predators of Vendaxa, a lushly fertile planet with one of the densest ecosystems in the galaxy. By day, acklay roam the Vendaxan plains, hunting for leathery shelled, nocturnal lemnai, which acklay pierce with their sharp claw-tips to gnaw out the fleshy interiors. Acklay are prized arena specimens because they are very difficult to capture. They starve if not fed often, giving them an appetite for many arena kills in a single day.

Geonosian arenas seat vast numbers of drones. Ruling Geonosians win praise for staging the most impressive beast-battles, called "venations," with exotic and wildly vicious creatures.

"Hand" for grappling and mating

Endoskeletal upper-limb

Protective bony nodules

Stomach stretches to accommodate food (and is acklay's most vulnerable area)

Exoskeletal claw

DATA FILE

◆ The Geonosian appetite for arena entertainment has completely wiped out some of the more popular beasts on Geonosis.

◆ Brave hunters can earn good money capturing dangerous galactic beasts alive for Geonosian venations.

Claw-tip

The acklay walks on hypertrophied fingertips, which form huge claws used for both locomotion and stabbing attacks. Waving these horrific hatchets wildly, the acklay can cut most beings to pieces without suffering a scratch.

Sensory hairs in hardened exoskeletal claw provide sensation

Piercing claw-tip is horn fused with solid bone

Semi-prehensile tail
wraps around
branches for
stability

Quills erect
during combat

Secondary
eyes for
heat vision

Nexu

Native to Cholganna, the nexu
lives and hunts in cool forests.
Its secondary eyes see in
infrared wavelengths, allowing it to spy the
tell-tale heat signatures of warm-blooded
prey, especially the arboreal octopi it relishes,
but also the stoutly-built bark rats that form
the bulk of its diet. The nexu seizes prey in its
broad, toothy mouth, then bites and shakes the
creature to death. Sharp quills on the nexu's
back discourage attack from above.

Fur for insulation
in cool environment

Short, secondary claw
for gripping treetrunks
on home planet

Wide gape

Sprawling stance allows broad
footing on leafy canopies

Primary claw for attacking prey

Fleshy and plodding, the reek is
nonetheless a strong beast and a powerful
fighter. The reek's powerful jaw muscles
are built to chop tough wood-moss
chunks into pieces, but its
bite can nip limbs off
even more easily.

Red coloration produced
by unnatural meat diet

Central horn
for goring
opponent (in
wild, used in
dominance
combat with
other reek)

Tough skin

Reek

Reek live on the Codian
Moon, where small
herds are highly
territorial over their patches of
wood-moss turf. Unfortunately
for the herbivorous reek, it
was discovered that the
beast can be starved into
carnivorism to provide
excellent entertainment
in the arena. Fed on
meat alone, the reek
will die, but arena
specimens are given
just enough plant
food to keep
them hungry
and strong.

Horn-teeth grow
continuously

Mottling identifies
subspecies

Cheek horns for dominance-
combat headlocks

Sprawling posture makes
reek relatively slow-moving

Front claws
for digging
wood-moss

Pullback for cutting sweep

Jedi in Battle

JEDI KNIGHTS use their powers of subtle perception to resolve conflicts through negotiation and diplomacy. They seek peace through justice, knowing that true harmony can rarely be forced upon a situation. Nonetheless, mystical philosophy has never blinded the Jedi to the practical need for force in intractable situations, and the most studied Jedi diplomats are capable of drawing their lightsabers in an eyeblink when crisis demands it. When war preparations are discovered on Geonosis, Mace Windu is quick to act, leading a Jedi expedition of all available fighters to rescue Obi-Wan Kenobi.

Horizontal parry

Different tentacles detect specific chemical signatures

Kit Fisto

As an amphibian Nautolan from Glee Anselm, Kit Fisto can live in air or water. His head tentacles are highly sensitive olfactory organs that allow him to precisely detect subconscious pheromonal expressions of emotion. This ability allows him to take instant advantage of an opponent's uncertainty.

Jedi utility belt

Even as a senior Council member, Windu wears standard robes

Jedi tunic allows ease of movement in combat

BULTAR SWAN

Jedi Knight Bultar Swan draws in her opponents by minimizing her physical movements, striking suddenly with a flawless attack that may be highly complex, yet executed in a single blaze of motion.

Power indicator

Electrum finish for Council senior only

Crystal chamber

Handgrip

Synthetic leather surcoat

Lightsaber traditionally worn at left

Jedi boots offer excellent traction

As a senior member of the Jedi Council, Mace Windu built a new lightsaber for himself. Displaying the highest standards of precision, it represents Mace's mature abilities as a Jedi leader.

Mace Windu

A Form VII instructor, Mace Windu is one of the best living lightsaber fighters in the Jedi Order. Only high-level masters of multiple forms can achieve and control Form VII. This dangerous regimen cuts perilously close to the Sith focus on physical combat ability.

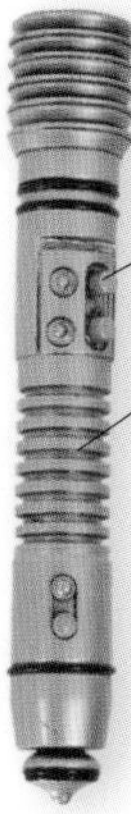

Blade projection
plate

Activator

Activator
matrix

Handgrip
ridges

Blade length
adjust

Blade length
adjust

Radiator
casing segment

**KIT FISTO'S
LIGHTSABER**

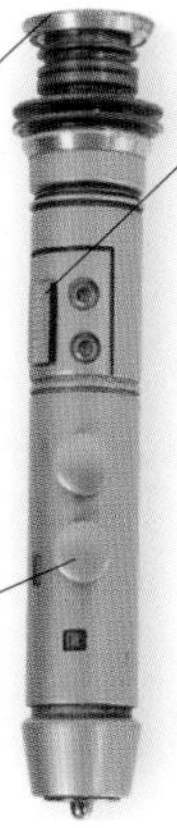

**BULTAR SWAN'S
LIGHTSABER**

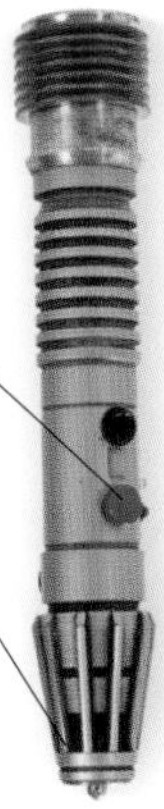

**PLO KOON'S
LIGHTSABER**

JEDI WEAPONS
Every hand-built
lightsaber expresses
the individuality of
its builder, although
there are few
differences in
function.

Shaak Ti

Shaak Ti fights at her best in group combat
as she is biologically adapted for moving in
dense crowds. She darts with
ease through chaotic melees,
where others struggle amidst
the complexity of movements.

Hollow montrals
sense space
ultrasonically

Barriss Offee

The Padawan learner of Luminara
Unduli, Barriss specializes in tandem
fighting. She uses the Force to
harmonize her actions perfectly
with her partner, making for a
pair that is more powerful
than the sum of its parts.

Intense
gaze is
half-inward

Common
lightsaber design

Mirialan
tattoos

Two-handed
grip for
control

Jedi in battle must resist
the temptation to use the
evil power of hate
and anger, even
against Sith enemies.

Headdress conceals
extrasensory organs
sensitive to dryness

Tattoo represents
dedication to
a physical
specialization

Luminara
Unduli

Through many years of
practice, Luminara has
increased her joints'
flexibility to easily allow
extreme lightsaber moves
that are impossible for
ordinary humanoids.

DATA FILE

◆ Special lightsaber
disciplines take advantage
of non-humanoid abilities
such as 360-degree vision.

◆ Jedi train constantly
with their lightsabers,
whether alone on long
field assignments or with
colleagues at the Temple.

Lightsaber Combat

THE LIGHTSABER is a powerful symbol of discipline as well as a weapon. In the hands of the untrained, the lightsaber is worse than useless against modern blasters, and may even injure its user. But in the hands of a Jedi, the lightsaber can become as powerful as any weapon turned against it, deflecting energy bolts back at attackers in a deadly hail and leaving the Jedi wielder untouched. In its highest form, lightsaber combat becomes a subtle and intricate art, but every Jedi begins by learning its first principles.

THE SEVEN FORMS
Seven forms of lightsaber combat have been developed since the foundation of the Jedi Order. Each represents a distinct approach or philosophy, and has its particular strengths. Jedi may specialize in dedication to a particular form or build their own fighting style with elements of multiple forms, although this takes special discipline.

Attack and parry zones

Slashing attacks to the neck are considered zone 2 or 3 attacks

1 head

2 right arm and side

3 left arm and side

4 back

5 right leg

6 left leg

Ready stances

In a ready stance, a Jedi is prepared for combat. Lightsaber forms include many ready stances, but the one called "Jedi ready" is the most common: dominant foot back, blade held in parry position on dominant side.

DEFENSIVE NEUTRAL
In this stance, feet are positioned evenly and the lightsaber is held upward in front of the body. This position presents the maximum amount of blade for deflection of blows or bolts, and maximizes the visual impact of the blade to an opponent as a warning sign. (A Jedi hopes to avoid conflict.)

Blade held toward opponent's eyes

AGGRESSIVE NEUTRAL
In this stance, feet are placed evenly with the point of the blade closest to enemy. It presents the minimum visual blade target for attack and tracking.

Body Zones

Attacks and parries are described in terms of the body zone they concern. "Attack 1" is a blow to the opponent's head, "parry 2" the block of an attack to your right arm or side, and so on. Attack zones are those you see on your opponent, while parry zones are those of your own body. So to go from attack 3 to parry 3, your blade must move from your right side to your left.

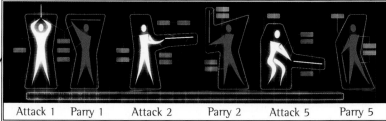

| Attack 1 | Parry 1 | Attack 2 | Parry 2 | Attack 5 | Parry 5 |

IDEAL FORM
In ideal form, attacks are horizontal side swipes and parries are made with the blade upright, pushing the point of the enemy's blade safely away. This rule is reversed for attack and defense of the head, where the attacker slashes down and the defender holds his blade parallel to the ground.

To develop lightning reflexes and tight control, Jedi face each other in drills called velocities. The tenth velocity sequence takes each opponent through a series of attacks and parries and is repeated in turn at ever greater speed until one opponent is felled or yields with the declaration, "Solah!"

Attack 1/Parry 1	Attack 6/Parry 6	Attack 5/Parry 5	Attack 3/Parry 3	Attack 2/Parry 2

Foundations

Jedi in training run lightsaber velocities endlessly to increase their key skills and physical stamina. Building on these basics, Jedi can go beyond what is physically possible, allowing the Force to flow through them. A Padawan practices for the trials of passage using dulon: Solo sequences of moves in which the opponents are only envisioned. The patterns of velocities and dulon prepare a Jedi for the unpredictable realm of live combat.

Two-handed grip gives best control

The Sith use synthetic lightsaber crystals, which generate a stronger blade when energized by the dark side of the Force. The advantage is slim, but the very appearance of a red blade is a symbol of hateful power.

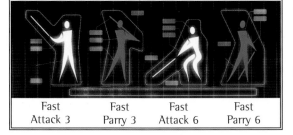

Fast Attack 3	Fast Parry 3	Fast Attack 6	Fast Parry 6

LIVE COMBAT FORM

In contrast to ideal form, in live combat, blade attitude for attack is often angled downward to minimize body movement and increase speed. But keeping in mind the ideal distinction between attack and defense attitudes improves precision.

Parry 4

Parry 1

KAI-KAN
Great lightsaber duels have been studied throughout the ages by sword-masters. Kai-kan are dangerous re-enactments of these combats that only well-trained Jedi attempt.

Drop stance

Push-down parry 3

In advanced lightsaber combat, the Force plays a role larger than physical skill alone. Combatants use Force powers for attack and defense, while Sith attempt to break a Jedi's inner spirit.

JEDI MOVES

JUNG: 180-degree turn
JUNG MA: 360-degree spin to gain power for an attack
SAI: Force-assisted jump to evade an attack to the legs
SHUN: One-handed grip, spinning lightsaber 360 degrees to gain speed for an attack

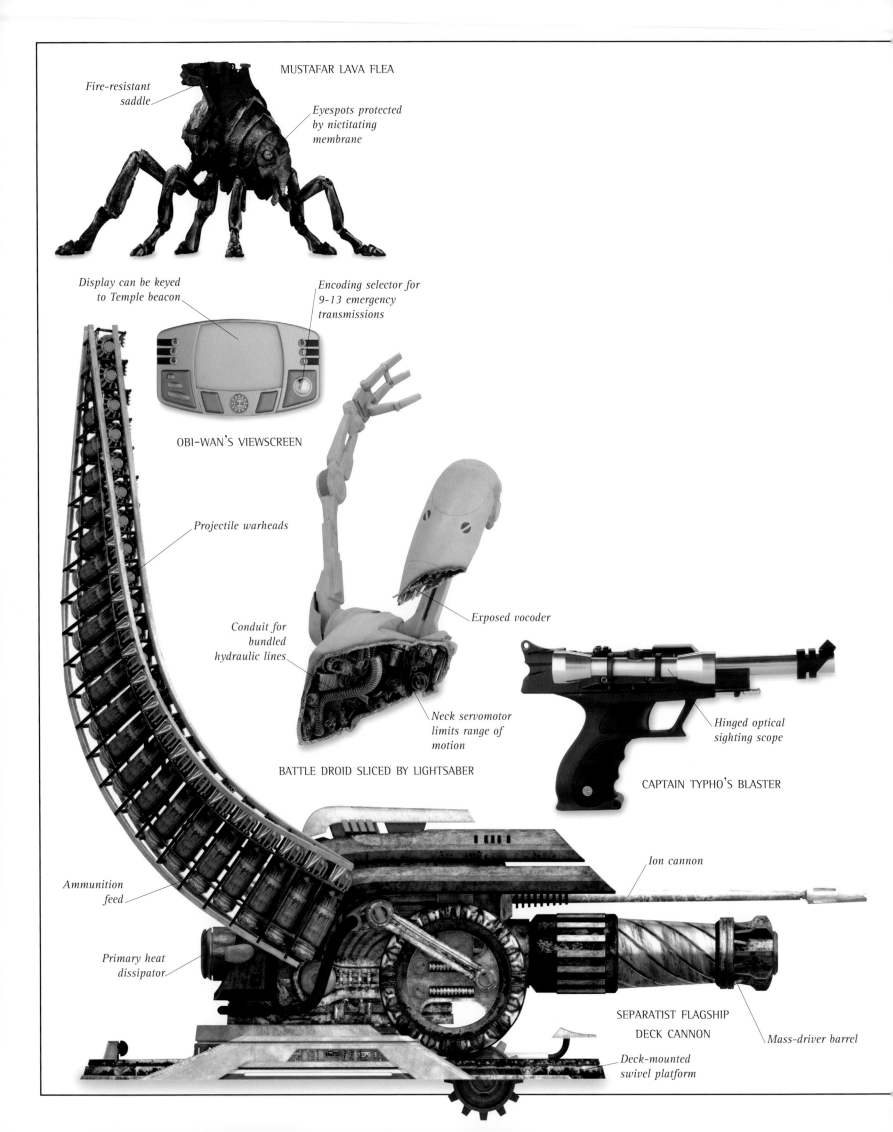

MUSTAFAR LAVA FLEA

Fire-resistant saddle

Eyespots protected by nictitating membrane

Display can be keyed to Temple beacon

Encoding selector for 9-13 emergency transmissions

OBI-WAN'S VIEWSCREEN

Projectile warheads

Exposed vocoder

Conduit for bundled hydraulic lines

Neck servomotor limits range of motion

BATTLE DROID SLICED BY LIGHTSABER

Hinged optical sighting scope

CAPTAIN TYPHO'S BLASTER

Ammunition feed

Primary heat dissipator

Ion cannon

SEPARATIST FLAGSHIP DECK CANNON

Mass-driver barrel

Deck-mounted swivel platform

EPISODE III
REVENGE OF THE SITH

Sᴛᴀʀ WARS: REVENGE OF THE SITH is at once the concluding chapter to events that have shaped the Prequel Trilogy—the era of the Republic—and a tragic prologue to the Dark Times—the 19-year period that witnesses the consolidation of power by Sith Lords Sidious and his pieced-together executioner, Darth Vader. Detailed in this chapter are the key players in the fall of the Jedi Order, the ascendancy of the dark side of the Force, and the emergence of the dreaded Empire, founded on a mad lust for power and fortified by weapons the likes of which the galaxy has never seen. Brought to life in film stills and original art are the exotic locations that serve as stages for this episode, the hardware of galactic warfare, and profiles of the many subsidiary characters caught up in this numbing climax.

Revenge of the Sith is a tale forged in chaos, informed by deceit, betrayal, heartbreak, and the death of heroes. A story almost 30 years in the making, and one that will be told and retold here, and in galaxies far, far away....

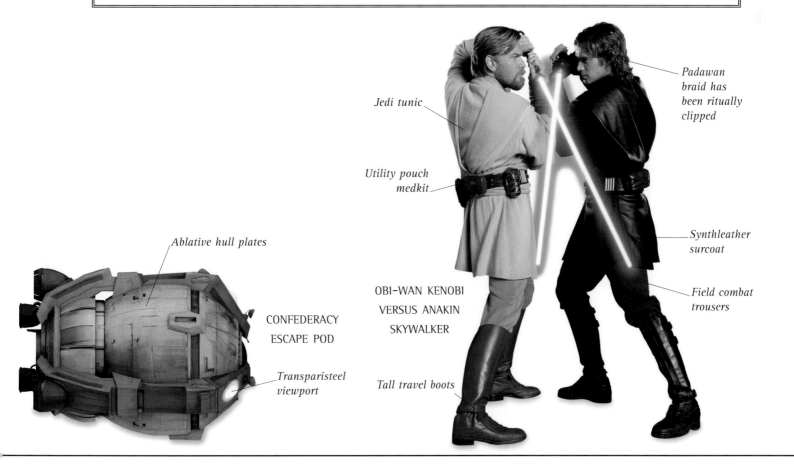

Padawan braid has been ritually clipped

Jedi tunic

Utility pouch medkit

Synthleather surcoat

Ablative hull plates

CONFEDERACY ESCAPE POD

OBI-WAN KENOBI VERSUS ANAKIN SKYWALKER

Field combat trousers

Transparisteel viewport

Tall travel boots

Galactic War

FOR THREE YEARS the Clone Wars have raged across the stars. In deep space and on a host of disparate worlds, the forces of the Republic and those of the Confederacy of Independent Systems (CIS) battle for supremacy. On one side stands a droid army led by a former Jedi named Count Dooku; on the other, an army of cloned soldiers led by the Jedi themselves, the galaxy's one-time guardians of peace. Few can explain why the conflict began, and fewer still understand what is at risk. In fact, the war is being waged by advocates of the dark side of the Force against those who call the Force their ally.

Coruscant

The varied denizens of Coruscant experienced the war from a safe distance, confident in the belief that Supreme Chancellor Palpatine could keep the fighting confined to the outer systems. But in such a conflict no world can remain untouched. So, finally, the war stabs even at the galactic capital itself, with a daring move by the Separatist forces, led by General Grievous, to abduct the Supreme Chancellor, raising the stakes to higher than they have ever been.

Above Coruscant, Republic and Separatist warships attack each other, after Grievous's MagnaGuards and battle droids have abducted Palpatine. Anakin and Obi-Wan Kenobi speed to Palpatine's rescue.

Utapau

An Outer Rim world of vast, arid plains and immense sinkholes, Utapau is a peaceful planet with few ties to either the Republic or the CIS. But, like Coruscant, the planet cannot escape the long reach of the war, and finds itself dragged to the forefront when droid forces under General Grievous's command invade and occupy. The Pau'an and Utai populations know that the liberation of their planet is in the hands of the Jedi Knights.

Kashyyyk

For countless millennia the skillful and resourceful Wookiees have lived in harmony with the towering wroshyr trees that dominate Kashyyyk's lush forests. But the Clone Wars bring changes even here, first with an invasion by Trandoshan slavers in league with the Separatists, then by legions of battle droids dispatched by Grievous to subjugate the entire planet.

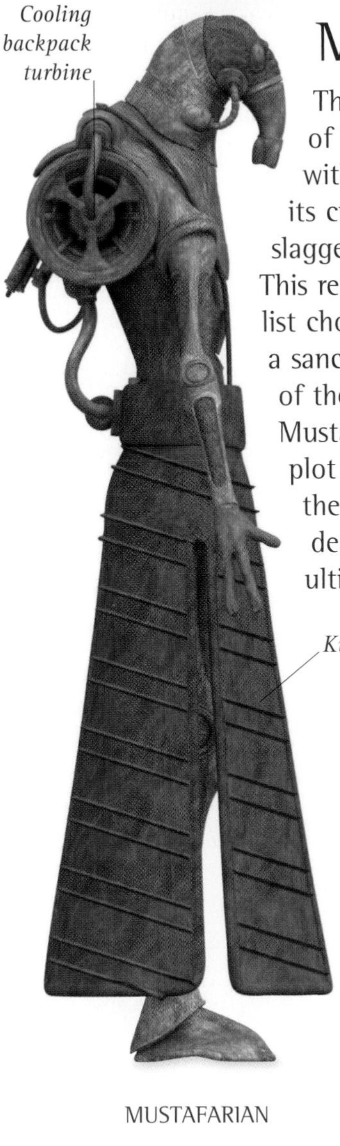

Polarized T-visor
reduces glare

Battle-damaged
chest plastron

Mustafar

The sulphurous skies
of Mustafar are filled
with fire and ash and
its craggy surface is
slagged by ceaseless floes of lava.
This remote planet is the last in a long
list chosen by Darth Sidious to serve as
a sanctuary for the hounded members
of the Separatist Council. On hellish
Mustafar the final acts of the Sith
plot will be played out, resulting in
the deaths of enemies, the
deaths of friends—and,
ultimately, the death of love.

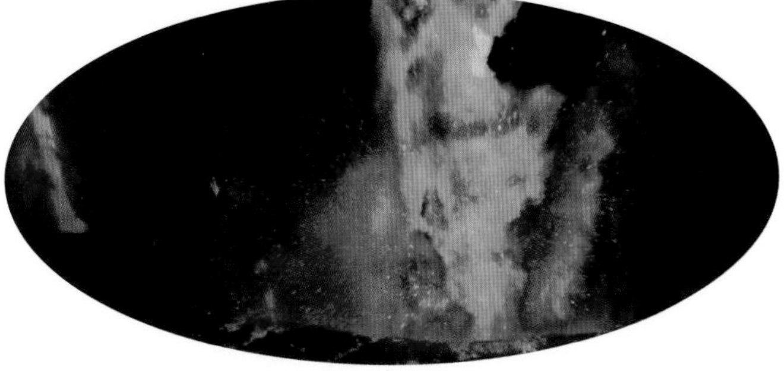

Cooling
backpack
turbine

Kubazian skirt

Standard
DC-15
blaster has a
folding stock

CLONE TROOPER
Symbol of the
Grand Army of the
Republic, the clone
trooper has become a
ubiquitous presence on
embattled worlds
throughout the galaxy.
In the grim theater that
is the Clone War, the
trooper is also a mindless
actor in a diabolical plot
to topple the galaxy
into darkness.

In service to the long-snouted aliens who oversee
the Separatists' smelting facilities on Mustafar, agile
lava fleas leap across the fiery surface.

MUSTAFARIAN

Anakin Skywalker

JEDI KNIGHT

AS THE CLONE TROOPER has become the emblem for the Grand Army of the Republic, Anakin Skywalker—dashing pilot and audacious Jedi Knight—has become the symbol of the Jedi Order and poster boy of the entire war effort. Praised by Supreme Chancellor Palpatine, applauded by the Senate, glorified on the HoloNet News, the "Hero With No Fear" is held by many to be the warrior-savior of the Republic. It is therefore only fitting that Anakin should rescue Palpatine from the evil clutches of General Grievous aboard the giant flagship as it attempts to flee Coruscant.

Electrostatic fingertips allow some feeling

Ideal for outwitting the in-close weaponry of Grievous's flagship, *Invisible Hand*, Anakin's Jedi Interceptor slips along its turreted hull and infiltrates a docking bay.

Ribbing and clamps ensure tight fit

Due to communication blunders among Republic forces, Grievous's flagship is blown in half with Palpatine aboard. Anakin and R2-D2 guide what remains of the ship to a controlled crash on Coruscant.

Armored shielding bulks glove and protects electromotive lines

Alloy ligaments provide pronation and supination

Electrodrivers for pistons

Glove auto-seal

ANAKIN'S GLOVE

R2-D2 in astromech socket

JEDI STARFIGHTER
Anakin asked that his starfighter be painted yellow, allegedly in tribute to the Podracer he flew as a youth, but perhaps to call attention to himself in battle.

Interface modules link prosthesis to surviving nerves

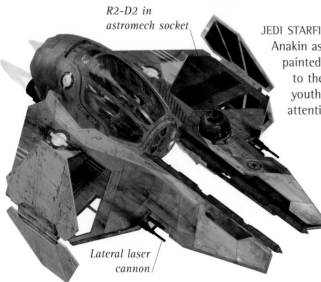

Lateral laser cannon

Cyborg Limb

Some Jedi Council members believe that when Anakin lost his right arm to Count Dooku, he lost some of his humanity. The result has been a chip on his shoulder to go with the prosthesis. In fact, Anakin has always been at ease with technology, and tinkers with his arm as he does his starfighter.

Even though Anakin is envious of Obi-Wan's place on the Jedi Council, they remain the best of friends and the most dynamic of Jedi partners, especially during the Outer Rim sieges.

Anakin believes that the political decisions should be made quickly and decisively. He is free to air his convictions to Supreme Chancellor Palpatine, who is a mentor to him in the ways of the real world.

Gauntlet worn in combat

Synthleather surcoat

Aggressive stance

Chosen One?

Torn by a desire to accomplish great things, Anakin is fearful of change. While he is generally believed to be the Chosen One alluded to in an ancient Jedi prophecy, Anakin frequently finds his hands tied, in the same way that the Senate binds the hands of Supreme Chancellor Palpatine. Nevertheless, he is determined to honor Obi-Wan, and to live up to the title the Jedi have seen fit to bestow upon him.

Utility pouch for emergency rations

Double-Agent

When Palpatine appoints Anakin to the Jedi High Council to serve as his voice, the Council counters by ordering Anakin to spy on the Supreme Chancellor. In addition, the Council withholds from Anakin the title of Master, despite his accomplishments and his mastery of the Force. Discouraged to learn that the Jedi are not above duplicity, Anakin no longer feels guilty about the fact that he has kept secrets from them.

Anakin hasn't seen Padmé—or Coruscant—in almost five months. Their forbidden marriage is yet another lie Anakin has had to maintain since the start of the Clone Wars—a secret he is reluctant to share even with Palpatine, much less with Obi-Wan.

Tunic apron

Military grade trousers

Grappling hook and line

MUSTAFAR

On Mustafar, Anakin's love for Padmé and Obi-Wan mutates to hatred when he convinces himself that his wife and his former Master have betrayed him. A Sith now, having accepted Darth Sidious as his Master and Darth Vader as his name, Anakin shows no remorse in Force-choking Padmé, and engaging Obi-Wan in a duel to the death.

DATA FILE

◆ Anakin's facial scar is a reminder of his encounter with Dooku-trained Asajj Ventress.

◆ Anakin was named a Jedi Knight after his actions on the planet Praesitlyn, where he almost single-handedly saved a Republic communications facility.

UTILITY POUCH

Durable grip-sole boots

General Kenobi

IMPERTURBABLE IN BATTLE, in deep space or planetside, General Obi-Wan Kenobi still prefers negotiation to conflict. The war, however, has given him a longer view of things. Where even his lightsaber technique once reflected an affinity for deflection, his style has since become bolder and more lethal. The cause, many say, is the influence of Anakin Skywalker, and indeed Obi-Wan has become Anakin's champion to those on the Council who dread the power of the Chosen One. As a result of his military successes in the Outer Rim, General Kenobi has been granted the title "Master," and named to the Council. Even so, he feels that his education in the Force is just beginning.

Spacious, pressurized cockpit module

R4-P17 received a full body at the start of the war

Jedi/Bendu-inspired emblem, symbol of the Republic

JEDI INTERCEPTOR
Obi-Wan hates piloting, and has scant regard for astromech or other droids. Yet, he remains Anakin's steadfast wingmate in battle, trusting Anakin to pull them through tricky situations. Just as Anakin has learned patience from Obi-Wan, Obi-Wan has been spurred on to take risks.

Return Bout

Wingtip to wingtip flying is only one aspect of Obi-Wan and Anakin's friendship and mutual trust. They attack Count Dooku in concert aboard the Separatist command cruiser, lulling him into a false sense of confidence by using standard lightsaber tactics, only to shift to advanced forms, forcing a confused Dooku to retreat.

Despite his failure to take Dooku into captivity, Obi-Wan is held in great esteem by the members of the Jedi Council, who conclude that Obi-Wan is the only person skilled enough to capture the elusive and dangerous General Grievous on Utapau.

Rangefinder lock

Cushioned eyecup

JEDI MACROBINOCULARS

Projection platform

Duranium cinch-locks

Casing ring

HOLOPROJECTOR

SEPARATIST BINDERS

Can be uncoupled by the Force

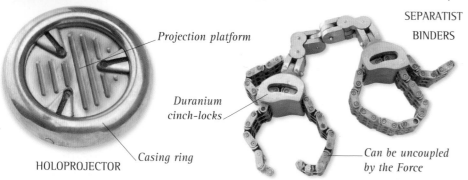

Leaving Anakin to face the hordes of media correspondents that flock to the flagship's crash site, Obi-Wan confers with Yoda regarding their fears that the Sith have been controlling the war from the beginning, and that Darth Sidious himself may be someone close to the Supreme Chancellor.

Powerful tail,
10 meters
(33 feet) long

Spines for defense

Crest present in
both male and
female

Five-clawed
feet provide
excellent
purchase

Unusually grave
expression

Robe is Obi-Wan's
sixth since start
of war

BOGA

On Utapau, Obi-Wan selects a
varactyl that he senses has
a constant commitment
to obedience and care for her rider.
Boga clambers to the tenth level of
Pau City with a swiftness that surprises
even Obi-Wan, only to fall later in
a hail of blaster fire unleashed by
turncoat Clone Troopers.

REBREATHER

The A99 Aquata Breather
Obi-Wan had used on Naboo
13 years earlier serves him all
the more on Utapau.

Compressed-air
tank

Obi-Wan knows that Anakin pines for
Senator Padmé Amidala. Throughout the
war, Obi-Wan has watched Anakin grow
more powerful, willful, and conflicted.

Jedi Tradition

Honoring the wishes of his former
Master, Qui-Gon Jinn, Obi-Wan has
made Anakin his life's focus, and has
instilled in Anakin his belief that the
dark side can be defeated and the
Force brought back into balance.
Yet Obi-Wan worries about
Anakin's refusal to surrender
the past, especially his fixation
with his mother's death.

Security recordings
are stored in the
Jedi Temple
data room

Obi-Wan's worst fears for Anakin are
realized when a Jedi Temple security
recording proves that Anakin has
turned to the dark side, pledged
himself to the Sith, and has
been responsible for the
murder of many Jedi
Knights and
younglings.

Traditional
blue blade

Fabric looks
heavier than it is

DATA FILE

◆ Shortly before the end of the war,
Obi-Wan and Anakin attempt but fail to
capture Dooku's dark-side apprentice,
Asajj Ventress, who remains at large.

◆ Partnered with Obi-Wan during most
of the war, R4-P17 is destroyed by buzz
droids during the Battle of Coruscant.

Jedi Knight

OBI-WAN SHARES Anakin's eagerness to confront Count
Dooku and repay him in kind for the defeat they suffered on
Geonosis. As a Jedi, though, Obi-Wan refuses to let his
emotions cloud his better judgment, and fixes his attention
on Supreme Chancellor Palpatine. "Rescue not mayhem," he
counsels Anakin. Rendered unconscious during the duel,
Obi-Wan does not witness the Count's death. However, he
persuades himself that his willful former Padawan was
forced to act in self-defense and has not skirted close to
what the Jedi consider the dark side of the Force. Obi-Wan
suspects that Palpatine has convinced Anakin that anything
which is possible must be allowed.

*The fight between Obi-Wan
and Anakin leads to the
collapse of Mustafar's shields*

*Utility belt houses pouches
for rebreather, comlink,
and liquid-cable launcher*

Swordmaster

Though a master of the Jedi lightsaber style
known as Ataru, in which deflection is prized
above aggression, Obi-Wan's true style is Soresu,
which encourages a practitioner to place himself
at the eye of the storm. Soresu is well served by
Obi-Wan's innate capacity for patience and
perception, but the key to mastery is audacity,
a talent he has learned from Anakin.

Obi-Wan and Anakin have been partnered for so
long that they can all but read each other's minds
and predict what each other will do.

In Anakin's flair for the
dramatic and his disregard
for the rules, Obi-Wan
finds troubling echoes of
Qui-Gon Jinn. Although
Obi-Wan's student, Anakin
helped mold his Master into
the great Jedi Qui-Gon
always thought Obi-Wan
might be. This is ironic when
Kenobi is forced to fight his own
apprentice whom Qui-Gon ordered
to be trained in the Jedi arts.

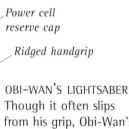

*Power cell
reserve cap*

Ridged handgrip

OBI-WAN'S LIGHTSABER
Though it often slips
from his grip, Obi-Wan's
lightsaber will remain in
his possession for his
19 years of self-exile on
Tatooine, watching over
young Luke Skywalker.

DATA FILE

◆ Obi-Wan is not without his secrets,
including a relationship with Jedi Siri
Tachi, who died saving Padmé.

◆ Obi-Wan is mystified by
Anakin's attachment to R2-D2,
and even more by the astromech's
apparent attachment to Anakin.

*Leading foot is
firmly planted*

Dooku—Sith Apprentice

THE TITLE OF COUNT has no real meaning to Dooku, the former Jedi. It is simply the name of the political leader of the Confederacy of Independent Systems, which itself is nothing more than a fabrication, conceived by Darth Sidious as part of his plan to topple the Jedi Order and reinstate the Sith. For more than a decade now, "Dooku" has thought of himself as Darth Tyranus, apprentice to Sidious and destined to sit at his left hand as joint master of the galaxy.

Signature look of superiority

Costly hand-woven tunic was made on Vjun

A shackled Palpatine watches Dooku and Anakin duel aboard the Separatist flagship. In fact, the abduction is an elaborate ruse, engineered to ensnare Anakin and test him to determine whether he can be turned to the dark side.

Dooku's Jedi and Sith pasts meet as Anakin scissors two lightsabers at his neck. Too late, Dooku realizes Anakin is more powerful than he could have imagined.

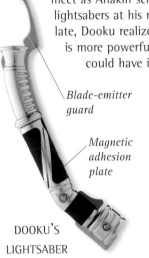

Blade-emitter guard

Magnetic adhesion plate

DOOKU'S LIGHTSABER

Easily Replaceable

Sidious had promised to intervene in the duel, in the unlikely event that Anakin gained the upper hand. But intervention, too, was never part of the real plan. Blinded by pride, Dooku has failed to grasp that, like Darth Maul before him, he is little more than a placeholder for the apprentice Sidious has sought from the beginning: Skywalker himself.

DATA FILE

◆ Dooku's turn to the dark side began with the murder of Jedi Master Sifo-Dyas, his former friend and confidant in the Order. Assuming control of the plans Sifo-Dyas had set in motion to create a clone army for the Republic, Dooku saw to it that all mention of the planet Kamino was erased from Jedi Archives.

Dress boots of rare rancor leather

Separatist Droids

IN THEIR MANAGEMENT of the war, Darth Sidious and Count Dooku carefully ensure parity between the Republic and the Separatists. By preventing either side from attaining firepower superiority, the Sith Lords protract the war just long enough to suit their ultimate goal—the restoration of the Sith Order. Further depleting the coffers of the Trade Federation, the Sith Lords order the production of new ordnance to counter the Republic's latest generation of nimble starfighters. Fearsome, fast, and highly maneuverable, the new breed of Separatist droids threatens the most skilled clone or Jedi pilot.

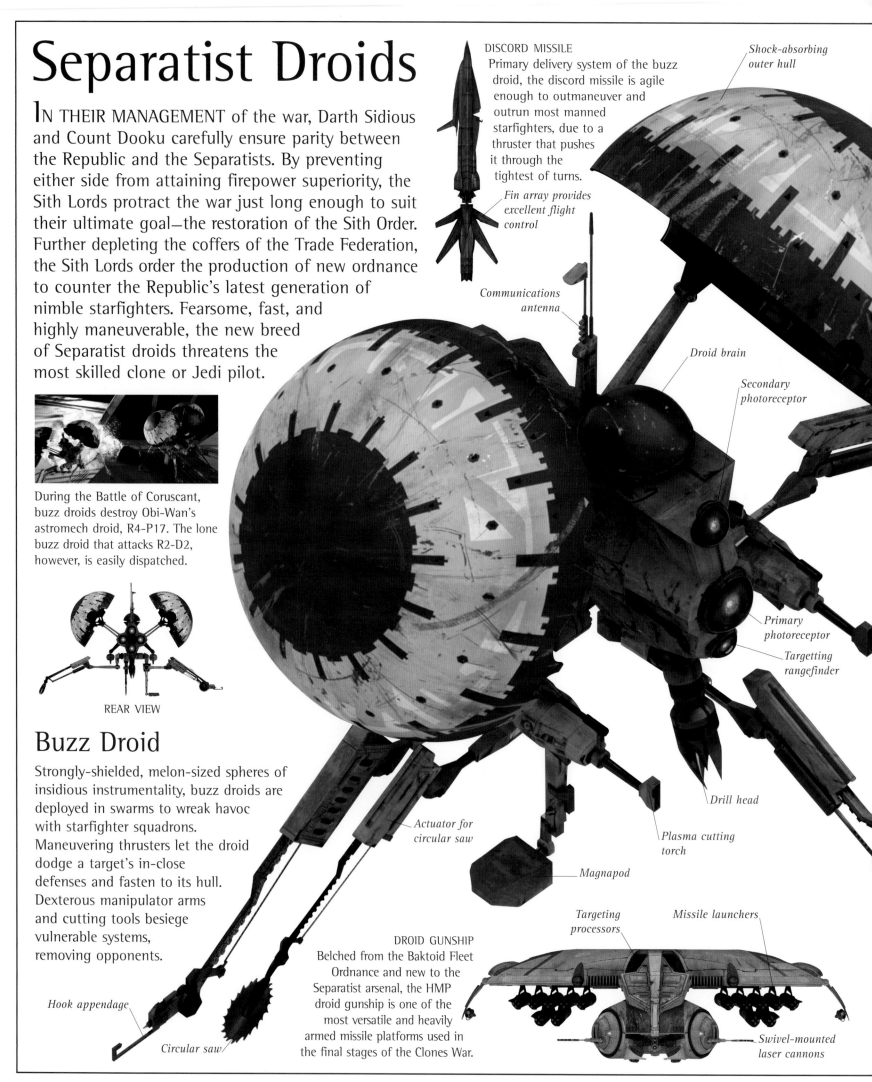

During the Battle of Coruscant, buzz droids destroy Obi-Wan's astromech droid, R4-P17. The lone buzz droid that attacks R2-D2, however, is easily dispatched.

REAR VIEW

Buzz Droid

Strongly-shielded, melon-sized spheres of insidious instrumentality, buzz droids are deployed in swarms to wreak havoc with starfighter squadrons. Maneuvering thrusters let the droid dodge a target's in-close defenses and fasten to its hull. Dexterous manipulator arms and cutting tools besiege vulnerable systems, removing opponents.

Hook appendage

Circular saw

DISCORD MISSILE
Primary delivery system of the buzz droid, the discord missile is agile enough to outmaneuver and outrun most manned starfighters, due to a thruster that pushes it through the tightest of turns.

Fin array provides excellent flight control

Shock-absorbing outer hull

Communications antenna

Droid brain

Secondary photoreceptor

Primary photoreceptor

Targetting rangefinder

Drill head

Plasma cutting torch

Actuator for circular saw

Magnapod

DROID GUNSHIP
Belched from the Baktoid Fleet Ordnance and new to the Separatist arsenal, the HMP droid gunship is one of the most versatile and heavily armed missile platforms used in the final stages of the Clones War.

Targeting processors

Missile launchers

Swivel-mounted laser cannons

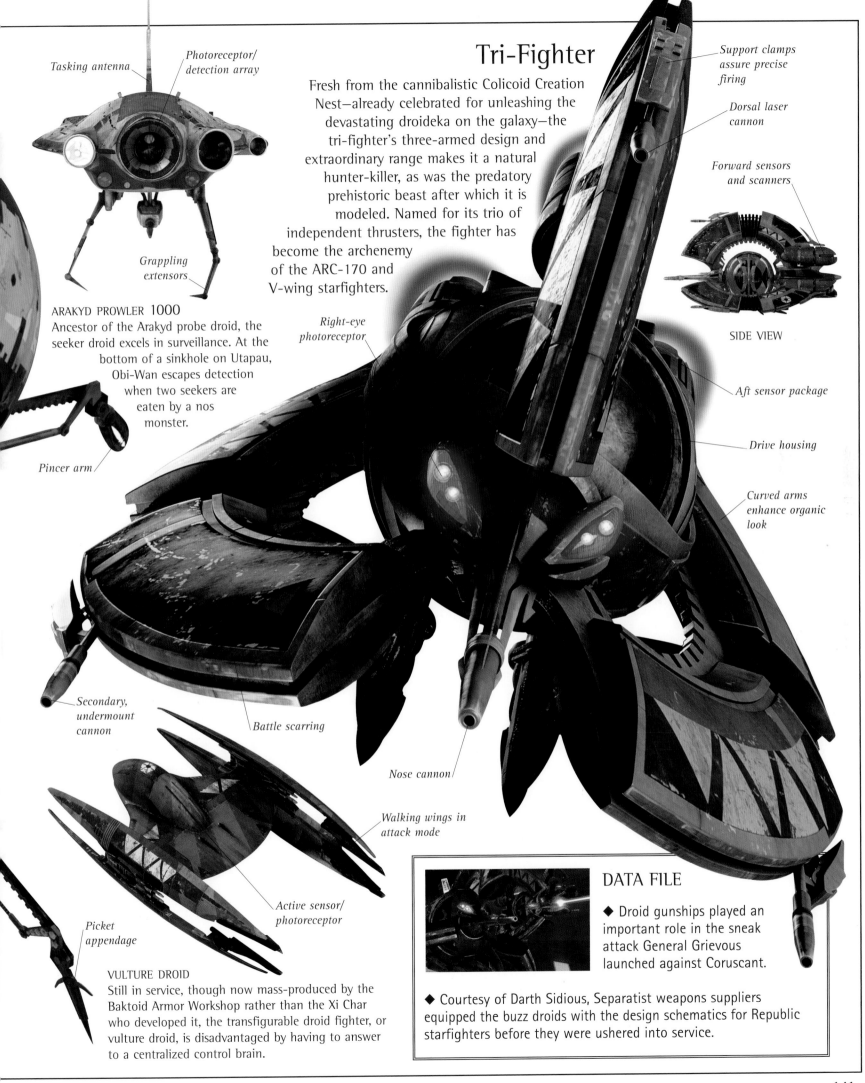

Tri-Fighter

Fresh from the cannibalistic Colicoid Creation Nest—already celebrated for unleashing the devastating droideka on the galaxy—the tri-fighter's three-armed design and extraordinary range makes it a natural hunter-killer, as was the predatory prehistoric beast after which it is modeled. Named for its trio of independent thrusters, the fighter has become the archenemy of the ARC-170 and V-wing starfighters.

Tasking antenna

Photoreceptor/ detection array

Grappling extensors

ARAKYD PROWLER 1000
Ancestor of the Arakyd probe droid, the seeker droid excels in surveillance. At the bottom of a sinkhole on Utapau, Obi-Wan escapes detection when two seekers are eaten by a nos monster.

Pincer arm

Right-eye photoreceptor

Support clamps assure precise firing

Dorsal laser cannon

Forward sensors and scanners

SIDE VIEW

Aft sensor package

Drive housing

Curved arms enhance organic look

Secondary, undermount cannon

Battle scarring

Nose cannon

Walking wings in attack mode

Active sensor/ photoreceptor

Picket appendage

VULTURE DROID
Still in service, though now mass-produced by the Baktoid Armor Workshop rather than the Xi Char who developed it, the transfigurable droid fighter, or vulture droid, is disadvantaged by having to answer to a centralized control brain.

DATA FILE

◆ Droid gunships played an important role in the sneak attack General Grievous launched against Coruscant.

◆ Courtesy of Darth Sidious, Separatist weapons suppliers equipped the buzz droids with the design schematics for Republic starfighters before they were ushered into service.

Separatist Ground Forces

THE SUPPLIERS OF SEPARATIST war machines have a long history of manufacturing droids to suit a wide range of uses and environments. The fearsome appearance of the military droids owes much to the fact that the insectoid species involved in the design phase use themselves as models. Faced with glowing photoreceptors that resemble eyes, stabilizers that mimic claws, and laser cannons that might be appendages, the soldiers of the Republic's non-clone ground forces almost forget that they are battling droids, and not living creatures.

BATTLE DROIDS
Mainstay of the Separatist infantry, battle droids are churned out on Techno Union foundry worlds. They answer to central computers, but words confuse them as much as bolts and lightsabers destroy them.

DROIDEKAS
One of the most feared armaments of the Separatist's surface arsenal, the droideka, or destroyer droid, is a self-shielded annihilator, able to deliver devastating packets of raw firepower. Droidekas help capture Obi-Wan and Anakin during their flight from the General's Quarters on Grievous's flagship, with a rescued Palpatine.

Pincer heat exhaust

Armorplast shielding

Reinforced alloy lifting rods

Communication/ sensor stalks

Blast shielding safeguards droid brain

Sensor bulb

Secondary photoreceptor

Targetting rangefinder

Pressurized bolt

Twin blasters

Pincers powered by proprietary motors

Lateral stabilizer

Prongs extend for added purchase

Crab Droid

Known to clone troopers as "The Muckracker," the crab droid is deployed on marshy worlds, such as Utapau. Heavily armored and ranging from surveillance drones that are one meter (three feet) tall to trailblazers that are six meters (twenty feet) tall, the droid can scuttle through muck to create tracks for infantry. Its front pincers also serve as vacuums, slurping up and spewing out lake-bed mud.

Duranium stabilizer can plunge into bedrock

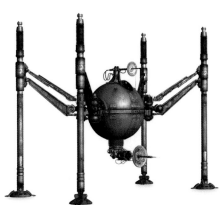

HOMING SPIDER DROID
The Commerce Guild's contribution to the ground war is the homing spider droid. It is an all-terrain weapon capable of precise targeting and sustained beam fire from its laser cannons. With surface-to-air and surface-to-surface abilities, it is a danger to Republic walkers and gunships.

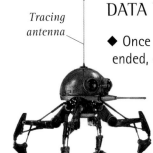

DATA FILE

Tracing antenna

◆ Once Darth Sidious announces that the war has ended, deactivation orders are sent to battle droids.

◆ Most Separatist war machines are deactivated at the end of the Clone Wars, but the dwarf spider droids are used by the Empire to enforce the submission of once-Separatist strongholds.

Hoop drive wheel

Hoop driver

Racks of heat-seeking missiles

Sequenced magpulse drive

Archduke Poggle the Lesser's super battle droid resembles a carapaced beetle, reared up on hind legs. Little more than an infantry droid in a durable shell, the improved model is single-minded about the task of killing.

HAILFIRE DROID
Once used by the InterGalactic Banking Clan for debt collection, the missile platform is a central component of the Separatists' rapid-deployment force. Retired from the battlefield due to its limited supply of 30 warheads, the swift, self-aware hailfire was later partnered with an air-mobile refresh droid, and regained its reputation for being the scourge of slow-moving targets.

NR-N99 Tank Droid

Once employed to persuade corporations of the wisdom of being acquired by the Corporate Alliance, the tank droid quickly became a staple in the Clone Wars, and was deployed to the Separatists' advantage on Geonosis, Kashyyyk, Cato Neimoidia, and many other worlds. An amphibious war machine, the tank can race across flat ground or shallow lakes. The circular-bodied automatons utilized early in the war were replaced by droid-piloted models, featuring superior firepower and targeting. Its treads provide amazing traction, and its side platforms are running boards for infantry droids.

Communications antenna

Tracking transmitter

Stereoscopic sensor

Drive axis hub

Primary drive tread

Modular ion cannon

Heat exchangers

Weapons outrigger

Pontoon tread

Laser cannon

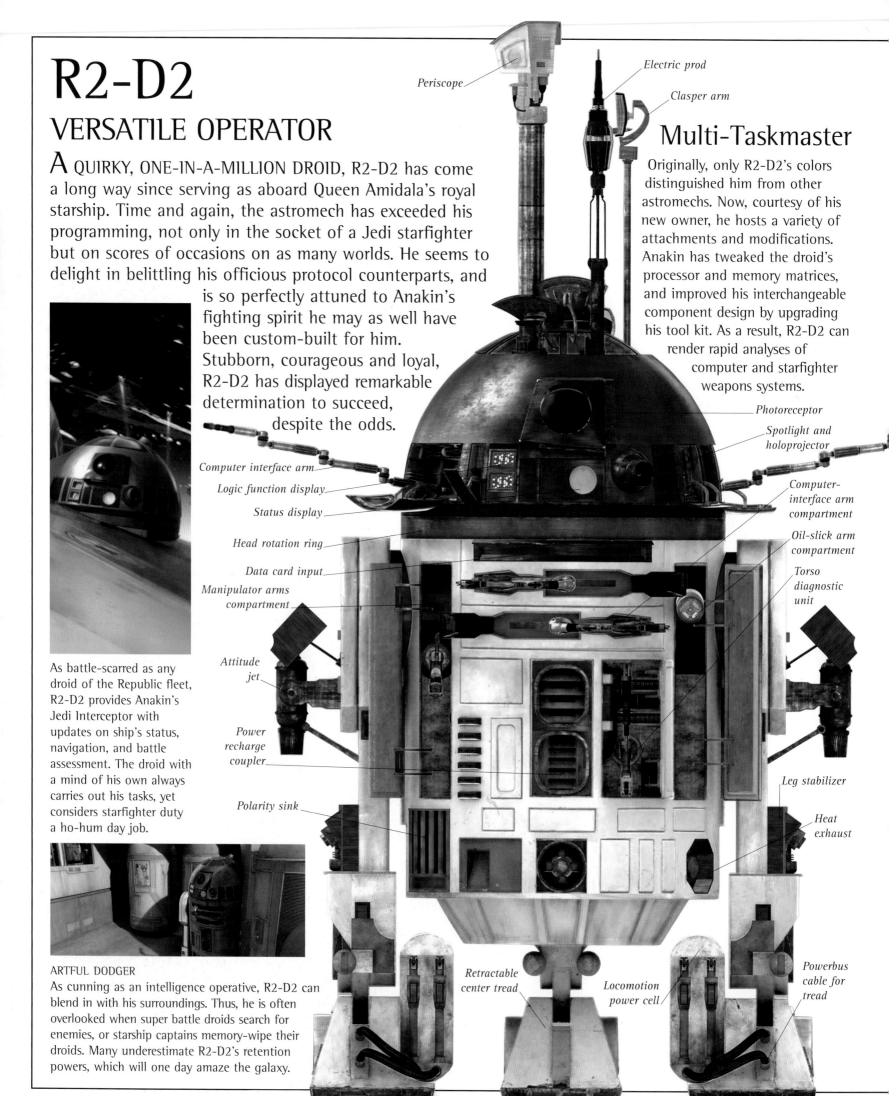

R2-D2
VERSATILE OPERATOR

A QUIRKY, ONE-IN-A-MILLION DROID, R2-D2 has come a long way since serving as aboard Queen Amidala's royal starship. Time and again, the astromech has exceeded his programming, not only in the socket of a Jedi starfighter but on scores of occasions on as many worlds. He seems to delight in belittling his officious protocol counterparts, and is so perfectly attuned to Anakin's fighting spirit he may as well have been custom-built for him. Stubborn, courageous and loyal, R2-D2 has displayed remarkable determination to succeed, despite the odds.

As battle-scarred as any droid of the Republic fleet, R2-D2 provides Anakin's Jedi Interceptor with updates on ship's status, navigation, and battle assessment. The droid with a mind of his own always carries out his tasks, yet considers starfighter duty a ho-hum day job.

ARTFUL DODGER
As cunning as an intelligence operative, R2-D2 can blend in with his surroundings. Thus, he is often overlooked when super battle droids search for enemies, or starship captains memory-wipe their droids. Many underestimate R2-D2's retention powers, which will one day amaze the galaxy.

Multi-Taskmaster

Originally, only R2-D2's colors distinguished him from other astromechs. Now, courtesy of his new owner, he hosts a variety of attachments and modifications. Anakin has tweaked the droid's processor and memory matrices, and improved his interchangeable component design by upgrading his tool kit. As a result, R2-D2 can render rapid analyses of computer and starfighter weapons systems.

Periscope

Electric prod

Clasper arm

Photoreceptor

Spotlight and holoprojector

Computer interface arm

Logic function display

Status display

Head rotation ring

Data card input

Manipulator arms compartment

Computer-interface arm compartment

Oil-slick arm compartment

Torso diagnostic unit

Attitude jet

Power recharge coupler

Polarity sink

Leg stabilizer

Heat exhaust

Retractable center tread

Locomotion power cell

Powerbus cable for tread

R4-G9

On Utapau, Obi-Wan relies on the astromech droid R4-G9 to trick the MagnaGuards into thinking that he is departing. The droid pilots the ship away, while Obi-Wan fades into the shadows.

Recharge power coupling

Head-to-head with a super battle droid in the Federation cruiser hangar, R2-D2 does not even flinch. Although outnumbered, his use of droid bath oil will win the day.

R2-D2 can create diversions when necessary. Held aboard the flagship's bridge, he activates his loudest and most colorful systems to create a pyrotechnic display that lets Obi-Wan recall his lightsaber.

Bronzium finish polished to a dazzling sheen

Audio sensor

Olfactory sensor

Bothersome to many, R2-D2's whistles, shrieks, and twitterings are understood by Anakin, though he relies on his viewpad display screen for translations of the astromech's sound effects.

R2-D2's bickering relationship with C-3PO changes aboard Bail Organa's starship, after C-3PO's memory is wiped to ensure the safety of Padmé's baby twins.

DATA FILE

◆ R2-D2's talent for never revealing more than he has to may be due to Anakin's modifications.

◆ After his memory wipe, C-3PO believes that he first worked with binary load-lifter droids.

A Beautiful Friendship

For R2-D2 and C-3PO, what began as a chance meeting on Tatooine will become an extended partnership, in service to Alderaanian starship captain, Raymus Antilles, and to Princess Leia Organa. Their daring exploits will become legendary, and take them across the galaxy. But only R2-D2 will have full access to their saddest memories.

Supreme Chancellor Palpatine

Hair is always immaculately arranged

Expression promises safety, security, justice, and peace

Senatorial collar

Cummerbund of high office

UNFLINCHING IN HIS ASSERTION that a Republic divided against itself cannot stand, Palpatine has devoted almost half of his unprecedented 13 years in office to vanquishing the Separatist threat. Gracious and unassuming before the outbreak of the Clone Wars, he has since become Democracy's fierce champion, sacrificing his private life to assume the burden of leading the Republic to victory, the Jedi at his right hand, the Grand Army of the Republic at his left. Determined to preserve the Constitution at all costs, he is quick to maintain that he will gladly relinquish the extraordinary powers the Senate has seen fit to cede him, once the Separatists have been eliminated.

The General's Quarters aboard *Invisible Hand* bear an eerie similarity to Palpatine's chambers in the Senate Office Building. When Anakin and Obi-Wan arrive, Count Dooku is there to welcome them. Neither Jedi realizes that Dooku and Palpatine are not enemies to each other, but confederates.

Aboard Grievous's devastated flagship, Palpatine shows remarkable strength and dexterity by negotiating a precarious elevator shaft and corridors turned topsy-turvy by ruined gravity projectors.

Beneath the Mask

To some, Palpatine's guileless smile belies the visage of a shadowy, self-serving politician. Isolated by a covey of advisors, he is frequently at odds with the Jedi Council regarding the course of the war. Adept at manipulating public opinion, he buoys the Republic with carefully controlled HoloNet reports. Bent on executing a hidden agenda, he uses the war to place himself in a position where his word is law.

DATA FILE

◆ Records of Palpatine's ancestry, immediate family members, and upbringing on Naboo have mysteriously vanished.

◆ Captain Panaka, former Head of Security for Queen Amidala, gave Palpatine information regarding Anakin and Padmé's secret marriage.

Ancient demagogue, Sistros

Lethorns have thickened over the years

Speaker's staff

Chagrian cowl

Umbarans conceal their emotions

Palpatine has counseled Anakin in worldly matters, and listened to his dark confessions regarding his anger, his infatuation with Padmé, his frustrations with the Jedi Council, and even his slaughter of a tribe of Sand People on Tatooine. Their almost familial relationship is a cause of great concern to the Council.

Secret Fraternity

Senate Speaker, Mas Amedda, and Aide to the Chancellor, Sly Moore, are two among a select few who understand that Palpatine is more than he appears and that the Chancellor's look of practiced humility belies that of a cunning manipulator of political power. Palpatine's duplicity could ultimately cost them their positions—and their lives.

SLY MOORE

Force pike

Contents unknown

SITH CHALICE

Palpatine declares the Republic an Empire and himself Emperor following the defeat of the Jedi responsible for the hideous change in his appearance.

IMPERIAL GUARD
With the creation of the Empire, the Red Guard becomes the Imperial Guard. Palpatine picked its members from non-clone military units.

Shadowcloak of the Ghost Nebula

MAS AMEDDA

Though his face is irreparably damaged, Palpatine's integrity and resolve are intact and he becomes authority personified. Safety, Security, Justice, and Peace are the bywords of the New Order.

General Grievous

The blade of Jedi Master Puroth

UNKNOWN TO THE JEDI until he battled them on the Separatist foundry world of Hypori, General Grievous was actually present at the Battle of Geonosis. The carnage for which he was responsible, however, was confined to the catacombs that undermined Archduke Poggle the Lesser's Stalgasin hive complex. Named Supreme Commander of the Droid Armies in the wake of Geonosis, Grievous brought new levels of butchery to the war, laying waste to entire worlds and populations, and leaving trails of blood wherever he ventured in the Outer or Mid Rims. Although he is a cyborg, Grievous does not consider himself a droid, and reacts savagely to any such inference—as his victims would attest.

Abetted by Darths Sidious and Tyranus, Grievous carried out the long-planned abduction of Palpatine from the Chancellor's bunker on Coruscant. Unaware that he is serving both Sidious and Palpatine, Grievous does not understand why he cannot assassinate Palpatine.

DATA FILE

◆ Grievous can dislocate his shoulders and split his two arms into four.

◆ The General is secretly humiliated at having been resurrected as a cyborg.

Duranium head

Phrik alloy

Impact-driven release

Retracted claws

High output magazine

BLASTECH CUSTOM
DT-57 "ANNIHILATOR"

Weapons of War

The uniwheel chariot Grievous pilots on Utapau is outfitted with a variety of weapons, including a powerful blaster, an energy staff of the sort wielded by his elite MagnaGuards, and a grappling hook, similar to the one he used at Coruscant to haul himself to freedom along the hull of his crippled flagship.

Power-assisted shaft

GRAPPLING HOOK

Palpatine lures Obi-Wan to Separatist-occupied Utapau. With Kenobi thus occupied, Anakin has no one to guide him and is more likely to listen to the dark side.

Weapons pack

Electromagnetic pulse generator

ENERGY STAFF

Transparisteel viewports

Hyperspace engine

Landing gear

TOP VIEW

FIGHTER
Escaping from Utapau, Obi-Wan learns that Grievous's starfighter is hyperspace-capable. After the clone trooper attack, he transmits a 9-13 Jedi emergency code over the HoloNet repeater.

Original mask
carved from
Mumuu skull

Sallow
reptilian
eyes

Engraved lines simulate
original mask's
karabba-blood war paint

Ultrasonic
vocabulator

Grievous's hatred of the Jedi goes
back to his former life as a Kaleesh
warlord. Grievous captured his
first lightsaber from a Jedi he
defeated, and his collection
has expanded ever since.

Electro-driven
arms can
split in half

Reinforced
knee plates

Leg drivers
house
crystal
circuitry

Upgraded
LX-44
legs

Alien Warlord

Grievous's reputation as a
warlord was forged during a
brutal war between the Kaleesh
and the Huk species. On the brink
of death following a shuttle crash,
Grievous was rebuilt. Neither Force-
sensitive nor a Sith, the cyborg general was trained in lightsaber
combat by Darth Tyranus, and is more than a match for most Jedi.

Powerful
magnetized
talons

Cape contains
sheath pockets
for lightsabers

Alien Cyborg

EVER ON THE ALERT for minions, Darth Sidious himself took an early interest in Kaleesh warlord Grievous. That interest continued through Grievous's reconstruction by Geonosian biotechs after his shuttle crash, with Sidious dispatching medical droids to participate in the surgical and cybernetic procedures. In the end, only Grievous's brain, spinal cord, and internal organs were transferred to the armor that would contain him as a cyborg.

Areas responsible for body coordination have been upgraded

Heuristic combat programming aids in Jedi arts training

Areas related to anger have been tampered with and areas responsible for memory have been altered

Interior of bleached armorplast death mask lined with pin-point electrodes

Grievous's own eyes enhanced with cybernetic implants

It was rumored that the shuttle crash in which the warlord nearly died had been arranged by Darth Tyranus.

Duranium teeth mimic those of Kalee's karabbac beast

Peripheral processors control speed and intensity of arm attacks

Duranium chest plates protect vulnerable gutsack

Gut sack is pressurized synthskin, allowing Grievous to survive in a vacuum

Ultrasonic vocabulator

Six-finger hands have two opposable thumbs

150

Trade Federation

GRIEVOUS'S FLAGSHIP, *Invisible Hand*, is a Trade Federation cruiser, originally intended for Neimoidian viceroy Nute Gunray and his advisors. Because Darth Tyranus had ordered the Neimoidians to surrender to Grievous exclusive control of their battle droid army, Gunray protested the reassignment of his personal cruiser, but his objections fell on deaf ears. As a consolation, Tyranus allowed Gunray to assign Neimoidian navigators and gunnery officers to the bridge crew.

Subordinate's miter

Mottled skin is sign of extreme stress

Tight-lipped expression of wariness

Half-closed eyes

Wave pattern weaved on mantle

Sumptuous brocaded robe

Grievous might have killed Gunray had Tyranus not intervened, warning the General that Sidious was determined to keep the Trade Federation under the Separatist umbrella.

DATA FILE

◆ On Geonosis, Gunray was not aware that Sidious was the real power behind the Confederacy of Independent Systems.

◆ The linear design of *Invisible Hand* was intended to compensate for defense weaknesses inherent in the Lucrehulk ring carriers.

Nute Gunray

The relationship between Viceroy Gunray and General Grievous got off to a rocky start when the two were first introduced on Geonosis by Count Dooku. Used to thinking of droids as utterly disposable, Gunray made the mistake of treating Grievous as just another in a long line of officer drones.

MagnaGuards

STRIDING DEFIANTLY across the surface-ravaged Huk worlds, Kaleesh warlord General Grievous was always accompanied by an elite group of warriors and bodyguards. Rebuilt as Supreme Commander of the Separatist army, he has to content himself with the Trade Federation's battle droids, which answer to a central control computer and are incapable of learning from their mistakes. Apprised of Grievous's disdain for these droids, Darth Tyranus authorizes Holowan Mechanicals to manufacture the Prototype Self-Motivating Heuristically Programmed Combat Droid, or IG-series 100 MagnaGuard, built to Grievous's specifications and trained by him.

The MagnaGuards score a victory on *Invisible Hand*, taking Anakin, Obi-Wan, and Supreme Chancellor Palpatine into custody after the trio are trapped in a ray-shielded stretch of corridor. But General Grievous's gloating is short-lived, however, after a diversionary move by R2-D2 sends the bridge into chaos.

Discharge capacitor

When the smoke clears, the MagnaGuards are in pieces. The remainder of Grievous's elite will suffer a similar fate on Utapau, in a warm-up round for Obi-Wan's match with the cyborg commander.

Inexpensive generic vocabulator *Armored brow ridge* *Primary photoreceptor* *Back-up photoreceptor*

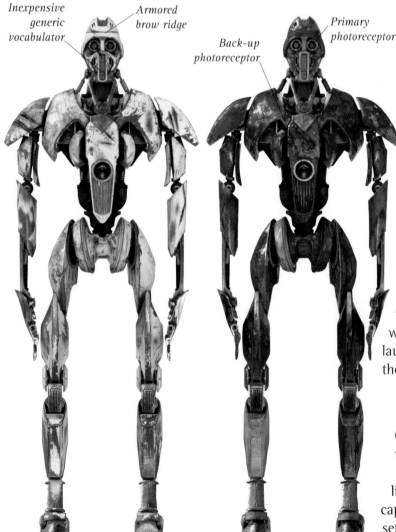

Model Guards

Holowan Mechanicals made several MagnaGuard models, distinguished by color: black, alabaster, blue, and the rare gray. Each two-meter (6.5-ft) tall droid specializes in a form of combat, and is equipped with an electrostaff or dedicated weapons, from grenades to rocket launchers. Headclothes pay tribute to those worn by Grievous's original elite.

Power cycling coil

Power cell

EMP field generator

Focusing rods

Electrostaffs

Constructed of costly phrik alloy and equipped with electromagnetic pulse-generating tips, the MagnaGuards electrostaffs are resistant to lightsaber strikes. While certain types of staff are capable of neutralizing ray shields, the standard staff serves primarily as a melee weapon, meting out fatal blunt-force injuries in the hands of its wielders.

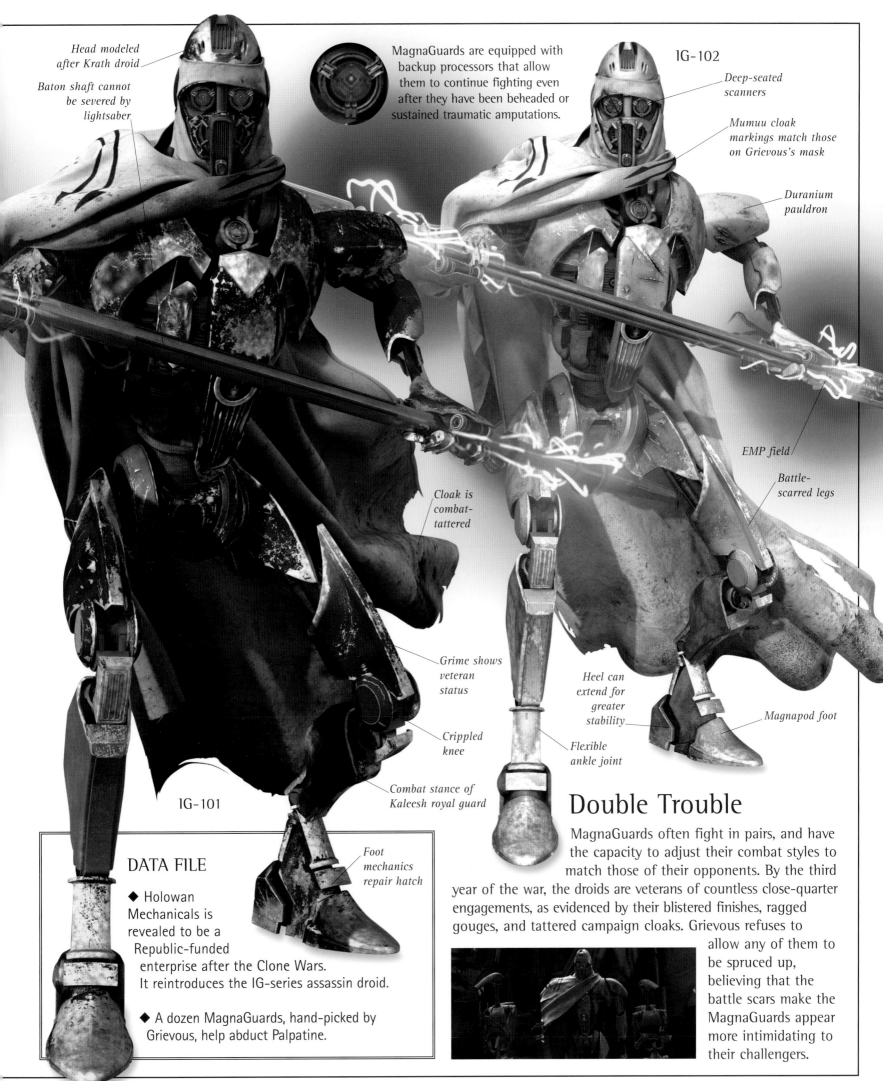

Head modeled
after Krath droid

Baton shaft cannot
be severed by
lightsaber

MagnaGuards are equipped with
backup processors that allow
them to continue fighting even
after they have been beheaded or
sustained traumatic amputations.

IG-102

Deep-seated
scanners

Mumuu cloak
markings match those
on Grievous's mask

Duranium
pauldron

EMP field

Battle-
scarred legs

Cloak is
combat-
tattered

Grime shows
veteran
status

Crippled
knee

Heel can
extend for
greater
stability

Flexible
ankle joint

Magnapod foot

IG-101

Combat stance of
Kaleesh royal guard

Double Trouble

MagnaGuards often fight in pairs, and have
the capacity to adjust their combat styles to
match those of their opponents. By the third
year of the war, the droids are veterans of countless close-quarter
engagements, as evidenced by their blistered finishes, ragged
gouges, and tattered campaign cloaks. Grievous refuses to

Foot
mechanics
repair hatch

DATA FILE

◆ Holowan
Mechanicals is
revealed to be a
Republic-funded
enterprise after the Clone Wars.
It reintroduces the IG-series assassin droid.

◆ A dozen MagnaGuards, hand-picked by
Grievous, help abduct Palpatine.

allow any of them to
be spruced up,
believing that the
battle scars make the
MagnaGuards appear
more intimidating to
their challengers.

Coruscant Ground Crew

WITH TENS OF THOUSANDS of ships arriving on Coruscant at any given moment, an army of landing-platform personnel stands by to assist in off-loading, refueling, and basic maintenance. Considered by many to be work fit more for droids than flesh-and-bloods, most so-called ground crew workers are poorly educated and underpaid.

Emitter for flame-retardant foam

Emergency running lights

Ablative cockpit canopy

FIRE-SUPPRESSION SHIP
Two members of Fire Team Three, a daredevil burn-off brigade, died during the attempt to extinguish the flames engulfing the Separatist flagship when it plunged into Coruscant's upper atmosphere.

Annunciator and siren

TOUCHDOWN
Anakin's ability to pilot the deteriorating flagship to safety is extraordinary. To avoid adding to the massive damage Coruscant has already sustained, he guides *Invisible Hand* to a seldom-used landing platform in the industrial sector.

Heat-resistant faceplate

Integrated heads-up display

Blast-proof goggles

FIRE FIGHTER

MECHANIC

Plastoid helmet contains comlink

Generic utility suit

Breathmask for oxygen supply

BACKPACK UNIT
Fire-suppression is a high-risk job. Due to the exotic nature of the fuels that power some cargo landers and shuttles, shipboard fires often become infernos, costing lives.

High-pressure emitter nozzle

Backpack is made of lightweight alloy

Discharge trigger

Heat-resistant and weatherproof housing

Fire Brigades

At the highest end of the ground-crew spectrum are the skilled workers of Coruscant's fire-fighting teams. Some are headquartered mid-level in the sheer cityscape, while others patrol the autonavigation lanes that striate the upper reaches of the galactic capital's skies.

Boot-guards impregnated with lead

Slop footwear

DATA FILE

◆ After the war, many clone troopers retired from service because of battlefield injuries, innate deterioration, or accelerated aging.

◆ These troopers will be reassigned to boost landing platform-maintenance and emergency rapid-reaction squads.

Coruscant High Life

CORUSCANT SEEMS MUCH AS it was ten years earlier, before anyone considered Count Dooku's Separatist movement a threat. However, clone troopers now stand guard at landing platforms and public buildings, and new laws allow searches and seizures of private property. The war has made many Coruscanti wealthy, and Senators still enjoy the kickbacks to which they have grown accustomed.

By good fortune or design, Palpatine managed to keep the surface battle from escalating. After his abduction, however, the mood in the capital grows tense, and disquieting rumors spread.

Command cap is as phony as rank

Artificially colored lekku

WAKS TRODE

Wide-angle vision

Sy Myrthian mantilla hides secret recording device

RYSTÅLL SANT

Crime-syndicate concubine hairstyle

GREEATA   CPT. FAYTONNI   KOYI MATEIL

OPERA DRESS
Nights at the opera are occasions for revelry and excess. Many patrons wear costumes that rival those worn by the performers.

DELVA RACINE

Privileged Few

Many new restaurants and clubs have opened on Coruscant. But the elite prefer to gather at the Galaxies Opera House for performances by troupes from many star systems. Palpatine often attends, if his schedule permits, preferring Galaxies to the older opera house patronized by wealthy members of the Valorum family.

DATA FILE

◆ A Mon Calamari performance is in progress when Anakin arrives at Palpatine's private box, where he is told that clone intelligence has discovered the whereabouts of Grievous.

◆ It is thought that Baron Papanoida may be a double agent.

BROOKISH BOON

Padmé—Tragic Heroine

TIME AND AGAIN Padmé has found herself at the center of galactic events. Her illegal presence on Geonosis to effect the rescue of Obi-Wan Kenobi is seen by some as the spark that ignited the Clone Wars. Padmé has earned a reputation for boldness, but now she is torn by choices she has made in her private life, and she sometimes dreams of retiring into seclusion on Naboo. However, her activist side is not easily suppressed.

Elaborate coiffure originated on Naboo

Heirloom suspensas

Rich cape enfolds Padmé completely

In the three years since their secret marriage on Naboo, Padmé and Anakin have found refuge in each other's embrace. But their trysts have been brief and clandestine. They haven't met in five months when Palpatine's abduction returns Anakin to Coruscant.

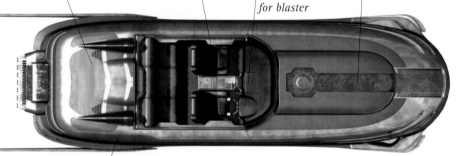

Anti-tracking device

Tractor field seats

Secret compartment for blaster

Souped-up engine

Aerodynamic yet classic styling

CLASSIC SPEEDER
Padmé's classic-style speeder whisks her to and from the landing platform where her starship is berthed. Anakin has modified the speeder's engine.

Senator

Padmé's voice in the Senate is still as powerful as it was before the start of the war. While Anakin commands legions of clone troopers in the Outer Rim, Padmé and other members of the Loyalist Committee attempt to find peaceful resolution to the ongoing conflict. Yet her critics say that she has turned a blind eye to the increasingly oppressive climate on Coruscant, to the loss of rights guaranteed by the Constitution, and to the growing power of Palpatine.

DATA FILE

◆ Handmaidens Moteé and Ellé were chosen because they resemble Padmé. They know of her marriage to Anakin, and often facilitate the couple's meetings by serving as decoys.

◆ After the massacre at the Jedi Temple, the official explanation is that Padmé and many Senators had been killed by the Jedi.

Ensconced in Naboo's platform in the Senate Rotunda, Padmé witnesses the death of democracy, as Palpatine proclaims the Republic an Empire, and himself Emperor for life. The ovation he receives shows that anyone can fall victim to the machinations of an evil leader.

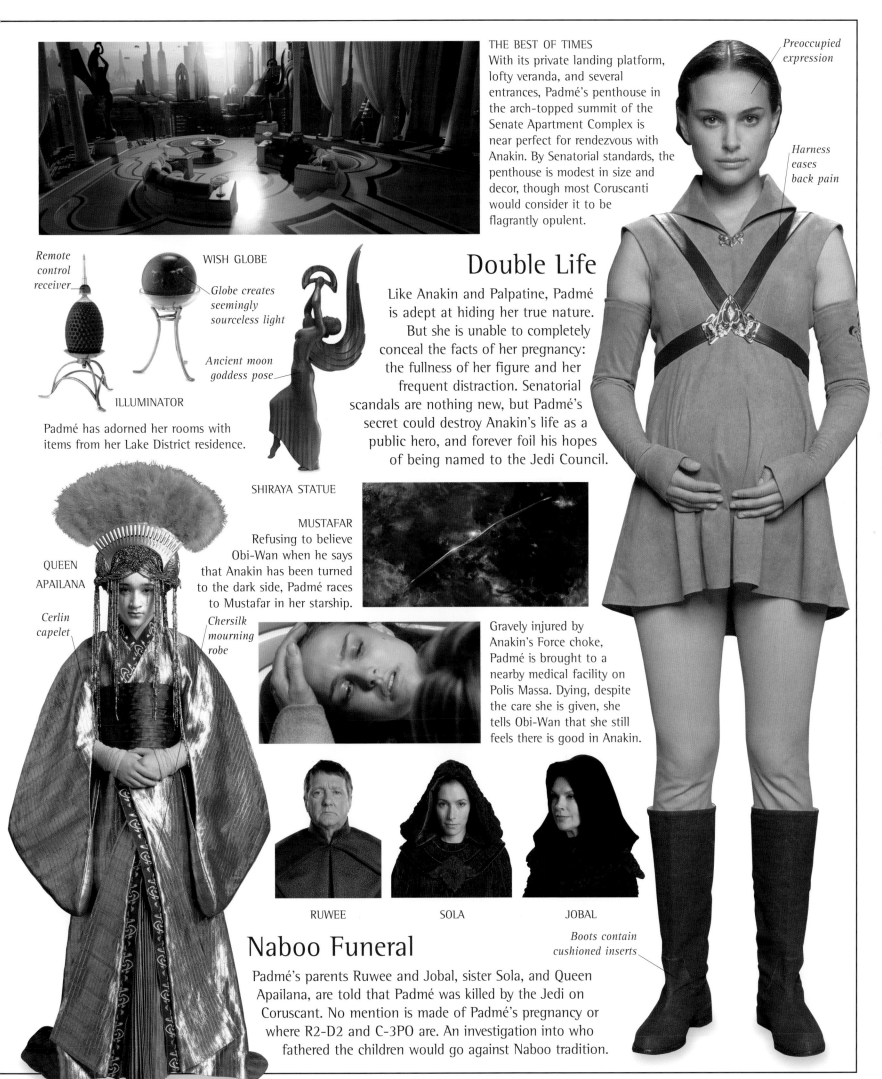

THE BEST OF TIMES
With its private landing platform, lofty veranda, and several entrances, Padmé's penthouse in the arch-topped summit of the Senate Apartment Complex is near perfect for rendezvous with Anakin. By Senatorial standards, the penthouse is modest in size and decor, though most Coruscanti would consider it to be flagrantly opulent.

Preoccupied expression

Harness eases back pain

Remote control receiver

WISH GLOBE

Globe creates seemingly sourceless light

Ancient moon goddess pose

ILLUMINATOR

Padmé has adorned her rooms with items from her Lake District residence.

SHIRAYA STATUE

Double Life

Like Anakin and Palpatine, Padmé is adept at hiding her true nature. But she is unable to completely conceal the facts of her pregnancy: the fullness of her figure and her frequent distraction. Senatorial scandals are nothing new, but Padmé's secret could destroy Anakin's life as a public hero, and forever foil his hopes of being named to the Jedi Council.

MUSTAFAR
Refusing to believe Obi-Wan when he says that Anakin has been turned to the dark side, Padmé races to Mustafar in her starship.

QUEEN APAILANA

Cerlin capelet

Chersilk mourning robe

Gravely injured by Anakin's Force choke, Padmé is brought to a nearby medical facility on Polis Massa. Dying, despite the care she is given, she tells Obi-Wan that she still feels there is good in Anakin.

RUWEE   SOLA   JOBAL

Boots contain cushioned inserts

Naboo Funeral

Padmé's parents Ruwee and Jobal, sister Sola, and Queen Apailana, are told that Padmé was killed by the Jedi on Coruscant. No mention is made of Padmé's pregnancy or where R2-D2 and C-3PO are. An investigation into who fathered the children would go against Naboo tradition.

The Senate
FAILING DEMOCRARY

WHERE GREED AND CORRUPTION defined the pre-war Senate, dereliction of duty and indolence have been the bywords since. Reasoned discourse and spirited debate are now viewed as archaic practices, impediments to the "efficient streamlining of the bureaucratic process." In the climate of fear spawned by the war, most Senators find it easier—some say safer—to place their personal convictions on hold, and to ratify any piece of legislation that cedes greater power to Supreme Chancellor Palpatine or to any of the committees responsible for overseeing the war effort. Typically, the Senate is so busy modifying the Republic Constitution that it has completely abandoned its role as a balancing arm of the government.

Republic Senate

Executive Annex Dome

SENATE BUILDING
Rising from the center of the Legislative District, the Senate comes under attack by vulture fighters and droid gunships during General Grievous's sudden raid on Coruscant. While the building emerges unscathed, nearby edifices, landing platforms, and plazas suffer major damage. In the Nicandra Counterrevolutionary Signalmen's Memorial Building alone, fatalities number in the thousands.

FANG ZAR

Sern Prime topknot

High-status beard

Senatorial gown

Fashionable translator

Kuati turban

Formal shoulder sash

GIDDEAN DANU

Hairstyle is a plea for peace

MALÉ-DEE

Visdic body wrappings

Molf-tasseled overcloak

TERR TANEEL

CHI EEKWAY

Giddean Danu and Malé-Dee are among a group of Senators opposing Palpatine. They believe that he may respond if he is told that there are other disaffected Senators.

Noble Politicians

Palpatine and his parties of aides and red-robed guards have not cowed all the Senators. A loyal group has signed "The Petition of the Two Thousand," which states in no uncertain terms that the time has come for the Supreme Chancellor to yield some of the emergency powers that were granted him. It also demands that he open cease-fire negotiations with representatives of the Confederacy of Independent Systems.

SPY CAM

Coruscanti have demonstrated a great willingness to surrender personal freedoms in the name of safety. Even severe security measures are now accepted without question. Inside the Senate, new procedures allow for eavesdropping by hovercams.

Control antenna

Telephoto lens

Mon Mothma

Unknown to Palpatine, the two Senators most responsible for drawing up the Petition of the Two Thousand are Bail Organa, representing the Core world Alderaan, and Mon Mothma, daughter of a former governor of Chandrila. Politically savvy but very headstrong, Mon Mothma encourages Bail to draw outspoken Padmé Amidala into their confidence, convinced that Padmé's well-known loyalty to Palpatine can work to the petitioners' advantage.

Antique Chandrilan headpiece

Serene expression

Hanna pendant

Privacy screens can no longer be activated in the Senate Rotunda. Many delegates are therefore afraid to whisper their reactions, let alone speak their minds. Hovercams slink about, relaying recordings to security chief Armand Isard.

Sarrish Defense Force tunic

Calamarian collar gives moisture

Beak can crack shellfish

VEEDAAZ AWMETTH

MEENA TILLS

GUME SAAM

Large, flat teeth for methodical chewing

Costly Andalian cloak

Formal Senate robes

ASK AAK

SOLIPO YEB

SWEITT CONCORKILL

Shimmersilk mantle

Heads of State

Even before the abrupt end to the Clone Wars, many Senators representing Outer Rim worlds avoided Coruscant. They feared retribution for having forged trade agreements with species identified with the Separatist movement. By contrast, those Senators who were shrewd enough to remain on Coruscant and side with Palpatine found themselves rewarded in the post-war years.

DATA FILE

◆ Until the election of Princess Leia Organa to the Imperial Senate, Mon Mothma is the youngest Senator ever to hold office.

◆ Mon Mothma, Bail Organa, and his adopted daughter, Leia, will all play pivotal roles in the formation of the Rebel Alliance.

Cranial plates
revealed by
angry scowl

Rarely bared claws

Ancient
lightsaber

Homespun robe

Bloused
pants

Tridactyl feet
spread wide

Yoda
JEDI WARRIOR

WHEN YODA FIRST ARRIVED at the Jedi Temple more than 800 years ago, memories of the Jedi–Sith War and the waning of the Dark Times were still fresh. Since then, this Jedi Master has witnessed the full flowering of the Jedi Order, and of the Republic itself. For the past two centuries, however, Yoda has been aware of a gradual re-emergence of the dark side. As the end of the Clone Wars draws near, he foresees that the most significant dangers to the Jedi Order have yet to be faced.

Accepting finally that the war has been nothing more than a manipulation by the Sith to undermine the Jedi Order, Yoda decides to act on his instincts.

Yoda's staff is a gift from the Wookiees

Master

Yoda has guided hundreds of Jedi to knighthood. But some Jedi believe that he has failed to provide the Order with enlightened leadership. For these same Jedi, Yoda has placed too much trust in the prophesized ability of the Chosen One to restore balance to the Force.

Safe aboard the *Tantive IV*, Yoda learns of the clone trooper attack on the Jedi Temple. He concludes that Mace and the others failed to defeat Darth Sidious.

GIMER STICK

When Yoda arrives at Palpatine's holding office beneath the Senate Rotunda, he is in no mood for interference. Before the Chancellor's red guards can so much as brandish their force pikes, Yoda flattens them with a Force push.

DATA FILE

◆ Jedi learner, Zett Jukassa, is one of many to die in the Temple attack.

◆ In his extended lifetime, Yoda has visited countless worlds, some of which are so remote as to be unknown. One such world is the swamp planet, Dagobah.

In his contest with Sidious, Yoda realizes he is overmatched and deserts the fight, perhaps because his spirit has been broken by so many Jedi deaths. However, he remains determined to achieve victory over the dark side.

Increasingly troubled by the gathering of the dark side around the Chancellor, the Jedi Council resolve to capture General Grievous and then force Palpatine to abdicate.

Second heart is needed to nourish large brain

Antiox breath mask

PLO KOON

High parry stance

LUMINARA UNDULI

Djem So attack stance

AAYLA SECURA

Kai-Kan drop stance

BARRISS OFFEE

FEMALE WARRIORS
Jedi Aayla Secura and Barriss Offee die in attacks by clone troopers on the murky world of Felucia. Light-years distant, Luminara Unduli is lost on the Wookiee world of Kashyyyk.

Jedi Leaders

Sensor processor and guidance computer

Since Geonosis, the Jedi have led legions of clone troopers into combat on hundreds of worlds. As a result, they are spread thinly throughout the galaxy. When clone commanders receive Palpatine's traitorous Order 66, Masters, Knights, and Padawans are taken by surprise. They are assassinated by the troopers with whom they have served.

Escape pods loft Yoda to safety from Kashyyyk, and to sanctuary on Dagobah.

On Polis Massa, late-Jedi Master, Qui-Gon Jinn, begins tutoring Yoda on how to survive death with one's consciousness intact. In time, Yoda tells Obi-Wan of this, and that he, too, will soon begin training with Qui-Gon.

KI-ADI-MUNDI

ESCAPE POD

Mace Windu—Stoic Jedi

Somber expression

Coarseweave tunic

Traditional hooded robe

GIFTED WITH A TALENT for seeing to the very heart of a matter, Mace Windu has long nursed suspicions about Palpatine. Shortly before the Chancellor's abduction, Mace worried openly that Palpatine had fallen under the influence of the as-yet unidentified Sith Lord, Darth Sidious. But Yoda cautioned that the Senate would need proof of the Chancellor's treachery. Mace's concern blossoms into certainty when Palpatine refuses to tender a peace offer to the Separatists, even after Count Dooku has been killed.

After Palpatine defies tradition by appointing Anakin to the Jedi Council as his voice, Mace, Obi-Wan, and Yoda discuss the Sith threat to the Republic. They reluctantly decide to order Anakin to act as a double agent in the Chancellor's office.

Modulation circuitry for amethyst blade

Power cell

WINDU'S LIGHTSABER
Mace's lightsaber technique synthesizes deadly Form VII with a newly created form known as vaapad. A Force-user who practices this form may skirt close to the dark side.

Determined Jedi

Anakin's revelation—that Palpatine and Darth Sidious are one and the same—hollows Mace to the core. Not days earlier, he and other Jedi had risked their lives against Grievous's droid forces to prevent Palpatine from being abducted. Grasping that the abduction and the war itself has been nothing more than a deception, Mace leaps into action, promising to take Palpatine into Jedi custody, dead or alive.

DATA FILE

◆ Mace's precognitive abilities give him keen insight into individuals and events.

◆ Yoda agreed that Mace should arrest Palpatine if the Supreme Chancellor was discovered to have had dealings with Darth Sidious.

Lightsaber Masters

Most of the Jedi are deployed on distant worlds, but Mace manages to assemble a trio of celebrated swordmasters to assist him in arresting Palpatine: Agen Kolar, a Zabrak known among the Jedi to strike first and ask questions later; Saesee Tiin, a solitary Iktotchi who has never chosen a Padawan learner; and Kit Fisto, Nautolan master of Form I lightsaber technique, who distinguished himself on Geonosis and Mon Calamari, and who partnered Mace in battling Grievous on Coruscant.

When Anakin Skywalker was a boy, Mace came to accept he could be the Chosen One and eventually advocated that he be trained as a Jedi. A decade later, Mace has his doubts about Skywalker, and is disturbed by his relationship with Palpatine.

Horns regenerate over time

Tough skin impervious to winds of homeworld

Well-developed horns

Nautolans are amphibious

Chemically sensitive tentacles

KIT FISTO

SAESEE TIIN

Entering Palpatine's quarters in the Senate Office Building, Mace doesn't fully grasp that Palpatine has been waiting a lifetime for just such a contest. Accusing the Jedi of treason, the Sith Lord conjures a lightsaber from the sleeve of his robe, and the fight is on.

Mace's Jedi team advances on Palpatine, confident that they can defeat Sidious. Allowing vaapad to flow through him, Mace leaps to engage the Sith Lord, unaware that the person who will figure most in his own death is not Sidious, but Anakin.

Iridonian field boots

AGEN KOLAR

Deadly Confrontation

Only four Jedi of Mace's generation have fought a Sith Lord. Qui-Gon Jinn is dead; Yoda and Obi-Wan are on Kashyyyk and Utapau; and Anakin cannot be relied on, now that Sidious has tempted him with apprenticeship. Before Mace realizes what has happened, Kolar, Tiin, and Fisto have fallen to Sidious's blade.

Raised hood for stealth

Anakin—Fallen Jedi

WHILE ANAKIN SKYWALKER'S SLIDE to the dark side seems abrupt, the tragedy is rooted in his upbringing as a slave on Tatooine, and in the death of his mother, abducted and tortured by a band of Tusken Raiders. His experiences during the Clone Wars have eroded his faith in both the Jedi and the Senate, neither of which he believes capable of restoring peace and order to the galaxy. Though manipulated and exploited by Chancellor Palpatine, Anakin ultimately agrees to apprentice himself to the Sith Lord, in order to prevent Padmé Amidala from dying.

Anakin takes a significant stride toward the dark side when he kills the defeated Count Dooku aboard the Separatist flagship. Urged to greater violence by Palpatine—then forgiven by him—Anakin gives in to his rage and craving for vengeance.

The Dark Side

Blinded by fear and anger, Anakin fails to realize how easily he has played into Palpatine's hands. Anakin pledges his allegiance to the Supreme Chancellor—now revealed to be Darth Sidious—and the Sith. In so doing, he rejects his destiny as the Chosen One, and seals the fate of the Jedi order.

Anakin's frightening visions foretell Padmé's death during childbirth on a world remote from Coruscant.

While its design suggests that of a fortress, the Jedi Temple has stood as a symbol of peace and justice for more than 40 generations. But with so many Jedi deployed on far-flung worlds, the Temple is relatively unprotected.

The computer room houses controls for the Temple's network of communications systems. The Jedi beacon enables near-instantaneous contact between the Temple and Jedi in the field, without relying on the HoloNet.

Tholoth headdress

Hollow montrals sense space

STASS ALLIE

Characteristic pigmentation of the Togruta species

SHAAK TI

Dubbed Darth Vader by Sidious, Anakin embarks on a murderous rampage through the halls of the Temple that has been his home for 13 years. He and hundreds of clone troopers kill Jedi swordmaster Cin Drallig, as well as teachers, teens, and younglings.

Evidence of Anakin's slaughter bloodies the stately halls of the Temple. Administrators and students pose little threat to Palpatine's plans but Anakin does not care. Carrying out the executions is Anakin's way of swearing allegiance to the dark side and ensuring his family's survival.

Stass Allie and Shaak Ti

With almost all able-bodied Jedi Knights deployed far from Coruscant, the training of young Jedi has been cut. Those who remain in residence are left to fend for themselves. Even the Temple's finest swordmaster is no match for Anakin Skywalker and the stormtroopers of the 501st Legion. Not one Jedi knight or youngling will survive the horrific onslaught.

Sidious assures his new apprentice that the murders of those he loves will allow him to tap deeply into the powers afforded by the dark side of the Force. The Jedi must be the first to die—and that means all of them.

DATA FILE

◆ Anakin knew his atrocities were being monitored, but he was confident his actions would help him to attain a position of power where he was answerable only to Palpatine.

◆ Yoda and Obi-Wan recalibrate the beacon's Return-to-Coruscant code to save Jedi survivors.

Elite Clones

THE KAMINOANS, WHO BUILT the clone army, believed the Jedi Knights were too few in number to serve as an elite force or as field commanders for millions of soldiers. So they provided some of the clones with enhanced programming and extra training, which allowed them to function as special forces or chain-of-command links between the Jedi and standard troopers. These clones displayed initiative and leadership ability, and closely resembled their bounty hunter template.

Advanced Recon

The Kaminoans created a select number of clone troopers to be trained personally by bounty hunter Jango Fett. Designated Advanced Recon Commandos (ARCs), they worked in teams to execute special missions. Elite ARC squads were deployed soon after the war began on Muunilinst and other strategic worlds. They operated autonomously, but reported to Jedi Generals.

Clone commanders use names in addition to numerical designations. This practice was initiated by the Jedi themselves, as well as other progressive-thinking officials in the Republic, to foster a growing fellowship. Thus, CC 2224 came to be called Cody; 1004, Gree; and 1138, Bacara.

Color denotes legion affiliation

Reinforced tactical boots

COMMANDER CODY

Standard-issue DC-15A rifle

DC-15A standard blaster

POLARIZED MACROBINOCULARS

Heat dispersion vent

ARC pauldron

Spare blaster magazines

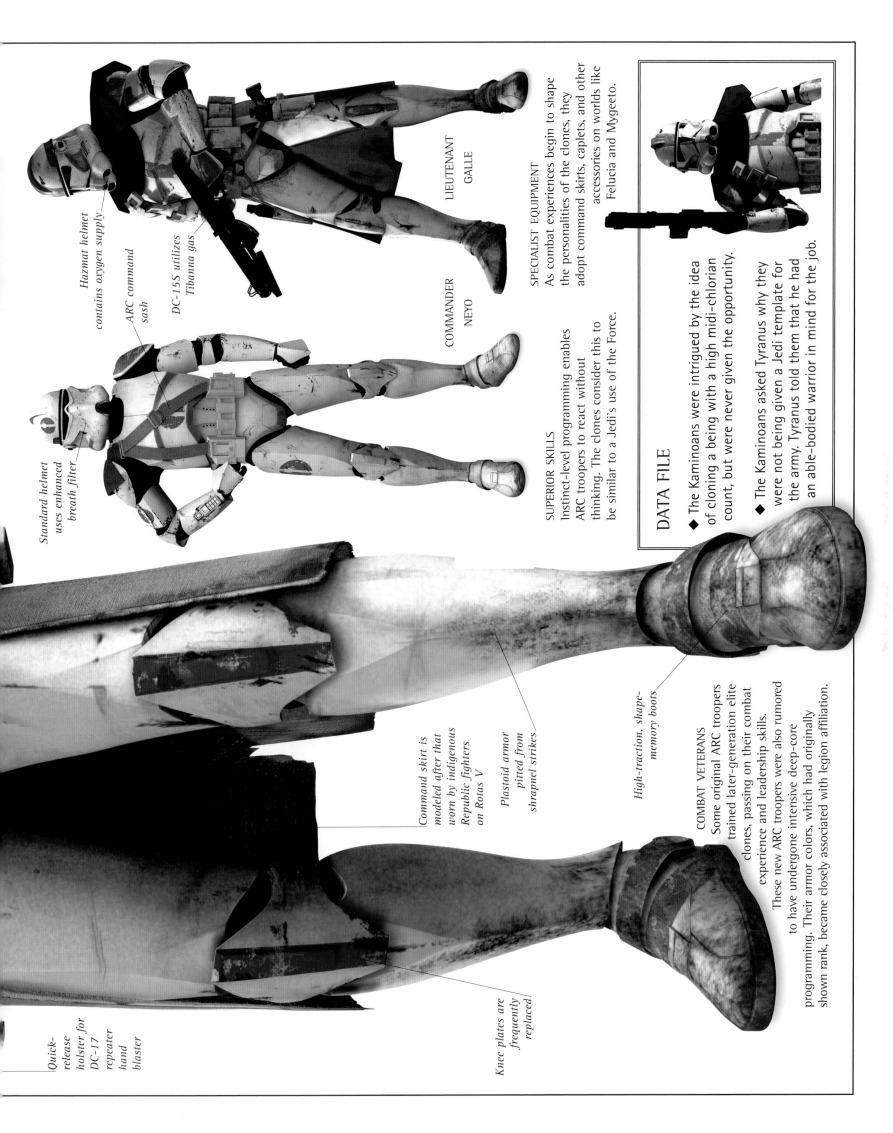

Quick-release holster for DC-17 repeater hand blaster

Knee plates are frequently replaced

Command skirt is modeled after that worn by indigenous Republic fighters on Rotas V

Plastoid armor pitted from shrapnel strikes

High-traction, shape-memory boots

COMBAT VETERANS

Some original ARC troopers trained later-generation elite clones, passing on their combat experience and leadership skills. These new ARC troopers were also rumored to have undergone intensive deep-core programming. Their armor colors, which had originally shown rank, became closely associated with legion affiliation.

Standard helmet uses enhanced breath filter

Hazmat helmet contains oxygen supply

ARC command sash

DC-15S utilizes Tibanna gas

LIEUTENANT GALLE

COMMANDER NEYO

SPECIALIST EQUIPMENT

As combat experiences begin to shape the personalities of the clones, they adopt command skirts, caplets, and other accessories on worlds like Felucia and Mygeeto.

SUPERIOR SKILLS

Instinct-level programming enables ARC troopers to react without thinking. The clones consider this to be similar to a Jedi's use of the Force.

DATA FILE

◆ The Kaminoans were intrigued by the idea of cloning a being with a high midi-chlorian count, but were never given the opportunity.

◆ The Kaminoans asked Tyranus why they were not being given a Jedi template for the army. Tyranus told them that he had an able-bodied warrior in mind for the job.

Clone Specialists

THE GRAND ARMY'S need for specialization is not limited to the production of support droids. Select clone troopers are trained in the use of new speeder bikes, rocket packs, and all-terrain vehicles. Others are trained in long-range reconnoitering, assassination, underwater demolition, and computer slicing. Recruited from mercenary groups and crime cartels, the instructors subject the troopers to live-fire exercises in which many clones die. The results, however, are teams of combat specialists that can be deployed in a host of environments, and against rare Separatist non-droid forces.

Tinted visor reduces glare by 70%

Air-supply hose made of tempered plastoid

Front-carry forced-ox rebreather

Flight data records pouch

Flightsuit clings to kneecap armor

Thermal outer boot worn over flight slipper

Projectile cannon

Laser cannon

Split wings

ARC-170

Clone Pilot

LAAT-gunship pilots were part of the war from the start, but a new breed of pilots was required to fly the hyperspace-capable ARC-170 and V-wing starfighters. Squadron pilots trained together, receiving programming on Kamino before being sent to Coruscant system worlds for advanced schooling.

Aggressive ReConnaissance-170 starfighters led by Clone Commander Odd Ball fly with Skywalker and Kenobi during the Battle of Coruscant.

Swivel-mounted saddle and blaster

Laser cannon

Reverse-articulation coupler

POD WALKER
Descended from the All Terrain Personal Transport, the AT-AP (All Terrain Attack Pod) is armed with blaster cannons. Deployed with mechanized platoons, the scout's adjustable leg-suspension system gives stability and maneuverability.

DATA FILE

◆ Sheathed in Katarn armor and trained by Mandalorian instructors, Republic commandos operate in teams to recruit and train provincial forces, or execute sabotage missions. On Kashyyyk, the commandos of Delta Squad free Tarfful from Trandoshan captivity.

Shock Trooper

Coruscant designation

Upgraded breath filter and annunciator

To the increasing frustration of the Jedi, Palpatine's War Council Advisory Panel, along with Senate committees under the aegis of the HomeWorld Security Command, is responsible for the deployment of clone specialists. On Coruscant, red-emblazoned shock troopers patrol public plazas and keep watch on government buildings and landing platforms. Citizens of the capital world are required to present their identity cards on demand.

Powerful turbofan

Forward blasters

Terrain-laser scanner

SWAMP SPEEDER

SPEEDER TYPES
By the end of the war, several varieties of the speeder bike have been introduced, including the swamp and the BARC. Driven by a powerful turbofan, the swamp speeder can seat two clones, side-by-side.

Repulsorlift engine

Legion designation

BARC SPEEDER

Enhanced helmet comlinks

Motion detection scanner

Control yoke

In the wake of the Jedi's failed attempt to arrest Palpatine, shock troopers accompany him to the Senate. Already, a list of possibly traitorous Senators is being compiled.

Heat dissipater

Visor adapted for greater visibility

Linkage

Stock holds power-charge magazine

Shaped charges

Repeating blaster

Reverse articulated legs

AT-RT
The spry All Terrain Recon Transport is an essential element of Grand Army mechanized units and reconnaissance platoons. It is equipped with enhanced communication arrays to provide forward command bases with updated situation reports.

DC-15 rifle

Camouflage armor is developed for jungle worlds. Some clones are shocked that not all environments are as clean as Kamino.

Clone Troopers

THE CLONE TROOPERS REMAIN the symbol of the war effort and the backbone of the army but, their armor gouged, dented, and smeared with the mud of a hundred worlds, they are no longer the white knights they appeared to be at the start of the war. Patched and repaired, they are returned to the front lines time and again to continue the fight for truth, justice, and, of course, the Republic way.

Helmet features built-in comlink antenna

"T" visor features heads-up display

Bodysuit glove

Shock-absorbing plastoid armor

Folding stock for braced firing

DATA FILE

◆ Aging at twice the rate of normally birthed humans, only two-thirds of the original army of clone troopers are alive. Clones are also being grown on other worlds, with cells procured from new templates.

Hundreds of rounds fired on one gas cartridge

Magnatomically-sealed knee plate

Laser cannon on Republic Star Destroyer

Blaster gas cartridges carried on utility belt

Armor emblazoned with legion color

Despite the fact that clone armor is frequently referred to as a "body bucket," troopers think of their plastoid shell as a portable shelter, which protects them against exploding laser cannons.

Clone troopers obey the commands of their Jedi generals, but ultimately they answer to Republic Chancellor and commander-in-chief, Palpatine. The mission to lay waste to the Jedi Temple is therefore obeyed immediately, especially as they are still being led by a Jedi Knight.

Action Figure

Like their clone template, Jango Fett, troopers are 1.78 meters (5 ft 10 in) tall, and their rallying cry remains: "One man, but the right man for the job!" However, three years of fighting has individualized many of the survivors. Informed by the campaigns in which they served, the wounds they sustained, and the scars they wear, troopers speak, react, and smell differently, and have acquired unique skills.

Courage, loyalty, obedience, and victory are the words that clone troopers live and die by. Though officer status was predetermined by the Kaminoans, battlefield promotions are not unknown.

Support Droids

WHEN THE KAMINOANS were growing the clone army, they also designed vessels and vehicles to bolster the troops. In making this new technology, they were guided by their thorough analysis of existing armies, such as those amassed in secret by the Trade Federation, Corporate Alliance, and Commerce Guild, and of potential planetary sectors in which sudden discord might erupt. As the war evolves and expands, taking worlds of varied climate and terrain into its dark embrace, so, too, does the need for larger ships, more powerful artillery, and a wider range of logistical and support droids.

PINCER LOADER
Bulked by multiple layers of durasteel, the IW-37 pincer—also known as the Salvager—employs its grasping arm to insert cargo or armaments into tight spaces, such as the compartment holds of Jedi interceptor starfighters.

Broadcast antennas communicate with other droids in binary

Primitive cognitive module

Remote sensor

Large central photoreceptor

Signal receiver

Wide-angle scanner

HOVER LOADER
Employed on landing platforms throughout Coruscant, hover loaders are a common feature at the Jedi Temple embarkation area, assisting in light-duty cargo relocation or, more often, droid traffic control. Hover loaders are also deployed at hyperspace ring stations to assist in the refueling of Jedi and clone-piloted starfighters.

Positioning arms

Graspers fasten to hyperspace rings

Hands made for handling cargo skids or missiles

Massive magnapod feet

Durasteel legs powered by hydraulics

Ordnance Lifter
Cybot Galactica's military version of their binary load lifter, the Ordnance Lifter stands three meters (9 ft 10 in) tall on powerful durasteel legs anchored by magnapod disks. Arms built for handling cargo skids or missiles flank a primitive cognitive module, capable of accepting verbal commands.

DATA FILE
◆ The owners of Sienar Systems, Kuat Drive Yards, Baktoid Armor Workshops, and Haor Chall Engineering are paying attention to the Clone Wars, in the hope of placing themselves profitably for the inevitable peace.

Utapauns

THE PEACEFUL OUTER RIM WORLD OF UTAPAU is shared by two indigenous and symbiotic near-human species. Comprising thirty percent of the population, the languid Pau'ans constitute Utapau's modest patrician class, and serve as city administrators and bureaucrats. Humble by nature, the stubby Utai make up the labor class. Unaffiliated with either the Republic or the CIS, the Utapauns remain neutral in the war until Darth Sidious sends General Grievous and the Separatist Council to their world as a temporary sanctuary. The Utapauns accept occupation with resignation, while preparing for rebellion.

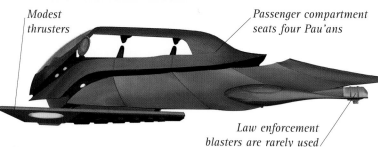

Utapau's most remote moon is inhabited

Utapau and its brood of small moons orbit in the remote Tarabba Sector. Huge sinkholes house cities that cling to the rocky walls of crevasses that fracture much of the planet's inhospitable surface.

Modest thrusters

Passenger compartment seats four Pau'ans

Law enforcement blasters are rarely used

SCOOP SKIMMER
An airspeeder used on Utapau, scoop skimmers are chiefly used as transport vehicles but some are equipped with light blasters. Scoop skimmers can also be found in the skies of Coruscant.

Shield conforms to profile

Distended eyes

Varactyl muck boots

LANDING PLATFORM
Obi-Wan lands in Pau City and is met by Tion Medon, who assures him that nothing strange has occurred. While Obi-Wan's Jedi Interceptor is refueled, Tion whispers that Separatists have taken control of Utapau.

Utai

Utapau's immense sinkholes were home to the Utai long before climactic change drove the lordly Pau'ans from the planet's surface. Distended eyes provide the Utai with keen night vision, perfectly suited to the crevasses that fissure Utapau. The Utai tamed the varactyl, and still serve as wranglers for the dragon mounts.

Flexible neck supports armor-plated skull

Mid-body ridge of spines displayed during courting ritual

Clawed feet adapted for scaling rocky cliffs

Long crooked legs

Four meters (13 ft 1 in) tall at the shoulder, the varactyl is an obliging herbivore. Utai leatherworkers handcraft high-backed saddles, sized for Pau'ans and Utai and perfect for riding at any angle.

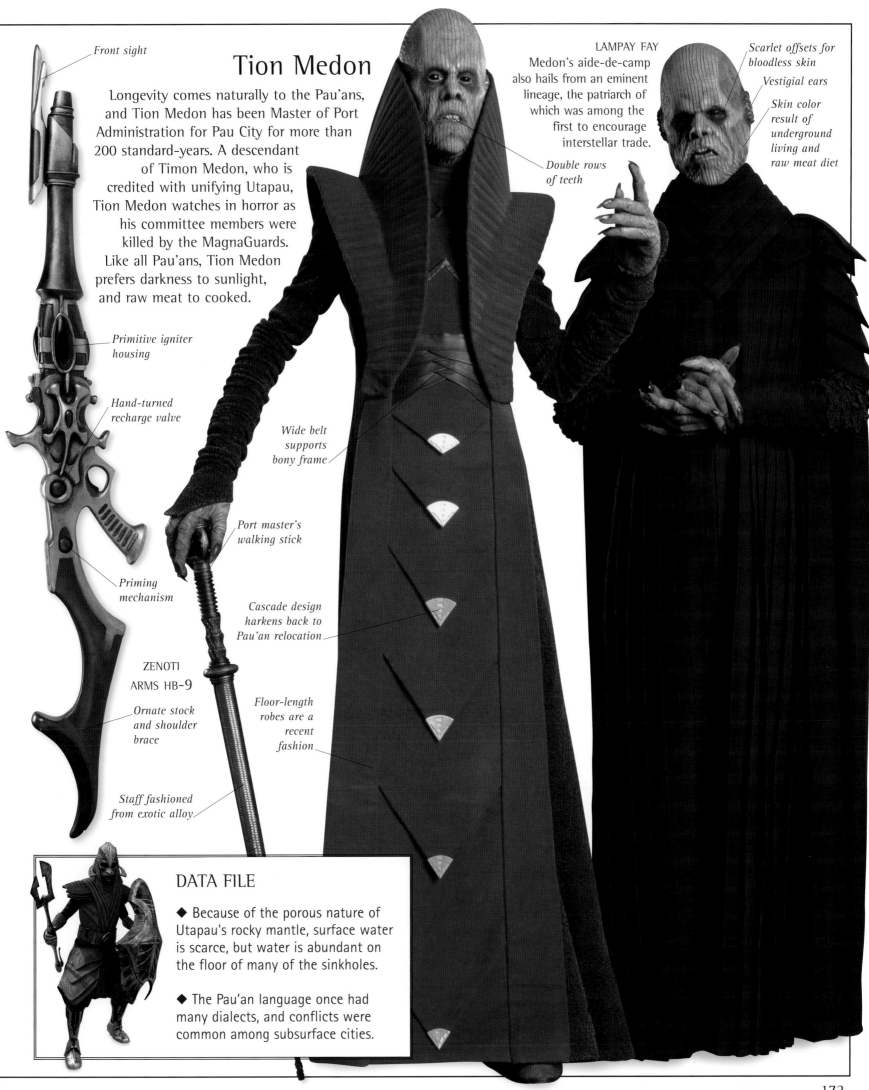

Tion Medon

Longevity comes naturally to the Pau'ans, and Tion Medon has been Master of Port Administration for Pau City for more than 200 standard-years. A descendant of Timon Medon, who is credited with unifying Utapau, Tion Medon watches in horror as his committee members were killed by the MagnaGuards. Like all Pau'ans, Tion Medon prefers darkness to sunlight, and raw meat to cooked.

Front sight

Primitive igniter housing

Hand-turned recharge valve

Priming mechanism

ZENOTI ARMS HB-9

Ornate stock and shoulder brace

Wide belt supports bony frame

Port master's walking stick

Cascade design harkens back to Pau'an relocation

Floor-length robes are a recent fashion

Staff fashioned from exotic alloy

LAMPAY FAY
Medon's aide-de-camp also hails from an eminent lineage, the patriarch of which was among the first to encourage interstellar trade.

Double rows of teeth

Scarlet offsets for bloodless skin

Vestigial ears

Skin color result of underground living and raw meat diet

DATA FILE

◆ Because of the porous nature of Utapau's rocky mantle, surface water is scarce, but water is abundant on the floor of many of the sinkholes.

◆ The Pau'an language once had many dialects, and conflicts were common among subsurface cities.

Battle of Utapau

WHEN TION MEDON DISCREETLY alerts Obi-Wan Kenobi that General Grievous and his droid forces have seized Pau City, windswept Utapau's long history of political neutrality comes to an end. Obi-Wan commandeers a cliff-scrabbling varactyl to infiltrate the droid army's secret base, then boldly confronts Grievous, who is unaware that his Jedi adversary has already summoned the Grand Army to Utapau. The native Pau'ans and Utai quickly join the fight to defend their planet.

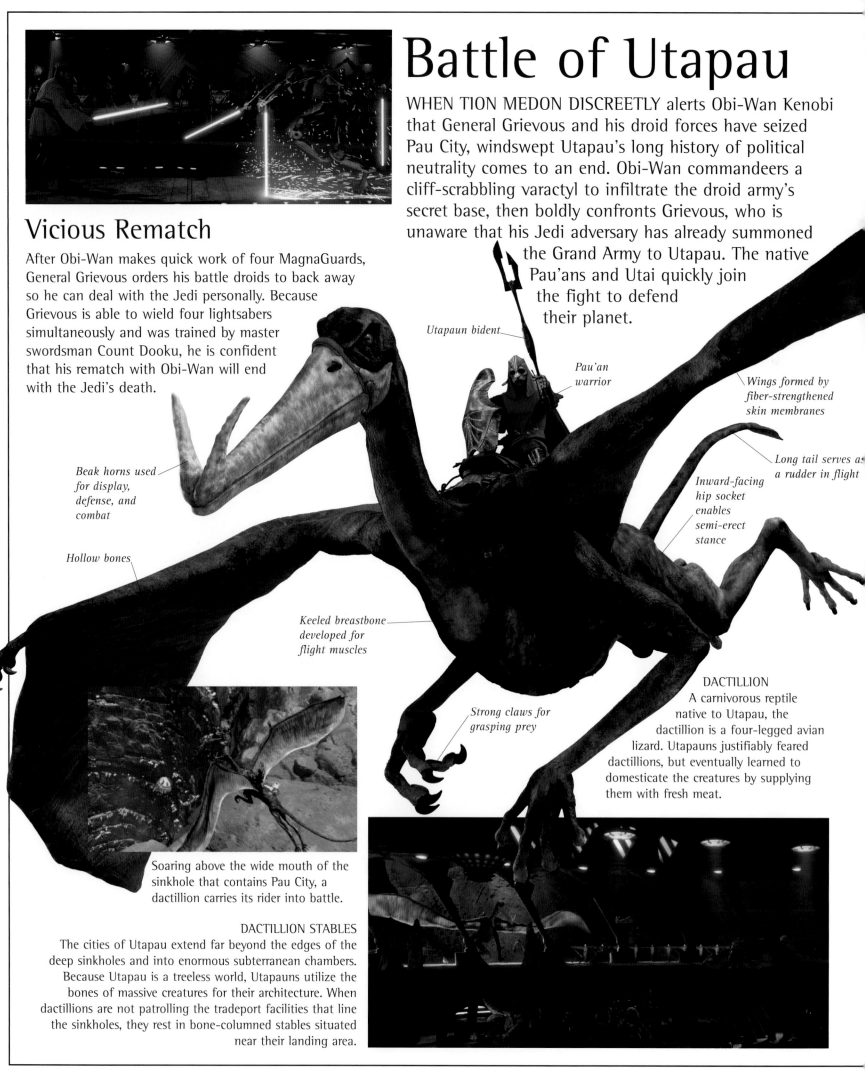

Vicious Rematch

After Obi-Wan makes quick work of four MagnaGuards, General Grievous orders his battle droids to back away so he can deal with the Jedi personally. Because Grievous is able to wield four lightsabers simultaneously and was trained by master swordsman Count Dooku, he is confident that his rematch with Obi-Wan will end with the Jedi's death.

Beak horns used for display, defense, and combat

Hollow bones

Keeled breastbone developed for flight muscles

Utapaun bident

Pau'an warrior

Wings formed by fiber-strengthened skin membranes

Long tail serves as a rudder in flight

Inward-facing hip socket enables semi-erect stance

Strong claws for grasping prey

DACTILLION
A carnivorous reptile native to Utapau, the dactillion is a four-legged avian lizard. Utapauns justifiably feared dactillions, but eventually learned to domesticate the creatures by supplying them with fresh meat.

Soaring above the wide mouth of the sinkhole that contains Pau City, a dactillion carries its rider into battle.

DACTILLION STABLES
The cities of Utapau extend far beyond the edges of the deep sinkholes and into enormous subterranean chambers. Because Utapau is a treeless world, Utapauns utilize the bones of massive creatures for their architecture. When dactillions are not patrolling the tradeport facilities that line the sinkholes, they rest in bone-columned stables situated near their landing area.

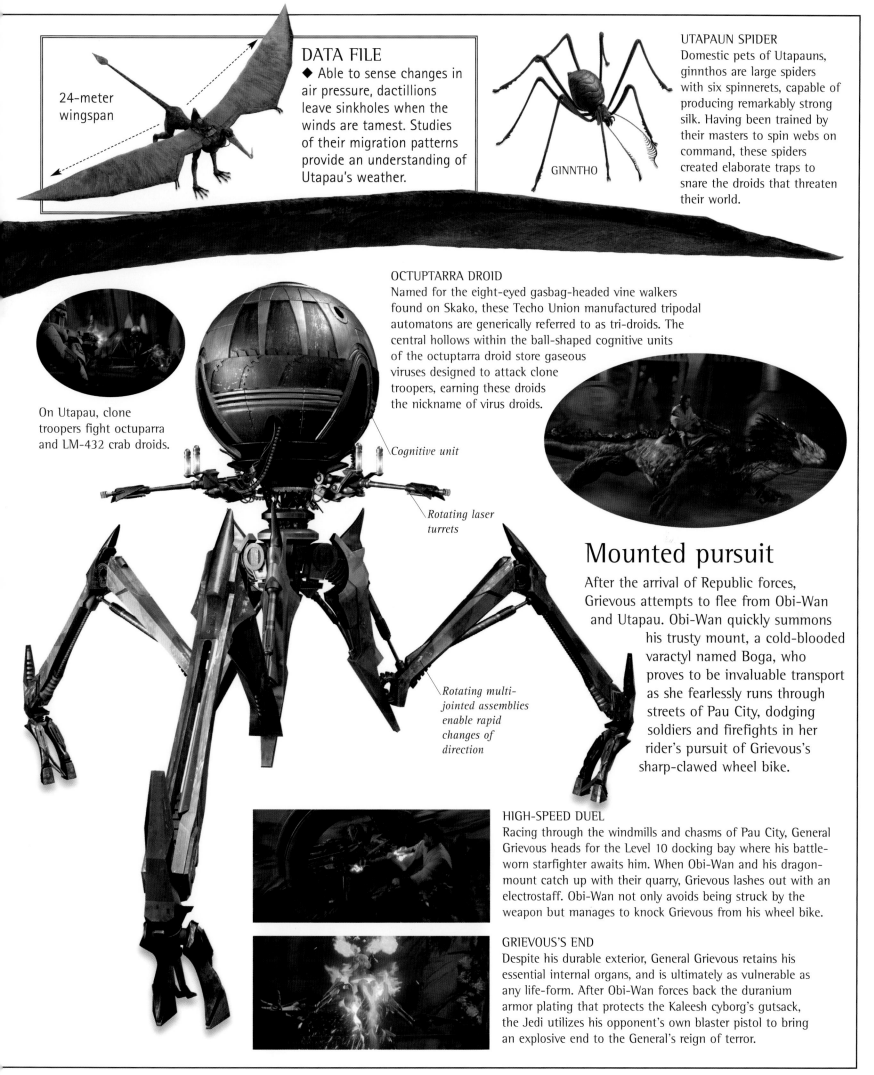

24-meter wingspan

◆ Able to sense changes in air pressure, dactillions leave sinkholes when the winds are tamest. Studies of their migration patterns provide an understanding of Utapau's weather.

UTAPAUN SPIDER

Domestic pets of Utapauns, ginnthos are large spiders with six spinnerets, capable of producing remarkably strong silk. Having been trained by their masters to spin webs on command, these spiders created elaborate traps to snare the droids that threaten their world.

GINNTHO

OCTUPTARRA DROID

Named for the eight-eyed gasbag-headed vine walkers found on Skako, these Techo Union manufactured tripodal automatons are generically referred to as tri-droids. The central hollows within the ball-shaped cognitive units of the octuptarra droid store gaseous viruses designed to attack clone troopers, earning these droids the nickname of virus droids.

On Utapau, clone troopers fight octuparra and LM-432 crab droids.

Cognitive unit

Rotating laser turrets

Rotating multi-jointed assemblies enable rapid changes of direction

Mounted pursuit

After the arrival of Republic forces, Grievous attempts to flee from Obi-Wan and Utapau. Obi-Wan quickly summons his trusty mount, a cold-blooded varactyl named Boga, who proves to be invaluable transport as she fearlessly runs through streets of Pau City, dodging soldiers and firefights in her rider's pursuit of Grievous's sharp-clawed wheel bike.

HIGH-SPEED DUEL

Racing through the windmills and chasms of Pau City, General Grievous heads for the Level 10 docking bay where his battle-worn starfighter awaits him. When Obi-Wan and his dragon-mount catch up with their quarry, Grievous lashes out with an electrostaff. Obi-Wan not only avoids being struck by the weapon but manages to knock Grievous from his wheel bike.

GRIEVOUS'S END

Despite his durable exterior, General Grievous retains his essential internal organs, and is ultimately as vulnerable as any life-form. After Obi-Wan forces back the duranium armor plating that protects the Kaleesh cyborg's gutsack, the Jedi utilizes his opponent's own blaster pistol to bring an explosive end to the General's reign of terror.

Chewbacca

COMPARATIVELY SHORT, EVEN SLIGHT, for a Wookiee, 200-year-old Chewbacca was born in the city of Rwookrrorro, several hundred kilometers from Kachirho, in an area of exceptionally tall wroshyr trees. His mother, father, and several cousins still reside there. A mechanic, holo-game competitor, and catamaran and fluttercraft pilot, Chewbacca learned his skills at Rwookrrorro's landing pad, and helped design and build the Wookiee escape pods. When it comes to outwitting droids or clone troopers, Chewbacca is ready with a plan.

Arms raised in gesture of dismay

Wookiee Explorer

Chewbacca has explored his homeworld from pole to pole, and is acquainted with even the wildest reaches of Kashyyyk's phenomenal forests. Restless by nature, he has also visited scores of planets, and is a veteran of numerous adventures, including run-ins with Trandoshan slavers. More compassionate than fierce, he nevertheless proves himself an able and cunning warrior.

Kashyyyk is distant from Coruscant, but close enough to hyperlanes to serve as a way-station for merchants. The Wookiees trade precious hardwoods for technology.

Ammunition bandoleer

On the ground and on Kachirho's loftiest tree platforms, Wookiees gaze into the night sky, which the ships of the Separatist fleet have strewn with harsh light. Chewbacca is no stranger to combat, but he worries that Kashyyyk may not be able to defend itself against the invasion force, and will fall to the Confederacy.

Jet engine exhaust nozzle

Centermount fuel feeder

Solid fuel is heated inside feeder

Tandem seating in hulls

Windscreen

Pouch contains dismantled bowcaster

Knife-edged keel for maneuverability

Rudder assembly

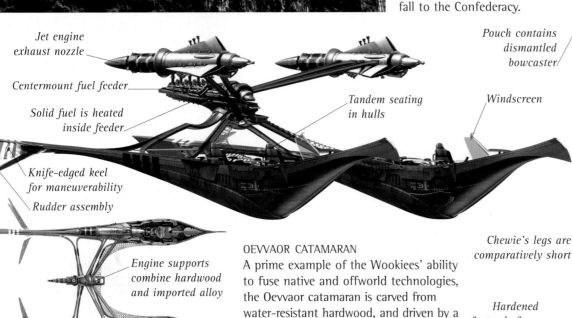

Engine supports combine hardwood and imported alloy

TOP VIEW

OEVVAOR CATAMARAN
A prime example of the Wookiees' ability to fuse native and offworld technologies, the Oevvaor catamaran is carved from water-resistant hardwood, and driven by a pair of powerful engines. Sought by rich buyers, no two catamarans are the same, and many have lasted for a millennium.

Chewie's legs are comparatively short

Hardened footpads from exploring Kashyyyk

DATA FILE

◆ Chewbacca will have his revenge on the Empire with the death of the Emperor and the destruction of the second Death Star during the battle of Endor. Jointly commanded by Chewbacca and General Han Solo, an Alliance task force will restore peace to Kashyyyk.

KASHYYYK CLARION

Immense lung capacity required to sound call

Hammered bronzium jacket inlaid with cerulean gemstone

ELDER'S STAFF

Wood is over six centuries old

Mouth emits bellow that can be heard for 20 kilometers (12 miles)

Elaborately engraved stem

CEREMONIAL PIPE

MASTER CARVERS

Wookiees turn their dexterous hands to carving at an early age, fashioning household items, musical instruments, and tools. The Kashyyyk clarion is made from the horn of a bantha, and jacketed with hand-hammered bronzium.

Wookiees are prized by slavers as much for their strong backs as for their keen intellects. Resourceful and fiercely loyal, Wookiees do not live as long as some species, but several residents of Kachirho and Rwookrrorro can recall when Yoda was a mere Jedi Knight.

Fangs puncture even durable Trandoshan skin

Respected elder

Emblem of the Kachirho clan

Wookiees can pull a person's arm from its socket

Water-shedding hair covers Wookiees like a cape

The Gathering

The clarion call to defend Kachirho summons young and old, from all areas of Kashyyyk. Despite the victory at the tree-city, Kashyyyk will became enslaved to the Empire soon after the end of the Clone Wars, and thousands of Wookiees, including Chewbacca, will be exported to remote worlds to serve as laborers. Even captivity, however, will not dampen Chewbacca's abiding fondness for humans.

GUANTA

LACHICHUK

MERUMERU

Tarfful

TARFFUL HAS SERVED AS LEADER of the Wookiee city of Kachirho for longer than a human lifetime. He has already experienced captivity, having fallen into the clawed hands of Trandoshan slavers who have long been enemies of the Wookiees, and who had cut a deal with Count Dooku. Standing over two meters (seven feet) tall, Tarfful is literally looked up to by many, and so assumes the role of commander when Separatist forces invade.

Unlike most areas of Kashyyyk, where the wroshyrs tower so high above the surface that Wookiees seldom leave their tree-caves, Kachirho rises from the shore of a large fresh-water lagoon.

Locks of hair banded by precious metal rings

Decorative pauldron

Kashyyyk long-gun heat dissipater

Ferocious visage

Teeth bared for war cry

Kashyyyk Landing

Tarfful is well-known on the planet of Kashyyyk. When word spreads that Kachirho is under siege by the Confederacy's droid forces, Wookiees from throughout the region hurry to defend the arboreal city, which gracefully spirals around the trunk of a 300-meter (984-feet) high wroshyr tree.

Shield depicts emblem of Kachirho

Stylized eyespots of Kashyyyk borer beetle

Clan pectoral cinches crossed bandoleers

Orb-igniter

Tarffful is left-handed

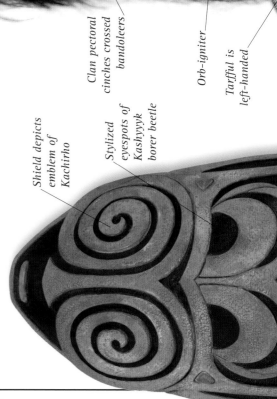

Powerful thighs
from swimming

Thick calve
muscles from
climbing trees

Fur protects
upper foot

Beetle
carapace
markings

Long-gun lacks
sights or beads

Bronzium-alloy
barrel

Indentation from
injury suffered in
captivity

WAR SHIELD

Wide
muzzle

Able Leader

Rescued from captivity by a team of
Republic clone commandos, Tarfful
pledged that he would fight to the
death any who threatened to enslave the
Wookiees or to occupy Kashyyyk. Yoda is
considered by the citizenry of Kachirho to be
a member of their extended honor family,
for subverting an earlier Trandoshan scheme to
lure hundreds of Wookiees into slavery, and is
welcomed back to Kashyyyk with open arms.

DATA FILE

◆ Trandoshans are a reptilian
humanoid species from a world
in the same planetary system
as Kashyyyk.

◆ Wookiees cannot speak Basic, and
few species in the galaxy can mimic
the complex roars and barks that
comprise their language,
Shyriiwook. Even so, Wookiees
have a way of making their
intentions clearly understood.

Wookiee Weapons

THE WOOKIEE LANGUAGE contains over 150 words for wood, many of them devoted to grain, moisture content, and factors that can influence warping, twisting, and checking. Shipboard logs cite instances of Wookiees effecting temporary repairs of starship drives using pieces of wood. Commentators have classified even their blasters as "art," and yet the language has no word for "artist." Wookiees view their innate talents for carving and engraving as mere survival skills.

KLORRI-CLAN BATTLE SHIELD
Carved with symbolic motifs and banded with bronzium, the two thousand-year-old Klorri-clan battle shields are normally displayed only during important rituals and ceremonies.

Crest is ancient sun symbol

Hair can be threaded through perforated flange

PAULDRON

HELMET

Blaster gas cartridges

MILITARY WEAR
Armor, harnesses, and other examples of military gear evolved from ceremonial clan regalia, in the same way that most Wookiee implements of war have their origin in hunting. Halter and shoulder-slung bandoleers typically hold power packs, blaster gas canisters, and bowcaster quarrels.

AMMO HALTER

BOWCASTER MECHANICS
The bowcaster works on the principle of magnetic acceleration. A pair of spherical polarizers generate positive and negative pulses that power the weapon's tensile metal bowstring. Enveloped in energy when it emerges from the barrel, the quarrel could be mistaken for a blaster bolt.

Polarizer

Bowcaster

The traditional bowcaster still enjoys wide use as a ranged weapon. The original bowcaster had few metal parts, and employed a length of braided kshyy vine to fire a wooden quarrel. The stock was adorned with clan or tree-city emblems, or inlaid with semi-precious stones or mosaics of contrasting hardwood.

Metal bowstring

Stock is tapered for line-of-sight accuracy

Battery pack is mortised into stock

Rear sight

Bowstring catch

Tensile bowstring

Blaster gas lines

Ribbed launch shaft

Conduction chamber housed in shaft

Front sight

Power pack

Stock recoil spring

Safety catch

Conduction chamber

Magnetic acceleration coil

Barrel

Trigger

DATA FILE

◆ The Battle of Kachirho might not have gone as well for the Wookiees had Yoda not been there to lend his lightsaber to the fray. Similarly, the battle might not have gone as well for Yoda had the Wookiees not peppered the area around the tree-city with launch-capable escape pods, in case Kachirho had to be evacuated.

Sure-Shot

Tremendous strength is required to cock and control bowcasters. Traveling circuses use bowcasters in feats-of-strength competitions. Chewbacca's, however, is more tribute than traditional, with an automatic recocking system and low-light scope. Consequently, his bandoleer houses more power packs than most.

Ring-grip peculiar to southern hemisphere tree-cities

DISRUPTOR

Bowcaster easily dismantled

Automatic recocking system

Bronzium alloy blast suppressor

Accelerator

SIDE-ARM

Polarizers positioned forward of barrel

BLASTERS

Of the array of blasters fashioned by Wookiee weaponsmiths, several models are favorites and are now mass-produced in workshops all over Kashyyyk. Blaster technology has influenced traditional weapons as well, with the over-under bowcaster featuring a built-in blaster.

Quarrel autofeed mechanism

Shortened stock

SLUG-THROWER

CHEWBACCA'S BOWCASTER

Blaster gas cartridges

Polarizer

Electromagnetic coil for ultra-power blasts

Front sight

Barrel

Lowered rear sight

Order 66

DESPITE THEIR INTUITIVE POWERS, the Jedi were unaware that the cloned soldiers of the Grand Army had been trained to obey, without question, numerous emergency protocols that could be activated by Supreme Chancellor Palpatine. After Palpatine was almost arrested by the Jedi Coucil on Coruscant, he initiated Order 66—a secret directive to assassinate Jedi throughout the galaxy. Upon receiving Order 66, clone commanders instantly identified the Jedi as traitors to the Republic and proceeded to murder them.

Jedi Aayla Secura is ambushed by her own troops on Felucia.

A Felucian ground beetle, also known as a gelagrub

Felucia

On numerous worlds, clone troopers utilize indigenous creatures as mounts and beasts of burden, such as the large ground beetles of Felucia. It was partially due to their care for such creatures that some Jedi assume that clones possess sensitivity that could be likened to compassion. Order 66 reveals that though the clones could behave as such, their ultimate loyalty is to Palpatine.

Ocellus detects changes in light intensity

Gelegrubs eat constantly to maintain their natural sunscreen

Prolegs offer steady locomotion

← - - - - - - - - - - 4 meters - - - - - - - - - - →

Cato Neimoidia

One of the wealthiest worlds in the galaxy, Cato Neimoidia is the primary base for Trade Federation forces allied with the Confederacy of Independent Systems. Jedi Master Plo Koon helps to secure the planet during the Clone Wars.

Palpatine contacts Captain Jag who served under Jedi Master Plo Koon on assignment at Cato Neimoidia. Receiving the secret directive in the cockpit of his ARC-170, Jag immediately orders his squadron to to shoot down the Jedi.

Jedi Master Plo Koon is piloting his customized Delta-7 Jedi starfighter when his wingmen attack on Cato Neimoidia.

After his wingmen attack, Plo Koon's damaged starfighter spins out of control before crashing into the Neimoidian cityscape.

Shielded backpack

Breath warmer cover made of synthmesh

Freeze-proof alloy

Semi-translucent skin can metabolize UV-filtering chemicals from Felucia's native plant life

Mygeeto

Stronghold of the InterGalactic Banking Clan, Mygeeto is a frigid world covered by crystallized glaciers. Palpatine dispatches a group of Coruscant-trained members of the 501st Legion to supplement the snow-armor clad Galactic Marines on Mygeeto.

After Clone Commander Bacara receives Order 66 on Mygeeto, he directs his Galactic Marines to open fire on Jedi Master Ki-Adi-Mundi. Because of their deep-core learning programs, the clones neither hesitate nor feel remorse for assassinating their leader.

DATA FILE
◆ Order 66 triggered the deaths of thousands of Jedi throughout the galaxy, an event that came to be known as the Jedi Purge. Among the casualties were Jedi Master Stass Allie, killed by her wingmen on recaptured Saleucami.

Clone Battle Tanks

ALTHOUGH THE GRAND ARMY of the Republic possesses starships with weapons capable of planetary bombardment, such assaults typically drain ships of their energy systems. To conserve resources and execute assignments with greater precision, the Grand Army uses drop ships to deploy tanks on planetary surfaces. As the heavily armored tanks are designed for various terrains, strategists consult all available information to determine which vehicles to use. Many of the massive ships are designed to walk on hydraulic legs, but their inherent disadvantages led to the development of new repulsorlift and wheeled tanks.

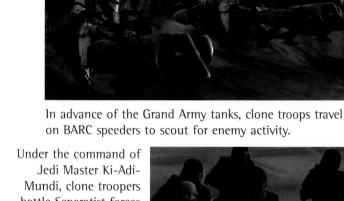

In advance of the Grand Army tanks, clone troops travel on BARC speeders to scout for enemy activity.

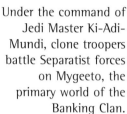

Under the command of Jedi Master Ki-Adi-Mundi, clone troopers battle Separatist forces on Mygeeto, the primary world of the Banking Clan.

Although civilizations with repulsorlift technology generally regard wheeled vehicles as archaic, the Republic Army's Clone Turbo Tanks can traverse rough terrain at higher speeds than walking vehicles, and can turn in a smaller radius than similarly sized repulsorlifts.

UT-AT "Trident"

Following a disastrous campaign in which the pounding movements of Republic walkers caused a bridge to collapse, the Grand Army commissioned repulsorlift tanks, such as the Unstable Terrain Artillery Transport, nicknamed "Trident" for its three forward weapons.

Anti-infantry laser turret

Artillery storage

Secondary turrets

Blast-proof armor plating

Air vent

Republic insignia

AT-OT WALKER

Stifle-joint cover

Knee-joint cover

Forward-mounted heavy laser cannon

AT-OT WALKER
Manufactured by Kuat Drive Yards, the 14.3-meters-long All Terrain Open Transport is an open-bed cargo walker with thick armor plating. Each AT-OT stands 5.8 meters tall, and has two forward-mounted laser cannons and two tail cannons for defense.

UT-AT "TRIDENT"

Tandem cockpit seats for one driver and one gunner

Because AT-OTs have exposed carriages, passengers are vulnerable to attack from above. However, the vehicles are excellent for carrying troops through dense forests to the outer perimeters of battlefields. On Felucia, AT-OT drivers navigated their tanks past formations of luminous fungi.

Medium laser cannon

Vents reduce nozzle pressure effects on emerging projectile

Scanning devices

Repulsorlift skis

DATA FILE
◆ After Kashyyyk is invaded by CIS droids, Jedi Master Yoda leads the Grand Army on a mission to prevent them from obtaining data on dormant hyperspace routes. The Grand Army's HAVw A6 Juggernauts (also known as Clone Turbo Tanks) combat Corporate Alliance tank droids.

Bail Organa

SENATOR FOR PACIFIC ALDERAAN, Bail Organa believes that the peace he enjoys on his homeworld may account for his growing concerns about the conflict on Coruscant. He is particularly concerned about the extra powers the Senate has given to Chancellor Palpatine and the loss of freedom on the galactic capital. Bail is seen as a voice of reason in the Senate, although just as often he is shouted down by his pro-war peers.

When Palpatine proclaims himself Emperor, Padmé cautions Bail to conceal his true feelings. She asks him to bide his time until the circumstances are right. Most of all, in private, she tells him to place his faith in the future and in the Force.

Candid Senator

With Padmé, Mon Mothma, Fang Zar, and other Loyalists, Bail argued against the Military Creation Act, only to put aside his feelings after the Battle of Geonosis and support the war effort. To no avail, Bail argued against the installation of surveillance holocams in the Senate Building and, later, against the Reflex Amendment that extended Palpatine's far-reaching authority.

BAIL ORGANA'S
IDENTITY TAG

Blaster fires incapacitating bolts only

TARGET BLASTER
Bail has grown used to showing his identity tag at building entrances on Coruscant. Seemingly passive, his resoluteness will be passed on to his adopted daughter.

Sheltay Retrac has been Bail's aide for two years

Alderaanian long coat

Wool produced in Alderaan's Killik region

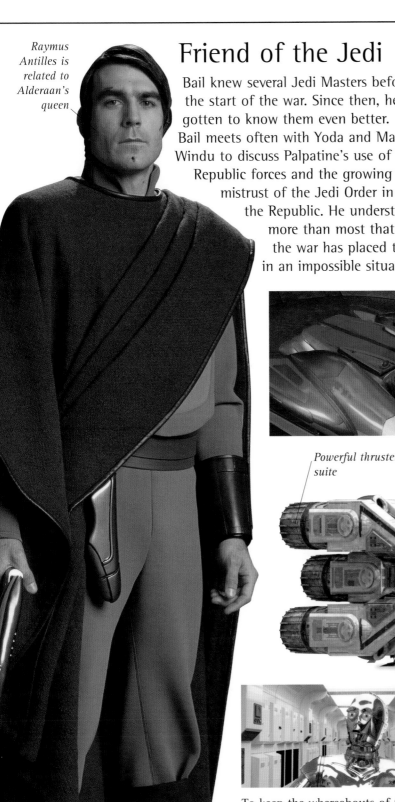

Raymus Antilles is related to Alderaan's queen

Friend of the Jedi

Bail knew several Jedi Masters before the start of the war. Since then, he has gotten to know them even better. Bail meets often with Yoda and Mace Windu to discuss Palpatine's use of Republic forces and the growing mistrust of the Jedi Order in the Republic. He understands more than most that the war has placed the Jedi in an impossible situation.

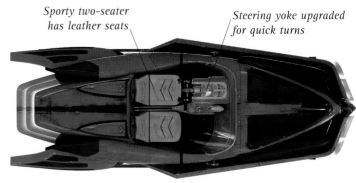

Sporty two-seater has leather seats

Steering yoke upgraded for quick turns

CUSTOM SPEEDER
With its design based on an older model, Bail's speeder comes in handy for spiriting Yoda to safety after he abandons the fight with Darth Sidious in the Senate building.

Bail believes in the Force and is the first civilian to arrive at the Jedi Temple after Anakin and his legion of clone troopers have gone on a killing spree. After witnessing a young Jedi fall to hails of blaster fire, Bail narrowly escapes with his own life.

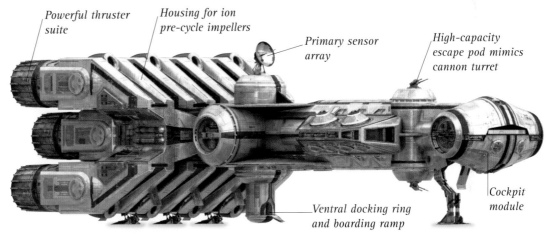

Powerful thruster suite

Housing for ion pre-cycle impellers

Primary sensor array

High-capacity escape pod mimics cannon turret

Ventral docking ring and boarding ramp

Cockpit module

To keep the whereabouts of Obi-Wan and Yoda secret after they have gone into exile, Bail orders that C-3PO's memory be wiped.

DIPLOMATIC STARSHIP
Bail's Corellian-made cruiser, *Tantive IV*, is commanded by Captain Raymus Antilles. In order to preserve its legacy as a diplomatic vessel, Bail refuses to outfit the ship with ranged weapons. On and off for the next 20 years, the starship will be home to C-3PO and R2-D2.

DATA FILE

◆ Bail will die when Grand Moff Tarkin orders the Death Star to destroy Alderaan.

◆ Using a Jedi homing beacon, Bail is able to contact Yoda and Obi-Wan after they are betrayed by clone commanders Gree and Cody.

◆ Bail and his wife, Breha, are childless.

Overcome by grief for what has transpired since the kidnap of Palpatine, Bail watches medtechs at the Polis Massa facility struggle to save Padmé's life after they have delivered her twins. After her death, Bail offers to raise Leia Amidala Skywalker in the house of his wife, the Queen of Alderaan.

Separatist Council

EARLY IN THE WAR, following the Separatists' first round of conquests, Count Dooku revealed to the Council members that the real power behind the Confederacy of Independent Systems was the Sith Lord, Darth Sidious. Three years later during the Outer Rim Sieges, with the Republic victorious at Separatist strongholds, Sidious orders that the Council members be placed under the personal protection of General Grievous. Housed on Utapau while Grievous strikes at Coruscant, the Council is then relocated to volcanic Mustafar.

The "hive mentality" characteristic of many of the Separatists works in Sidious's favor, in that once a leader is won over, the rest of his or her species follows. Their spinelessness makes it easier for the Sith Lord to order the murder of his former allies.

WAT TAMBOR

Vocabular/annunciator

Hides within oily Koorivan cloak

Cranial crown

PASSEL ARGENTE

Attitude of prayer

DENARIA KEE (AIDE)

SHI'IDO (AIDE)

Elaborate breast plate doubles as body armor

PO NUDO

Tusks

Primary Aqualish eyes

TECHNO UNION
Wat Tambor has suffered several close calls during the war, falling into Republic captivity on Metalorn and narrowly escaping an assassination attempt by Boba Fett on Xagobah. With his homeworld of Skako in Republic hands, Tambor has no option but to place his trust in Sidious.

CORPORATE ALLIANCE
Passel Argente had hoped to play a secondary role in the war, but quickly found himself pressed into service by Dooku. Unknown to Passel, many of his Alliance subordinates have been relocating their distribution companies to a cluster of star systems in the galaxy's Tingel Arm, also known as the Corporate Sector.

HYPER-COMMUNICATIONS CARTEL
Aqualish Po Nudo helped to influence dozens of unscrupulous Senators and steered resource-rich Ando into the Separatist fold in the months prior to the Battle of Geonosis. In gratitude, the Banking Clan and the Techno Union appointed him head of the Hyper-Communications Cartel. This organization oversees a CIS analogue of the Republic HoloNet.

Endgame

The Separatist facility on volcanic Mustafar was thought to be impregnable. But that was before Darth

Sidious sent his new apprentice, Darth Vader, to assassinate the members of the Council. With the Jedi killed, and the chief Separatists soon to follow, no one will stand in Sidious's and Vader's way when they seize total control of the galaxy.

DATA FILE

◆ The Separatist movement ignored all Republic laws prohibiting the amassing of weapons, warships, and soldiers.

◆ The Separatists prevented Republic eavesdropping by using an InterGalactic Banking Clan code.

Strong neck muscles support heavy cranium

Heritage miter

RUTE GUNRAY

RUNE HAAKO

SAN HILL

Troubled posture

Cato Neimoidian yoke collar

Command headdress

CAT MIIN (AIDE)

Now paralyzed wings folded behind back

ARCHDUKE POGGLE THE LESSER

SHU MAI

Neck rings

BANKING CLAN
San Hill was taken into Republic custody and allowed to escape. Having financed the resurrection of the Gen'dai warrior Durge, as well as the rehabilitation of Grievous, Hill feels that Darth Sidious owes him a great debt.

GEONOSIAN INDUSTRIES
With hundreds of thousands of his fellow Geonosians employed in the construction of Darth Sidious's battle station, Poggle the Lesser is confident that the best is yet to come.

TRADE FEDERATION
More than any other members of the Council, the Neimoidian Viceroy, Nute Gunray, and his chief attaché, Rune Haako, feel they have a special agreement with Darth Sidious. This is mainly because the Trade Federation was the first organization to be drawn into helping the Sith Lord's evil plans.

COMMERCE GUILD
With her homeworld of Castell absorbed into the Republic, Gossam Presidente Shu Mai's talent for bribery is useless against Vader.

Polis Massans

MYSTERY SURROUNDS THE CAUSE of the cataclysm that fractured the Outer Rim planet now known as Polis Massa. Evidence of the civilization that flourished on the formerly arid world is scant, but on one of the largest of the planetary chunks, an archaeological dig has been in progress for so long that the humanoid aliens supervising the dig are themselves referred to as Polis Massans. Most of the prize artifacts uncovered thus far have come from deep within the asteroid, and so seasoned spelunkers—cavers—comprise the majority of the archaeological team. The medical facility to which Padmé is taken was built primarily to suit the needs of the investigators. Known for their discretion, the Polis Massans ask few questions of Bail or the Jedi Masters.

Obi-Wan, Padmé, R2-D2, and C-3PO rendezvous with Yoda and Bail Organa at the Polis Massa medical facility. The fact that the facility is remote suits the purposes of the Jedi, who are determined to keep secret the birth of Padmé's children. The medtechs who assist in delivering the twins are baffled by their inability to save her life. But sometimes a broken heart simply cannot be mended.

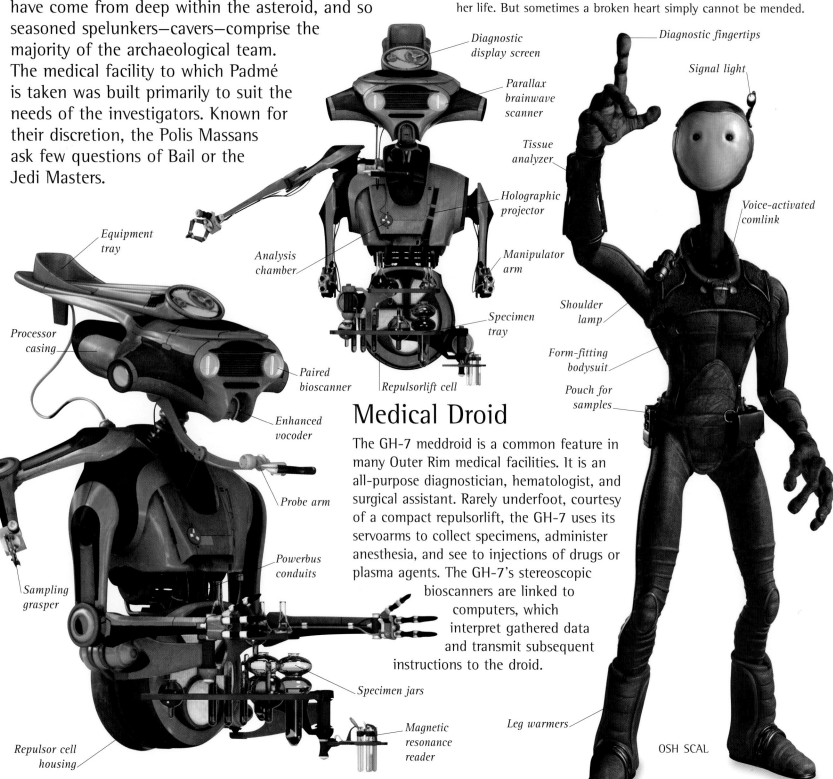

Equipment tray

Processor casing

Paired bioscanner

Enhanced vocoder

Probe arm

Sampling grasper

Powerbus conduits

Specimen jars

Repulsor cell housing

Magnetic resonance reader

Diagnostic display screen

Parallax brainwave scanner

Tissue analyzer

Holographic projector

Analysis chamber

Manipulator arm

Specimen tray

Repulsorlift cell

Diagnostic fingertips

Signal light

Voice-activated comlink

Shoulder lamp

Form-fitting bodysuit

Pouch for samples

Leg warmers

OSH SCAL

Medical Droid

The GH-7 meddroid is a common feature in many Outer Rim medical facilities. It is an all-purpose diagnostician, hematologist, and surgical assistant. Rarely underfoot, courtesy of a compact repulsorlift, the GH-7 uses its servoarms to collect specimens, administer anesthesia, and see to injections of drugs or plasma agents. The GH-7's stereoscopic bioscanners are linked to computers, which interpret gathered data and transmit subsequent instructions to the droid.

MIDWIFE DROID

Non-threatening aspect

Warming cushion

The current Polis Massan team has had limited contact with humans, and knows little about delivering human children. After consulting their databanks, the medtechs select as midwife a padded droid, equipped with a thermal cushion and paddle appendages with which to cradle the newborns.

Nutrient reservoir

Repulsorlift

Cradling paddle

DATA FILE

◆ The Polis Massan exobiologists learned cloning from the Kaminoans.

◆ While investigating a planet in the Subterrel sector, the thin-bodied aliens chanced to run into Besalisk Dexter Jettster, who was impressed by the Kaminoan saberdarts the team was using to subdue predatory wildlife.

Fearing the worst for Padmé, Bail orders Captain Antilles to delete all data about Mustafar from Padmé's starship computer. With Anakin believed dead, Bail wonders what the Jedi will do with the twins, whom Padmé has named Luke and Leia.

Head lamp

Surgical hood

Sign language gesture

Remote control

Deep-focus eyes

Mildly telepathic brain

Droid summoner

Osmotic membrane face

Caver's harness

Surgical hood seal

Sample containers

Alien Medics

Only two of the technicians that help deliver the Skywalker twins are trained physicians. The rest are exobiolologists, natives of a Subterrel sector world. They are attached to the archaeological team to analyze artifacts for organic tissue, suitable for cloning. Padmé's condition is judged to be so critical that the techs have no time to change out of their caving jumpsuits.

Utility belt

Remote control unit

Warming line

Suit reveals body growth-rings

Knee pads

DZNORI XAM

SELIF XAM

MANEELI TUUN

Mustafar

A tiny, fiery planet in the Outer Rim, Mustafar maintains an erratic orbit between two gas giants, Jestefad and Lefrani. Although the gravitational forces of the greater worlds have transformed it into a geological chaos, Mustafar is rich in unique and valuable mineral allotropes which have long been mined by the Techno Union. Because of this affiliation, and due to the natural interference created by its surface and atmosphere to standard scanners and navigational systems, Mustafar is deemed an ideal hideout for Separatist leaders.

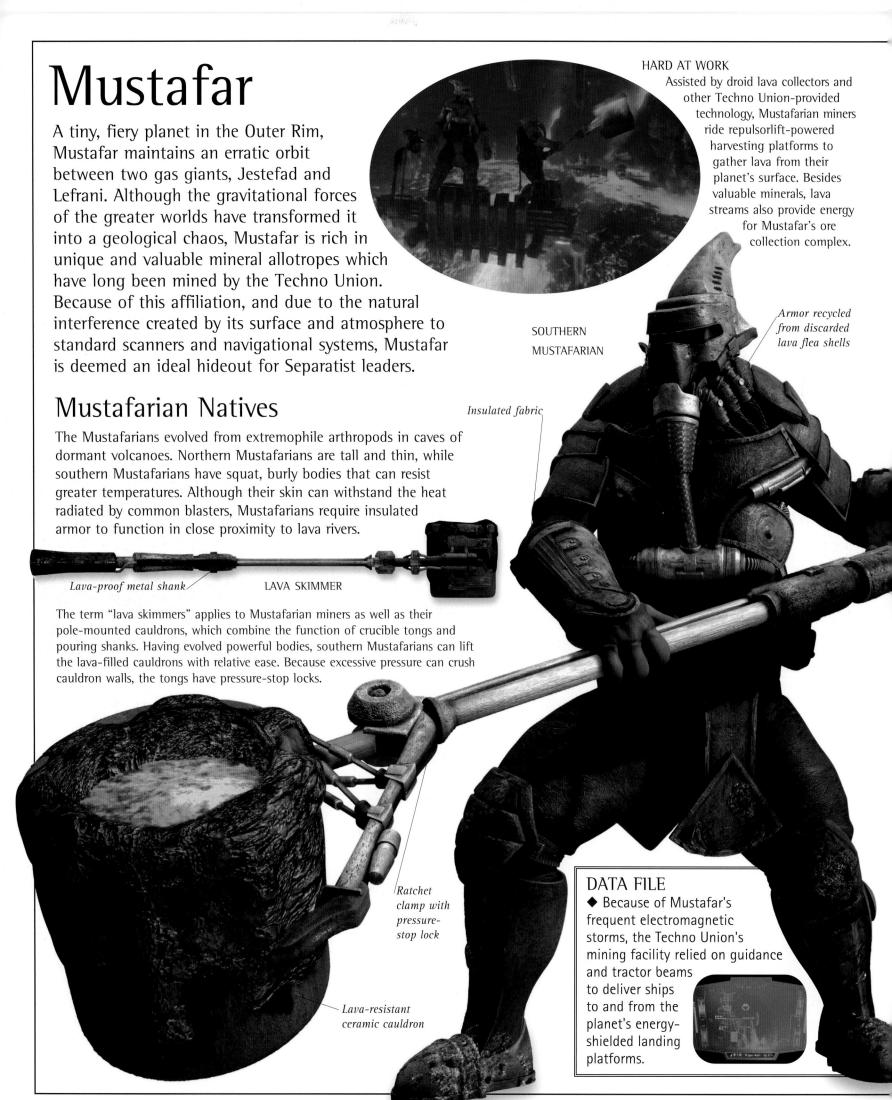

HARD AT WORK
Assisted by droid lava collectors and other Techno Union-provided technology, Mustafarian miners ride repulsorlift-powered harvesting platforms to gather lava from their planet's surface. Besides valuable minerals, lava streams also provide energy for Mustafar's ore collection complex.

SOUTHERN MUSTAFARIAN

Armor recycled from discarded lava flea shells

Mustafarian Natives

The Mustafarians evolved from extremophile arthropods in caves of dormant volcanoes. Northern Mustafarians are tall and thin, while southern Mustafarians have squat, burly bodies that can resist greater temperatures. Although their skin can withstand the heat radiated by common blasters, Mustafarians require insulated armor to function in close proximity to lava rivers.

Insulated fabric

Lava-proof metal shank   LAVA SKIMMER

The term "lava skimmers" applies to Mustafarian miners as well as their pole-mounted cauldrons, which combine the function of crucible tongs and pouring shanks. Having evolved powerful bodies, southern Mustafarians can lift the lava-filled cauldrons with relative ease. Because excessive pressure can crush cauldron walls, the tongs have pressure-stop locks.

Ratchet clamp with pressure-stop lock

Lava-resistant ceramic cauldron

DATA FILE
◆ Because of Mustafar's frequent electromagnetic storms, the Techno Union's mining facility relied on guidance and tractor beams to deliver ships to and from the planet's energy-shielded landing platforms.

MUSTAFARIAN LAVA FLEA
Among the earliest cavern-dwelling native creatures to venture across Mustafar's hostile surface, lava fleas are enormous hard-shelled arthropods that have been domesticated as mounts for Mustafarians. Feeding on soft, mineral-rich rocks, the fleas grow up to 4.3 meters tall, and can leap up to 30 meters in a single bound. Natural armor protects them from Mustafar's searing rock terrain.

Despite access to Techno Union-provided repulsorlifts, most Mustafarians prefer to travel by lava fleas. During the more than 300 years that the Techno Union has owned Mustafar, the Mustafarians have witnessed enough mechanical breakdowns to be cautious of any technology that has a melting point.

Lava-proof jointed mechanisms are expensive, and the Techno Union's droid lava collectors are extremely costly for their size. However, the investment is insignificant compared to the enormous profits gained from mining rare heavy elements.

Shock-resistant exoskeleton

Trochanter enables incredible jumping ability

Eyes distinguish between light and darkness

NORTHERN MUSTAFARIAN

Stereoscopic binocular sensors

DROID LAVA COLLECTOR
Manufactured on Mustafar, droid lava collectors employ repulsorlift technology, energy shielding, and durable armor to carry their molten loads to the mining complex. Like Trade Federation battle droids, mining droids are not autonomous and are controlled via remote signals.

Repulsorlift thruster cooling vents

Lava rich in precious ores

Fateful battle

After learning that Anakin Skywalker has become Darth Vader, Obi-Wan Kenobi tracks his former friend to the Techno Union's mining complex on Mustafar. Their lightsaber duel rages across various levels of the facility, but ends on the bank of a lava river, where Obi-Wan easily defeats the recently-appointed Sith Lord and leaves him to his fate.

Only the dark side of the Force allows Darth Vader to cling to life after being mortally wounded; he is barely alive when his charred remains are recovered by Darth Sidious.

Reinforced rings provide grip

High torque limbs

Darth Sidious

THE SITH HAVE WAITED a millennium for the birth of one who is powerful enough to return them from hiding. Darth Sidious is that one—the Sith's revenge on the Jedi order for having nearly eradicated the practitioners of the dark side of the Force. Trained by Darth Plagueis, Sidious, in his guise as Palpatine, understood that the corrupt Republic and the subservient Jedi Order could be brought down by playing to the weaknesses of the former: its mindless bureaucracy and attachment to power.

Sith hood and mantle

Face deformed by Sith lightning

Sidious does not consider himself evil but rather a savior. After the destruction of the Jedi order, he has no need to reveal his Sith identity, for he is now the beloved Emperor Palpatine, who has restored peace to the galaxy.

Sidious has one more task to perform before his conquest is complete: to kill Yoda. Then the light side of the Force will be eclipsed, and the Jedi order will cease to exist.

Precious aurodium cap and blade emitter

Blade-length adjust

Phrik alloy casing

LIGHTSABER
Sidious's Sith lightsaber is usually concealed within a neuranium sculpture that adorns his chambers in the Senate Office Building. A wall panel in the office depicts a legendary battle between the Sith and the Jedi.

Voluminous Sith robes

Two Faces

"Always two there are"—not only master and apprentice, but persona and true face. Unmasked by deflected lightning during his duel with Mace Windu, the Sith Lord's true face is revealed to the world. But for the Senate, the Jedi could not damage Palpatine's reputation.

DATA FILE

◆ A powerful practitioner of the dark side of the Force, Sidious uses Sith lightning to attack his enemies. It causes terrible pain.

◆ Sidious's act as the mild-mannered Chancellor Palpatine is so convincing that even the Jedi are taken in.

Darth Vader will represent the Sith, serving as Palpatine's liaison with the planetary system governors he has installed. He will also keep the military commanders in line—at least until work is completed on the Death Star.

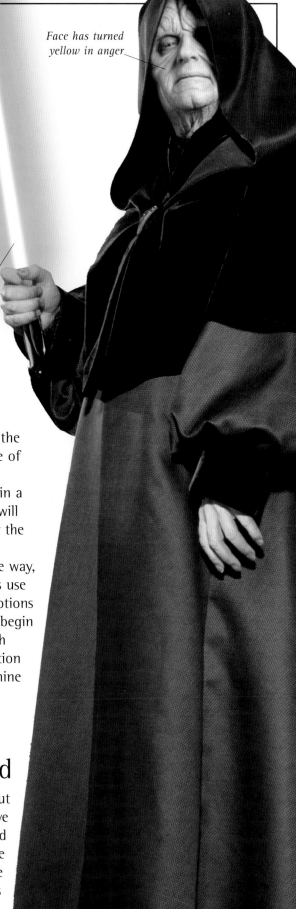

Face has turned yellow in anger

Vials of injectable bacta and bota

Injector power cells

Wireless defibrilator

Filtration transpirators

Resuscitating ventilator

Sith lightsaber

Injector head

Adaptors for pressor field generator

Cardiovascular monitors

Injector handle

Medical Kit

Plucked from death on the black-sand bank of one of Mustafar's lava rivers, Darth Vader is placed in a medical capsule that will keep him alive during the hyperspace jump to Coruscant. Along the way, Darth Sidious makes use of various special potions and implements to begin the process of Darth Vader's transformation into the man-machine he is destined to become.

Sith Lord

Darth Sidious isn't worried about any Jedi who managed to survive Order 66. Even united, Yoda and Obi-Wan pose no threat to the Dark Lords of the Sith. Soon the Jedi will be remembered only as archaic warriors, practicing a sad religion, and memories of the Republic will disappear. For Sidious, everything is proceeding according to plan.

Emperor Palpatine's shuttle can jump to lightspeed without having to use a hyperspace ring. The same is true of the V-wings that form his special escort.

Dark robes hide Sidious's identity

Darth Vader

FOLLOWING THE ATROCITIES he commits on Coruscant, Darth Vader is sent to Mustafar to "take care of the Separatist Council." There, he carries out his task with homicidal glee, executing one member after the next, saving an imploring Nute Gunray for last. His bloodlust temporarily sated, Vader learns that Padmé has followed him across the stars. But when she rebuffs his offer to rule the galaxy at his side, and it is revealed that Obi-Wan has accompanied her, Vader nearly chokes his wife to death with the Force, before engaging his former Master in a deadly duel above the planet's rivers of lava.

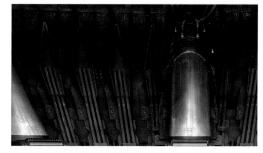

SURGICAL RECONSTRUCTION CENTER
Following his battle with Obi-Wan, Darth Vader was taken to a rehabilitation chamber on Coruscant. For all his powers, Vader's body remains mortal and he would have died without extensive surgical reconstruction.

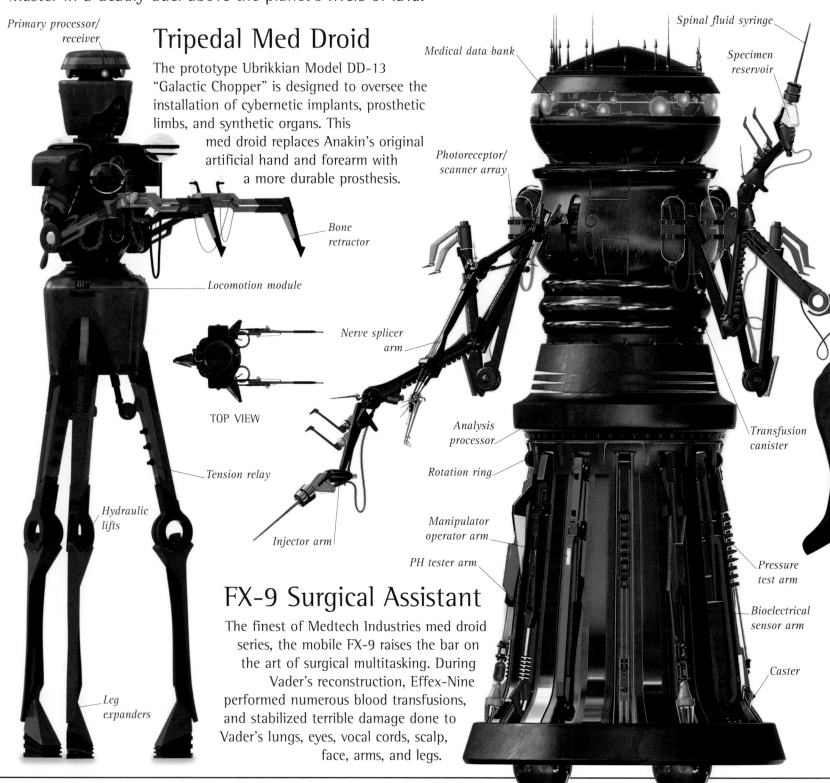

Tripedal Med Droid

The prototype Ubrikkian Model DD-13 "Galactic Chopper" is designed to oversee the installation of cybernetic implants, prosthetic limbs, and synthetic organs. This med droid replaces Anakin's original artificial hand and forearm with a more durable prosthesis.

Primary processor/receiver

Bone retractor

Locomotion module

Nerve splicer arm

TOP VIEW

Tension relay

Hydraulic lifts

Injector arm

Leg expanders

Medical data bank

Spinal fluid syringe

Specimen reservoir

Photoreceptor/scanner array

Analysis processor

Transfusion canister

Rotation ring

Manipulator operator arm

PH tester arm

Pressure test arm

Bioelectrical sensor arm

Caster

FX-9 Surgical Assistant

The finest of Medtech Industries med droid series, the mobile FX-9 raises the bar on the art of surgical multitasking. During Vader's reconstruction, Effex-Nine performed numerous blood transfusions, and stabilized terrible damage done to Vader's lungs, eyes, vocal cords, scalp, face, arms, and legs.

Dark Lord of the Sith

Awakened from his life-altering reconstruction on a gleaming table in Sidious's laboratory, Anakin learns that Padmé is dead—most likely by his own hand. His subsequent scream destroys nearly everything in the lab, including most of the med droids. The realization that he has killed the person he loved most will haunt him for the rest of his life.

Power indicator

Sith crystal chamber

Activator

Bloodshine Sith blade

Blade power adjuster

NEW LIGHTSABER

Vader will build a new lightsaber, powered by a synth-crystal supplied by Sidious that will yield a crimson blade.

Plastoid girdle protects abdominal organs

Function indicators

SYSTEMS STATUS BELT

Laser scalpel arm

Voice projector/ respiratory intake

Locking helmet

Vision enhancement receptors

Hermetic collar

Control function panel

System function display

DATA FILE

◆ As a result of having artificial arms, Darth Vader will never be able to conjure Sith lightning—nor be invulnerable to it.

◆ After Palpatine's creation of the Empire, academies for the training of non-clone Imperial officers will appear.

Ribbed multi-ply trousers

Shin armor protects prosthesis

Boots adhere to artificial limb

While Sidious is pleased to find that Anakin's rage has survived intact, Darth Vader is not what Sidious was expecting, and not the perfect apprentice to perpetuate the legacy of the Sith.

Cervical rib

Tail bone

Sand creature claw

TATOOINE SAND
CREATURE BONES

Multi-function
tool sheath

LUKE SKYWALKER'S
BELT POUCH

Magnetic
insulator

Neural
spine

Posterior
zygapophosis

SAND CREATURE
NECK VERTEBRA

Plastoid
composite
alloy

DEATH STAR TROOPER'S
HELMET

Chime
mount

Screamer gong

Tryna
chime

O'Tawa cymbals

Resonator

Gong
stand

Centressar
strings

DRUMHELLER
HARP

Intercomlink

Communications
antenna

Flash
shield

DEATH STAR GUNNER'S HELMET

Seilith
music
charms

Blade length
adjust

Activator
assembly

Harp
base

Emitter
shroud

DARTH VADER'S LIGHTSABER

EPISODES IV–VI
CLASSIC TRILOGY

EPISODE IV: A NEW HOPE heralds a new generation of characters that have grown up under Emperor Palpatine's iron fist. Luke Skywalker is an unlikely hero, having never left his sleepy desert home-planet of Tatooine. Upon receiving a distress call from the beautiful Princess Leia he enlists the aid of Obi-Wan Kenobi, Han Solo, and Chewbacca to rescue her from the forces of the Empire. As the adventure unfolds so do the mysteries of Luke's past. He must face up to his destiny to be a Jedi Knight, just as his father was before him.

In Episode V: *The Empire Strikes Back,* the battle to restore the Republic continues. With the Rebels' success in destroying the Death Star still fresh, the Emperor is keen to exact revenge. Using his henchman, Darth Vader, the battle for power continues unabated even when both Vader and Luke Skywalker learn the truth of their relationship.

Episode VI: *Return of the Jedi* sees Luke struggle with his internal emotions. By learning to control his anger and hate, he masters the Force and begins to control his own destiny as well as that of the galaxy....

THE EMPEROR'S CANE

Primary crystal

LIGHTSABER ENERGY CORE

Ploong sounder

Peel rod

Fanfar

Kloo horn

Band pants

Support post

Tone mode selectors

Handgrip

FIGRIN D'AN AND THE MODAL NODES

LUKE SKYWALKER'S BELT POUCH

Special Technology

For thousands of years high technology has existed throughout the galaxy, ebbing and flowing with the rise and fall of civilizations. The development of technology has taken many different and uneven paths, and what is a natural extension to one culture may be overlooked by another for ages. Traditional technology such as the Jedi lightsaber may remain constant for centuries. Alternatively, military pressures may bring new innovations in areas which have remained unchanged for millennia. As cultures meet and interact, advanced devices fall into the hands of otherwise primitive groups, and many creatures use technology of which they have no real understanding.

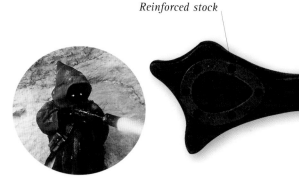

Reinforced stock

ION BLASTERS
Complex electronic components can be disrupted by ion blasts. Ion cannons can disable spacecraft without damaging them, while custom-built Jawa ionization blasters stun droids in the same way.

DARTH VADER'S LIGHTSABER

Magnetic stabilizing ring

Ring tuning flange

Lightsaber designs often relate to personal histories. Darth Vader's lightsaber looks much like the one he used as a Jedi learner, only darker. Luke Skywalker's lightsaber, on the other hand, follows the type used by Luke's mentor Ben Kenobi.

OBI-WAN KENOBI'S LIGHTSABER

LUKE SKYWALKER'S SECOND LIGHTSABER

Blade length adjust · *Energy modulation circuits* · *Cycling field energizers* · *Focusing crystals* · *Primary crystal* · *Primary crystal mount* · *Diatium power cell* · *Power field conductor* · *Handgrip attachment*

Blade emitter shroud

Blade arc tip · *Blade power adjust* · *Blade energy channel* · *Crystal energy chamber* · *Energy gate* · *Power vortex ring* · *Belt ring*

Focusing crystal activator · *Inert power insulator*

Lightsabers

Lightsabers tend to follow a similar basic structure, although many are very individualized by their Jedi builders. While the pure energy blade has no mass, the electromagnetically generated arc wave creates a strong gyroscopic effect that makes the lightsaber a distinct challenge to handle. Operating on the complex principle of tightly controlled arc-wave energy, it requires focusing elements made from natural or synthetic crystals, the latter being traditionally associated with the Sith. A lightsaber must be assembled by hand, as there is no exact formula for the crucial alignment of the irregular crystals. The slightest misalignment will cause the weapon to detonate on activation.

Luke Skywalker and Darth Vader duel in Cloud City

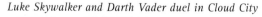

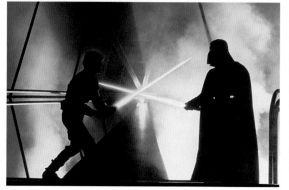

The legendary lightsaber is the ancient traditional weapon of the Jedi Knight, guardians of justice for so many generations. Building a working lightsaber is one of the threshold tests for Jedi initiates: accomplishing the impossibly fine alignment task proves their Force sensitivity.

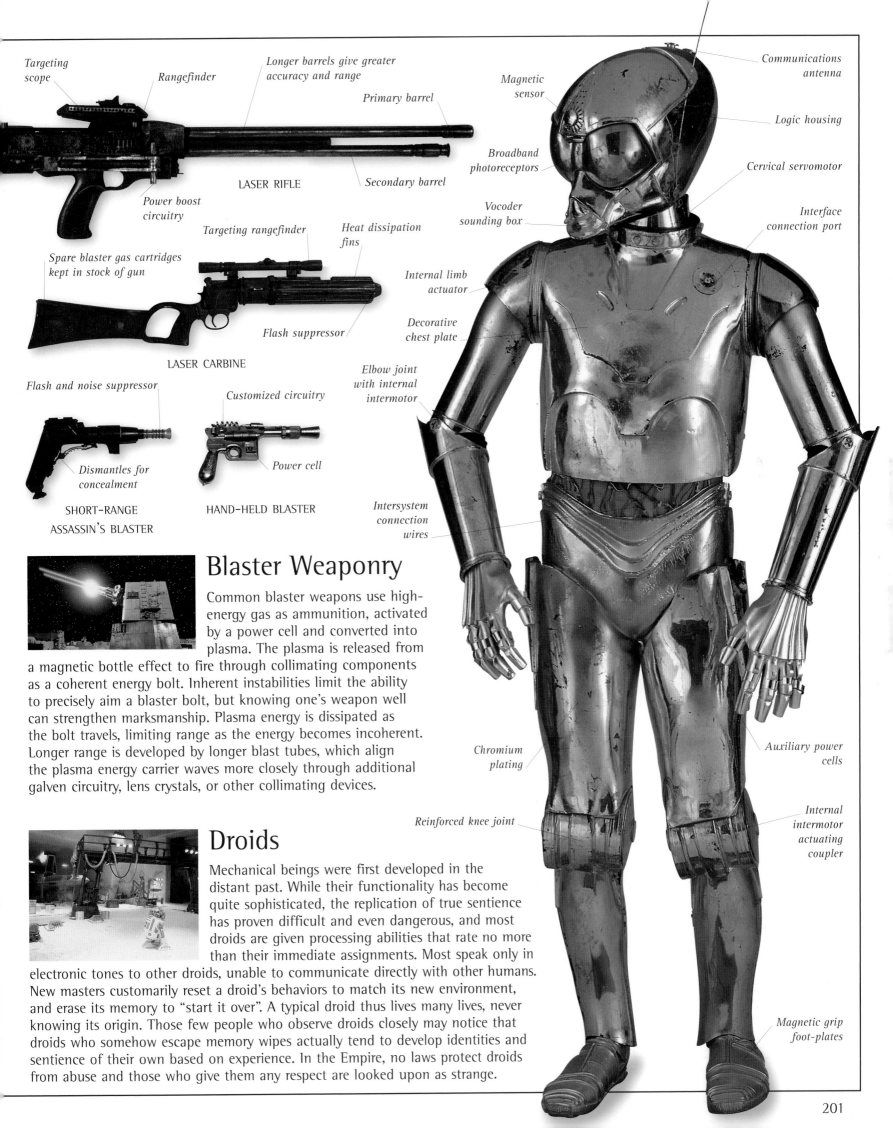

Targeting scope

Rangefinder

Longer barrels give greater accuracy and range

Primary barrel

LASER RIFLE

Power boost circuitry

Secondary barrel

Spare blaster gas cartridges kept in stock of gun

Targeting rangefinder

Heat dissipation fins

Flash suppressor

LASER CARBINE

Flash and noise suppressor

Customized circuitry

Dismantles for concealment

Power cell

SHORT-RANGE ASSASSIN'S BLASTER

HAND-HELD BLASTER

Communications antenna

Magnetic sensor

Logic housing

Broadband photoreceptors

Cervical servomotor

Vocoder sounding box

Interface connection port

Internal limb actuator

Decorative chest plate

Elbow joint with internal intermotor

Intersystem connection wires

Blaster Weaponry

Common blaster weapons use high-energy gas as ammunition, activated by a power cell and converted into plasma. The plasma is released from a magnetic bottle effect to fire through collimating components as a coherent energy bolt. Inherent instabilities limit the ability to precisely aim a blaster bolt, but knowing one's weapon well can strengthen marksmanship. Plasma energy is dissipated as the bolt travels, limiting range as the energy becomes incoherent. Longer range is developed by longer blast tubes, which align the plasma energy carrier waves more closely through additional galven circuitry, lens crystals, or other collimating devices.

Chromium plating

Auxiliary power cells

Droids

Mechanical beings were first developed in the distant past. While their functionality has become quite sophisticated, the replication of true sentience has proven difficult and even dangerous, and most droids are given processing abilities that rate no more than their immediate assignments. Most speak only in electronic tones to other droids, unable to communicate directly with other humans. New masters customarily reset a droid's behaviors to match its new environment, and erase its memory to "start it over". A typical droid thus lives many lives, never knowing its origin. Those few people who observe droids closely may notice that droids who somehow escape memory wipes actually tend to develop identities and sentience of their own based on experience. In the Empire, no laws protect droids from abuse and those who give them any respect are looked upon as strange.

Reinforced knee joint

Internal intermotor actuating coupler

Magnetic grip foot-plates

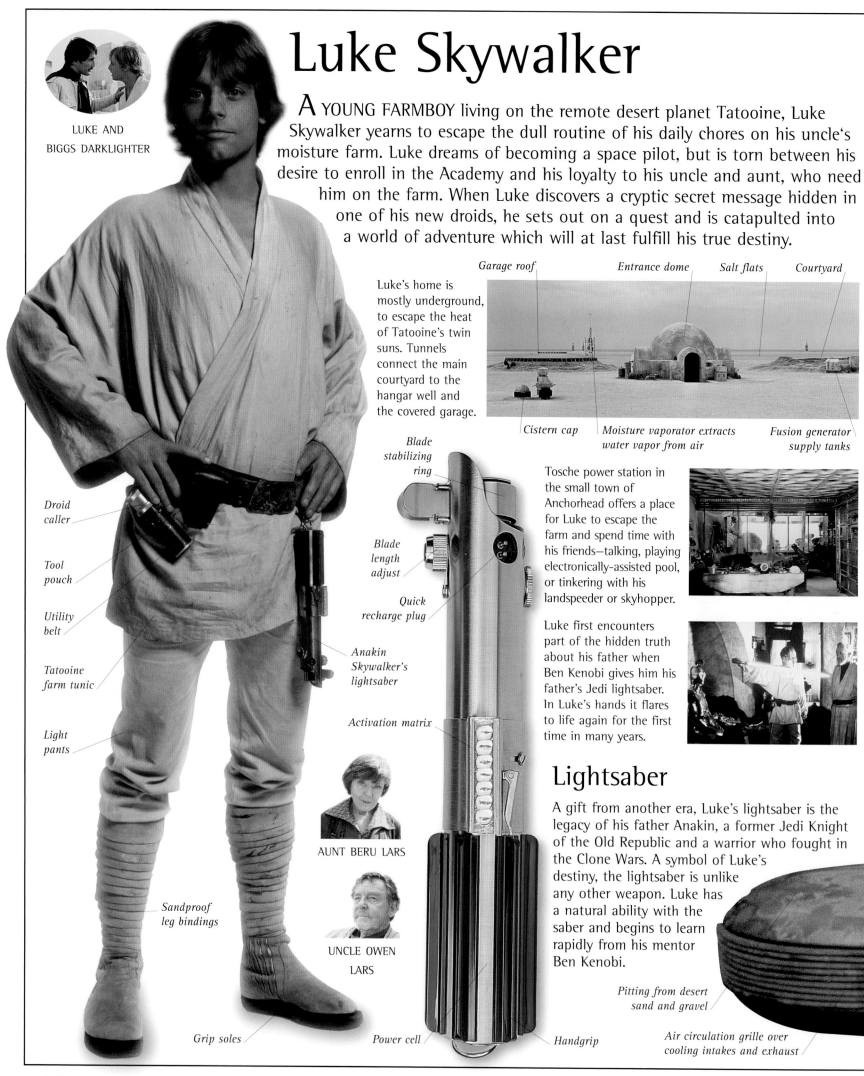

Luke Skywalker

LUKE AND
BIGGS DARKLIGHTER

A YOUNG FARMBOY living on the remote desert planet Tatooine, Luke Skywalker yearns to escape the dull routine of his daily chores on his uncle's moisture farm. Luke dreams of becoming a space pilot, but is torn between his desire to enroll in the Academy and his loyalty to his uncle and aunt, who need him on the farm. When Luke discovers a cryptic secret message hidden in one of his new droids, he sets out on a quest and is catapulted into a world of adventure which will at last fulfill his true destiny.

Luke's home is mostly underground, to escape the heat of Tatooine's twin suns. Tunnels connect the main courtyard to the hangar well and the covered garage.

Garage roof

Entrance dome

Salt flats

Courtyard

Cistern cap

Moisture vaporator extracts water vapor from air

Fusion generator supply tanks

Tosche power station in the small town of Anchorhead offers a place for Luke to escape the farm and spend time with his friends—talking, playing electronically-assisted pool, or tinkering with his landspeeder or skyhopper.

Luke first encounters part of the hidden truth about his father when Ben Kenobi gives him his father's Jedi lightsaber. In Luke's hands it flares to life again for the first time in many years.

Blade stabilizing ring

Blade length adjust

Quick recharge plug

Anakin Skywalker's lightsaber

Activation matrix

Droid caller

Tool pouch

Utility belt

Tatooine farm tunic

Light pants

Sandproof leg bindings

AUNT BERU LARS

UNCLE OWEN LARS

Lightsaber

A gift from another era, Luke's lightsaber is the legacy of his father Anakin, a former Jedi Knight of the Old Republic and a warrior who fought in the Clone Wars. A symbol of Luke's destiny, the lightsaber is unlike any other weapon. Luke has a natural ability with the saber and begins to learn rapidly from his mentor Ben Kenobi.

Grip soles

Power cell

Handgrip

Pitting from desert sand and gravel

Air circulation grille over cooling intakes and exhaust

DATA FILE

◆ Luke's best friend was Biggs Darklighter, who left Tatooine to enlist in the Academy. Biggs graduated with a commission on the freighter *Rand Ecliptic*. Luke is reunited with Biggs on the flight deck of the Rebel base at Yavin 4, where he learns that Biggs has become a Rebel pilot. The friends fly and fight together in the critical attack on the Death Star.

◆ Sandstorms scour the surface of Tatooine for days at a time, but farm work on the vaporators still has to be done. Luke wears a desert poncho and goggles for protection on windy days.

Model includes decor and enhanced components Luke hopes to get when he can afford them

Emblem Luke would like to add

Pneumatic projectile gun for blasting womp rats

Display base

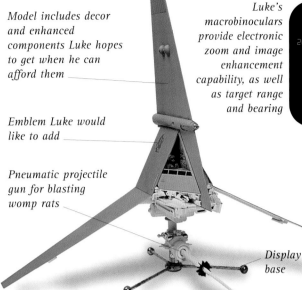

Luke's macrobinoculars provide electronic zoom and image enhancement capability, as well as target range and bearing

While working on a vaporator, Luke uses his macrobinoculars to observe a space battle between two ships far overhead.

Luke owns a suborbital T-16 skyhopper (his own model of it is shown above), which he races through the narrow ravines of Beggar's Canyon with his friends, blasting womp rat dens in sheltered hollows. Having narrowly made it through both Diablo Cut and the Stone Needle, Luke has proven himself an excellent pilot. He cannot search for R2-D2 in the skyhopper because his uncle has grounded him for reckless flying.

The kitchen of the Lars home is typical of moisture farms, with many moisture-saving devices. The kitchen passage leads up to the dining room, which opens onto the main courtyard.

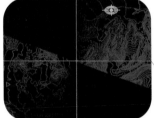

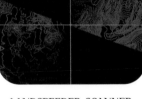

R2-D2 appears on the landspeeder scanner

LANDSPEEDER SCANNER

Luke's Landspeeder

Luke's X-34 landspeeder hovers above the ground, suspended by low-power repulsorlifts which keep the craft floating even when parked. Three turbines boost the repulsor drive effect and jet the 'speeder across the wide open spaces of the desert. The windshield can be closed to a sealed bubble, but Luke hasn't been able to fix the back half, so he keeps the cockpit open.

Crash damage

Repulsor drive generators

LANDSPEEDER – SIDE AND REAR

Thrust turbine vent

Velocity sensor

Power boost circuits

Hood panel

Duraplex windshield

Steering wheel

Cockpit

Cushioned seats

Storage well

Turbine mount

Repulsor field generator housing

Repulsor vents

Primary repulsor exhaust

Steering turbine engine with cowling removed

Turbine jet exhaust

Skywalker: Pilot and Jedi

LUKE SKYWALKER first climbs into the cockpit of an X-wing starfighter to fly as "Red Five" in the attack on the first Death Star. Fighting for the Alliance in the years afterward, Luke takes his X-wing and other craft into battle and adventure against space pirates and Imperial ships, bringing victories for the hard-pressed Rebels and becoming one of their most innovative leaders. His Force abilities are awakened by Master Yoda and, over the years, Luke grows towards the moment when he will become a Jedi Knight at last.

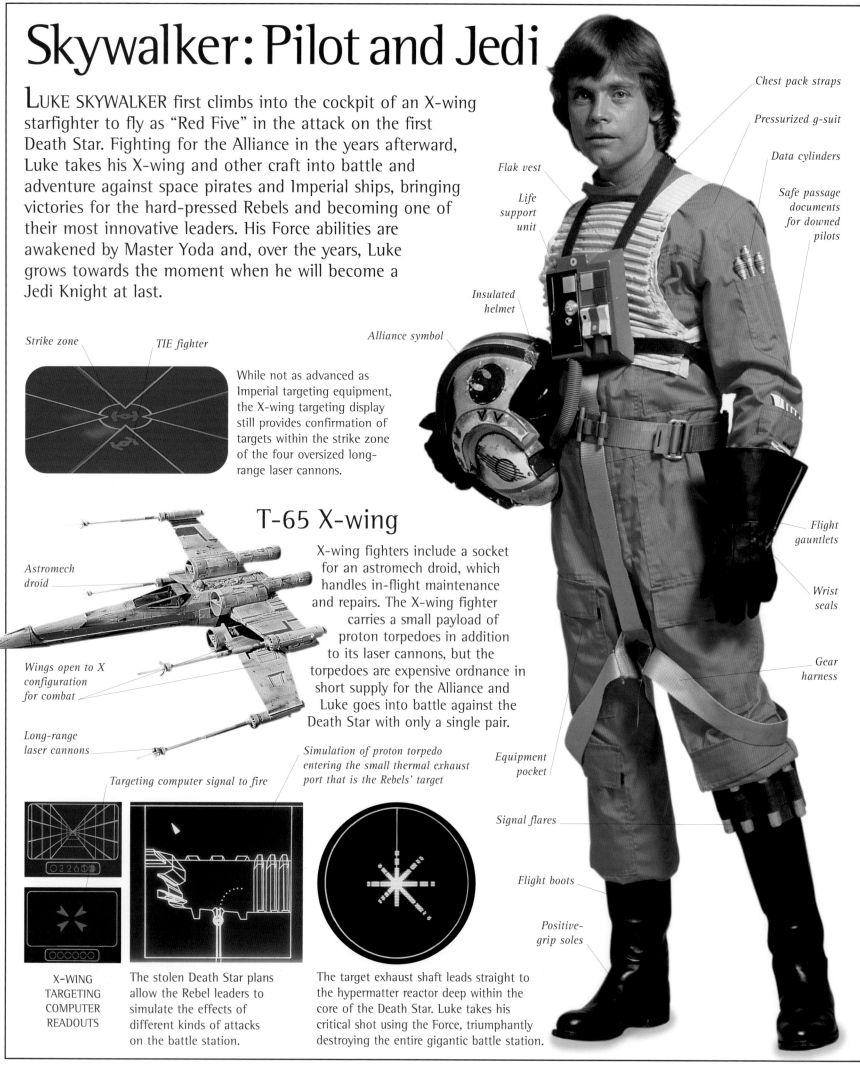

Chest pack straps

Pressurized g-suit

Data cylinders

Flak vest

Safe passage documents for downed pilots

Life support unit

Insulated helmet

Alliance symbol

Strike zone

TIE fighter

While not as advanced as Imperial targeting equipment, the X-wing targeting display still provides confirmation of targets within the strike zone of the four oversized long-range laser cannons.

Flight gauntlets

Wrist seals

T-65 X-wing

Astromech droid

X-wing fighters include a socket for an astromech droid, which handles in-flight maintenance and repairs. The X-wing fighter carries a small payload of proton torpedoes in addition to its laser cannons, but the torpedoes are expensive ordnance in short supply for the Alliance and Luke goes into battle against the Death Star with only a single pair.

Gear harness

Wings open to X configuration for combat

Long-range laser cannons

Targeting computer signal to fire

Simulation of proton torpedo entering the small thermal exhaust port that is the Rebels' target

Equipment pocket

Signal flares

032600

Flight boots

Positive-grip soles

X-WING TARGETING COMPUTER READOUTS

The stolen Death Star plans allow the Rebel leaders to simulate the effects of different kinds of attacks on the battle station.

The target exhaust shaft leads straight to the hypermatter reactor deep within the core of the Death Star. Luke takes his critical shot using the Force, triumphantly destroying the entire gigantic battle station.

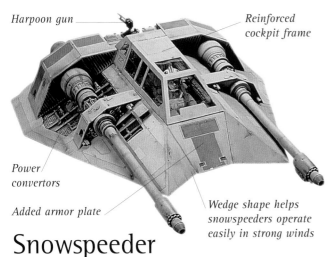

Harpoon gun

Reinforced cockpit frame

Power convertors

Added armor plate

Wedge shape helps snowspeeders operate easily in strong winds

Snowspeeder

Luke helped the Alliance acquire its squadron of defense speeder craft, equipped with armor plating and heavy-duty blaster cannons. Laboriously modified to operate in the frozen temperatures of Hoth, the snowspeeders have no defensive shields and must rely on agility and speed in battle. Luke, as a wing commander, leads the Rogue Squadron of snowspeeders against the Imperial Blizzard Force AT-ATs.

Luke's bravery takes him into situations which wipe out his equipment, but he never gives up. Blasted from the sky on Hoth, Luke struggles out of his cockpit before the snowspeeder is crushed by an AT-AT.

Jedi Knight

Having faced the challenge of his father's identity, Luke develops his abilities with the Force according to the teachings of his mentors Ben Kenobi and Yoda. Though he walks his path alone and without fellow initiates, Luke strives to fulfill his destiny and become a Jedi. Returning to Dagobah, he learns from Yoda that he has almost achieved that noble level at last. Centering his determination, Luke moves on to face the darkest challenges of the Emperor and Darth Vader, holding in his heart the galaxy's hope for freedom.

In a quad-laser turret of the *Millennium Falcon*, Luke faces a storm of TIE fighters as the *Falcon* escapes the original Death Star. Despite his inexperience, Luke adapts quickly and destroys two fighters, matching Han Solo's tally and winning the Corellian's respect.

Intercomlink headset

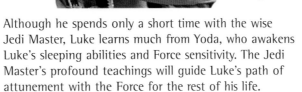

Yoda

At first, Luke bridles at Yoda's demanding training techniques

Although he spends only a short time with the wise Jedi Master, Luke learns much from Yoda, who awakens Luke's sleeping abilities and Force sensitivity. The Jedi Master's profound teachings will guide Luke's path of attunement with the Force for the rest of his life.

Black Jedi clothing

Mechanical hand

Utility belt

Lightsaber hook

DATA FILE

◆ Traveling to Dagobah in search of the Jedi Master Yoda, Luke has nothing to go on but his instincts and a vision message from his departed mentor Ben Kenobi.

◆ Returning to his home world of Tatooine, Luke leads the rescue of Han Solo from Jabba the Hutt. Doubted by both his friends and enemies, Luke proves himself and his extraordinary abilities in battle against the Hutt's forces, bringing the fire of Jedi protection and justice back to the galaxy.

The Shadow of Darth Vader

Growing up, Luke never knew much about his father. Ben Kenobi revealed that Luke's father had been a Jedi Knight, a space pilot, and a warrior, but the secret of his father's death remained clouded by the evil figure of Darth Vader. Only in close combat with Vader does Luke learn the truth that will pose his greatest challenge with the Force.

Princess Leia Organa

STRONG-WILLED and a woman of action, Princess Leia Organa of Alderaan uses her position in the Galactic Senate as a cover for diplomatic aid to the Rebel Alliance. Able to travel throughout the galaxy on her consular ship *Tantive IV*, Leia brings aid to beleaguered planets and secretly makes connections for the Rebellion. A beautiful and pensive young woman, she understands only too well her crucial position at a fateful time for the galaxy, and she hides her personal feelings behind stern discipline and dedication to her cause. As the adoptive daughter of Viceroy Bail Organa, Leia was trained for her royal position by the finest minds on Alderaan. The Princess was highly educated in martial and political arts in a lifelong preparation for her role.

Stolen Imperial blaster

Symbolic belt worn by Alderaan royalty

Traditional gown of the Alderaan royal family

Travel boots

Primary sensor array

Twin turbolasers

Command bridge

Escape pods

Tantive IV

Serving Leia as it did her father, the Tantive IV is a Corellian Corvette, a common ship design seen throughout the galaxy. Blending in anonymously amongst galactic space traffic, so many Corvettes have been converted for smuggling or covert uses that they are often called "Blockade Runners."

While on a secret mission to summon the aid of the Jedi Knight Obi-Wan Kenobi, Leia is trapped on board her diplomatic starship. Knowing she will be captured, she nonetheless fights to the end, and does what she can to ensure that her message will reach Obi-Wan, via R2-D2, even if she herself cannot.

A princess alone within the soulless metal depths of the Death Star, Leia was incarcerated by Darth Vader after her capture. She held firm against every torture.

Princess Leia's influence, royal connections, and diplomatic abilities obtained much of the vital communication and scanning equipment in the Rebel command center on the Fourth Moon of Yavin.

On-duty braids

Rank insignia

Heated vest

White insulated jumpsuit

Boot bindings

Military snow boots

Within the frozen command center of Echo Base, Leia watches the scanners intently for any sign of Imperial detection. Her concerns are always with her people.

When Echo Base is discovered and invaded by Imperial forces, Leia inspires the Rebel pilots, staying at her command post and directing the evacuation even when the base begins to collapse around her.

Although her background has given her little training in mechanical hardware work, Leia does her best to help with repairs when the *Falcon* is in trouble.

Amidst the fabulous beauty of Cloud City, Leia has only a brief time to share with the *Falcon*'s flashy rogue captain before they are all in ensnared in Darth Vader's trap.

Ice Princess

Trading her ceremonial gown for an insulated jumpsuit, Leia still wears symbolic white as the princess of a lost planet in the corridors of Hoth's Echo Base. As the Alliance faces new challenges, she remains a key command figure, directing deployments and determining key strategic moves, with General Rieekan and other Alliance leaders.

Jabba's Slave

Braving the dangers of Jabba's palace in her quest to rescue Han Solo, Leia knew she could face torture or death if captured. Though she did not anticipate the grueling experience of serving as Jabba's slave girl, she endures her captivity with fierce spirit and keeps ready to turn on Jabba when the time is right.

Where dozens of professional assassins had failed, Leia succeeds in putting an end to the contemptible crime lord Jabba the Hutt.

Slave girl harness

Lashaa silk

Jerba leather boots

DATA FILE

◆ Princess Leia is the youngest person ever to hold a seat in the Galactic Senate. Intelligent and a strong leader, Leia is used to taking charge and making things happen.

◆ Trained in military discipline, techniques, and strategy, Leia is an excellent tactician and an expert shot with a blaster. She virtually never misses.

◆ As princess of Alderaan, Leia is a noble leader of her people; as a senator she represents her entire home planet in the Galactic Senate, stirring much sympathy for the Rebellion. Within the Rebel Alliance the princess is a beloved leader and symbol of hope.

Rebel Leader

Rank insignia

Trusty light target pistol

Exposed as a Rebel, Princess Leia's career as a recognized diplomat is over, but she contributes more than ever to the strength of the Alliance. No longer content to be just a great symbol, a leader, and a negotiator, Leia also returns to action in the field, proving that she is still one of the best shots in the Alliance.

Forest Diplomat

Leia's good spirit and natural gift for diplomacy help her to win the confidence of the Ewoks she meets on Endor. By swapping her combat uniform (right) for clothes they make for her, she helps win humble allies that will topple the Empire.

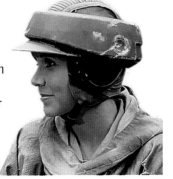

Han Solo

MERCENARY PIRATE, smuggler captain, and cocksure braggart, the overly confident Han Solo is a rugged individual of the Galactic Rim. From impoverished beginnings, Solo worked up through petty thievery to gain a commission in the Academy, from which he was later expelled. A Corellian pilot of the finest caliber nonetheless, Solo gained control of his destiny when he won his ship, the *Millennium Falcon*, in the best game of sabacc he ever played. His reputation as a gunfighter matches his renown as captain of the *Falcon*. Reckless and foolhardy, he is also courageous and daring, a match for any adventure.

Customized blaster pistol

Corellian spacer black vest and light shirt

Faced at gunpoint by one of Jabba's minions in the Mos Eisley Cantina, Han Solo keeps his cool and slowly draws his blaster under the table. The regulars could have warned Greedo that Han was the wrong man to threaten. Only one of them would walk away from the table.

Scope settings and adjustment

Scope

Flash suppressor

Enhanced blast delivery circuits

Cooling unit

Final stage collimator

Power pack

Trigger

Power pack

Power pack release lever

Low-power pulse warning

HAN SOLO'S DL-44 PISTOL

Droid caller

Blaster power cell

Captain's pants

Corellian blood stripe

Captain Solo's loyal friend and first mate is the imposing Wookiee Chewbacca. Each has risked his life for the other in many tight situations. Between Han's fast draw and Chewbacca's violent strength, the two are not to be trifled with.

Quick-draw holster

Holster thigh grip

One of Han's regular employers has been the crime lord Jabba the Hutt. When Han had to jettison a cargo to avoid arrest, he incurred Jabba's wrath and was unable to pay him back. This has led to Jabba posting a deadly bounty on Han's head that will haunt him until he resolves the situation.

DATA FILE

◆ As a child Solo was raised by space gypsies, never knowing who his real parents were. He learned tricks and self-reliance from his adoptive community.

◆ Solo's last-minute rescue of Luke Skywalker saved the Rebel Alliance and won him one of the highest medals of honor, along with Chewbacca and Luke Skywalker.

Action boots

FALCON QUAD-LASER SCOPE

Upper quad-
laser cannon

Main sensor
rectenna

Starboard
docking ring

Cockpit

Hyperspace
integrator

Millennium Falcon

This battered and aging YT-1300 light freighter
has had a long history in the hands of several
captains. Han's extensive modifications to the
ship have made it one of the fastest vessels in
hyperspace. Even at sublight speeds its velocity
and maneuverability are extraordinary for a ship
of its class. The *Falcon* sports Imperial military-
grade armor, quad-laser cannons, a top-of-the-
line sensor rectenna, and many other illegal and
customized hot-rod components. The ship serves
them as a unique home and powerful workhorse.

Han proves to Leia that
there is more to being a
scoundrel than having a
checkered past. A princess
and a guy like him?

Han had heard spacer's tales about the
legendary titan space slug, but he scoffed
at them as nothing more than ghost
stories. His narrow escape from the belly
of a live space slug restores his distrust
in anything being really safe.

Solo, Rebel Leader

After the victory at Yavin, Han eventually
accepts a commission as captain in the
Rebel Alliance. At frozen Echo Base
on Hoth, he volunteers for difficult
perimeter patrol duty even though
he does not like tauntauns or the
cold. Han is a natural leader and
serves as an inspiration to many
of the troopers around him.

Heavy weather parka

REBEL SENSOR
PACK

Extensible
antenna

Stentronic
wave monitor

Power
indicator

Range cycle
computer

Power
cells

Stolen Imperial
electrobinoculars

HOTH EQUIPMENT
With their patrol craft paralyzed by
the icy cold, the Rebels must survey
the snow plains of Hoth with hand-
carried gear. Han Solo is an expert
at keeping a low profile
and seeing others
before they see him,
and has helped
design the Echo Base
perimeter survey plan.

With the *Falcon* on the run and in
need of repairs, Han Solo lands at
Bespin to meet the ship's previous
owner Lando Calrissian, not knowing
for certain how Lando will react.

Han in Carbonite

Trapped in a plot by Darth Vader to ensnare
his friend Luke Skywalker, Han Solo is taken
to the industrial bowels of Cloud City and
flash-frozen in carbonite to test the process
meant to immobilize Luke. Carbon-freezing is
a way of bonding condensed Tibanna gas for
transport, but can be used to keep life forms
in suspended animation when the painful
process of freezing does not kill them.

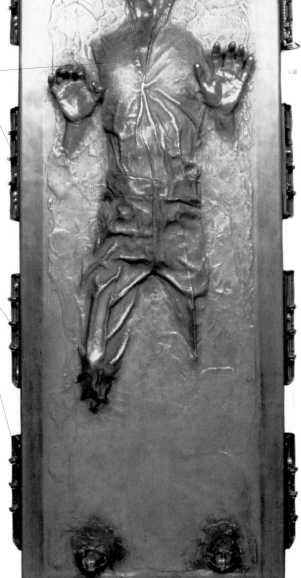

Carbonite
frame

Life
system
monitor

Flash-blasted
carbonite
matrix

Carbonite
flux monitor

Gas ratio
monitor

Carbonite
integrity
monitor

Chewbacca
WOOKIEE CO-PILOT

A MIGHTY WOOKIEE from the planet Kashyyyk, Chewbacca was recued from slavery by Han Solo. Teaming with him to repay the traditional Wookiee life debt, Chewbacca later "adopted" the wayward Corellian and became his best friend. The great Wookiee now uses his mechanical abilities to keep Solo's heavily modified spaceship flying, and serves as both a fiercely loyal co-pilot and a trusty fellow adventurer.

Chewie enjoys a good fight and likes the action that Solo gets them into, but sometimes acts as his partner's conscience.

Han Solo and Chewbacca make a dauntless pair of spacers, following adventure where it leads them. The two fight well together, knowing each other's strengths and relying on each other's abilities. Han's ego may get them into trouble or Chewie's temper may start fights, but the two of them together know when to blast 'em and when to run.

Although the *Millennium Falcon* cockpit is small for his great frame, Chewbacca is at ease with the myriad controls and copilots the ship with confidence. Deferring to Han's outstanding marksmanship, Chewie usually flies the ship while Han mans a gun turret during pursuit space combat.

BOWCASTER AMMUNITION
The traditional Wookiee bowcaster uses a magnetic accelerator to fire explosive quarrels, which are enveloped in a penetrating energy shell as they are fired. The bowcaster has a range of 50 meters and requires immense strength to cock.

Blue eyes

Sensitive nose

Bandolier

Padding

Quarrel

Insulated lining

Six-shell ammo case

Ammo case lid

Detonator pin

Energy shell flare material

Shell casing

Accelerator lock surface

QUARREL

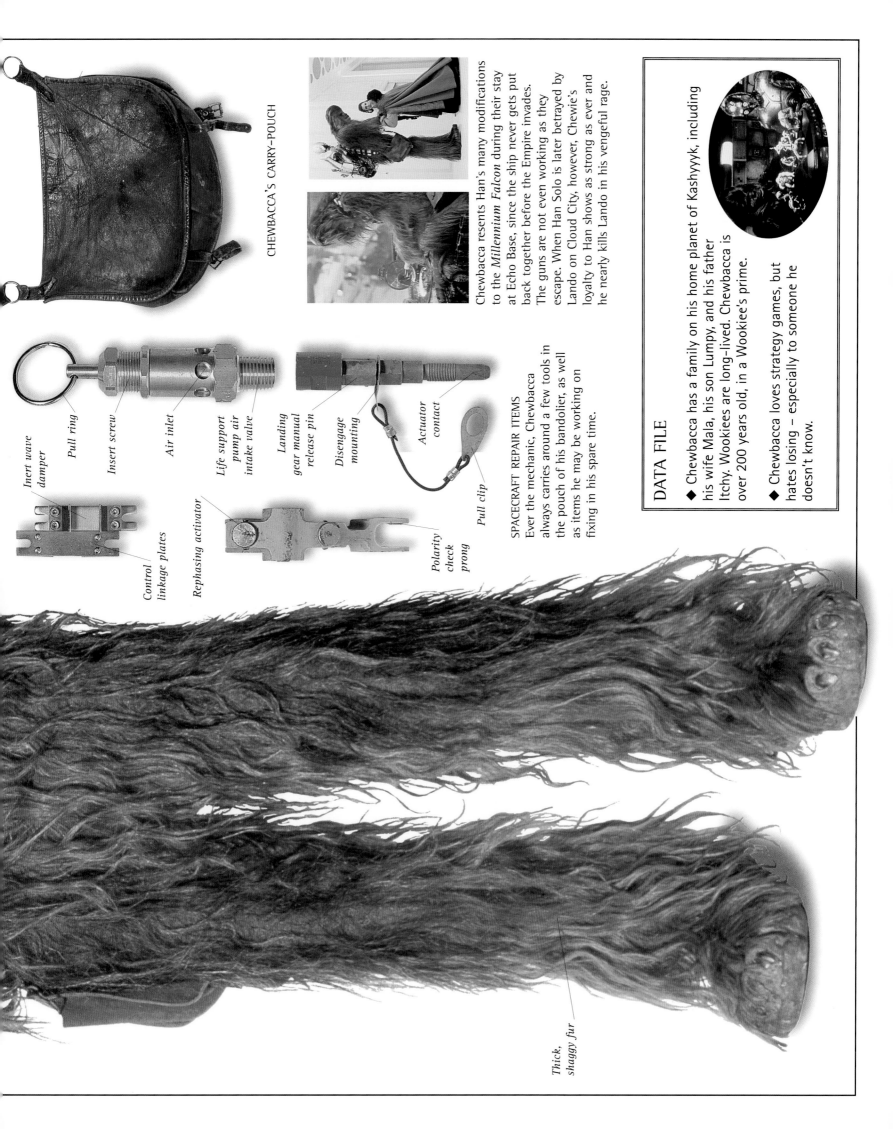

CHEWBACCA'S CARRY-POUCH

Inert wave damper

Pull ring

Insert screw

Air inlet

Life support pump air intake valve

Landing gear manual release pin

Disengage mounting

Actuator contact

Pull clip

Control linkage plates

Rephasing activator

Polarity check prong

SPACECRAFT REPAIR ITEMS
Ever the mechanic, Chewbacca always carries around a few tools in the pouch of his bandolier, as well as items he may be working on fixing in his spare time.

Chewbacca resents Han's many modifications to the *Millennium Falcon* during their stay at Echo Base, since the ship never gets put back together before the Empire invades. The guns are not even working as they escape. When Han Solo is later betrayed by Lando on Cloud City, however, Chewie's loyalty to Han shows as strong as ever and he nearly kills Lando in his vengeful rage.

DATA FILE

◆ Chewbacca has a family on his home planet of Kashyyyk, including his wife Mala, his son Lumpy, and his father Itchy. Wookiees are long-lived. Chewbacca is over 200 years old, in a Wookiee's prime.

◆ Chewbacca loves strategy games, but hates losing – especially to someone he doesn't know.

Thick, shaggy fur

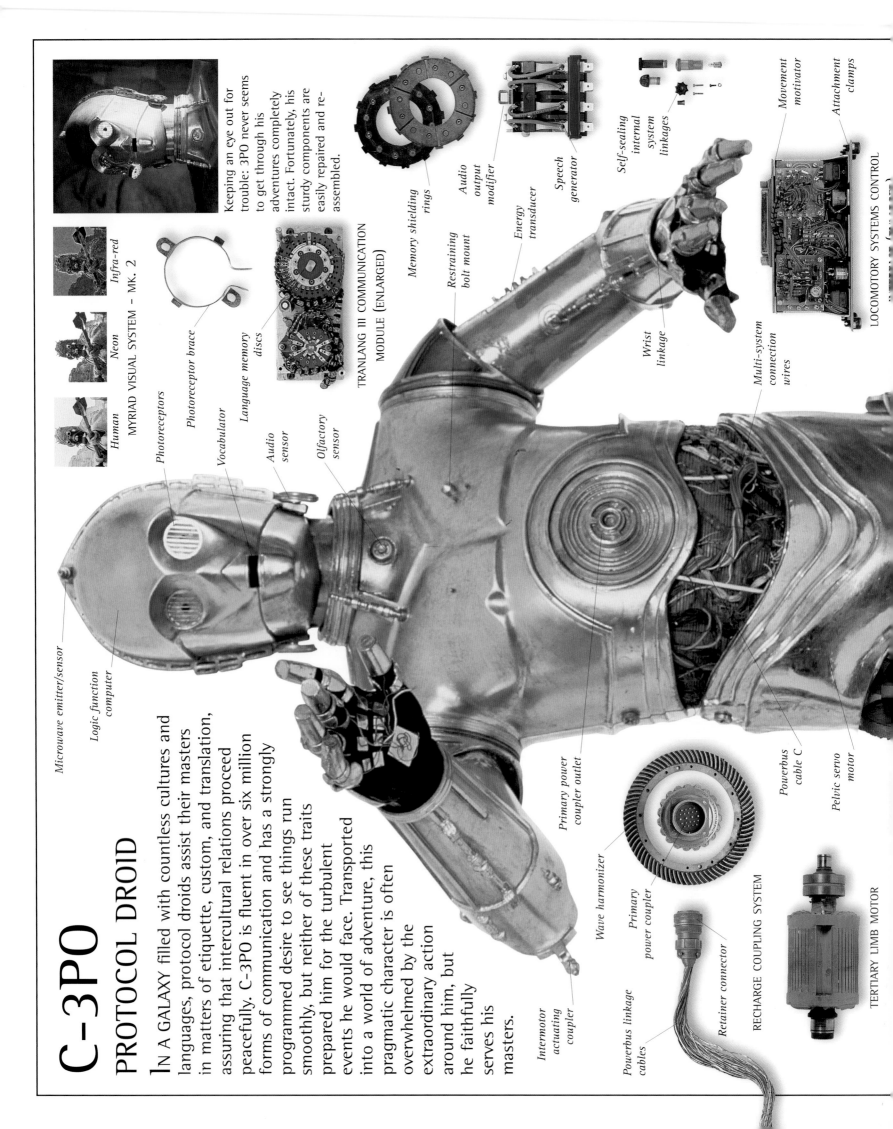

C-3PO
PROTOCOL DROID

In a galaxy filled with countless cultures and languages, protocol droids assist their masters in matters of etiquette, custom, and translation, assuring that intercultural relations proceed peacefully. C-3PO is fluent in over six million forms of communication and has a strongly programmed desire to see things run smoothly, but neither of these traits prepared him for the turbulent events he would face. Transported into a world of adventure, this pragmatic character is often overwhelmed by the extraordinary action around him, but he faithfully serves his masters.

Keeping an eye out for trouble: 3PO never seems to get through his adventures completely intact. Fortunately, his sturdy components are easily repaired and re-assembled.

Human   Neon   Infra-red

MYRIAD VISUAL SYSTEM – MK. 2

TRANLANG III COMMUNICATION MODULE (ENLARGED)

Memory shielding rings

Restraining bolt mount

Audio output modifier

Energy transducer

Speech generator

Self-sealing internal system linkages

Movement motivator

Attachment clamps

Wrist linkage

Multi-system connection wires

LOCOMOTORY SYSTEMS CONTROL

Photoreceptors

Photoreceptor brace

Vocabulator

Language memory discs

Audio sensor

Olfactory sensor

Microwave emitter/sensor

Logic function computer

Primary power coupler outlet

Powerbus cable C

Pelvic servo motor

Wave harmonizer

Primary power coupler

Intermotor actuating coupler

Powerbus linkage cables

Retainer connector

RECHARGE COUPLING SYSTEM

TERTIARY LIMB MOTOR

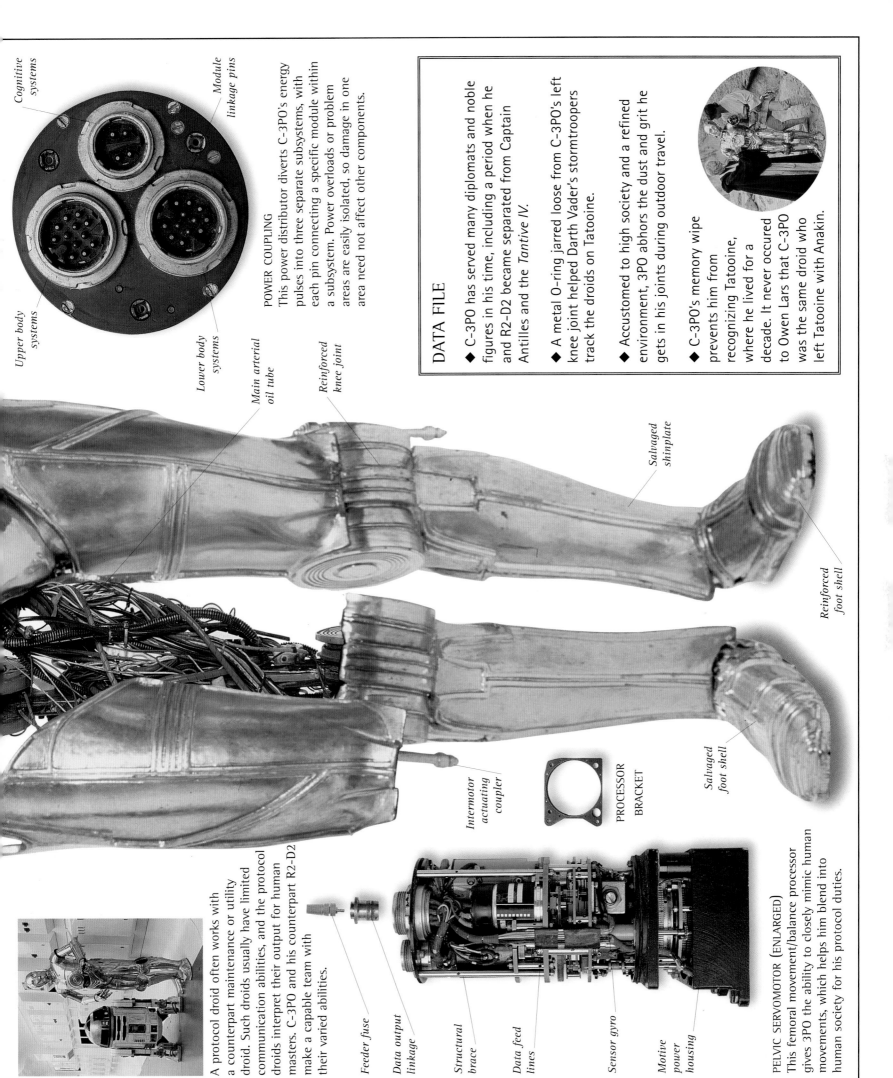

Cognitive systems

Module linkage pins

Upper body systems

Lower body systems

Main arterial oil tube

Reinforced knee joint

POWER COUPLING

This power distributor diverts C-3PO's energy pulses into three separate subsystems, with each pin connecting a specific module within a subsystem. Power overloads or problem areas are easily isolated, so damage in one area need not affect other components.

DATA FILE

◆ C-3PO has served many diplomats and noble figures in his time, including a period when he and R2-D2 became separated from Captain Antilles and the *Tantive IV*.

◆ A metal O-ring jarred loose from C-3PO's left knee joint helped Darth Vader's stormtroopers track the droids on Tatooine.

◆ Accustomed to high society and a refined environment, 3PO abhors the dust and grit he gets in his joints during outdoor travel.

◆ C-3PO's memory wipe prevents him from recognizing Tatooine, where he lived for a decade. It never occured to Owen Lars that C-3PO was the same droid who left Tatooine with Anakin.

Salvaged shinplate

Reinforced foot shell

Salvaged foot shell

Intermotor actuating coupler

PROCESSOR BRACKET

A protocol droid often works with a counterpart maintenance or utility droid. Such droids usually have limited communication abilities, and the protocol droids interpret their output for human masters. C-3PO and his counterpart R2-D2 make a capable team with their varied abilities.

Feeder fuse

Data output linkage

Structural brace

Data feed lines

Sensor gyro

Motive power housing

PELVIC SERVOMOTOR (ENLARGED)

This femoral movement/balance processor gives 3PO the ability to closely mimic human movements, which helps him blend into human society for his protocol duties.

R2-D2
ASTROMECH DROID

DESIGNED AS a sophisticated computer repair and information retrieval droid, R2-D2 is a highly useful astromech unit filled with apparatus of all sorts. His long history of adventures has given him distinct personality and quirkiness. R2 exhibits a strong motivation to succeed in his assigned tasks, displaying stubborn determination and inventiveness that are extraordinary for a utility droid. A protocol droid like C-3PO must translate his electronic beeps and whistles for human masters, but that doesn't stop R2 from trying to communicate anyway, and he usually manages to get his points across, even without an interpreter. Highly loyal, R2 is never reluctant to risk damage or destruction to help his masters and accomplish missions.

Princess Leia entrusted R2-D2 with the stolen Death Star plans and her urgent message to Obi-Wan Kenobi, which R2 faithfully found a way to deliver. Hologram recording and projection is one of R2-D2's standard capabilities.

An on-board R2 unit is a vital component of the Incom T-65 X-wing. The droid's in-flight adjustments allow for optimum performance. Most pilots would want to use the available droid in the best condition, but Luke Skywalker grows attached to R2-D2 and chooses the droid to accompany him in the attack on the Death Star.

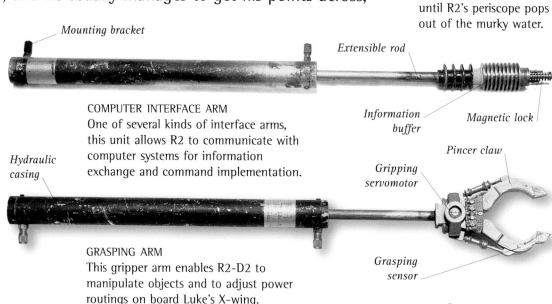

Mounting bracket

Extensible rod

COMPUTER INTERFACE ARM
One of several kinds of interface arms, this unit allows R2 to communicate with computer systems for information exchange and command implementation.

Hydraulic casing

Information buffer

Magnetic lock

Pincer claw

Gripping servomotor

GRASPING ARM
This gripper arm enables R2-D2 to manipulate objects and to adjust power routings on board Luke's X-wing.

Grasping sensor

Insulated casing

Overload breaker

Contact prongs

POWER CHARGE ARM
A power output arm allows R2-D2 to recharge dead machinery or pulse electricity through damaged circuits for diagnostic tests.

Power regulator

Charge capacitor

Pressurizing system

Adjustable spray nozzle

Lubricant filter

Rotation servomotor

Lubricant heating coil

Pressure delivery tube

LUBRICANT APPLICATION ARM

Arm Extensions

R2-D2's extension arms include everything from welding tips to cutter devices, clamps, and magnetic depolarizing leads. Many such devices are built into his various compartments, and an interchangeable component design allows him to be equipped with still others for special tasks.

When R2-D2 disappears into a swamp on Dagobah, Luke thinks he may have lost his companion for good ... until R2's periscope pops out of the murky water.

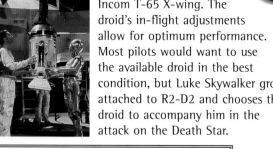

R2-D2 uses his fire extinguisher inventively to conceal his friends from attacking stormtroopers.

DATA FILE

◆ Durable and strongly built, R2-D2 has been around even longer than his counterpart C-3PO.

◆ R2-D2 resorts to innovative deceit when necessary, which makes 3PO throw up his hands in dismay. One of R2's deceptions began all of Luke's adventures.

Life-scan mesh

Primary photo receptor and radar eye

Data card input

Inert alloy plate

Processor state indicator

Holographic projector

Signal amplifier

Logic function display

HOLOGRAM PROJECTOR BULB

Overload heat vent

MOTIVATOR HOUSING AND VENT

Sensory input head

Reinforced rod

Computer interface and lubricant application arms compartment

Head rotation ring

Spacecraft linkage data slot

Hydraulic extension

Actuating coupler

Spacecraft linkage and control arms

Acoustic signaler

System ventilation

Stored experiences

MEMORY CHIP

Main logic processor connection

SCANNER ANTENNA

Charge arm compartment

MAIN POWER COUPLING

Systems diagnostic input receptors

Grasping arm compartment

Interference pulse stabilizers

Heat exhaust

Polarity sink

Recharge power coupling

Astromech units are standard droid types, and Jabba's personnel found a fitting that would allow R2-D2 to serve drinks on board Jabba's sail barge.

Locomotion power cells

Durasteel shell

Powerbus cables

Third tread (retractable)

Motorized all-terrain treads

215

Lando Calrissian

THE DASHING Baron Administrator of Cloud City has a past that few on Bespin would suspect. As a rogue and con artist, Lando built his early fortunes from modest beginnings, becoming a daring smuggler captain with a good head for business and a bad habit of gambling. He flew the *Millennium Falcon* for years before losing the ship to Han Solo in a sabacc match. The same game later won Lando control of the fabulous gas mining colony on Bespin. As the flamboyant leader of Cloud City, Lando combines his sense of style with a new-found sense of responsibility and has come to enjoy his role as Baron Administrator.

Winning smile

Borrowed Rebel blaster

Tarelle sel-weave shirt

Baron Administrator state belt

Aeien silk lining

Royal emblems

Baron's cape

Handmade Liwari shoes

Cloud City

Suspended high above the core of the gas giant Bespin, Cloud City was once the headquarters of great royal leaders. The city's glorious past has filled the skyline with monumental majesty and ethereal beauty. The city is supported on a single giant column which stems from a processing reactor at its base. In the city's hollow air shaft core are gigantic directional vanes that control the facility's location in space.

Broadcast antenna

Microphone

Signal processor

COMLINK

Handgrip

Cloud City is home to industrious citizens and advanced technology. Facilities throughout the city process for export the rare anti-gravitational tibanna gas from the exotic atmosphere of Bespin.

Calrissian is forced to betray Han Solo and his friends to Darth Vader in order to preserve Cloud City's freedom. When Lando learns that Vader has no intention of keeping the bargain, he plots a rescue and escape with his aide Lobot.

General Lando

Having become a renegade on the run from the Empire, Lando fell in with the Rebels after leaving Cloud City. His penetrating judgment at the Battle of Taanab won Lando promotion within the ranks, and the former con artist and baron became a general within the Alliance. He once more wears a cape of honor and authority. Grown beyond his self-centered past, Lando still finds adventure but now contributes his abilities to a greater cause.

Electro-stun extensible bayonet

Stun attachment wire

Vibro blade

Vibration generator

Blade release switch

Rank insignia

Dress cape

Rank plaque

City central computer link

Alliance general's uniform

Sidearm blaster

Wrist comlink

Lobot

Equipped with cybernetic implants, the Chief Administrative Aide of Cloud City keeps in direct contact with the city's central computer. Able to monitor a vast array of details at once, Lobot is an ideal assistant to Lando Calrissian. Lobot takes great satisfaction in making Cloud City a well-run success.

Cyborg unit

By turning against the Imperial forces of Darth Vader, Lando loses everything he has built as Baron Administrator of Cloud City. Racing through the corridors of the city with Leia and Chewbacca, Lando witnesses Boba Fett lift off with Han Solo, and barely escapes with his life from the city he once ruled.

Grip

Blade/electro-stun power unit

Reinforced lance pole

VIBRO-AXE POLEARM

Disguised as a lowly skiff guard at Jabba's palace, Lando braves the very heart of danger to rescue Han Solo. His old con man skills are put to good use, and no one at the palace ever suspects him until it is too late.

DATA FILE

◆ Using a comlink and his security code, Lando can address all parts of Cloud City from any central computer terminal.

◆ Lando uses an old underworld contact on Tatooine to secure a guard job at Jabba's palace.

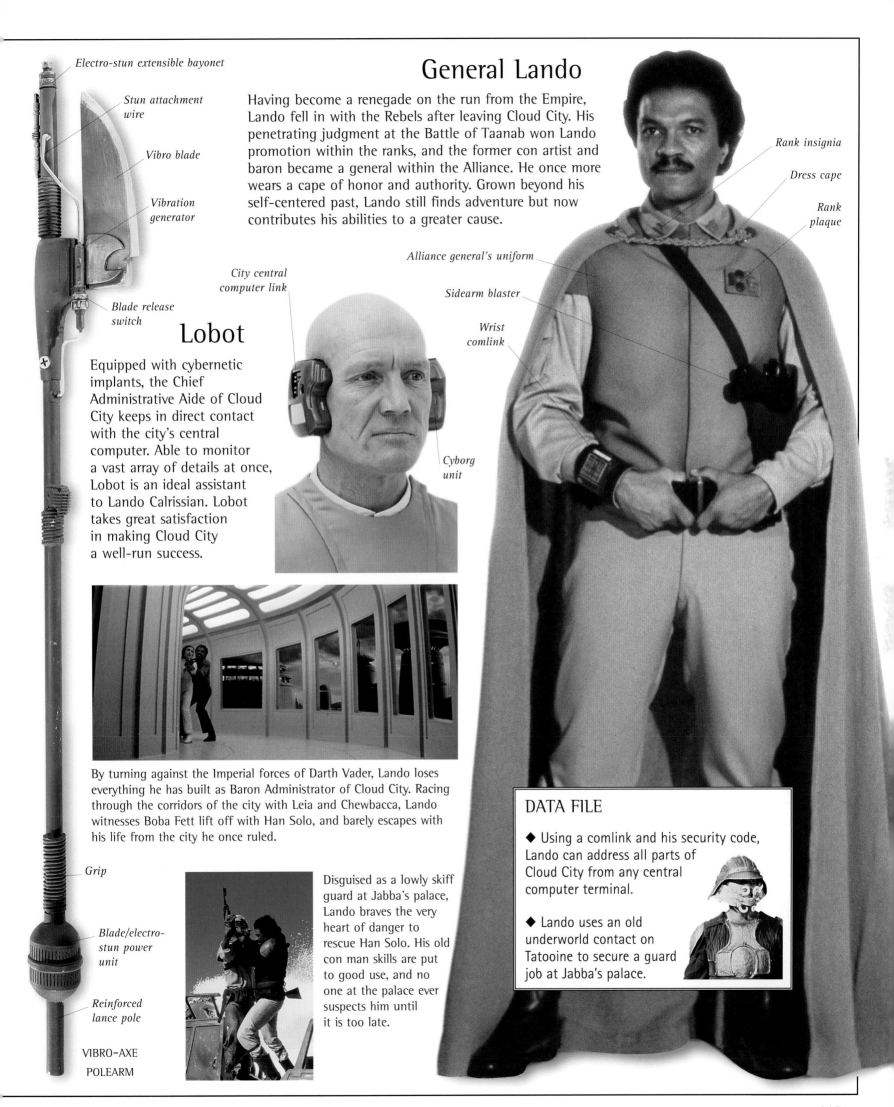

Obi-Wan Kenobi
JEDI IN EXILE

FAR OUT in the remote Jundland wastes lives the hermit Ben Kenobi. Ben is a figure of mystery to the Tatooine settlers, dismissed by many as a crazy wizard. In truth Kenobi is a Jedi Knight, a great warrior of the Old Republic who fought in the Clone Wars. One of Kenobi's students turned to the dark side of the Force, betraying the Jedi and assisting the rise of the Emperor. Crushed by his failure with the man who became Darth Vader, Kenobi retreated to Tatooine, watching over the young Luke Skywalker and waiting for the time to reveal Luke's birthright as the son of a Jedi. Kenobi's powers make him a threat to the Empire even in his elder years.

Hooded cloak

Jedi robes

In accordance with Jedi philosophy, Kenobi lives simply. In his hut are only a few scant reminders of his former life and great exploits. It is here that Kenobi gives Luke his father's lightsaber.

Hovering training remotes are used by Jedi and also by gunfighters to sharpen reflexes and develop coordination. They can be set to varying degrees of aggressiveness and their shock rays adjusted from harmless to painful.

Air jet

Shock ray emitter

Tracking sensor

TRAINING REMOTE

On board the Death Star, Kenobi uses his technical knowledge and Jedi mind powers to disable a crucial tractor beam without being noticed. This is his first return to such heroic action in many years.

Even after he is struck down by Vader, Kenobi returns in spirit to guide Luke on his path to becoming a Jedi. On Hoth and near death, Luke sees Kenobi just before being rescued by Han Solo.

It is Kenobi who first awakens Jedi abilities in Luke and begins to train him, but Luke can learn from him only briefly before Kenobi faces his final lightsaber duel. Afterward, as Luke learns the ways of the Force, he is able to meet Ben again in spirit.

DATA FILE

◆ Ben Kenobi once rescued Luke when the boy had become lost in the Tatooine wilderness with his friend Windy. In spite of this, Owen Lars forbade Kenobi from ever coming near their farm again.

◆ Luke Skywalker returns to the home of Ben Kenobi to build his own lightsaber after losing his father's in the battle on Cloud City.

Yoda
SKYWALKER'S TEACHER

NOT TO BE JUDGED by his small size, the wise Jedi Master Yoda is very powerful with the Force. At almost 900, his years of contemplation and training have given him deep insight and profound abilities. One of his greatest challenges is the training of Luke Skywalker, who arrives on Dagobah an impatient would-be Jedi. In the short time he has with Luke, Yoda must instill in him the faith, peace, and harmony with the Force that will fulfill Luke's potential and guard him from the dark path of temptation, anger, and evil. To his final student Yoda imparts the heart of the ancient Jedi traditions that are the galaxy's last hope.

Jedi robes

Through the Force, Luke Skywalker is able to see his mentors Yoda and Obi-Wan, as well as a youthful apparition of his father Anakin, all finally at peace due to Luke's heroic efforts. United in the Force, their Jedi spirits are restored and complete.

On Dagobah, Yoda uses his attunement with the natural world to live peacefully on the resources around him. His gimer stick, for example, serves as a walking staff as well as a source of pleasant gimer juice, which can be chewed out of the bark.

HEALING MOTHER-ROCK

Dagobah

A remote planet of swamps and mists, inhospitable Dagobah hides a tremendous variety of life forms, including gnarl trees, butcherbugs, and swamp slugs. This inhospitable setting provides a good hiding place in the dark days of the Empire.

YARUM SEED
tea-making variety

MUSHROOM SPORES

GALLA SEEDS

SOHLI BARK

Green skin

Sensitive ears

Gimer stick

Tridactyl feet

Yoda spends his days in meditation, seeing ever deeper into the infinite tapestry that is the living vitality of the Force. Like Obi-Wan, he hides behind an assumed identity of harmless craziness. Yoda uses this persona to test Luke upon his arrival on Dagobah. As Obi-Wan once told Luke, "Your eyes can deceive you. Don't trust them."

DATA FILE

◆ Yoda's house expresses his oneness with nature, using no technological appliances or fittings. All the furnishings in the house of clay, sticks, and stones were handcrafted by Yoda himself.

◆ In the days before the sinister Empire, Yoda held a seat within the Jedi high council on the Republic's capital world of Coruscant.

Rebel Leaders

HARD-PRESSED for ships and weapons, the Rebel Alliance relies on its capable leaders to make the most of every asset. Living up to the highest standards of virtue and duty, they come from many backgrounds – from nobility and powerful government positions to mechanics, pilots, and merchants who have answered the call of justice and freedom. A good Rebel leader can overcome the Empire's numeric advantage with inventive tactics, or find the words and deeds needed to bring new allies into the fight for freedom. The Alliance recognizes merit, and capable individuals soon find themselves in positions of authority.

Carlist Rieekan

The grim General Rieekan keeps the seven hidden levels of Echo Base in a state of constant alert, ever wary of discovery by Imperial forces. The terrible cold of Hoth made patrolling the perimeters of the base difficult until Rebel craft could be adapted to the ice.

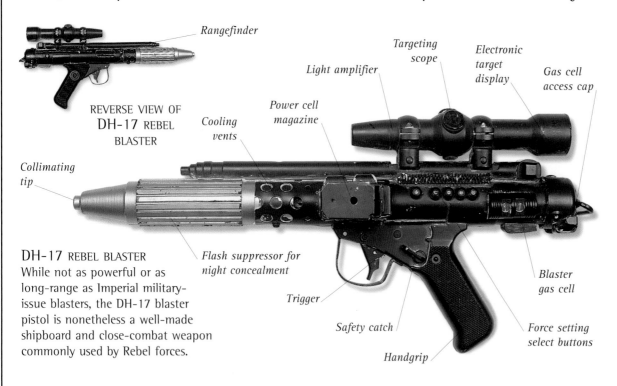

Rangefinder

REVERSE VIEW OF
DH-17 REBEL
BLASTER

Targeting scope

Light amplifier

Electronic target display

Gas cell access cap

Cooling vents

Power cell magazine

Collimating tip

DH-17 REBEL BLASTER
While not as powerful or as long-range as Imperial military-issue blasters, the DH-17 blaster pistol is nonetheless a well-made shipboard and close-combat weapon commonly used by Rebel forces.

Flash suppressor for night concealment

Trigger

Safety catch

Handgrip

Blaster gas cell

Force setting select buttons

The frozen world of Hoth is home to Echo Base, where the Rebels retreat after the discovery of their base on the Fourth Moon of Yavin. Hoth provides protection only for a short time before an Imperial probe droid detects the Rebel presence.

Jan Dodonna

General Jan Dodonna is a dauntless master tactician, commanding the Rebel assault on the Death Star in the Battle of Yavin. While the stolen plans provided a complete technical readout of the Death Star, the station seemed invulnerable. General Dodonna identified the one best hope of penetrating the station's defenses and bombing a small thermal exhaust port. His strategy enabled a small fleet of 30 one-man fighters to annihilate a battle station over 160 kilometers wide.

The Rebel forces won their first victories against the Empire from hangars hidden deep within ancient temples in the remote, jungled Fourth Moon of Yavin.

The tactical display at the Massassi base on Yavin 4 tracks the Death Star as it orbits Yavin, closing in to destroy the Rebel stronghold. The display offers limited ability to zoom in and monitor the movements of the ships in battle.

Reinforced midrib

Pre-Rebellion squadron insignia

Rebel unit marking

REBEL HELMET
Battle leaders are as vital to the Rebellion as strategic masterminds. The battered helmet of X-wing squadron Red Leader Garven Dreis testifies to his extensive battle service.

Admiral Ackbar

Commander of the Rebel fleet, the cautious Admiral Ackbar hails from the ocean world of Mon Calamari. Once a slave to Grand Moff Tarkin, Ackbar was rescued by Rebels and convinced his people to join the Alliance. The giant Mon Cal star cruisers contributed by his people are the largest ships in the Rebel fleet.

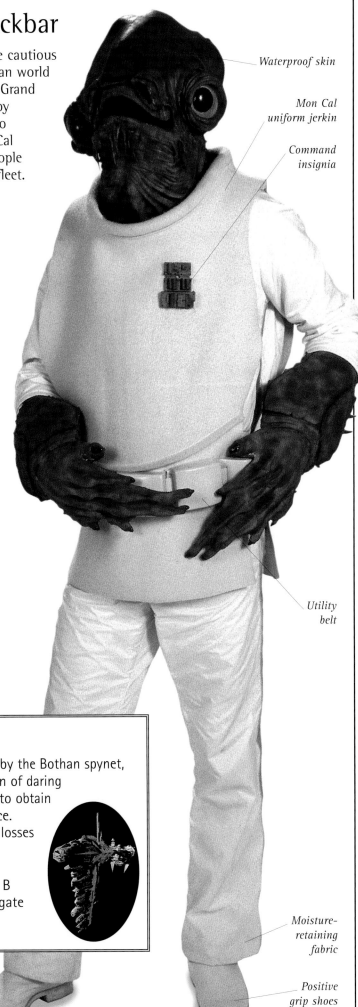

Waterproof skin

Mon Cal uniform jerkin

Command insignia

Utility belt

Moisture-retaining fabric

Positive grip shoes

Admiral Ackbar commands the Rebel fleet from his seat in his personal flagship, the Headquarters Frigate, a Mon Calamari star cruiser contributed to the Alliance by his people.

Chandrillian Freedom Medal

Their secret bases discovered or destroyed, the Rebels fled into space to escape the Empire. The Alliance maintains a mobile command center on board the Mon Cal Headquarters Frigate, from where the actions of the fleet are directed.

Mon Mothma

Mon Mothma is the highest leader of the Rebellion. As a member of the galactic Senate, Mon Mothma championed the cause of freedom until the Emperor's evil closed in around her. Abandoning the Senate, she built the Rebel Alliance and continues to strengthen it through her diplomacy and negotiations.

DATA FILE

◆ The Rebellion is greatly aided by the Bothan spynet, a galaxy-wide secret organization of daring operatives who claim to be able to obtain nearly any information, for a price. Bothan teams will endure heavy losses to accomplish their objectives.

◆ This 300-meter-long Nebulon B escort craft serves as medical frigate for the Rebel fleet.

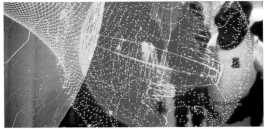

A tactical monitor in the Alliance command center displays the defensive shield projected around the second Death Star from the Forest Moon of Endor. This display also reveals interior areas of the Death Star.

Rebel Warriors

ALTHOUGH SOME MEMBERS from the Rebel Alliance are deserters of the Imperial forces and military academies, many are young volunteers with little or no experience in combat. Some have only recently ventured from their homeworlds, most of which have greatly suffered under the oppressive Imperial regime. However, Rebel leaders recognize the value of anyone willing and able to fight, especially those with specific knowledge and skills. New recruits receive basic training in handling weapons, communications, and emergency medical relief, and are quickly acclimated to a wide range of posts, from engineering and vehicle maintenance to security and acquisitions.

Yavin Base Briefing Room

As the Death Star approaches the Rebel Alliance's secret base on Yavin 4, Rebel pilots assemble in their retrofitted briefing room within an ancient Massassi temple. Desperate for pilots, the Alliance assigns flight-simulator-trained volunteers and anyone with suborbital flying skills to X-wing and Y-wing starfighters.

BIGGS DARKLIGHTER
Reunited with his friend Luke Skywalker at Yavin, Biggs participated in the assault on the first Death Star.

WEDGE ANTILLES
A native of Corellia, Wedge fought at the Battle of Yavin, the Battle of Hoth, and the Battle of Endor.

DOROVIO BOLD
A top cadet at the Academy, Bold joined the Alliance after she learned Alderaan was destroyed by the Empire.

GRIZZ FRIX
Recruited from the Alliance's Support Services, Frix honed his flying skills in an old airspeeder on Devaron.

DEREK "HOBBIE" KLIVIAN
An Imperial Academy deserter, Hobbie continued to serve with Rogue Squadron after the Battle of Hoth.

DAK RALTER
An idealistic young pilot from Kalist VI, Dak was Luke's tailgunner at the Battle of Hoth.

ZEV SENESCA
After Luke Skywalker and Han Solo became lost on Hoth, they were located by pilot Zev Senesca.

KEIR SANTAGE
A Rogue Squadron veteran, Santage was once rescued from an Imperial detention center by Wedge Antilles.

ECHO BASE TROOPS
After the Battle of Yavin, the Alliance relocates their secret headquarters to the ice planet Hoth. Anticipating an Imperial invasion, the Rebels modify their weapons (such as tripod-mounted blasters) to function in frigid temperatures.

INTELLIGENCE AGENT
An Alliance spy and scout, Colonel Airen Cracken (later promoted to General) flies support missions for General Madine's commandos. Under the command of General Calrissian at the Battle of Endor, he serves as a gunner on board the Millennium Falcon.

Cal Alder (above left) serves as a Rebel Alliance scout with Major Bren Derlin (above right) at Echo Base. After the Empire discovers the Rebel base, Derlin helps to coordinate the mass evacuation from Hoth.

Hands-free comlink

Communications badge

Lightweight flak vest

DL-21 BLASTER PISTOL

Targeting scope

Flared muzzle can produce scattered energy charges

Rebel Blasters

Because BlasTech Industries refuse to enter an exclusive agreement with the Empire and continue to provide weapons to the public sector, the resemblance between some Imperial and Rebel blasters is no coincidence. Both the BlasTech DL-21 blaster pistol and A280 blaster rifle are used by Rebel forces on Hoth and Endor.

Safety lever inside trigger guard

Electronic sight adjusts for windage and elevation

Handgrip

A280 BLASTER RIFLE

Integrated muzzle compensator

Ribbed front-grip pump

Power charge system

Carry strap

Fire-resistant tactical gloves

Special Forces

Charged with carrying out specific military objectives, Alliance Special Forces (SpecForces) brigades are trained for specialized services, ranging from zero-gravity combat to stealthy demolitions. SpecForce wilderness fighters are trained to use their terrain for the best tactical advantage in combat. During the Battle of Endor, wilderness fighters wear full forest-camouflage fatigues to infiltrate an Imperial base.

WILDERNESS FIGHTER

DATA FILE
◆ General Cracken mans the Millennium Falcon's upper quad laser cannon at the Battle of Endor.

Tactical system double-magazine canister

Tauntauns

THE SNOW LIZARDS called tauntauns are one of the few forms of life that thrive in the frozen conditions of the ice planet Hoth. Several different breeds of tauntaun live in various terrains on Hoth, from herds moving across moss-covered tundra to the solitary mountain tauntauns and small packs of lichen-eaters dwelling deep within the ice caves. Tauntauns survive the intensely cold nights by slowing their metabolisms almost to a standstill, and can die if forced into activity once the night cold descends.

TAUNTAUN HEAD

TAUNTAUN SKULL

Tauntaun Patrols

Tauntauns serve the Rebel troops of Hoth's Echo Base more reliably than patrol vehicles, which are often halted by the winds and cold. Snow-dwelling tauntauns were domesticated and trained early on during the construction of Echo Base. Tauntauns make obedient and hardy mounts, but they secrete thick oils and have an unpleasant odor. Patrol riders learn to ignore this, and ride their tauntauns on constant lookout for Imperial forces.

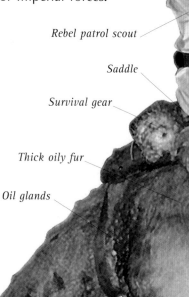

Horns for dominance combat

Ears

Cap warmer

Reins

Rebel patrol scout

Tough lips for scraping lichen

Saddle

Survival gear

Thick oily fur

Oil glands

Internal organs protected within layers of fat and muscle

Hoth

Hoth is uninhabitable except for a subarctic band circling its equator. The Rebels' Echo Base is located on the snowy northern edge of this band. Most tauntauns live in the equatorial tundra and subsist on lichen and ice worms.

Stirrups

Claws for clearing ice from lichen

Tail for balance when running

Strong leg muscles

Tridactyl feet

DATA FILE

◆ Tauntauns are irritated by the ultrasonic frequencies of certain droids, such as this tactical 3PO unit, and tend to swat them with their tails. The droids of Echo Base have learned to be careful.

◆ Many of the Rebels' tauntaun patrol mounts were discovered living in the ice caves that became Echo Base.

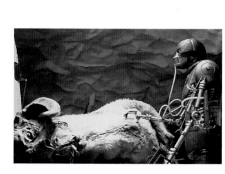

On several occasions, tauntauns were killed in the stables of Echo Base by wampa ice creatures stalking the caverns and corridors at night. The medical droids analyzed the wounds and determined their origin.

Medical Droids

THE REASSURING PRESENCE of a medical droid is a welcome sight to any injured Rebel trooper. Medical droids are equipped with encyclopedic memory banks and statistical analyzing algorithms, allowing them to be sure of the best course of treatment in any situation. Dependable and knowledgeable, they can often restore health even to critically injured patients.

Multi-wave visual sensors

Logic center

Vocoder unit

The synthetic chemical bacta can heal grievous flesh wounds. Patients are immersed in tanks of the bacta mix, which is constantly filtered and revitalized.

Magnetic diffraction scanner

Medical data banks

Visual sensor

High-speed data output transmitter

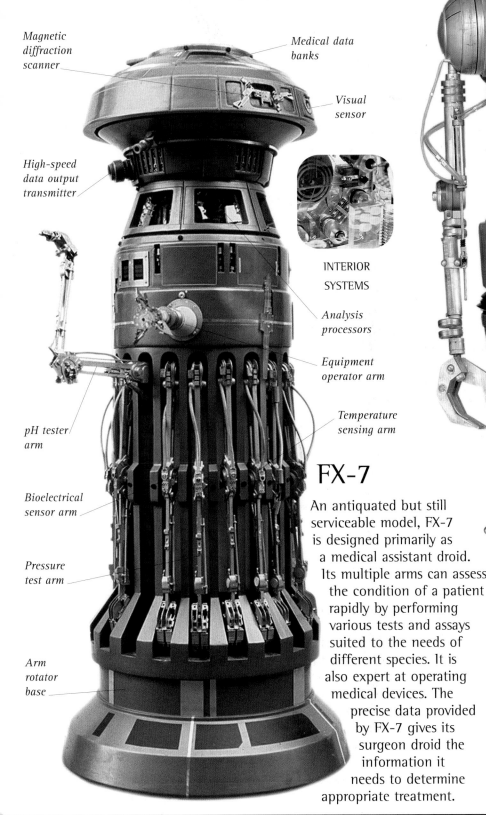

INTERIOR SYSTEMS

Analysis processors

Equipment operator arm

Temperature sensing arm

pH tester arm

Bioelectrical sensor arm

Pressure test arm

Arm rotator base

Precision servomotor

Auxiliary data input

Data banks

Hydraulic lines

Transparent body shell

Hydraulic system pumps

Wrist rotator

Fine motion hand

Knee assembly

FX-7

An antiquated but still serviceable model, FX-7 is designed primarily as a medical assistant droid. Its multiple arms can assess the condition of a patient rapidly by performing various tests and assays suited to the needs of different species. It is also expert at operating medical devices. The precise data provided by FX-7 gives its surgeon droid the information it needs to determine appropriate treatment.

2-1B

An excellent surgeon and field medic, 2-1B is able to perform extremely precise operations that leave little or no scar. 2-1B's long experience with humans makes him considerate as well as beneficial, and he seems actually to care about his patients.

DATA FILE

◆ Precise hydraulic systems using several liquids at different temperatures give 2-1B a gentle touch.

◆ 2-1B treated Luke Skywalker for his injuries on Hoth. Luke requested that the droid treat him again after he lost his hand on Cloud City.

Darth Vader

A GRIM, FORBIDDING FIGURE, Darth Vader stalks the corridors of the Imperial Navy. Once regarded as mad human wreckage, with the increasing favor of the Emperor, Vader has risen in power and influence to become a much-feared military commander. Grand Moff Tarkin was one of the few who recognized Vader's capabilities in spite of his bizarre appearance and eccentric conduct, and as Tarkin's right-hand man, Vader attained a new level of respect amongst the upper echelons of the Imperial military. Unable to survive without the constant life support provided by his suit, Vader is nonetheless a powerful figure whose knowledge of the dark side of the Force makes him unnerving and dangerous.

Magnetic sensor pits

Speech projector and respiratory intake

Respiratory vent

Neck vertebra replaced with metal

Outer cloak

Vision enhancement receptors

Vader is hardly pleased when his pursuit of Princess Leia's starship delivers him to the orbit of Tatooine, his despised homeworld, where he last saw his mother. As Leia is entirely unaware of her true heritage, Vader fails to realize he has captured his own daughter.

Armored breast plate to shield badly injured chest

Cybernetic replacement internal organs

Control chestplate

Control function connectors

Artificial cyborg lower arm

Vader allows no one to assist him with his accoutrements. In a special isolation chamber, mechanical arms assist in the removal and replacement of certain of his suit components.

CHESTPLATE
Vader's life support systems are monitored and controlled through this central panel of chestplate controls on his suit. Slots allow the insertion of diagnostic cards for periodic system checkouts, while switch panels allow function modification.

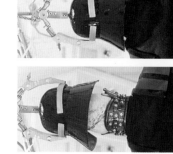

System function indicator

Secondary system function box

Control activator; only when this is pushed will Vader's chestplate controls work

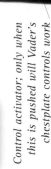

DARTH VADER'S BELT

Electromagnetic clasp

Synthetic belt strap

Primary system function box

DATA FILE

◆ Over time Vader has advanced in his ability to manipulate the dark side of the Force, and has used it to sustain his own damaged body as well as to persuade opponents of his will. Under the Emperor's tutelage, Vader learns to kill with mere suggestion.

◆ Despite the fact that much of his body was replaced by machine components after his battle against Obi-Wan Kenobi on Mustafar, Darth Vader retains an incredibly high count of midi-chlorians.

◆ Vader incurs the wrath of high officers by piloting his own fighter into combat.

Vader plotted with the Emperor to sway Luke to the dark side. In an intense lightsaber battle, Vader tempted Luke with the proposal that the two of them join to overthrow the Emperor. Where Vader's loyalties really stood at this time is lost in the darkness filling his soul.

Body heat regulators

Outer helmet locking surface

Helmet air pump

Multiple power cells

Hermetic seal

Power distributor

Electrical system radiators

Neck support

Hermetic seal

Voice processor

Nutrient feed tube

Air processing filter

Primary environmental sensor

Armored boots binding cyborg elements to flesh

INTERIOR OF VADER'S HELMET

Vader's helmet is the most important part of his life support suit, connecting with a flat backpack to cycle air in and out of Vader's broken lungs and keeping his hideously damaged skull in shape.

Anakin Skywalker

The horror and tragedy of Darth Vader are revealed when he tells Luke Skywalker "I am your father." Vader hopes to bring Luke down the same dark path of hate and anger that destroyed Anakin Skywalker. Instead he finds that Luke is committed to finding redemption for his father in spite of all that Vader has become.

Imperial Leaders

THE EMPEROR'S WILL is enforced by the might of the Imperial Space Navy and its assault forces. Imperial military commanders carry out the orders of the Emperor and hold the true positions of power in the New Order. The price for failure can be death, but ambition for the highest posts keeps competition fierce amongst officers. While bureaucracy and political whims can place incapable men in high posts, many of the Empire's commanders are formidable military talents in a system that values ruthless efficiency.

TRACKING MONITOR
This Death Star tracking monitor shows the Fourth Moon of Yavin emerging from behind the planet itself into firing range.

Superlaser

Exhaust port

THE FIRST DEATH STAR
The Death Star contains a hypermatter reactor that can generate enough power to destroy an entire planet. Invulnerable to large-scale assault, the space station has a fatal weakness in a small thermal exhaust port (connecting directly to the main reactor) which can be bombed by a small fighter craft.

Docking bays

Aboard the original Death Star, this conference room can project holographic tactical readouts for evaluation by Tarkin and his Imperial strategists.

SUPERLASER TARGETING DISPLAY

DEATH STAR GUNNERS
Obeying the orders of their superiors, gunnery crew leaders ensure that the titanic energies of the Death Star laser systems do not overload or hit phase imbalances that would cause huge internal explosions.

Imperial Navy emblem

Grand Moff Tarkin

Governor of the Imperial Outland Regions, Grand Moff Wilhuff Tarkin conceives the horrific Death Star superweapon as part of his doctrine of Rule by Fear. The Imperial Outlands contain systems too scattered to police effectively, but the fear of the Death Star will subjugate systems across the galaxy.

Officer tunic

Imperial officer's disc

Rank insignia plaque

Imperial code cylinder

Officer's disc

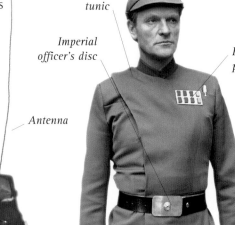

Antenna

Transceiver

Shielded lens

DEATH STAR GUNNER'S HELMET

Neutral-alloy helmet

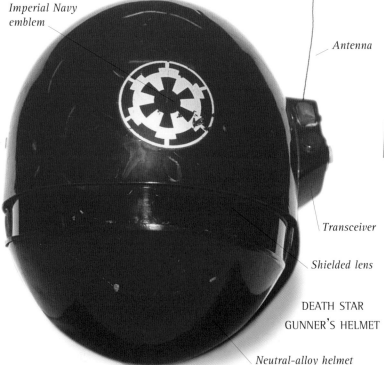

ADMIRAL PIETT

ADMIRAL OZZEL

General Veers

General Maximillian Veers masterminds the devastating Imperial assault on Echo Base, commanding the action in person within the lead walker cockpit. A cunning and capable individual, Veers is a model Imperial officer.

Tunic

CAPTAIN NEEDA

MOFF JERJERROD

Emperor Palpatine

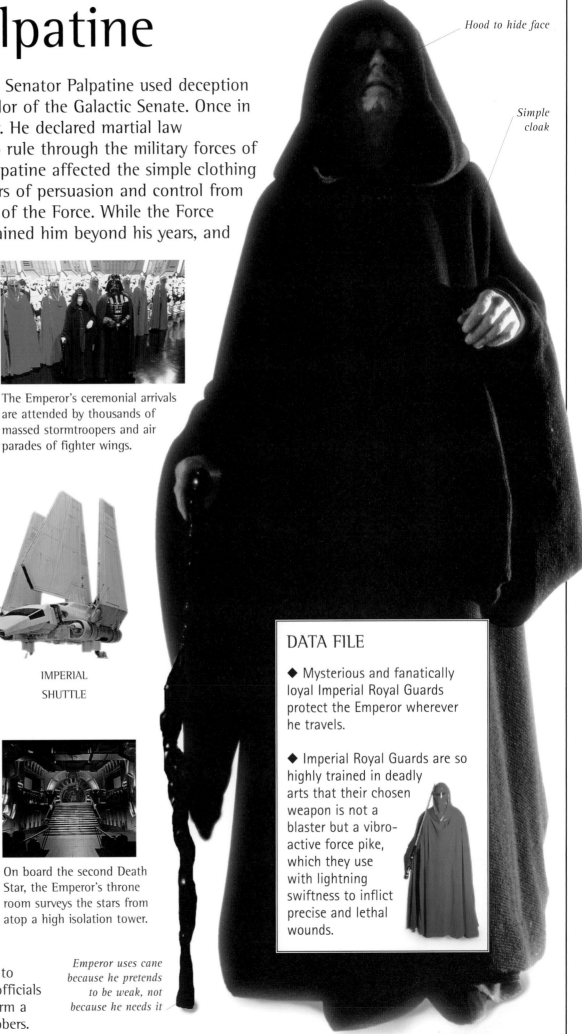

Hood to hide face

Simple cloak

IN THE LAST DAYS of the Republic, Senator Palpatine used deception to become elected Supreme Chancellor of the Galactic Senate. Once in office he appointed himself Emperor. He declared martial law throughout the galaxy and began to rule through the military forces of the newly-created Imperial Navy. Palpatine affected the simple clothing of a simple man, but drew his powers of persuasion and control from the blackest depths of the dark side of the Force. While the Force has twisted his face, it has also sustained him beyond his years, and even in his old age the Emperor remains a figure of terrible power.

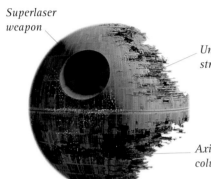

Superlaser weapon

Unfinished structure

Axial power column

The Emperor's ceremonial arrivals are attended by thousands of massed stormtroopers and air parades of fighter wings.

THE SECOND DEATH STAR
The Emperor conceived the second Death Star as a colossal trap, which would use a false image of vulnerability to lure the Rebel fleet into fatal combat.

Coruscant headwear

IMPERIAL SHUTTLE

On board the second Death Star, the Emperor's throne room surveys the stars from atop a high isolation tower.

Imperial Dignitaries

The Emperor's favor can elevate individuals to positions of fantastic galactic power. High officials owe their posts to Palpatine's whim, and form a society of twisted sycophants and back-stabbers.

Emperor uses cane because he pretends to be weak, not because he needs it

DATA FILE

◆ Mysterious and fanatically loyal Imperial Royal Guards protect the Emperor wherever he travels.

◆ Imperial Royal Guards are so highly trained in deadly arts that their chosen weapon is not a blaster but a vibro-active force pike, which they use with lightning swiftness to inflict precise and lethal wounds.

Officer's disc

Disciplined expression commands respect

Belt buckle contains secret data-storage compartment

Rank insignia plaque

Imperial Personnel

Following the Clone Wars, Palpatine did nothing to halt the massive military build up that had produced an army of troopers and enormous weapons of destruction. Citizens of many worlds were eager to join the newly formed Imperial Space Navy. The Empire initially found innumerable recruits among cadets of the Academy, an elite educational and training institution with campuses throughout the galaxy.

Chain of Command

Just as Darth Vader serves as the Emperor's lieutenant, Chief Bast is the chief personal aide to Grand Moff Tarkin aboard the first Death Star. Although some self-important officers made the mistake of assuming that Vader is subservient to Tarkin, Bast witnesses how Vader deals with fools, and always shows his respect.

DETENTION BLOCK GUARDS
While the Emperor's policy of subjugating non-human races is protested by the Rebel Alliance, Imperial soldiers such as Lieutenant Shann Childsen seize any opportunity to uphold Imperial ideals. Childsen supervises troopers and prisoners at detention area AA-23 on the first Death Star.

STORMTROOPER COMMANDERS
Because the Emperor rarely leaves his palace on Coruscant, relatively few Imperial personnel ever actually see their leader. On the second Death Star, Darth Vader commands an assembly of Imperial officers and stormtroopers to greet the Emperor's shuttle.

Imperial Officer

Many Imperial officers received training at an Imperial Academy such as the prestigious Raithal Academy in the Core Region. Cadets endure harsh discipline, lengthy field exercises, and rigid indoctrination into Imperial political ideology. With few exceptions, Imperial officers are ethnocentric humans who fully support the Emperor's policy of subjugating nonhuman races.

Durasteel-toed boots

DEATH STAR TROOPER
An elite fighting force selected from Imperial Navy Troopers, Death Star Troopers such as Sergeant Torent serve as security guards, monitored sensor arrays, and handle hangar traffic control.

Command console

Built at the starship yards of Fondor, the Executor is Darth Vader's personal flagship, and serves as his primary headquarters during his search for Luke Skywalker and the Rebel Alliance. Utilizing probe droids and sophisticated long-range scanners, the Executor's crew track a signal from the Hoth system that leads them straight to the Rebels' secret headquarters.

BRIDGE CREW
Flight data officers, tracking systems specialists, and combat supervisors work in sunken data pits on either side of the elevated platform that bisects the Executor's bridge. Because the location of their stations inhibit their ability to see through the bridge's viewports, the crew can focus on their consoles without unnecessary distraction.

DATA FILE
◆ The Imperial shuttle carries Darth Vader to his flagship, the 19,000-meters-long Super Star Destroyer Executor.

IMPERIAL INTELLIGENCE
Assigned to Grand Moff Tarkin, Colonel Wullf Yularen is an officer of the Imperial Security Bureau (ISB). His mission is to ensure absolute loyalty to the Emperor.

TEST PILOT
After the Battle of Yavin, thousands of Imperial Academy cadets are rapidly advanced into service, so veteran personnel are soon dealing with fresh-faced officers. Captain Yorr serves as a test pilot on various TIE prototype ships.

SECURITY OFFICER
Imperial starships and battle stations require security forces to control access areas. On the first Death Star, docking bay security officer Captain Khurgee orders a scanning crew to search every part of the captured Millennium Falcon.

Imperial Stormtroopers

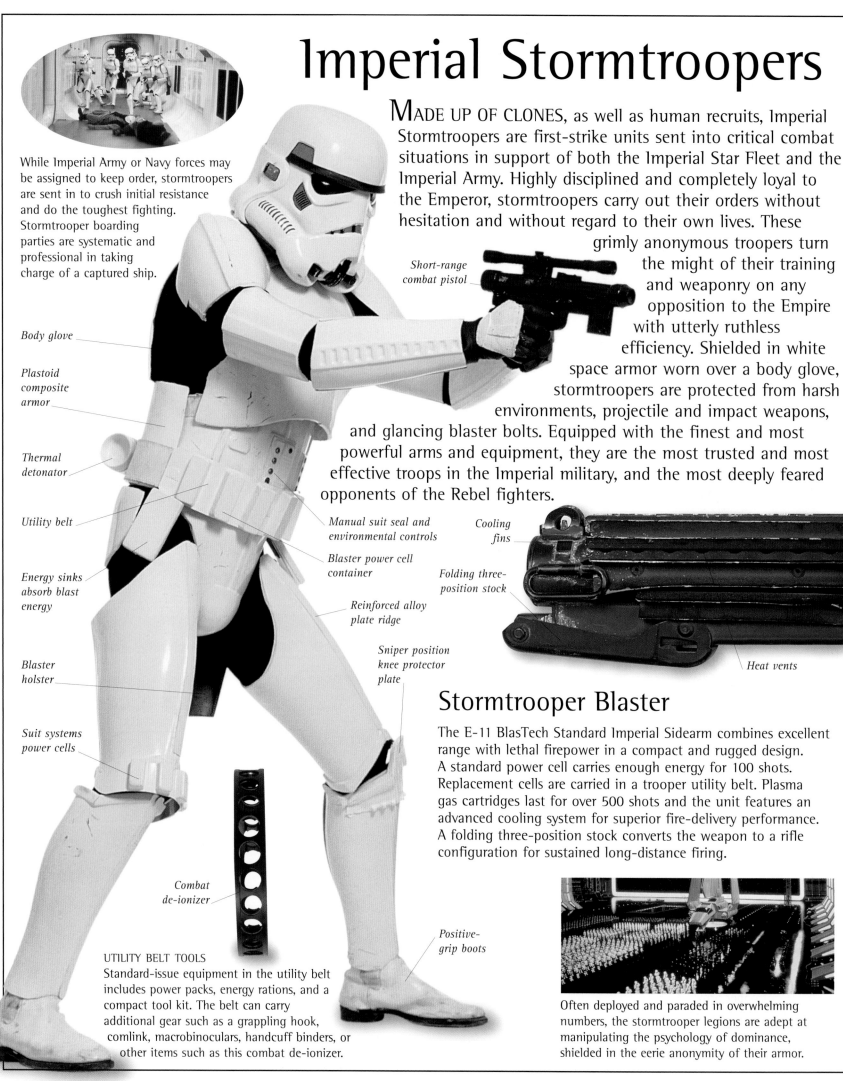

While Imperial Army or Navy forces may be assigned to keep order, stormtroopers are sent in to crush initial resistance and do the toughest fighting. Stormtrooper boarding parties are systematic and professional in taking charge of a captured ship.

MADE UP OF CLONES, as well as human recruits, Imperial Stormtroopers are first-strike units sent into critical combat situations in support of both the Imperial Star Fleet and the Imperial Army. Highly disciplined and completely loyal to the Emperor, stormtroopers carry out their orders without hesitation and without regard to their own lives. These grimly anonymous troopers turn the might of their training and weaponry on any opposition to the Empire with utterly ruthless efficiency. Shielded in white space armor worn over a body glove, stormtroopers are protected from harsh environments, projectile and impact weapons, and glancing blaster bolts. Equipped with the finest and most powerful arms and equipment, they are the most trusted and most effective troops in the Imperial military, and the most deeply feared opponents of the Rebel fighters.

Body glove

Plastoid composite armor

Thermal detonator

Utility belt

Energy sinks absorb blast energy

Blaster holster

Suit systems power cells

Short-range combat pistol

Manual suit seal and environmental controls

Blaster power cell container

Reinforced alloy plate ridge

Sniper position knee protector plate

Cooling fins

Folding three-position stock

Heat vents

Combat de-ionizer

Positive-grip boots

Stormtrooper Blaster

The E-11 BlasTech Standard Imperial Sidearm combines excellent range with lethal firepower in a compact and rugged design. A standard power cell carries enough energy for 100 shots. Replacement cells are carried in a trooper utility belt. Plasma gas cartridges last for over 500 shots and the unit features an advanced cooling system for superior fire-delivery performance. A folding three-position stock converts the weapon to a rifle configuration for sustained long-distance firing.

UTILITY BELT TOOLS
Standard-issue equipment in the utility belt includes power packs, energy rations, and a compact tool kit. The belt can carry additional gear such as a grappling hook, comlink, macrobinoculars, handcuff binders, or other items such as this combat de-ionizer.

Often deployed and paraded in overwhelming numbers, the stormtrooper legions are adept at manipulating the psychology of dominance, shielded in the eerie anonymity of their armor.

STORMTROOPER OFFICER'S CAP

Officer's disc

BELT BUCKLE

Officer's rank plaques

OFFICER'S RANK PLAQUES

CODE TRANSMITTER

Series code

Pocket clip

Data interface

CODE CYLINDERS

Reinforced helmet

Broadband communications antenna

Audio pickup

Stormtrooper Officers

In non-combat situations, stormtrooper officers wear distinctive black tunics and caps. Their insignia – officer's discs, rank plaques, and code cylinders – conform to the standards of the Imperial Navy. Code cylinders allow officers access to secure areas and computer systems. All stormtrooper officers are proven soldiers, and in combat they wear body armor like any other trooper. Officers in field units may wear colored shoulder pauldrons as high-visibility rank indicators.

Power cell

Range-finding sight

Accessory mounting rail

Setting adjust

Gas cartridge cap

Energy ration

Blast energy sink

Safety catch

Low-power pulse indicator

Magnatomic adhesion grip

In battle, stormtroopers are disciplined to ignore casualties within their own ranks. Notice is only taken from a tactical standpoint. They are never distracted by emotional responses.

DATA FILE

◆ A power pack and pressurized gas system in the stormtrooper armor backplate allows a trooper to survive even in the vacuum of space for limited periods. For extended exposure to open space, troopers wear space backpacks with extended life-support capacity.

◆ Stormtrooper armor is impervious to projectile weapons and blast shrapnel. It may be pierced by a direct blaster bolt, but will deflect glancing bolts and reduce damage from bolts absorbed.

STORMTROOPER ARMOR
Every component of a stormtrooper's armor and equipment is manufactured to the highest standards in the Empire. Their armor lasts indefinitely and may still be found half-buried at decades-old battle sites.

Stormtrooper Equipment

WHILE THE BRUTAL TRAINING and intense conditioning of stormtroopers accounts for much of their power and effectiveness, Imperial-issue stormtrooper equipment is also vital in making them the galaxy's most dreaded soldiers. Field troops carry gear such as pouches of extra ammunition (power packs and blaster gas cartridges) and comprehensive survival kits. Standard backpack sets can adapt troopers to extreme climates or even the vacuum of space. Component construction allows standard backpack frames to be filled with gear suited to specific missions, which may include micro-vaporator water-gathering canteens, augmented cooling modules, or a wide variety of base camp and field operative equipment.

Under able officers like Commander Praji, stormtrooper teams adapt to their environments. The unpredictable sandstorms of Tatooine can immobilize landing craft, but native dewback lizards carry search parties equipped with desert gear through any conditions.

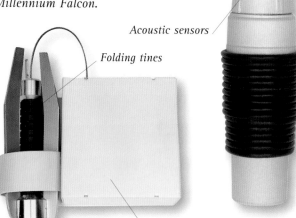

With high-powered backpack communications gear, troopers in Mos Eisley alerted orbiting Star Destroyers to intercept the escaping *Millennium Falcon*.

Acoustic sensors

Folding tines

GRAPPLING
HOOK

Fibercord reel

Comlink

The hand-held comlink supplements a stormtrooper's built-in helmet transmitter/receiver system with improved range and communication security. Comlink sets can be tuned with sophisticated encryption algorithms to work only with each other. Within or near Imperial bases, comlink signals are boosted and relayed automatically for optimal transmission.

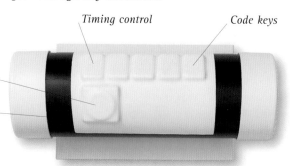

Timing control   *Code keys*

Detach control

Axidite shell

Thermal Detonator

Stormtroopers are usually issued a thermal detonator, carried at the back of the belt. Controls to set arming, timing, and blast intensity are not labelled so that enemy troops cannot use the powerful explosives if they are captured. While these detonators would not normally be used against intruders on board an Imperial ship or battle station, troopers carry their full set of standard equipment at all times to maintain combat readiness and familiarity with the feel of their gear.

Rangefinder

Electronic sight

BLASTECH DLT-20A
LASER RIFLE

Firing capacitor   *Cooling vents*   *Galven circuitry barrel*

Power charge system

Magnatomic adhesion grip

Laser Rifle

In field combat situations, the standard Imperial sidearm offers insufficient accuracy at long range. Field troops are issued blaster rifles, which improve the consistency and accuracy of blaster bolt trajectory by incorporating additional collimating rings and longer conduits of galven circuitry. Imperial blaster rifles are extremely rugged weapons, which give Imperial troops a deadly edge in battle. They are much prized on the black market.

DATA FILE

◆ Stormtrooper backpack gear can include boosted field communication sets, mortar launchers, and equipment for establishing security perimeters.

◆ Squad leaders, who lead units of seven troopers, wear orange shoulder pauldrons.

Activator

POWER CELLS
Small power packs plug into standard stormtrooper gear, including standard helmets and back plates as well as communication sets and other field equipment. Complex circuitry extracts the maximum power from the cell.

Stormtrooper Helmet

There are a number of different models of Imperial stormtrooper standard issue helmets, incorporating various specialized components and changing over time with new developments. In this model, enhanced optical equipment creates holographic images of the surrounding terrain, shielding the eye from excessive brightness and offering vision through many barriers such as smoke, darkness, and fire. Optical equipment in trooper helmets can range from simple eye lenses to these elaborate vision processors. The helmets are cooled and atmosphere-processed to keep the trooper operating at peak efficiency at all times.

4 layer construction

Outer plastoid composite armor

Inner insulator

Anti-laser mesh

Magnetic shielding layer

Comtech Series IV speaker uses three-phase sonic filtering for clear sound

Atmospheric cycling unit

Padding

Power cell

Atmosphere intake and processing unit

Used air exhaust

Artificial air intake

Mouth plate

Voice filtering unit

Comlink microphone

Artificial air supply nozzles

Specialist Stormtroopers

FOR ANY MILITARY SITUATION there is an appropriate class of Imperial soldier, well-equipped for environments that would challenge the standard stormtrooper. Certain Imperial troopers are selected at an early stage for specialization and conditioned with appropriate knowledge and psychological training. Once specialized, their psychological conditioning to their particular identity is so strong that a trooper almost never wishes to change his division.

Helmet

Polarized snow goggles

Breath warmer cover

Chest plate

Imperial sidearm

Heated pants

Rugged ice boots

Wrist comlink

Insulating belt cape

Legs less heavily armored, for mobility

The E-Web heavy repeating blaster can be broken down into its component parts and carried into difficult snow terrain or through restricted ice passages by a crew of only a few troopers. With weaponry such as this, specialized troopers can destroy any advantage the Rebels hope to gain from unusual terrain.

Adjustable attachment straps

Blast armor

Reinforced blast plate

External temperature monitor

Communication controls

Identity chip

Suit heater controls

Power cell monitor

SNOWTROOPER CHEST PLATE

Communications unit

Heater

Heater liquid pump

Power indicator

Accessory power outlet

Surplus power indicator

Homing beacon

Rations storage compartment

SNOWTROOPER BACKPACK

Heavy-duty power cell

Snowtrooper

Equipped with breath heaters under their face masks, snowtroopers are self-sufficient mobile combat elements. Their backpacks and suit systems keep them warm and exceptionally mobile for environments of ice and snow. They can survive for two weeks in deeply frozen environments on suit battery power alone.

The ground troops of General Veers' Blizzard Force on Hoth find themselves accompanied at the Echo Base invasion by the extraordinary figure of Darth Vader. Vader oversees the occupation of the base with the front line of the assault group.

Terrain sensor

Guidance vanes mounting strut

Forward guidance repulsor field directional vanes

Speeder bike

The light repulsorlift Imperial speeder bike carries one or two riders at high velocities for reconnaissance and antipersonnel missions. An unusual turbine repulsorlift makes the bike stable even in extreme maneuvers. Forward-reaching repulsor fields help thread it through obstacles like trees, but their guidance must be used carefully because they are not strong enough to deflect the bike away from obstacles on their own.

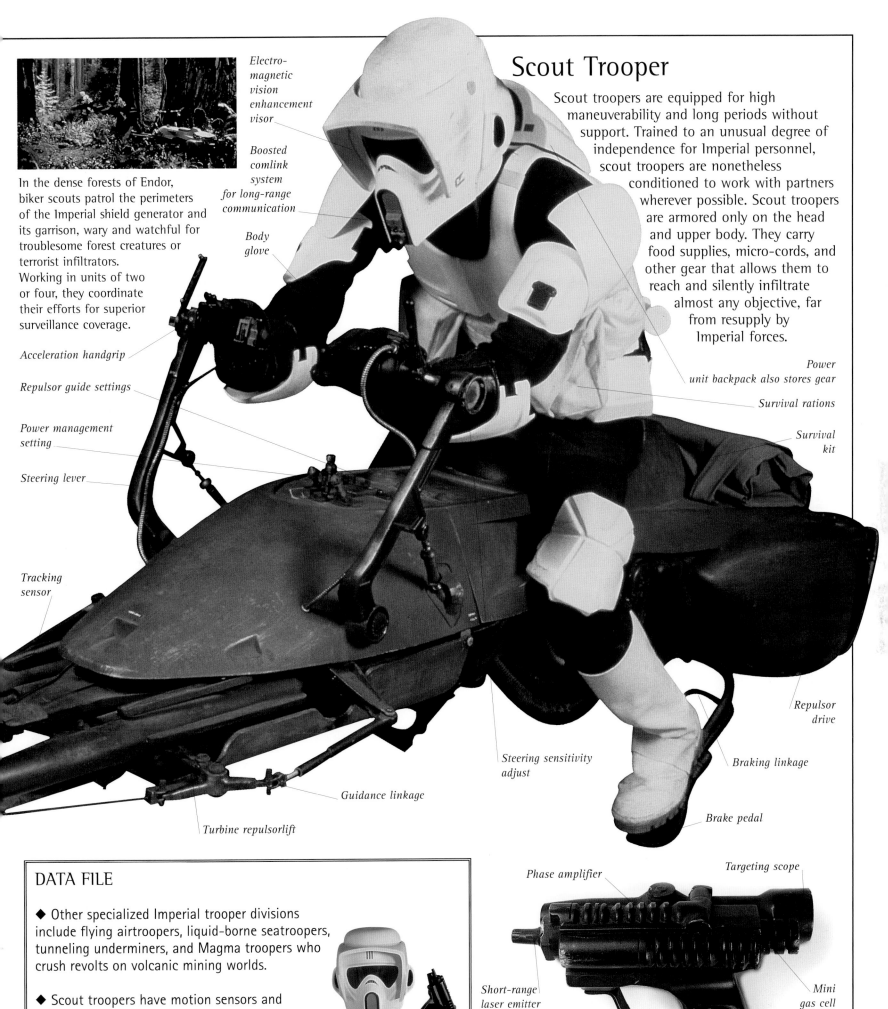

Scout Trooper

Scout troopers are equipped for high maneuverability and long periods without support. Trained to an unusual degree of independence for Imperial personnel, scout troopers are nonetheless conditioned to work with partners wherever possible. Scout troopers are armored only on the head and upper body. They carry food supplies, micro-cords, and other gear that allows them to reach and silently infiltrate almost any objective, far from resupply by Imperial forces.

In the dense forests of Endor, biker scouts patrol the perimeters of the Imperial shield generator and its garrison, wary and watchful for troublesome forest creatures or terrorist infiltrators. Working in units of two or four, they coordinate their efforts for superior surveillance coverage.

Electro-magnetic vision enhancement visor

Boosted comlink system for long-range communication

Body glove

Acceleration handgrip

Repulsor guide settings

Power management setting

Steering lever

Tracking sensor

Power unit backpack also stores gear

Survival rations

Survival kit

Repulsor drive

Steering sensitivity adjust

Braking linkage

Guidance linkage

Brake pedal

Turbine repulsorlift

DATA FILE

◆ Other specialized Imperial trooper divisions include flying airtroopers, liquid-borne seatroopers, tunneling underminers, and Magma troopers who crush revolts on volcanic mining worlds.

◆ Scout troopers have motion sensors and enhanced macrobinocular viewplates allowing them to see energy emissions, night vision, and designated target magnification.

Phase amplifier

Targeting scope

Short-range laser emitter

Mini gas cell

Grip retainer guard

SCOUT TROOPER BLASTER

Imperial Pilots

IMPERIAL FIGHTER PILOTS are an elite group within the Imperial naval forces. Only ten percent of those accepted into training graduate with commissions. Through their intense psychological conditioning, pilots are entirely dedicated to target destruction and know that their mission comes above all other concerns, including those of personal survival and aid to threatened wingmen. Each pilot knows he is expendable. TIE pilots are trained to regard the TIE craft as the most expressive instrument of Imperial military will, and they exult in their role, taking pride in their total dependence on higher authority.

Reinforced flight helmet

Ship-linked communications

Gas transfer hose

Life support pack

Vacuum g-suit

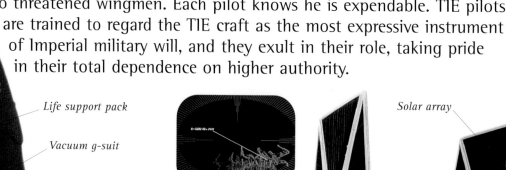

Solar array

Fueling port

TARGETING READOUTS
TIE targeting systems are superior to anything available to Rebel fighters. The advanced readouts of these Seinar systems track targets in high resolution.

TIE Fighter

The standard TIE fighter carries no deflector shield or hyperdrive equipment and employs high-performance ion engines energized by solar array "wings." This lightweight design makes the craft lethally agile, but leaves the pilot defenseless and unable to travel far from his base station. TIE pilots view shields as tools of cowards.

Air scrubber

Emitter aperture

Energy-shielded fabric

JAMMING UNIT

TIE FIGHTER FUELING PORT
TIE fighter fuel is a radioactive gas under high pressure. The twin ion engines of the ship have no moving parts, making the TIE easy to maintain.

Positive gravity pressure boots

DATA FILE

◆ Pilots rely on their self-contained flight suits to stay alive in space, as TIE fighters contain no life support systems.

◆ TIE fighters have no landing gear and are launched from special hangar racks.

AT-AT Pilots

Drawn from hardened combat soldiers, All Terrain Armored Transport (AT-AT) pilots are conditioned to believe themselves invincible. Though they no longer need their armor and life-support suits, they continue to wear them – perhaps as part of their combat history. AT-AT pilot training makes these men masters at guiding the mighty walkers through irregular terrain or city streets, wreaking destruction and terror.

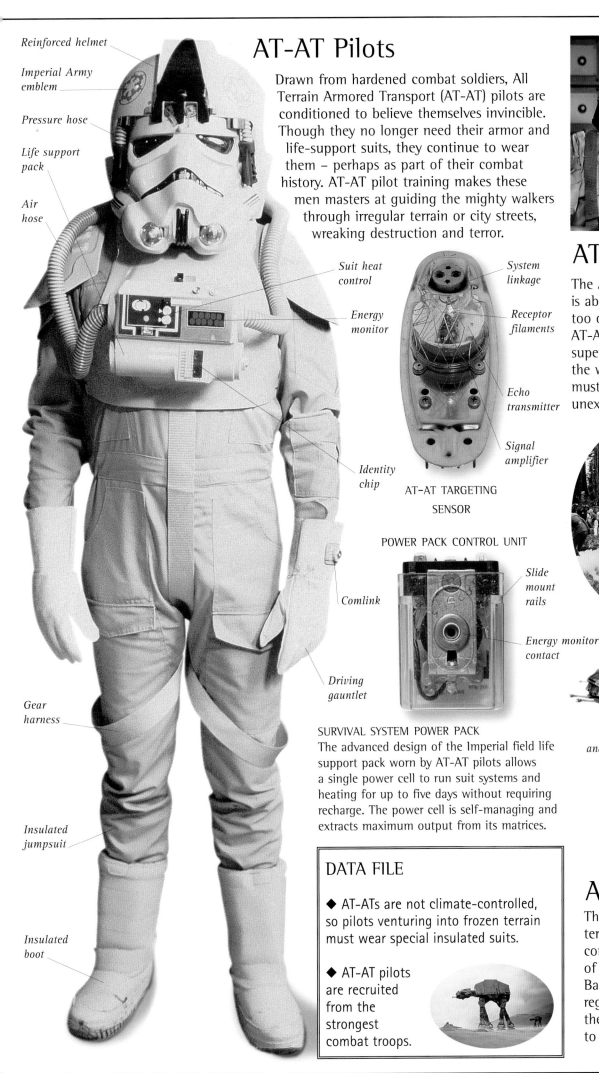

Reinforced helmet

Imperial Army emblem

Pressure hose

Life support pack

Air hose

Suit heat control

Energy monitor

Identity chip

Comlink

Driving gauntlet

Gear harness

Insulated jumpsuit

Insulated boot

System linkage

Receptor filaments

Echo transmitter

Signal amplifier

AT-AT TARGETING SENSOR

POWER PACK CONTROL UNIT

Slide mount rails

Energy monitor contact

SURVIVAL SYSTEM POWER PACK

The advanced design of the Imperial field life support pack worn by AT-AT pilots allows a single power cell to run suit systems and heating for up to five days without requiring recharge. The power cell is self-managing and extracts maximum output from its matrices.

DATA FILE

◆ AT-ATs are not climate-controlled, so pilots venturing into frozen terrain must wear special insulated suits.

◆ AT-AT pilots are recruited from the strongest combat troops.

AT-ST Walker Pilots

The All Terrain Scout Transport (AT-ST) is able to move in and through terrain too dense or irregular for full-size Imperial AT-AT walkers. Their pilots are chosen for superior sense of balance and dexterity with the walker controls, since scout walkers must be able to move quickly through the unexpected to accomplish their missions of reconnaissance and anti-personnel hunting.

Forests and rugged inclines are easily managed by the small, gyroscopically-stabilized AT-ST, or scout walker. Its range is limited since it is too small to carry a full-size locomotion power generator and fuel.

Command and navigation center

Assault troops staging area

AT-AT Walker

These gigantic machines are used as terror weapons. Their powerful walking controls can only be operated by pilots of great physical strength. Until the Battle of Hoth, AT-ATs were widely regarded as invincible in combat, and their mere appearance was often enough to drive enemy forces into fearful retreat.

Imperial Droids

THE EMPIRE'S MILITARY FORCES adapt common droid models to suit specific Imperial purposes and also commission specialized new forms, including illegal assassin and torture droids. Imperial droids are programmed with extremely harsh identity parameters, restricting their abilities for independent action and focusing them tightly on their assigned tasks. This can make them oblivious to external circumstances. Imperial droids are pure machines which rarely develop anything approximating personality.

When Princess Leia refused to discuss the location of the hidden Rebel base, Darth Vader brought in a torture droid. Leia had heard rumors of such atrocities, but hoped they were not true. Subjected to the machine's horrible manipulations, Leia somehow maintained her resistance even near the point of death from the pain.

Mouse Droid

While often used to carry messages, MSE (or "mouse") droids are also used in vast Imperial ships and battle stations to lead troops through long mazes of corridors to their assigned posts. Since they each include complete readouts of their assigned sections, they are programmed to melt their processors instantly upon capture. This gives them an odd combination of paranoia and self-importance.

Electroshock assembly

Sonic piercing needle

Chemical torture turret

Searing flesh pincers

Acid jet

Durite housing

Biofeedback monitors

Life energy monitors

Drug injector

Sonic torture device

Hypnotic power strip

Function commence indicator

Magnetic fault sensor

Circuit fault detector

Logic housing

Audio receptor

Victim analysis photoreceptor

Lower repulsor projector

Motorized leg

Victim pain response monitors

Arc emitter

R4-19

When patrolling the corridors of the Death Star, computer maintenance and repair units go about their tasks automatically, servicing only the equipment and areas permitted to them. Their perception limited for security reasons, they are oblivious to all but their programmed work.

Interrogator Droid

Illegal by the laws of the Republic, this interrogation droid is one of the technological horrors concocted behind the curtains of Imperial secrecy. Completely without pity, this nightmare machine surgically exploits every physical and mental point of weakness with flesh peelers, joint cripplers, bone fragmenters, electroshock nerve probes, and other unspeakable devices. It injects drugs to heighten excruciating pain and erase mental resistance while forcing victims to remain conscious.

Probe Droid (Probot)

Carried to their destination planets in hyperdrive pods, intelligent and eerie probe droids relentlessly search the galaxy for evidence of Rebel presence. Floating above the ground on repulsorlifts and drifting mysteriously on silenced thrusters, probots are equipped with myriad sensors and investigative instincts. They are programmed to find out a location's secrets, communicating their discoveries to distant Star Destroyers via high-frequency HoloNet transceivers.

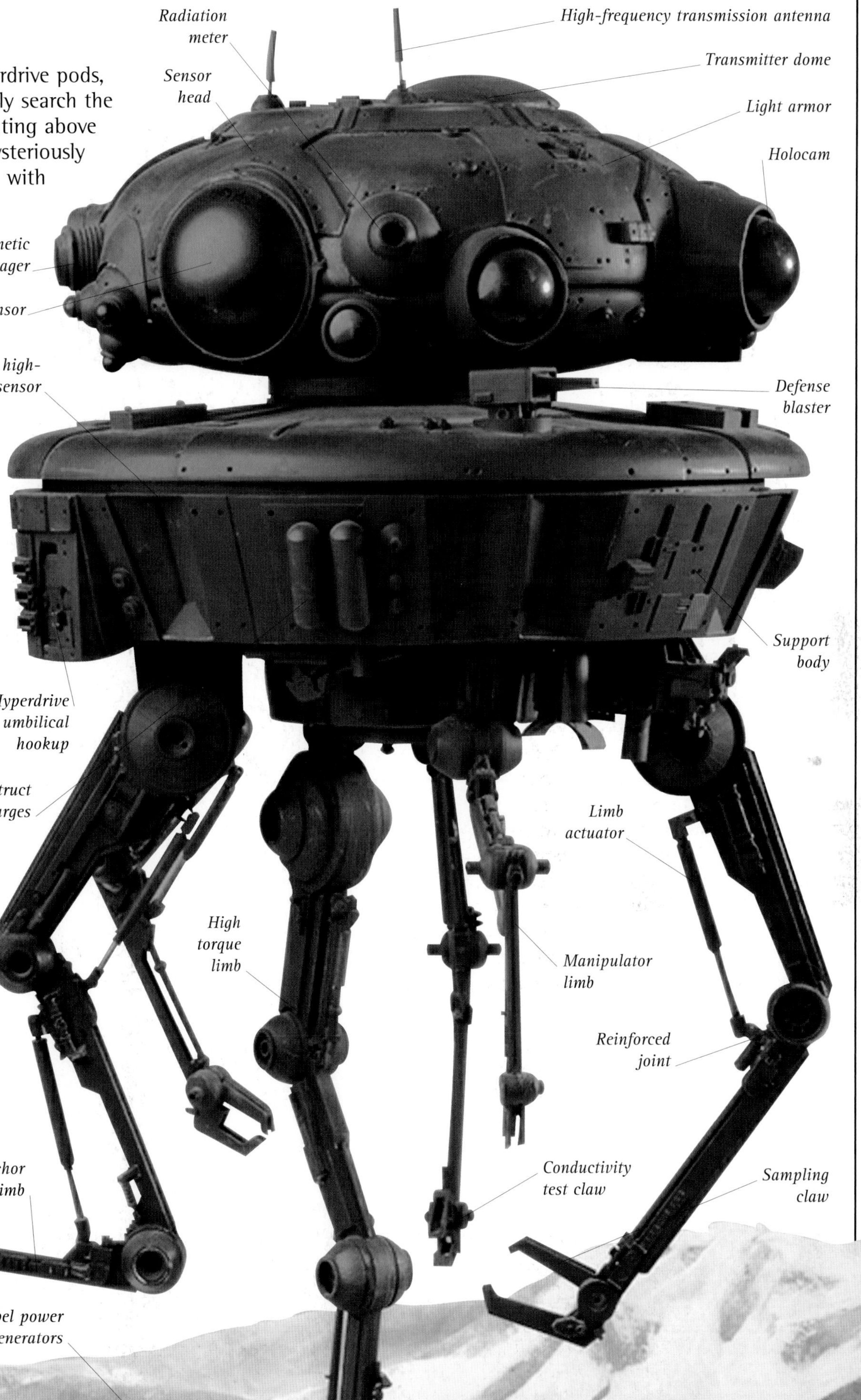

The Imperial Mark IV patrol droid IM4-099 moves through the streets of Mos Eisley on the lookout for criminal activity or illegal signal emissions. It is equipped with no weapons, but sounds an alarm and transmits an alert on detection.

DATA FILE

◆ Many Imperial utility droids are equipped with secret spy devices that allow human overseers to monitor military personnel, ensuring obedience.

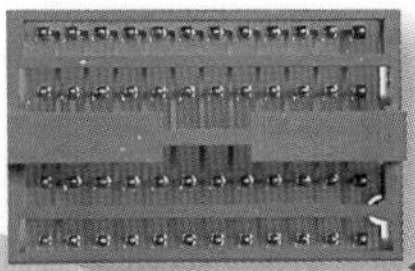

PROBOT SENSOR
PLATE

A probot sent out from the Star Destroyer *Avenger* detects the Rebel base on Hoth and sends its images of the power generators back to Darth Vader.

Radiation meter

High-frequency transmission antenna

Sensor head

Transmitter dome

Light armor

Holocam

Magnetic imager

Motion sensor

360-degree high-sensitivity sonic sensor

Defense blaster

Support body

Hyperdrive pod umbilical hookup

Self-destruct charges

Limb actuator

High torque limb

Manipulator limb

Reinforced joint

Anchor limb

Conductivity test claw

Sampling claw

Rebel power generators

VISUAL IMAGE

ULTRAVIOLET SCAN

MAGNETIC IMAGING SCAN

241

Jabba the Hutt

AT THE CENTER of an extensive crime empire is the repellent crime lord Jabba the Hutt. Equipped with a cunning criminal mind, Jabba has built his syndicate through a long history of deals, threats, extortion, murders, and astute business arrangements. Unlike many of his competitors, Jabba is highly intelligent, and rarely overlooks details or dangers. Once bold and daring, he has settled back in his old age to a life of debauchery in his palace on Tatooine. Jabba enjoys violent entertainment almost as much as he enjoys profits, and he arranges deadly gladiatorial games and creative executions on a regular basis.

Jabba's palace is equipped with many security devices, including a semi-intelligent droid gatewatcher built into several of the entrances.

JABBA'S TATTOO, OF YORO ROOT PIGMENT

Telepath response unit

Brain support unit

Locomotion unit

Neurix tube

Spider leg

Detachable brain jar

Disembodied monk brain

Manipulator claw

B'OMARR MONK
Automated droid legs carry disembodied monks through the palace. The oldest spider droids have four legs, while more recent models have six.

Alkhara's Tower

Main citadel

Western Keep

The desert palace of Jabba the Hutt was originally a monastery constructed long ago by the mysterious B'omarr monks. Over the years, bandits took control of parts of the citadel, adding portions even as the monks went about their secret ways in the nether reaches of the structure. As Jabba's headquarters, the fortress holds a wide variety of gangsters, assassins, travelers, crooked officials, entertainers, and servants.

Oola

Oola was kidnapped from a primitive clan by Jabba's majordomo Bib Fortuna, and trained by other Twi'lek girls in the art of seductive dance. Although Jabba finds her highly desirable, Oola refuses to give in to him.

Lekku (head-tail)

DATA FILE

◆ Jabba maintains a lavish estate in Mos Eisley, where he stays when conducting business at the spaceport. Wherever he is, he likes to eat nine meals a day.

◆ Although few suspect it, the creature called Buboicullaar, or Bubo, (right) is actually intelligent. He once ate a detonation link needed for a bomb, foiling an attempt to assassinate Jabba.

Jabba the Hutt

Jabba Desilijic Tiure, known to all as simply Jabba the Hutt, comes from the planet Nal Hutta, where he was raised (by his father, also a crime lord) to crave power and wealth. Hutts are notorious for their ruthless and amoral ways, and they often exploit their physical power to control weaker species. Hutts run most of the galaxy's large criminal syndicates.

Muscular body can move like a snail or slither forward

Accompanied by lookouts on sand skiffs, Jabba's sail barge *Khetanna* carries the Hutt on journeys to Mos Eisley or to places of execution and gladiatorial combat staged for the crime lord's amusement.

Internal mantles shape a Hutt's head

Hutt skin secretes oil and mucus, making Hutts difficult to seize

Body has no skeleton

Hookah pipe

Naal thorn burner

Hermi Odle

Ephant Mon

Jabba's palace is filled with bizarre creatures like his personal armorer, the Baragwin Hermi Odle. The former gun-runner Ephant Mon is Jabba's only real friend: the Hutt once saved his life.

Salacious Crumb

When Jabba first found this Kowakian monkey-lizard stealing his food, he tried to eat him, but later he became amused by the creature's antics. Salacious has since taken on the job of Jabba's court jester.

Salacious Crumb

Movable dais

Jabba's Entourage

CROWDED AROUND JABBA is a wide variety of individuals — sycophants, co-conspirators, hired thugs, and beings of mystery. The crime lord's extensive syndicate offers opportunity to many types, just as Jabba's power and wealth draw many to secretly scheme against him. The Hutt regards the inevitable plots as amusement, pitting the different schemers against each other before compassing their destruction. Amidst all the power plays and convoluted ambitions, many are individuals simply doing their jobs and ignoring the web of intrigue around them. Each in the retinue have their own stories, and curious paths have led every one of them to the desert palace.

Sensory brain areas

Scary red eyes

Sharp, pointed teeth

Lekku (head-tail; one of two)

Dagger (concealed in robe)

Slaver bracelet

Traditional Ryloth robe made from Jalavash worm silk

Soft-soled shoes for silent movement

Rock wart sting juice (dried)

Chall granules

Krayt dragon venom

Taulek style handle

TWI'LEK DAGGER AND POISONS

Poisoned blade

Suction-tipped fingers

Manipulative mouth tentacles

Vand belt

Desert cloak

Moisture-retaining robe

Bib Fortuna

Jabba's Twi'lek majordomo supervises the affairs of both the desert palace and the Mos Eisley estate. Before working with Jabba the Hutt, Bib Fortuna grew wealthy as a slave trader of his own people and became a hunted criminal as a spice smuggler. As Jabba's chief lieutenant, he plots to kill his boss behind a facade of obsequious manners. Fortuna's control within the organization and his tendency to resort to underhanded means with friends and foes alike make him a powerful and dreaded, if cowardly, individual.

A clever Qarren from Mon Calamari, Tessek views the world of Jabba's palace with a clear and calculating mind. As Jabba's accountant, he embezzles money into a secret fund and plans (like several others) to assassinate Jabba and take over his organization.

Jabba finds Bib Fortuna serviceable but not up to the standards of his best majordomo, Sevan Domna, who was killed in an assassination attempt on Jabba decades ago.

Barrel

Simple optical targeting scope

Heat sink

Phase
amplifier

Trigger

Recharge
valve

SKIFF GUARD'S BLASTER

DATA FILE

◆ Jabba knows that Tessek is plotting against him, as the plan was revealed by one of the B'omarr monks with whom Jabba sometimes secretly confers.

◆ Bib Fortuna and a now-murdered associate brought to Jabba his rancor monster, discovered in a mysterious crashed ship in the Tatooine desert.

◆ Jabba doesn't like humans and there are few who have spent long periods amongst his palace entourage. More welcome are such types as Rodian hunters, the occasional sociopathic Snivvian (right), and grim Weequay thugs.

Nostrils

Thick
oily pelt

Hooked
claw

Calloused
skin

Most Eloms are sympathetic to the Rebellion, but this vile opportunist carries out extortion activity for Jabba, interacting with few others at the palace.

Jabba's skiff guards serve as escorts and lookouts, fully exposed on the skiffs to wind, sun, and enemy fire. New hires generally get skiff duty.

Retractable
eyes

Tusks

Coarse
fur

J'Quille is a brutal Whiphid from the cold planet of Toola, working as a manhunter for Jabba. He is actually a spy for a rival crime lord, and is planning to kill the Hutt with a slow-acting poison in his food.

Helmet

Sensitive nose

Thick
muscles

Weak eyes

Palace
garments

Fangs

Shoulder
armor

Gauntlets

Gamorrean Guards

Tough, brutish Gamorrean guards stand throughout Jabba's palace as sentries. Prone to violence, these slow-witted creatures are stubborn and loyal. The low intelligence of male Gamorreans is an asset to their employers, as they cannot be bribed or persuaded to betray. They prefer hand-to-hand combat weapons over blasters.

Heavy-duty
ax head

Vibro-lance

Sandals

Jabba's Entertainers

JABBA HAS COME TO SPEND a good deal of time in his palace, importing entertainers to amuse him in his courts. His wealth and lavish spending can attract real talent, but the palace reputation for danger and mayhem tends to keep out all but the desperate. The bands that do end up playing the palace are typically either slaves to debt, heavy spice users, or the singing dregs of galactic society. Some few are merely very poor judges of venue, and those that leave the palace intact almost always fire or eat their managers. Jabba's whims keep this odd flotsam of musicians and dancers hopping, one way or another.

Yarna d'al Gargan has been a dancer at the palace for years. She is the daughter of an Askaji tribal chief, brought by slavers to Tatooine, then bought by Jabba. While she still resents the Hutt, she is close to some palace regulars.

These singers were appalled to find out what life at Jabba's palace is really like. They put on a show of enthusiasm with each performance, desperately trying to figure out how to get out alive.

Umpass-stay

Power drum

Ak-rev

Jabba's drum master Ak-rev grew up in a Sriluurian monastery devoted to Am-Shak, the god of thunder, where he learned to play the thunder drums of the temple. Ak-rev is assisted by the Klatooinian Umpass-stay, who is secretly also a bodyguard for Jabba.

The Rodian Doda Bodonawieedo has become the favorite bard of Jabba's palace Gamorreans. At times he plays with the palace bands. Barquin D'an is the brother of Bith Figrin D'an of the Modal Nodes.

Barquin D'an with kloo horn

Traz

Lekku (head-tail)

Form-fitting szona body glove

Suction-tipped fingers

GREEATA

Hooves

RYSTÁLL SANT

Sounding cymbal

Resonator

Radion modulator

Plandl horn

Xloff horn

Troomic sound tube

Sub-woofer base

BONTORMIAN KLESPLONG

When he particularly likes a unique sound, Jabba keeps the instruments of some bands that ... don't need them anymore. These exotic instruments stay in the palace, and the Hutt sometimes orders the new bands to perform using them, even if they don't know how.

Sensua bindings

Dance shoes

The body shape of Hutts makes them unsuited to elaborate forms of dance, but Jabba has developed an appreciation for the sinuous and rhythmic movements of non-Hutt dancers. A good dancer can obtain the favor and indulgence of the Hutt, and those who are also expert at the arts of manipulation can find profit or opportunity among his entourage.

Lyn Me

A Twi'lek from the barren northern continent of Ryloth, Lyn Me practiced the arts of seductive dance to make her way off-planet. Max Rebo talked her into coming to Jabba's palace.

DATA FILE

◆ Quite a few more bands have arrived at the palace than have left. When really disappointed, Jabba feels entitled to feed bad musicians to his rancor.

◆ Known on his homeworld as Rapotwanalantonee, Max Rebo's Shawda Ubb plays a combination flute and water organ.

Droopy McCool

Totally oblivious to what's going on around him, this Kitonak hardly recognizes the stage name given to him by Max Rebo. A far-out quasi-mystic, he hardly fits in with the Rebo band but doesn't notice; he just plays his tunes. Lonely for the company of his own kind, he claims to have heard the faint tones of other Kitonaks somewhere out in the Tatooine dunes.

Sy Snootles

Misled by Jabba's enthusiastic appreciation, the egotistical singer Sy Snootles has a very inaccurate view of her own potential. As a vocalist she is too weird to make it anywhere mainstream. She will probably never discover this, since Jabba's favorite singers find it very hard to leave the palace.

Max Rebo

The blue Ortoloan known in the business as Max Rebo is a half-insane keyboard player completely obsessed with food. He accepted a contract with Jabba that pays only in free meals, to the outrage of his bandmates. He may have poor judgement as a band leader, but he is devoted to music and quite good at his chosen instrument.

Keen sense of smell

Ears store fat

Output speaker

Air intake

Fingertips can absorb food and drink

RED BALL JET ORGAN

Keyboard

Organ base

Air outlet pipes

The Sarlacc

SCIENTIFIC ANALYSIS has answered questions about many lifeforms in the galaxy, but some creatures continue to defy analysis, such as the Sarlacc. A rare, enormous beast, one Sarlacc rests in the basin of the Great Pit of Carkoon in the Northern Dune Sea on Tatooine. The Sarlacc's three-meter-wide mouth is the only part above ground level, and is otherwise completely concealed beneath the desert sands. While some xenobiologists argue over whether the Sarlacc is a plant or animal, most agree that the creature is far too dangerous to merit extended study.

The Sarlacc feeds on stray creatures that cannot escape the sandy slopes that surround its mouth, but not all of its meals are accidental. For many years, Jabba the Hutt delivered his enemies as "gifts" to the Sarlacc. Luke Skywalker was among the few to survive such a close encounter.

Touch-receptor tentacles

Rock-hard primary digestive glands

Beaked tongue swallows small prey whole

Inward-pointing teeth prevent victims from escaping

Tranquilizing poisons immobilize prey

Slower digestive route for more intellectually stimulating victims

Multiple hearts paired with multiple lungs

Sand trap

Site of Boba Fett's eventual escape

Moisture-gathering roots

Upper stabilizing limb senses movement in surrounding sands

Jabba was surprised by the sudden, coordinated revolt of his Rebel captives. While the battle raged over the Great Pit of Carkoon, the Sarlacc simply waited for bodies to fall.

Deadly Tongue

As the only visible aspect of the Sarlacc rests in the basin of the Great Pit of Carkoon, some mistakenly assume that the beak-tipped appendage at the basin's center is the creature's head. In fact, this eyeless protuberance is the Sarlacc's muscular tongue, which rises up from its mucous-lined mouth, seeking whatever savory morsels come its way.

Parasitic male remains attached to female for life

Unfortunate eopie

Acidic juices dissolve soft membranes and digest smaller molecules of food

Anchored root system

Careless anooba

The only known survivor of the Sarlacc's actual digestive system was Boba Fett, whose armored suit offered some protection from the creature as he used his weapons to blast his way out. It took years for Fett to recover from his wounds and regain his reputation.

Once swallowed, the Sarlacc's prey is incorporated into the biological system. It is believed that the Sarlacc absorbs the intellect of its victims, and is capable of sustaining their torment for thousands of years.

Still-sentient cocooned victims become part of the Sarlacc's collective intelligence

Transport tentacles place prey in specific areas of main stomach

Humanoid prey from one of Jabba's previous visits

The Sarlacc claimed numerous lives during the skirmish that became known as the Battle of Carkoon, but many escaped the conflagration which consumed Jabba's sail barge. It remains unknown whether the Sarlacc prefers its meals live or roasted.

Lower stabilizing limb

DATA FILE

u The Sarlacc is vulnerable to energy weapons, but most of its victims are unarmed. Those snared by the Sarlacc can only hope for rescue. Various factions have suggested that the Sarlacc should be destroyed, but more influential beings ensure its ongoing use as a most entertaining disposal system of their enemies.

Boba Fett

HAVING INHERITED JANGO FETT'S Mandalorian battle armor and arsenal of exotic weapons, Boba Fett assumes his father's mantle as a notrious and enigmatic bounty hunter. Over the years, Boba Fett has developed his own code of honor, and though he takes only certain assignments, he devotes himself to those few with fanatical skill. His cool and calculating ways combined with his manifold hidden capabilities have brought in many "impossible" marks, and earned his reputation as the best bounty hunter in the galaxy. From the concealed weapons covering his space suit to the disguised armaments of his starship *Slave I*, Boba Fett is unerringly a bounty's worst nightmare.

Slave 1

Rotating cockpit capsule

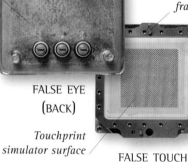

Jango Fett had heavily modified his personal starship but Boba Fett continues to improve the aging craft. Slave 1 is jammed with weapons and customized tracking equipment of every kind, as well as a stolen military sensor masking system to hide him from those he stalks. Four on-board power generators are required to run the many weapons systems that can suddenly deploy from hidden panels.

Boba Fett has worked for Darth Vader on several occasions, enough to have been called Vader's right-hand man. Vader finds Fett an intelligent, ruthless, capable ally, worthy to track Rebels and pursue Luke Skywalker.

Jet Backpack

Missile

Fett's backpack is an excellent combination jumper-pack and rocket launcher. The launcher can be fitted with a missile or with a grappling hook projectile (attached to a rope and winch). The jet jumper system holds rocket blasts for short flights or for escaping and surprising Boba's prey.

Missile boost charge

Jet Pack adjustment tool

Stabilizing gyro

Fuel tank

Directional servo

Missile launcher

Missile targeting rangefinder

Activation button

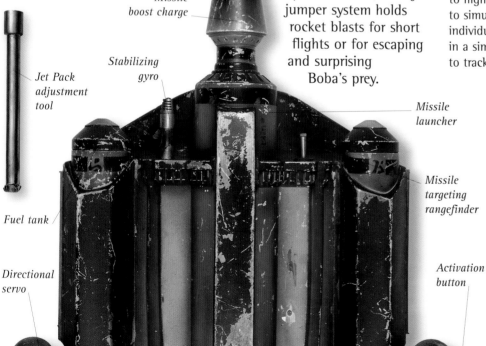

Directional exhaust nozzles

HoloNet transmitter

S-thread detection matrix

ION LIMPET
HOMING BEACON

Setting control

Organic alloy casing

Attachment magnet

Attachment frame

FALSE EYE
(BACK)

Touchprint simulator surface

FALSE TOUCH

Boba Fett uses these devices to track his marks and gain silent access to high security areas. A false touch pad clamps over touchprint locks to simulate the bioelectrical field and fingerprint of nearly any individual. A false eye pad can be applied to defeat retinal scan locks in a similar fashion. The ion limpet quietly uses the galactic HoloNet to track spacecraft throughout the known galaxy.

DATA FILE

◆ Fett is notorious for completely disintegrating those whom he has been hired to track down and kill.

◆ Working as a spy for Darth Vader, Boba Fett first encountered Luke Skywalker on a moon in the Panna system, where he almost tricked Luke into giving away the new location of the main Rebel base.

◆ Fett's services are famously expensive, but his honor cannot be bought. He only accepts missions which meet his harsh sense of justice.

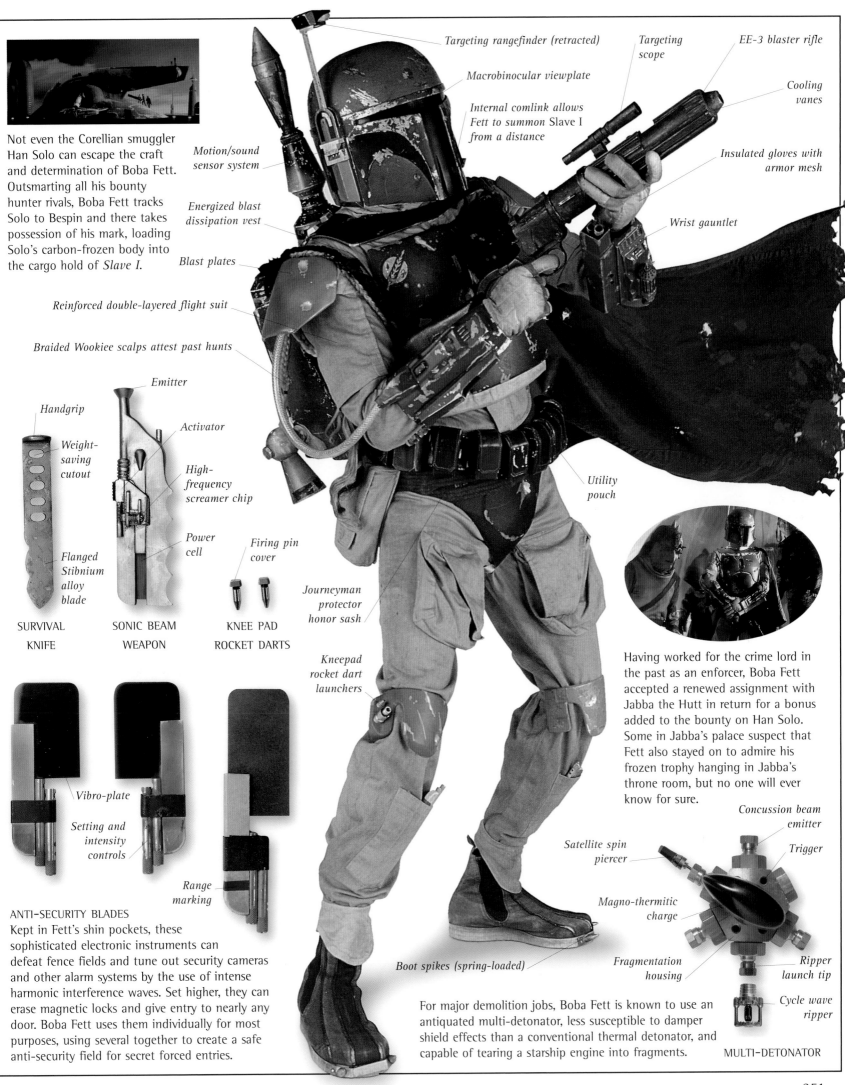

Targeting rangefinder (retracted)

Targeting scope

EE-3 blaster rifle

Macrobinocular viewplate

Cooling vanes

Internal comlink allows Fett to summon Slave I from a distance

Not even the Corellian smuggler Han Solo can escape the craft and determination of Boba Fett. Outsmarting all his bounty hunter rivals, Boba Fett tracks Solo to Bespin and there takes possession of his mark, loading Solo's carbon-frozen body into the cargo hold of *Slave I*.

Motion/sound sensor system

Insulated gloves with armor mesh

Energized blast dissipation vest

Wrist gauntlet

Blast plates

Reinforced double-layered flight suit

Braided Wookiee scalps attest past hunts

Emitter

Handgrip

Activator

Weight-saving cutout

High-frequency screamer chip

Power cell

Firing pin cover

Journeyman protector honor sash

Flanged Stibnium alloy blade

Utility pouch

SURVIVAL
KNIFE

SONIC BEAM
WEAPON

KNEE PAD
ROCKET DARTS

Kneepad rocket dart launchers

Having worked for the crime lord in the past as an enforcer, Boba Fett accepted a renewed assignment with Jabba the Hutt in return for a bonus added to the bounty on Han Solo. Some in Jabba's palace suspect that Fett also stayed on to admire his frozen trophy hanging in Jabba's throne room, but no one will ever know for sure.

Vibro-plate

Concussion beam emitter

Setting and intensity controls

Satellite spin piercer

Trigger

Range marking

Magno-thermitic charge

ANTI-SECURITY BLADES
Kept in Fett's shin pockets, these sophisticated electronic instruments can defeat fence fields and tune out security cameras and other alarm systems by the use of intense harmonic interference waves. Set higher, they can erase magnetic locks and give entry to nearly any door. Boba Fett uses them individually for most purposes, using several together to create a safe anti-security field for secret forced entries.

Boot spikes (spring-loaded)

Fragmentation housing

Ripper launch tip

Cycle wave ripper

For major demolition jobs, Boba Fett is known to use an antiquated multi-detonator, less susceptible to damper shield effects than a conventional thermal detonator, and capable of tearing a starship engine into fragments.

MULTI-DETONATOR

251

Bounty Hunters

THE RESTRICTIVE RULE of the Empire has made criminals of many, encouraging black-market smugglers and creating long blacklists of proscribed citizens of every kind. Imperial rewards posted for all such "enemies of the state" have made bounty hunting a thriving profession. Often criminal refuse themselves, many bounty hunters act in murderous and violent ways with the sanction of Imperial law. A few work with the legitimate intention of capturing criminals, but the profession as a whole is distinguished by outstanding slime.

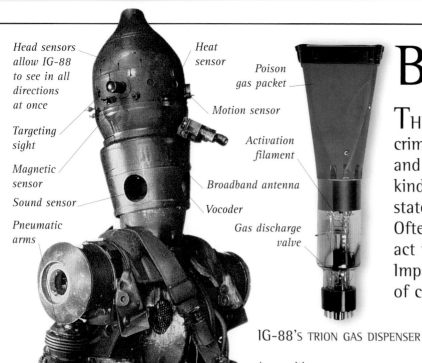

Head sensors allow IG-88 to see in all directions at once

Heat sensor

Poison gas packet

Motion sensor

Targeting sight

Activation filament

Magnetic sensor

Broadband antenna

Sound sensor

Vocoder

Pneumatic arms

Gas discharge valve

IG-88's TRION GAS DISPENSER

Ammunition bandolier

Flamethrower

Sonic stunner

"Butcher" vibro-blade

Explosive core

IG-88's CONCUSSION DISCS

Pulse cannon

Ammo packets

Worn due to use

Neural inhibitor projectile launcher

IG-88's BLADE EXTENSION SET

IG-88

This hideous assassin droid is one of a set of five identical robots which massacred their constructors moments after activation, and escaped their laboratories to stalk the galaxy. IG-88's incompletely formed identity leaves it obsessed with hunting and killing. Assassin droids are always hard to control and have long been illegal for good reason, since they pose a threat to any and all around them.

Blast armor

Acid-proof servo wires

An IG-88 droid tracked *Slave I* to Cloud City, intending to kill Boba Fett. Fett ambushed it in the scrap processing levels. He paralyzed it with an ion cannon, then finished it off, leaving the hulk for recycling.

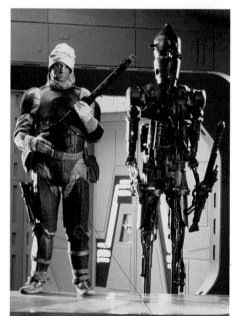

Dengar

Dengar

Trained as an Imperial assassin, Dengar underwent brain surgery that replaced his hypothalamus with circuitry, making him a nearly unfeeling killer. Now independent as a bounty hunter, he has claimed 23 bounties and carries a personal grudge against Han Solo for severe head injuries he suffered racing him through the crystal swamps of Agrilat long ago.

DATA FILE

◆ IG-88 droids have attacked Boba Fett several times, badly damaging *Slave I* but never claiming Fett himself. Fett has now destroyed three of the assassin droids.

◆ Rodians like Greedo come from a culture that favors bounty hunting as a sport, though Greedo found his match in Han Solo.

Poison-tipped needles

Firing chamber

Silencer tube

Release valve

Needle Barrel

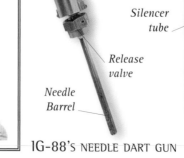

IG-88's NEEDLE DART GUN

4-LOM

Once a sophisticated protocol droid made to resemble the species it worked with, 4-LOM's programming degraded and it became a criminal, specializing in anticipating the moves of target beings. Teamed with the findsman Zuckuss, 4-LOM provides information and analysis to support his partner's mysterious ways.

Zuckuss

The bounty hunter Zuckuss uses the mystic religious rituals of findsman traditions dating back centuries on his gaseous homeworld of Gand. His uncanny abilities make other bounty hunters uneasy. Zuckuss is a tireless tracker and weirdly effective.

4-LOM   Zuckuss

Boba Fett   Bossk

Targeting laser

Vision-plus scanner

Speech scrambler

Body suit

Impact armor

Chest-mounted comlink

Audio pickup and broadband antenna

Glove spikes

Activation panel and timer settings

Plasmic core

Bandolier

Projectile detonator

Ogygian cloak

Ubese clan belt-clasp

Fragmentation shell

Ammo pouches

BOUSHH'S THERMAL DETONATOR

Shata leather pants

Boushh

Stun tip

Fire coils

Shock blade

BOUSHH'S LANCE BLADE AND STUN ATTACHMENTS

In a galaxy with so many bizarre creatures acting as bounty hunters (or claiming to be), it was easy for Princess Leia to adopt a convincing identity as a Ubese tracker, disguising herself with a dead hunter's helmet and garb. Leia's military training served her well as Boushh, and only Jabba suspected her real identity.

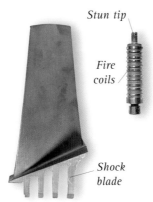

Bossk

A reptilian Trandoshan, the tough and resilient Bossk has gone from tracking runaway slaves to claiming bounties posted by the Empire – a count of 12 captures so far. Trandoshans can regenerate lost skin, fingers, and even limbs until they reach adulthood as Bossk finally has. Fond of skinning his quarry when possible, he is as vile and mean as bounty hunters get.

Jabba the Hutt's palace frequently brings bounty hunters together as the Hutt posts rewards for both captures and kills on a regular basis.

Traditional Ubese boots

Sand People
TUSKEN RAIDERS

FIERCE NOMADS OF TATOOINE, the Sand People or Tusken Raiders prowl areas like the Dune Sea and the Jundland Wastes, blending invisibly into the landscape. Masters of the desert, they survive where no one else can, protected from the suns by heavy clothing. Their savage and violent ways pit them against the moisture farmers and settlers in lonely, remote lands. They usually stay away from towns and cities, but in the dead of hot season, Raiders emerge from the wastes after the twin suns set to scavenge or steal from the edges of settlement zones. It is best to lock up tight at night – Sand People almost never come into a house but they will slay a lone resister outside.

Warrior spines

Head bandages

Eye protection lenses

Breath filter

Moisture trap

Poisoned blade

Gaderffi stick

Thick desert cloak

Sand gloves

Bandaged feet

Banthas

Banthas roam the dunes and wastes of Tatooine in herds. Sand People use these giant beasts to carry both riders and gear, forming close bonds with them, and even making them members of their clans. Sand People ride in single file to hide their numbers.

BLOODLETTING BLADE
Tusken Raider clan rituals may involve the sacrifice of animals, captives, or even condemned Sand People.

Rare water wells in canyons like Gafsa are sacred to the Tusken Raiders. Merely trespassing near one can provoke immediate violence. Intruders may be taken alive for sacrifice.

DATA FILE

◆ Tusken Raiders scavenge metal from wrecks to make their traditional terror weapon, the gaderffi (or gaffi) stick.

◆ While Sand People are nomadic, clans often have a particular cave or hollow where they gather to hold special ceremonies or to bury their dead.

Jawas

CONCEALED in dark robes that protect them from the twin suns, the timid and acquisitive Jawas scavenge scrap metal, lost droids, and equipment from refuse or the many crashed spaceships that dot the desert landscapes of Tatooine. Their glowing eyes help them see in the dark crevices where they hide, and their rodent-like faces are remarkably ugly. While there are a few Jawa settlements, most Jawas patrol the dunes and dusty rocks in gigantic sandcrawlers, ancient vehicles from a mining era long ago. Jawas can offer real bargains in the junk that they repair, but are notoriously tricky and will swindle the unwary buyer.

Droids that wander off or get thrown out as junk are favorite targets for the Jawas. Jawas always carry restraining bolts which they install to claim itinerant droids. A magnetic suction tube draws captured droids into the bowels of a roving sandcrawler.

Scoured and rusted from countless sandstorms and the blistering suns, sandcrawlers hold droid prisons, mineral ore and metal processors, and wrecked or salvaged junk of every kind.

Ionized gas filament compartment

ION POWER CHARGE CELL

Charge cell housing

Overload breakers

Ion regulators

Primary ion accelerator

Blast nozzle

Ion accelerator brace

Power transformer

Trigger

Stock

IONIZATION BLASTER

Power coupling

Mounting brace

Tread energizer

Neutral polarity node

Linkage pins

Mark II reactor drone magfield sensor ball

Contact cage

DROID PARTS
Jawa recycling talents are legendary. If a droid is too battered even for Jawas to repair, it is cannibalized for spare parts (above). New owners who open up a droid bought from Jawas may find internal parts of which its makers never dreamed.

Transmitter calls or halts a droid

Droid signal receiver

Setting adjust

Belt ring

Activator

Power cell

DROID CALLER

Ionization charge (inside belt pouch)

Glowing eyes

Heavy cloaks protect from sun glare

Bandolier

Droid caller

Tool belt

Mini-ionization pistol

DATA FILE

◆ The Jawa clans gather together once a year in a great salvage swap meet, where they trade droids, equipment, and stories of their adventures.

◆ When a Jawa sandcrawler arrives to sell and trade at the edge of a town, the droids hide, and people watch their 'speeders extra closely. Things tend to disappear when Jawas are around.

Ewoks

DEEP WITHIN the primeval forests of the emerald moon of Endor, the small, furry Ewoks live in harmony with the natural world around them. They build their villages high in the oldest trees, connecting their dwellings with wooden bridges and suspended platforms. Ewoks hunt and gather by day on the forest floor, retreating to their aerial villages by night, when the forest becomes too dangerous for them.

Sounding sticks

Retaining strap

Leather strap

Stone knife

HUNTING KNIFE

Sheath

Handle

CHURI BIRD CALLERS

Churi feathers

Gurreck skull headress

Stone club head

Authority stick

Striped pelt

Teebo

A watcher of the stars and a poet at heart, Teebo has a mystical alignment with the forces of nature. His subtle perception lets him see more than meets his dreamer's eye, but he is also a practical thinker. His sound judgment has led to his position as a leader within his tribe.

Hood

Spear

Thick fur

Wicket W. Warrick

A young loner, Wicket is off traveling when he encounters Princess Leia Organa in the forest. Helping her to the relative safety of his village, he comes to trust her and senses her goodness of spirit. When Leia's friends arrive, Wicket argues that they should be spared any abuse, but his solitary habits leave him with small influence amongst the village elders. Wicket's thorough knowledge of the forest terrain greatly assists the Rebels in their later attack on the Imperial forces.

Thickened head lends weight to blows

FIGHTING CLUBS

Talisman bag

Healing wand

SHAMAN'S KIT

An Ewok shaman builds a collection of many magical objects and medicinal cures for his work. A spirit staff helps summon dead ancestors for assistance, while the sick or injured are touched with a powerful healing wand. The forest vegetation offers many medicinal plants, which are kept with charms in a talisman bag.

SHAMAN'S GHOST RATTLE

Logray

A tribal shaman and medicine man, Logray uses his knowledge of ritual and magic to help and awe his people. He still favors the old traditions of initiation and live sacrifice. The trophies on his staff of power include the remnants of old enemies. Logray is suspicious of all outsiders, an attitude reinforced by the arrival of Imperial forces.

Churi skull

Staff of power

Trophy spine

Chief Chirpa

Leader of his tribe for 42 seasons, Chief Chirpa has the wisdom of long years. He leads his people with understanding, even though he has become a bit forgetful in his old age. His authority commits the Ewoks to their dangerous fight against the Empire.

Hood

Hunting knife

Chief's medallion

Medicine bag

Striped fur

DATA FILE

◆ While their technology is primitive, the Ewoks display resourceful ingenuity, constructing hang gliders and complex traps for Imperial occupation forces.

◆ Ewoks often wear the teeth, horns, and skulls of animals they have hunted as trophies.

The Cantina Crowd

THE MOS EISLEY SPACEPORT sees a wide variety of unusual people and things, but the Mos Eisley Cantina is known as the haunt of the weirdest clientele in town. Hardened professional spacers and bizarre outlanders from distant corners of the galaxy can be found here. It's no place for the squeamish, but for its regulars, the cantina provides a pan-galactic atmosphere that helps distract them from their various misfortunes and the miserable hole of Mos Eisley. The regular band suits many tastes, and as long as foolish outsiders don't step in and get their heads blown off, everyone can have their own version of a good time. Deals get made, things get drunk, and the wrong sorts of business go the right sorts of ways. The bartender maintains a semblance of order by threatening to poison the drinks of creatures that give him trouble.

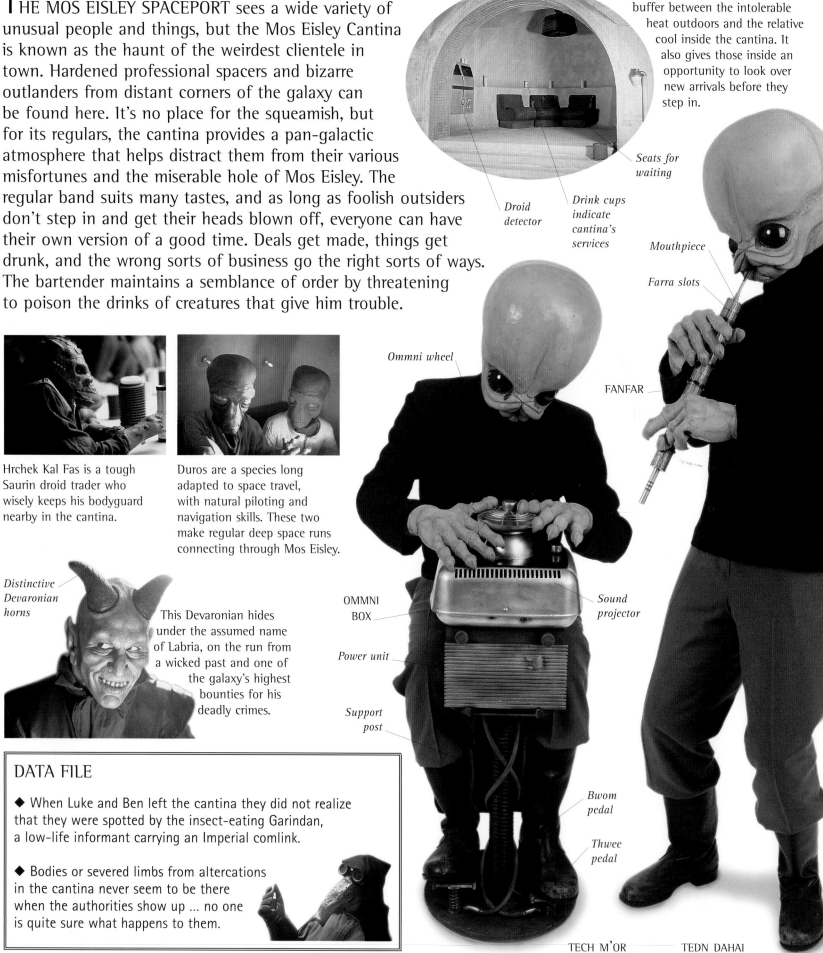

An entrance vestibule serves as a buffer between the intolerable heat outdoors and the relative cool inside the cantina. It also gives those inside an opportunity to look over new arrivals before they step in.

Seats for waiting

Droid detector

Drink cups indicate cantina's services

Mouthpiece

Farra slots

Ommni wheel

FANFAR

Hrchek Kal Fas is a tough Saurin droid trader who wisely keeps his bodyguard nearby in the cantina.

Duros are a species long adapted to space travel, with natural piloting and navigation skills. These two make regular deep space runs connecting through Mos Eisley.

Distinctive Devaronian horns

This Devaronian hides under the assumed name of Labria, on the run from a wicked past and one of the galaxy's highest bounties for his deadly crimes.

OMMNI BOX

Sound projector

Power unit

Support post

Bwom pedal

Thwee pedal

DATA FILE

◆ When Luke and Ben left the cantina they did not realize that they were spotted by the insect-eating Garindan, a low-life informant carrying an Imperial comlink.

◆ Bodies or severed limbs from altercations in the cantina never seem to be there when the authorities show up ... no one is quite sure what happens to them.

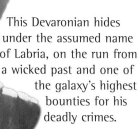

TECH M'OR   TEDN DAHAI

Living beneath Mos Eisley in abandoned tunnels, this Talz named Muftak works as a pickpocket. Talz are a primitive species who use few tools, and are taken into space only by slavers.

Day vision eyes (night vision eyes beneath)

The cantina's diverse selection of legal and illegal drinks draws unusual visitors. Lamproids and other marginal species are served blood mixes of questionable origin.

Figrin D'an and his Band

The Bith musicians most often heard in the cantina are highly intelligent creatures with sophisticated musical abilities – a band called the Modal Nodes. Even though they complain, the band members enjoy their out-of-the-way dive and are glad to be away from their home world of Clak'dor VII. The lead player is an expert gambler who lives well and pays off his occasional debts with his tunes, and meanwhile tries to keep his members out of trouble. They've been asked to play at Jabba's palace, but they're too smart for that.

Enlarged cranium

Large eyes

Mouth tube

KLOO HORN

Tone mode selectors

Respiratory folds

FIZZZ (OR DORENIAN BESHNIQUEL)

BANDFILL

Band jacket

Reciprocator horns

Ploong sounder

Peel rod

Power indicator

Peel rods

Band pants

Travel boots

FIGRIN D'AN

NALAN CHEEL

DOIKK NA'TS

Cantina Patrons

BECAUSE OF THE EMPIRE'S tyrannical control of the Core Worlds and its hatred of nonhumans, many citizens migrated or fled to Outer Rim planets such as Tatooine, which the Empire regarded as barely worth their attention. Although some beings have chosen to band together in this relatively lawless area of space, others have become cynical and look out only for themselves. The Mos Eisley Cantina is known to some locals and spacers as Chalmun's Cantina, as it is owned by Chalmun, a grizzled Wookiee and former street fighter. Except for droids, anyone with credits is welcome at the Cantina—but newcomers should be cautious of the more dangerous regulars.

In an alcove close to the bar, the Talz pickpocket Muftak, Bith mercenary and backup Kloo Horn player Lirin Car'n, and Sakiyan bounty hunter Djas Puhr, and fight-loving Myo discuss current events while listening to the band.

Diverse Clientele

Of the relatively few places where a methane-breathing Morseerian, a Jawa-speaking Bimm smuggler, a Saurin bodyguard, and a blood-sucking Anzati ever find common ground, the Cantina is a favorite hangout. The wide range of species that frequents the Cantina encourages the bartender to maintain an equally wide stock of beverages.

Imperial fugitive Yerka Mig

Mistryl Shadow Guards Shada D'ukal and Karoly D'ulin impersonating the con-artist Tonnika twins

Moreerian pilot Nabrun Leids

Bimm smuggler Rycar Ryjerd

Saurin bodyguard Sai'torr Kal Fas

Anzati bounty hunter Dannik Jerriko

MOMAW NADON
An exile from his homeworld Ithor, the "hammerhead" Momaw Nadon secretly supports the Rebellion.

DJAS PHUR
A Sakiyan bounty hunter, Puhr was also an occasional assassin employed by Jabba the Hutt.

BOM VIMDIM
An Advozse smuggler who works for corrupt officials, Bom Vimdim despises his own species.

"BRAINIAC"
The Siniteen nicknamed "Brainiac" is capable of calculating hyperspace coordinates in his head.

MYO
Employed by the Galactic Outdoor Survival School, Myo is a self-regenerating Abyssin from the planet Byss.

MODIFIED DL-21

*No safety
mechanism*

*Cooling vents on
flared muzzle*

*Comfortable grip for
Aqualish hand*

Blasters

Although blaster fights are discouraged in the Cantina, even the toughest customers agree that it would be downright unwise to enter the Cantina unarmed. The BlasTech SE-14C blaster pistol is the weapon of choice for both Dr. Evazan and Ponda Baba, who also packs a modified DL-21.

Power pack

*Optical
targeting scope*

SE-14C

Recharge valve

*Rapid-fire auto
trigger*

*Aqualish see better
underwater*

DR EVAZAN
Carrying multiple death sentences, the murderous Dr. Evazan is notorious for rearranging body parts on living creatures. Evazan and his partner Ponda Baba also enjoy brawling and gunning down defenseless beings.

*Length and
density of tusks
indicates age*

Wuher the bartender dives for cover as Dr. Evazan and Ponda Baba (having failed to provoke Luke Skywalker) make the mistake of attacking Luke and drawing their blasters on Ben Kenobi.

*Short-sleeved jacket
accommodates
flipper arms*

Teak Sidbam

A native of Ando, the flipper-handed amphibian Teak Sidbam was sometimes mistaken for fellow Aqualish Ponda Baba, who, being a different race, has manipulative fingers. A repossession agent, Sidbam was searching for a stolen freighter when he entered the Cantina.

*Shirt
torn by
broad
flippers*

*Skin
changes
color in
cold
water*

DATA FILE
◆ The mercenary Arleil Schous is a Defel, a species of shadowy aliens that have the natural ability to absorb visible light.

Creatures

The ghastly toothed sand creatures of Tatooine's deep deserts can grow to over 100 meters in length.

COUNTLESS VARIETIES of life forms inhabit the galaxy, many known only to those who have encountered them and myriads unclassified by galactic science. Long after dark, space pilots may trade tales over drinks about weird and horrible creatures on remote planets or in the far reaches of space. More than once these stories have turned out to be true, from the haunting howls of Hoth's stalking snow beast to the impossibly gigantic asteroid lurkers, closing their maws on fleeing starships. The doubtful traveler is often the last one to realize that a tentacle is already curled around his leg, about to draw him to some unspeakable death. In a galaxy full of creatures such as these, it pays to be careful.

Space Slug

Silicon-based space slugs survive in a vacuum, digesting minerals with a uranium-based metabolism. Recently a titan space slug was documented by an Imperial Star Destroyer on a pursuit mission in an asteroid field. The slug attacked and digested part of the Imperial vessel before being subdued.

Dianoga

Dianogas (or garbage squids) have spread throughout the galaxy, growing up to ten meters long and thriving especially in sewers. Feeding on refuse, these creatures are sometimes bred in space stations for waste processing. Older specimens are very aggressive, seizing prey in their seven muscular tentacles.

Space-living silicon-based parasites, mynocks attack the signal emitters and power cables of starships, feeding on the energy emissions. They can cause significant damage to ships they infest.

Mild-tempered rontos are used by settled Jawa clans on Tatooine as pack animals, bringing goods to cities for trade.

Tauntaun bones

Curving horns

Fanged maw

Camouflaging white pelt

Thick insulating fur

The worrt inhabits the wastelands of Tatooine, attacking almost any moving object. Jabba keeps worrts in the grounds outside his palace.

Manacles

The rock wart of Tatooine uses a painful neurotoxic venom in its bite and sting to kill even large prey.

Wampa

Standing three meters high, huge wampa ice creatures hunt tauntauns and other creatures on the snow plains of Hoth, where their howling wails blend with the icy winds at night. Cunning predators, wampas are normally solitary beasts, but they have been known to band together with uncanny intelligence in the face of threats like human settlements.

Rancor Monster

Standing five meters tall, this fearsome carnivore possesses an armored skin and colossal strength. Jabba keeps this beast in a pit beneath one of his palace courts, feeding it a live diet of unfortunate victims and watching its attacks for amusement. Jabba keeps the origin of his bizarre, freakish pet a mystery, though there are little-known legends of rancor-like monsters on the remote planet of Dathomir.

Powerful jaw muscles

Stubby hooves

Short legs

Tough, rigid hide can absorb blaster bolts

Digestive spittle

Claws

Long reaching arms

Wide grasp

Clutching fingers

The animal handler Malakili became an outlaw when some of his circus beasts escaped during a show and killed much of the audience. Jabba then hired him as keeper of the murderous rancor, which Malakili has grown fond of.

Gaffi stick: gift from some Tusken Raiders for killing a giant mutant womp rat that took over their clan cave

Old circus pants

Rancors are inherently benign and have been domesticated by the Witches of Dathomir, but Jabba takes every measure to encourage ferocious behavior from his own rancor. Consumed by rage and hunger, Jabba's rancor proved immune to Luke Skywalker's persuasive Jedi mind tricks when they battled in the creature's pit.

DATA FILE

◆ Dianogas change color to match their last meal, turning translucent if they have not eaten for a long time.

◆ Jabba's pet Hoover (below) looks harmless, but creeps up on sleeping victims to suck their blood at night, using its nose trunk to slither through clothing or around blankets.

263

Droid Technology

MECHANICAL DROIDS perform thousands of different servant functions, saving labor, doing precise or dangerous work, and taking as many different forms as there are tasks. Their abilities to think and communicate vary, from protocol droids designed to blend in with civilized society to utility droids that cannot communicate directly with humans. Droids are regarded as slaves and third-class citizens, held in contempt by those many who "don't like machinery that talks back." Those who give them a little respect can find that some droids have personalities and identities of their own.

DATA FILE

◆ Most droids have their memory banks periodically erased, which prevents them from developing personalities.

◆ The agromech droid R5-D4 "Red" blew his motivator so Owen Lars would have to take R2

Remote communications antenna

Photoreceptors made to look like Stacchati eyes

Stereo vocoder with sounding box

Old-model heavy arm plating

Standard protocol/ secretary droid legs

Decorative chest plate

Human-style manipulator hands

Binocular fine-focus vision

Photoreceptor movement servo

Reinforced body brace

CZ-1

This very old secretary droid was modified from a standard model to resemble the Stacchati species he once served. Abandoned on Tatooine and separated from his twin unit CZ-3 after a crash, CZ-1 broke down in the desert and was captured by Jawas. Presently his locomotors are sand-encrusted and too damaged for him to walk or move properly. Still optimistic, he hopes to be repaired and sold soon.

Jawas try to sell anything they can, prompting them to offer even this ancient droid R1-G4 to Owen Lars. A reactor drone such as this old droid would be at home in the engine room of a large starship, but would have little to do on a moisture farm.

WED-15-77

Capable of accomplishing very specific tasks with close supervision, this binocular Treadwell has a frustratingly small independent thought processor. It assists Luke on his uncle's vaporators but prefers working for Aunt Beru since she always asks it to do the same predictable jobs.

Extensible neck strut

Manipulator arm

Secondary manipulator arm

Equipment test arm

Rotation unit

Logic housing

Communications antenna

Treads

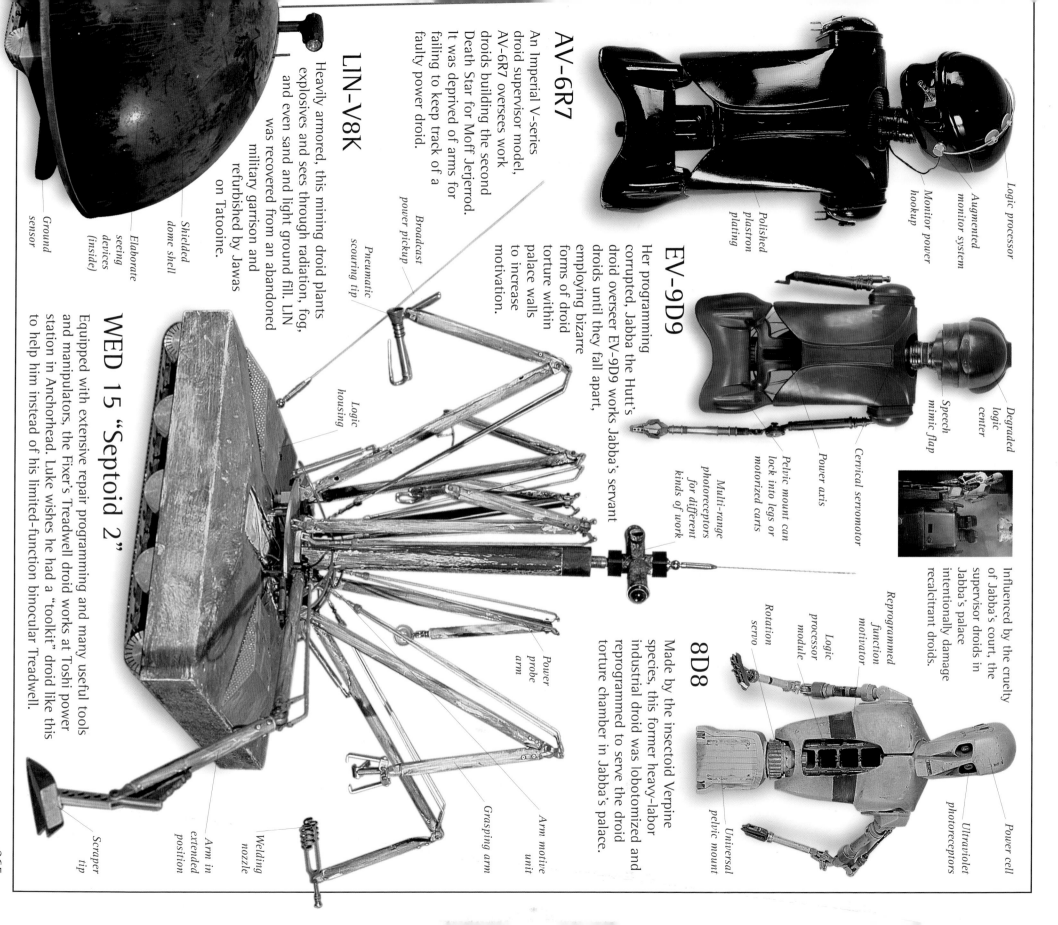

AV-6R7

An Imperial V-series droid supervisor model, AV-6R7 oversees work droids building the second Death Star for Moff Jerjerrod.

- Logic processor
- Augmented monitor system
- Monitor power hookup
- Polished plastron plating

EV-9D9

Her programming corrupted, Jabba the Hutt's droid overseer EV-9D9 works Jabba's servant droids until they fall apart, employing bizarre forms of droid torture within palace walls to increase motivation.

- Degraded logic center
- Speech mimic flap
- Cervical servomotor
- Power axis
- Pelvic mount can lock into legs or motorized carts
- Multi-range photoreceptors for different kinds of work

Influenced by the cruelty of Jabba's court, the supervisor droids in Jabba's palace intentionally damage recalcitrant droids.

8D8

Made by the insectoid Verpine species, this former heavy-labor industrial droid was lobotomized and reprogrammed to serve the droid torture chamber in Jabba's palace.

- Reprogrammed function motivator
- Rotation servo
- Logic processor module
- Universal pelvic mount
- Ultraviolet photoreceptors
- Power cell

LIN-V8K

Heavily armored, this mining droid plants explosives and sees through radiation, fog, and even sand and light ground fill. LIN was recovered from an abandoned military garrison and refurbished by Jawas on Tatooine.

- Ground sensor
- Elaborate seeing devices (inside)
- Shielded dome shell
- Broadcast power pickup
- Pneumatic scouring tip

WED 15 "Septoid 2"

Equipped with extensive repair programming and many useful tools and manipulators, the Fixer's Treadwell droid works at Toshi power station in Anchorhead. Luke wishes he had a "toolkit" droid like this to help him instead of his limited-function binocular Treadwell.

- Logic housing
- Power probe arm
- Arm motive unit
- Grasping arm
- Welding nozzle
- Arm in extended position
- Scraper tip

R2-D2 Expanded

VARIOUS OWNER MODIFICATIONS and sometime limited availability of non-standard optional features gives older model Industrial Automaton astromech droids a reputation for being laden with improvised, exotic, and obsolete assemblies. Although infrequent memory wipes can instill idiosyncratic behavior in most intelligent droids, aged astromechs such as R2-D2 are known for extreme quirkiness. Despite loyalty to his allies, R2 is notoriously good at keeping secrets and is not quick to reveal all of his technological capabilities.

DROID LOGIC
R2 lacks the intuitive and associative capabilities of many organic species, but his unique experiences, observations, and memories have distinctly affected his highly developed logic circuits. He is unusually innovative and decisive.

Imaharatronics logic display sensors

Data cable bus

Protective casing

Universal computer interface arm

Linear actuator provides height adjustment

Grasping arm

Hydraulic head extenders

Head rotation servomotor

Power distribution umbilical

Coupling for power distribution

Commutator

Extendible Neck

EXTENDIBLE NECK
Equipped with an extendible neck to allow his insertion into the droid socket of a Naboo N-1 starfighter, R2-D2 has long ignored this particular feature of his assembly, as its use generally invites unwelcome particles into his systems.

Four-way servomotor

Kerner optical holo control emitter

Fiber-optic data cable

VicksVisc holo-casing

Extendable fire extinguisher

Holographic Projector

By accessing data, R2-D2 can create three-dimensional displays of starship systems. To make a holographic recording of a proximal being or object, the droid's visual sensors are used in combination with his acoustic signaler; an automatic analysis of reflected sound waves creates a visual pattern that "fills in" the areas that R2 cannot see directly.

RECORDED MEMORIES
By sacrificing some free memory, R2 retains several holographic recordings in his system, including Princess Leia's desperate plea for help from Obi-Wan Kenobi and other messages that he regards as historically or personally significant.

Electromagnetic field sensor unit

Nelhal multijunction optical readers

Industries RGB photoreceptor lenses

Stears Data auxiliary visual imaging system

Extendible visual

Protective lens and filter

Gimbal provides tilt adjustment

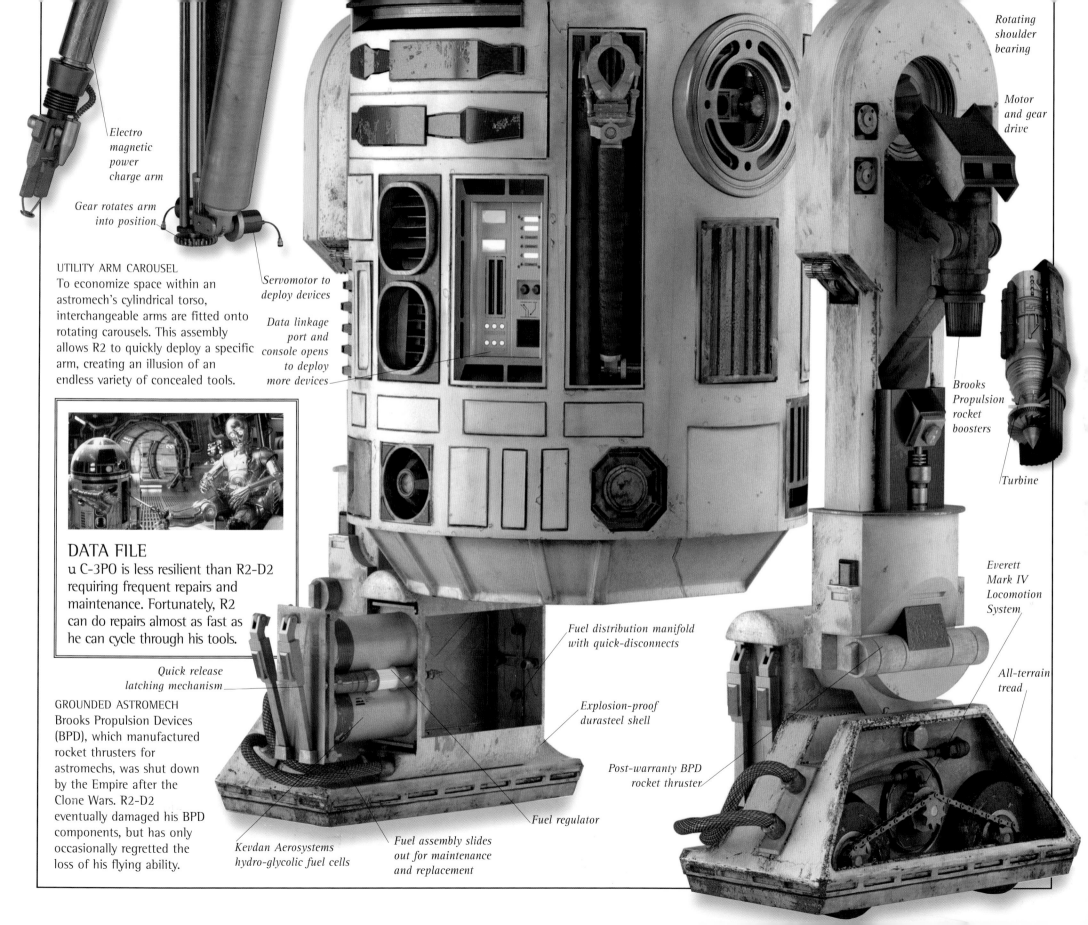

Rotating
shoulder
bearing

Motor
and gear
drive

*Electro
magnetic
power
charge arm*

*Gear rotates arm
into position*

UTILITY ARM CAROUSEL
To economize space within an
astromech's cylindrical torso,
interchangeable arms are fitted onto
rotating carousels. This assembly
allows R2 to quickly deploy a specific
arm, creating an illusion of an
endless variety of concealed tools.

*Servomotor to
deploy devices*

*Data linkage
port and
console opens
to deploy
more devices*

*Brooks
Propulsion
rocket
boosters*

Turbine

DATA FILE
u C-3PO is less resilient than R2-D2
requiring frequent repairs and
maintenance. Fortunately, R2
can do repairs almost as fast as
he can cycle through his tools.

*Everett
Mark IV
Locomotion
System*

*Quick release
latching mechanism*

*Fuel distribution manifold
with quick-disconnects*

*All-terrain
tread*

GROUNDED ASTROMECH
Brooks Propulsion Devices
(BPD), which manufactured
rocket thrusters for
astromechs, was shut down
by the Empire after the
Clone Wars. R2-D2
eventually damaged his BPD
components, but has only
occasionally regretted the
loss of his flying ability.

*Explosion-proof
durasteel shell*

*Post-warranty BPD
rocket thruster*

Fuel regulator

*Kevdan Aerosystems
hydro-glycolic fuel cells*

*Fuel assembly slides
out for maintenance
and replacement*

Glossary

ACADEMY Training institution for Exploration, Military, and Merchant Services.

AIRSPEEDER Repulsorlift-powered vehicle designed to operate inside a planet's protective atmosphere. Some airspeeders can soar more than 250 kilometers high at a speed of more than 900 kilometers an hour. Models include the T-16 skyhopper and Rebel-modified snowspeeders.

ASTROMECH All-around utility droids that carry out computer repairs and undertake information retrieval. Usually short, cylindrical, and tripedal, astromech droids specialize in starship maintenance and repair.

BLASTER Commonly used energy weapons, blasters have adjustable settings to fire beams of intense light that can stun, kill, or vaporize. Models range from handheld blaster pistols and rifles to large blaster cannons that require a crew to operate.

BOUNTY HUNTER Individuals who hunt criminals, outlaws, and predatory creatures for a reward. The Bounty Hunters' Guild upholds their creed, which states that no hunter can kill another hunter or interfere with another's hunt.

CARBONITE A strong but highly volatile metal used to preserve materials such as Tibanna gas, which is frozen in carbonite to allow long-distance transport.

CLONE WARS The interstellar battle fought between the Galactic Republic (which employed clone soldiers under the command of Jedi generals) and the Confederacy of Independent Systems.

COMLINK A personal communications transceiver that consists of a transmitter, receiver, and power source.

CONFEDERACY The common term used for the Confederacy of Independent Systems, an alliance of interstellar commerce factions committed to capitalism and the eventual abolition of all trade barriers.

CORE WORLDS Prestigious and densely populated, the Core Worlds border the central area of the galaxy, and were allied with the Republic before the rise of the Empire.

CREDITS Basic monetary unit used throughout the galaxy.

CYBORG A cybernetic organism, combining technological and organic parts.

DEATH STAR An Imperial moon-sized battle station, equipped with a planet-destroying superlaser.

EMPIRE The common term used for the Republic of the Galactic Empire, ruled by Emperor Palpatine.

ESCAPE POD A technological lifeboat, used by passengers and crew to abandon starships.

THE FORCE An energy field generated by all living things, and which binds the entire galaxy.

HOLOCRON Device used to store and access information for Force-sensitive beings.

HOLOGRAM Three-dimensional image constructed from waves of light. Used for recordings and communications.

HOLONET Interstellar network that allows holographic communication throughout the galaxy.

HYPERSPACE A dimension of space-time that can be reached only by traveling beyond light-speed velocity.

ION CANNON A weapon that fires bursts of ionized energy to damage mechanical and computer systems without causing structural damage.

JEDI Originally protectors of the Republic, Jedi are sensitive to the Force and able to manipulate its energies to help and serve others.

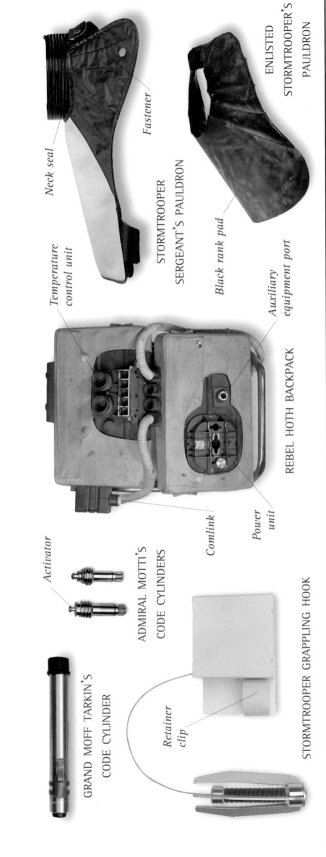

Temperature control unit

Neck seal

Fastener

STORMTROOPER SERGEANT'S PAULDRON

Black rank pad

Auxiliary equipment port

ENLISTED STORMTROOPER'S PAULDRON

REBEL HOTH BACKPACK

Comlink

Power unit

Activator

ADMIRAL MOTTI'S CODE CYLINDERS

GRAND MOFF TARKIN'S CODE CYLINDER

Retainer clip

STORMTROOPER GRAPPLING HOOK

Wupiupi pouch

TATOOINE MONEY BELT

CUT-AWAY STORMTROOPER HELMET

RATH RECORDER

Holographic memory cell

Condensing canteens

DESERT SURVIVAL BACKPACK

Sunshield roll

NABOO DETONATOR

Burnished alloy shell

HITMAN'S BLASTER

Flashy decor

SITH TRACER BEACON

LANDSPEEDER A repulsorlift vehicle used for traveling at low altitude over land.

LASER CANNON Often mounted on a ship or vehicle, this weapon shoots visible bolts of coherent light in a rapid-fire fashion. More powerful than a blaster.

LIGHTSABER The elegant weapon of the Jedi, lightsabers are swords with blades of pure energy that can cut through nearly any object. They can also be used to deflect fired energy bolts.

MIDI-CHLORIANS Microscopic organisms that exist in all living things, and can be detected and measured by a simple analysis of blood or other genetic material. Especially abundant in Force-sensitive beings, midi-chlorians allow Jedi and Sith to tap into the Force.

MOFF Title given to Imperial military commanders who ruled certain sectors of the galaxy, and who reported to Grand Moffs.

NAV COMPUTER Sometimes called a navicomputer, a nav computer is a specialized processing unit used to calculate lightspeed jumps and routes and trajectories through hyperspace and realspace.

OUTER RIM TERRITORIES A group of star systems that lie beyond the Core worlds.

PHOTORECEPTOR A device that captures light rays and converts them into electronic signals for processing by video computers. Photoreceptors are used as eyes in most droids.

PODRACER Essentially a control pod linked to two large repulsorlift engines, Podracers are high-speed vehicles used in professional racing tournaments. Podracer pilots are also called Podracers.

PROTON TORPEDO A projectile weapon that carries a proton-scattering warhead. Proton torpedoes can be fired from starfighters or shoulder-mounted launchers.

REBEL ALLIANCE The common term used for the Alliance to Restore the Republic, which rebelled against Palpatine's Galactic Empire.

REPUBLIC The common term used for the Galactic Republic, the united worlds of the galaxy, which eventually fell to the Galactic Empire.

REPULSORLIFT An engine that employs an antigravitational propulsion unit called a repulsor, repulsorlifts provide thrust for landspeeders and airspeeders, and are also used in small starships for docking and atmospheric flight.

SANDCRAWLER Engineered as ore haulers and mobile refineries, sandcrawlers are enormous vehicles that travel on treads. Abandoned sandcrawlers are typically salvaged

SEPARATISTS Initially a political movement by those who sought to break their alliance with the Galactic Republic, the Separatists officially united as the Confederacy.

SITH An ancient sect of Force-sensitive beings, the secretive Sith use their powers for evil. Their goal is to destroy the Jedi and conquer the galaxy.

SPICE A name given to a variety of drugs, including the glitterstim spice mined underground on the planet Kessel.

STARFIGHTER A combat starship, typically operated by a single pilot.

THERMAL DETONATOR A powerful hand-size bomb that disintegrates everything in its 20-meter blast radius.

TIBANNA GAS A rare gas that can produce greater energy yield in blasters. Tibanna gas is frozen in carbonite for export from refineries.

TRACTOR BEAM A modified force field that can immobilize and move objects. Tractor beams are generally used in spaceports to guide ships to safe landings, but can also be used to capture ships.

TRADE FEDERATION The commerce faction controlled by the Neimoidians, the Confederacy-allied Trade Federation was the largest commercial corporation in the galaxy.

Index

TRAMPER'S BAG — Recycled materials

CONDUIT PURGER — Nozzle emits flesh-eating gas

DIAGNOSTIC SCREEN — Systems check panel

NABOO OFFICER'S CAP — Traditional Naboo security emblem

MANDALORIAN GAUNTLET — Accessory weapon mount

TUSKEN RAIDER'S RIFLE — Rifled projectile barrel; Magnetic pulse accelerator; Automated dosing sensors

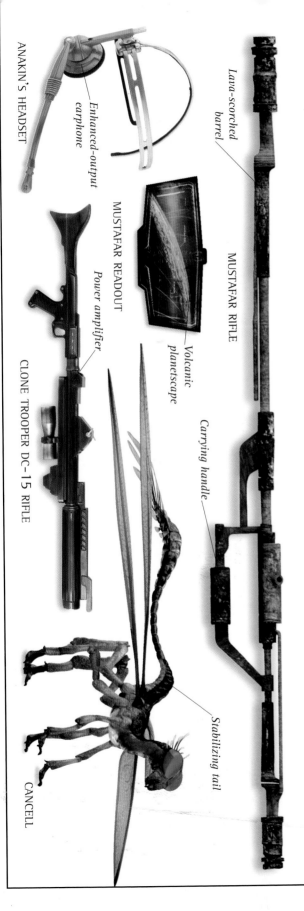

ANAKIN'S HEADSET

Enhanced-output earphone

Lava-scorched barrel

MUSTAFAR READOUT

Power amplifier

Volcanic planetscape

MUSTAFAR RIFLE

Carrying handle

CLONE TROOPER DC-15 RIFLE

Stabilizing tail

CANCELL

LONDON, NEW YORK, MUNICH,
MELBOURNE AND DELHI

DORLING KINDERSLEY

PROJECT ART EDITORS Dan Bunyan, Guy Harvey,
Nick Avery, Jane Thomas, and Iain Morris
PROJECT EDITORS Heather Scott,
Laura Gilbert, and David Pickering
SENIOR DESIGNER/BRAND MANAGER Lisa Lanzarini
PUBLISHING MANAGER Simon Beecroft
CATEGORY PUBLISHER Alex Allan
DTP DESIGNER Hanna Ländin
PRODUCTION Rochelle Talary and Nick Seston
INDEXER Marian Anderson

LUCASFILM LTD.

EXECUTIVE EDITOR Jonathan W. Rinzler
ART EDITORS Iain R. Morris and Troy Alders
CONTINUITY SUPERVISOR Leland Chee

First published in Great Britain in 2006 by
Dorling Kindersley Limited,
80 Strand, London WC2R 0RL

Published in Australia by Dorling Kindersley Limited,
250 Camberwell Road, Camberwell, Victoria 3124
A Penguin Company

09 10 10 9 8 7 6 5

Copyright © 2006 Lucasfilm Ltd. and ™.
All rights reserved. Used under authorization.
Page design copyright © 2006 Dorling Kindersley Limited

All rights reserved. No part of this publication may be reproduced,
stored in a retrieval system, or transmitted in any form or by
any means, electronic, mechanical, photocopying, recording
or otherwise, without the prior written permission
of the copyright owner.

Material in this book was previously published in:
Star Wars: The Visual Dictionary ®, ™, and Copyright © 1998 Lucasfilm Ltd.
Star Wars Episode I: The Visual Dictionary Copyright © 1999 Lucasfilm Ltd. & ™
Star Wars Attack of the Clones: The Visual Dictionary Copyright © 2002 Lucasfilm Ltd. & ™
Star Wars Revenge of the Sith: The Visual Dictionary Copyright © 2005 Lucasfilm Ltd. & ™

A CIP catalogue record for this book is available from the British Library.

ISBN 13: 978-1-40531-601-9   ISBN 10: 1-4053-1601-2

Colour reproduction by MDP, UK
Printed and bound in China by Hung Hing

DK Publishing would also like to thank:

Stacy Cheregotis, Tina Mills, Halina Krukowski, Christine Owens, Aaron Henderson, Paloma Añoveros,
Sarah Hines Stephens, Jane Mason, Cara Evangelista, Joanna Devereux, Cathy Tincknell, Cynthia O'Neill Collins,
Kim Browne, Jill Bunyan, Lauren Egan, Steve Lang, Lauren Britton, Nicola Torode, Louise Barrett and Katy Holmes

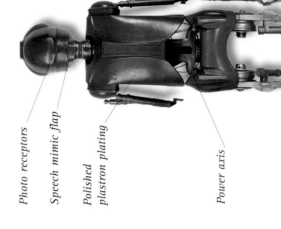

EV-9D9

Photo receptors

Speech mimic flap

Polished
plastron plating

Power axis

WATTO

Pit-droid head
plate serves as tin hat

Mind focused on profit

Ill-fitting
vest

Wings for flight

General
Grievous

Racing
cap

Webbed feet used to
walk on slushy algae
mats on homeworld

Long limbs
allow spider-
like movement
through
caves and up
giant trees

GASGANO

Primary
manipulator
arm

Armored
plating

Laser
cannons

Wheel claws

GRIEVOUS'S WHEEL BIKE

WHEEL BIKE
(SIDE VIEW)

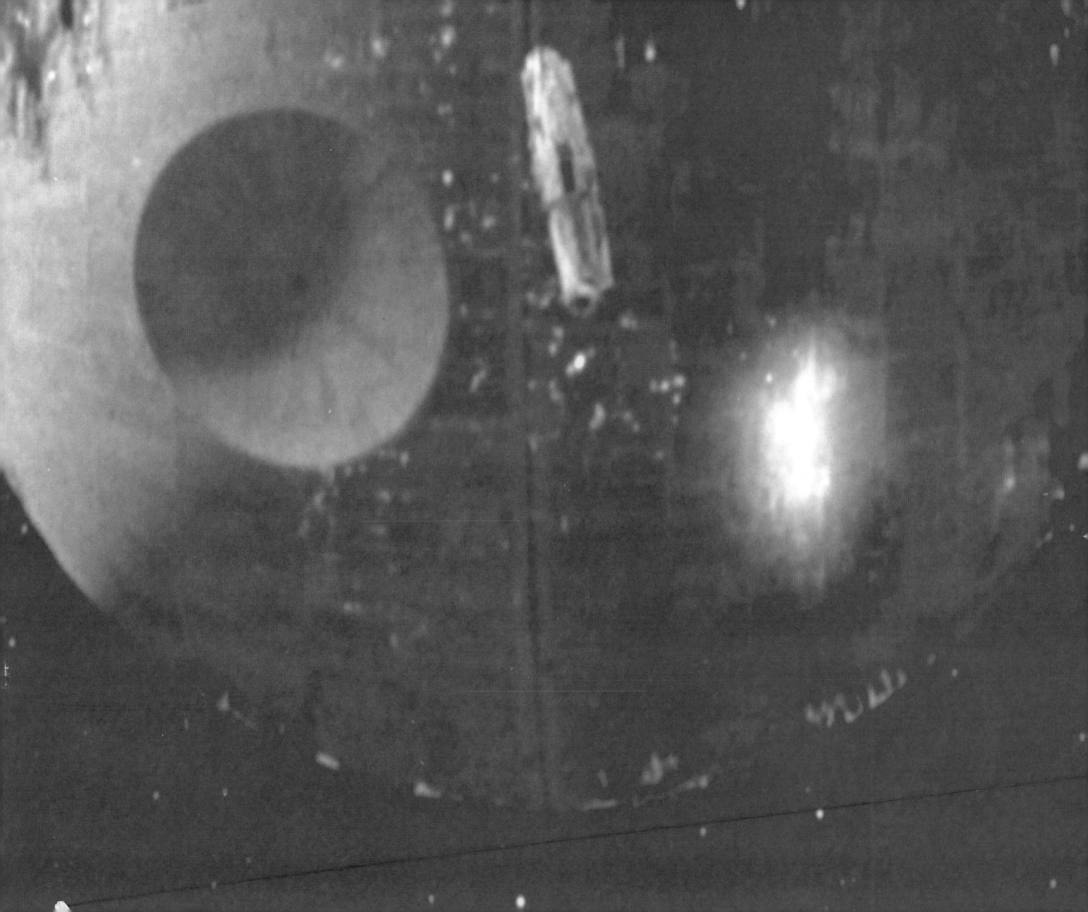